A CULTURAL HISTORY OF WESTERN EMPIRES IN THE RENAISSANCE

A Cultural History of Western Empires
General Editor: Antoinette Burton

Volume 1
A Cultural History of Western Empires in Antiquity
Edited by Carlos Noreña

Volume 2
A Cultural History of Western Empires in the Middle Ages
Edited by Matthew Gabriele

Volume 3
A Cultural History of Western Empires in the Renaissance
Edited by Ania Loomba

Volume 4
A Cultural History of Western Empires in the Age of Enlightenment
Edited by Ian Coller

Volume 5
A Cultural History of Western Empires in the Age of Empire
Edited by Kirsten McKenzie

Volume 6
A Cultural History of Western Empires in the Modern Age
Edited by Patricia Lorcin

A CULTURAL HISTORY OF WESTERN EMPIRES IN THE RENAISSANCE

Edited by Ania Loomba

BLOOMSBURY ACADEMIC
LONDON • NEW YORK • OXFORD • NEW DELHI • SYDNEY

BLOOMSBURY ACADEMIC
Bloomsbury Publishing Plc
50 Bedford Square, London, WC1B 3DP, UK
1385 Broadway, New York, NY 10018, USA
29 Earlsfort Terrace, Dublin 2, Ireland

BLOOMSBURY, BLOOMSBURY ACADEMIC and the Diana logo are
trademarks of Bloomsbury Publishing Plc

First published in Great Britain 2018
Paperback edition published 2023

Copyright © Ania Loomba and Contributors, 2018

Ania Loomba and Contributors have asserted their right under the Copyright,
Designs and Patents Act, 1988, to be identified as Author of this work.

Cover design: Raven Design
Cover image: Christopher Columbus received by King Ferdinand and Queen Isabella
on his return from the New World in 1493, chromolithograph © Everett Collection
Historical/Alamy Stock Photo

All rights reserved. No part of this publication may be reproduced or transmitted in any
form or by any means, electronic or mechanical, including photocopying, recording,
or any information storage or retrieval system, without prior permission in writing
from the publishers.

Bloomsbury Publishing Plc does not have any control over, or responsibility for,
any third-party websites referred to or in this book. All internet addresses given in
this book were correct at the time of going to press. The author and publisher regret
any inconvenience caused if addresses have changed or sites have ceased to exist,
but can accept no responsibility for any such changes.

A catalogue record for this book is available from the British Library.

A catalog record for this book is available from the Library of Congress

ISBN: HB: 978-1-4742-4260-8
PB: 978-1-3503-5822-5
ePDF: 978-1-3502-9028-0
eBook: 978-1-3502-9027-3

Series: The Cultural Histories Series

Typeset by RefineCatch Limited, Bungay, Suffolk
Printed and bound in Great Britain

To find out more about our authors and books visit www.bloomsbury.com
and sign up for our newsletters.

CONTENTS

Illustrations		vii
General Editor's Preface		xiii
	Introduction *Ania Loomba*	1
1	War *Thomas Dandelet*	27
2	Trade *Daniel Vitkus*	49
3	Natural Worlds *Vinita Damodaran and Richard Grove*	77
4	Labor *Michael Guasco*	101
5	Mobility *Jonathan Gil Harris*	127
6	Sexuality *Valerie Traub*	147
7	Resistance *Su Fang Ng*	181

8 Race *Jonathan Burton*	203
NOTES	225
FURTHER READING	229
NOTES ON CONTRIBUTORS	257
INDEX	261

ILLUSTRATIONS

INTRODUCTION

0.1 **Title page** of print series Theodoor Galle's *Nova Reperta* (New Inventions of Modern Times), 1600. Credit: Bettmann/Contributor/Getty Images.   3

0.2 Portrait of Sultan Mehmet II, 1480, by Gentile Bellini (1429–1507), oil on canvas. Credit: De Agostini Picture Library/Getty Images.   5

0.3 *Theatrum Orbis Terrarum*, 1570 by Abraham Ortelius, Title Page. Credit: Holmes Garden Photos/Alamy Stock Photo.   7

0.4 Vespucci "Discovering America" 1492 (*c.* 1600). Plate 2 from *Nova Reperta*, *c.* 1600. Artist Theodoor Galle. Credit: Historica Graphica Collection/Heritage Images/Getty Images.   8

0.5 Paolo Veronese, Allegory of the Battle of Lepanto, 1572. Saints implore the Virgin to grant victory to the Christian fleet; in answer an angel hurls burning arrows at the Turkish vessels. Credit: Leemage/Corbis via Getty Images.   16

0.6 Zheng He's sailing charts. Public domain.   21

CHAPTER 1

1.1 Rubens, Peter Paul (1577–1640). Caesar. Oil on canvas. Credit: bpk Bildagentur/Art Resource, NY. ArtResource: ART428755.   31

1.2 Rubens, Peter Paul (1577–1640). Emperor Charles V as Master of the World—allegory. Around 1607. Credit: Erich Lessing/Art Resource, NY. ArtResource: ART159759. 34

1.3 Anonymous, seventeenth century. Conquest of Mexico—The death of Montezuma at the hands of his own people on July 1, 1520. Spanish School, second half seventeenth century. Oil on canvas; 120 × 200 cm. This scene is considered to be part of the earliest of three complete cycles of paintings of the Conquest. Credit: Erich Lessing/Art Resource, NY. ArtResource: ART370950. 37

1.4 Velazquez, Diego Rodriguez (1599–1660). The surrender of Breda, June 2, 1625. During the Dutch War of Independence, Justin of Nassau hands the keys of the city to Ambrosio Spinola, commander of the Spanish troops. Credit: Erich Lessing/Art Resource, NY. 39

1.5 Struck gold medal of Charles II by John Roettier: the Increase of the Navy. London, England, AD 1667. D: 56 mm. The reverse of the medal shows "The Increase in the Navy" with the king's mistress, Frances Stuart, as Britannia. Copyright The Trustees of the British Museum/Art Resource, NY. ArtResource: ART307601. 43

1.6 Warin, Jean III (1604–72). Statue of King Louis XIV at the Salon of Venus in the Grands Appartements. Credit: RMN-Grand Palais/Art Resource, NY. ArtResource: ART387347. 46

CHAPTER 2

2.1 Engraving by Theodor de Bry in *Emblemata Nobilitati et vulgo scitu digna* (Frankfurt, 1592), p. 147 of 276 unnumbered pages. Credit: Getty Research Institute. 52

2.2 Frans Huys, Armed Four-Master Putting Out to Sea from *The Sailing Vessels (After Pieter Bruegel the Elder)* (Hieronymus Cock: Antwerp, c. 1555–6). Credit: Metropolitan Museum. 57

2.3 Castaway merchant in Geoffrey Whitney, *A Choice of Emblemes* (Leiden, 1586). Credit: Huntington Library, San Marino, California. 60

2.4 From John Blaxton, *The English Usurer* (London, 1634). Credit: Folger Shakespeare Library. 61

2.5 Portraits of King Henry the Navigator and Vasco da Gama from Richard Fanshawe's translation of *Camões's Lusiads* (London, 1655). Credit: Huntington Library, San Marino, California. 64

CHAPTER 3

3.1 Baldaeus Phillipus, English Fort of Bombay 1672. Credit: The Biodiversity Heritage Library. 81

3.2 Henrick Van Reede *Hortus Malabaricus* (1678–93). Credit: The Biodiversity Heritage Library. 85

3.3 Anonymous. Emperor Jahangir on a lion hunt, 1615. From the collection of the Aga Khan Museum. 95

CHAPTER 4

4.1 Title page depicting Atahualpa and numerous scenes of Native Americans mining for silver. From Theodor de Bry, *America*, pt. 6 (Frankfurt, 1596). Credit: John Carter Brown Library, Brown University. 104

4.2 Native Americans search for gold in a stream. Illustration derived from Gonzalo Fernandez de Oviedo y Valdés, *Historia general de las Indias* (Seville, 1535). From Giovanni Battista Ramusio, *Navigazioni e viaggi*, vol. 3 (Venice, 1556). Credit: John Carter Brown Library, Brown University. 105

4.3 Slaves process sugar cane and make sugar. Illustration derived from Girolamo Benzoni, *Historia del mondo nuovo*, pt. 5 (Venice, 1565). From Theodor de Bry, *America*, pt. 5 (Frankfurt, 1595). Credit: John Carter Brown Library, Brown University. 110

4.4 "How the Negro Slaves Work and Look for Gold in the Mines of the Region called Veragua" [Panama]. From the *Histoire naturelle des Indes*, manuscript, *c.* 1586, fol. 100r. The Pierpont Morgan Library, New York. MA 3900. Bequest of Clara S. Peck, 1983. Credit: Pierpont Morgan Library, New York. 116

4.5 A vagabond or criminal being whipped through the streets of town (*c.* sixteenth century). Woodcut engraving. From Raphael Holinshed, The first volume of the *Chronicles of*

England, Scotlande, and Irelande (London, 1577). Credit: Houghton Library, Harvard University.   121

CHAPTER 5

5.1 Title page of the second Italian edition, translated by Giovanni Battista Ramuno, of Leo Africanus, *La Descrittione dell'Africa* (Venice, 1554). Credit: Universitätsbibliothek Heidelberg.   131

5.2 Title page of Garcia da Orta, *Colóquio dos Simples* (Lisbon, 1578). Public domain. Accessed via Wikimedia Commons: https://upload.wikimedia.org/wikipedia/commons/5/5d/Garcia_de_Orta_book_cover.jpg   137

5.3 Copper engraving of Pocahontas wearing a tall hat. Engraving by Simon van de Passe, 1616. Credit: National Portrait Gallery.   141

5.4 The Harem court of the Khas Mahal, Agra Fort. Mariam Khan would have lived here in the 1610s when Jahangir had her married to Captain William Hawkins. Credit: Biswarup Ganguly. Accessed via Wikimedia Commons: https://commons.wikimedia.org/wiki/File:Harem_Court_-_Khas_Mahal_Complex_-_Agra_Fort_-_Agra_2014-05-14_4140.JPG   143

CHAPTER 6

6.1 Detail of hermaphrodite, Monstrous Races, woodcut by Michael Wolgemut, Wilhelm Pleydenwurff, and workshop, in Hartmanm Schedel, *Liber Chronicarum* (Nuremberg Chronicle) (Nuremberg: 1493). Credit: Courtesy of the Hatcher Library, University of Michigan.   153

6.2 "Elizabetha Angliae et Hiberniae Reginae, &c (Truth Presents the Queen with a Lance)," engraving by Thomas Cecil (*c.* 1625). © The Trustees of the British Museum.   155

6.3 "Europa Regina," or "Europa Prima Pars Terrae in Forma Virginis," engraving by Johan Putsch, in Sebastian Münster, *Cosmographia Universalis* (Basel: 1544). Credit: Stephen S. Clark Library, University of Michigan.   156

6.4 Southeast Asian yardball, in John Bulwer, *Anthropometamorphosis* (London: 1654). Credit: Hatcher Library, University of Michigan.   157

ILLUSTRATIONS   xi

6.5   "Hermaphroditorum officia," engraving by Le Moyne de
      Morgues, in Theodore de Bry, *Brevis narration eorum quae in
      Florida Americae* (Frankfurt am Main: 1591, xvii-r). Credit:
      Clements Library, University of Michigan.   162

6.6   "Doña Catalina de Erauso," Francisco Pacheco, *Historia de la
      monja alférez* by Joaquin Maria de Ferrer (Paris: 1829). Credit:
      Northwestern University Library.   165

CHAPTER 7

7.1   Jamestown Massacre. Woodcut by Mattäus Merian, 1628.
      Credit: MPI/Getty Images.   188

7.2   Theodore de Bry. Indians testing the immortality of the
      westerners, 1594. Credit: Rijksmuseum, the Netherlands.   189

7.3   Romeyn de Hooghe, Cornelis Speelman's victories in the
      Kingdom of Makassar, 1666–9. 1670. Credit: Rijksmuseum,
      the Netherlands.   198

7.4   Jan Luyken, Melaka besieged under the leadership of Cornelis
      Matelief de Jonge. 1683. Credit: Rijksmuseum, the Netherlands.   199

7.5   Three warriors from Banten, 1596. Soldiers equipped with spear,
      sword, shields, and musket. Printed from plates made for the
      original illustrations in the travel account of the First Voyage
      of Cornelis de Houtman to the East Indies in 1595–7.
      Credit: Rijksmuseum, the Netherlands.   200

CHAPTER 8

8.1   Mehmed Agha, *Shāhanshāhnāma of Lokman*, vol. 1. Istanbul,
      1581. Credit: Istanbul University Library, F. 1404, fol. 131b.   210

8.2   Prince Mehmed conversing with Vizier Mehmed Pasha,
      Shāhanshāhnāma of Lokman, vol. 2. Istanbul, 1592–7. Topkapi
      Palace Library, B. 200, fol. 83a. Credit: Getty Images/Werner
      Forman/Contributor.   210

8.3   The Somerset House Conference, 1604, by unknown artist.
      Credit: National Portrait Gallery.   211

8.4   Tiziano Vecelli (Titian). Portrait of Laura de'Dianti c. 1523.
      Public domain: GNU Free Documentation License.   211

8.5 Battle between the Turks, led by Suleiman the Magnificent, and the Hungarians at Mohacs, August 29, 1526, drawing from a manuscript. Credit: De Agostini Picture Library/Getty Images. 212

Every effort has been made to trace copyright holders and to obtain their permission for the use of copyright material. The publisher apologizes for any errors or omissions and would be grateful if notified of any corrections that should be incorporated in future reprints or editions of this book.

GENERAL EDITOR'S PREFACE

Histories of empire have been transformed in the last three decades by a combination of new methods, new archives, and a new generation of scholars who have come of age in a postcolonial world. The impact of these historical forces on how imperialism is understood has been remarkable. For decades the province of geopolitics, diplomacy and the "official mind," imperial history is now just as likely to be told from the bottom up as from the top down. The rise of cultural history has played a significant role in how we think about and narrate imperialism from the ancient world to the twentieth century. With an emphasis on evidence drawn from literature, the arts, life-writing, and a host of fragmentary sources, cultural historians think through patterns of representation and experience that shape the conditions in which histories of all kinds—economic, political, social—happen. They investigate often overlooked subjects and offer new angles of vision on familiar topics through a cultural lens. The ambition of *A Cultural History of Western Empires* is to advance conversations about the work of culture in shaping how empire took root, took shape, was maintained, and faced challenges whether its regimes were of long or short durée. Indeed, no thoroughgoing histories of the subject can afford to ignore the influence that culture has had on the shape of empires in local, regional, and global contexts.

The geographical remit of *A Cultural History of Western Empires* is indicated in its title. As compelling a topic as the wide variety of imperial formations is, and as interconnected as west and non-west have been along the axis of empire from Greece to Beijing and back again, the authors in this volume explore empire's cultural histories in a broadly western European setting. And while the differences between French and German and English imperial experiences are often notable, what is equally striking are the features that cultures of labor, trade, sexuality, race, war, mobility, natural worlds, and resistance share across imperial locales. Even allowing for specificities of time and place, there is a value to taking a very long view of the concept and practice of *imperium*—not simply to note commonalities or differences but to be able to discern through lines across such widely distinctive terrains as the Frankish kingdoms and the world of the post-Versailles settlement. In no small respect, attention to cultural forces, identities, rhetorics, tropes, relationships, and imaginaries make this kind of discernment possible. Reading for culture—which is to say, developing the capacity to plumb a variety of sources and archives for evidence of how meanings and forms were constantly made and struggled over across a range of domains—reveals the work of historical forces that have undergirded and, at times, have redirected or undone imperial power. Empire simply cannot be understood in all its limits and possibilities without an analysis of its cultural histories.

This is a work of scholarly synthesis rooted in the original scholarship and intellectual vision of the volume editors and their contributors. Its audience is students seeking a comparative, interdisciplinary, and evidence-based account of how empires worked at multiple scales. Readers will get a sense, then, of the cultural impact of large-scale territorial expansion and hegemony *and* of the meaning and experience of conquest and colonization in more intimate environments. Contributors have written their essays to make available a broad overview of their theme or topic. Each one draws on a range of materials and case studies to make a larger argument about the history of cultural formations and influences that pertain to their subject. The series is structured around six time periods: Antiquity, The Medieval Age, The Renaissance, The Enlightenment, The Age of Empire, and the Modern Age. These are conceptual and pedagogical, signaling a periodization that modern Western imperialism itself has played an important role in shaping and sustaining. Casting Rome as an imperial touchtone and colonized territories as "ancient" or "medieval" in temporal terms remains an important cultural resource for contemporary empire building, and it draws on a long cultural legacy that contributors both address and challenge. Each volume takes up the chronological parameters assigned in critical conversation with the historical evidence, allowing readers to see the pros and cons of thinking about empire itself as a maker—and breaker—of time periods. Of equal significance, each volume is organized with the same chapter titles so that readers can either follow a theme across time frames—mobility in the Enlightenment as compared to the twentieth century, for example—or read through a single period by exploring the range of thematic lenses on offer. This combination of diachronic and synchronic affords us a unique opportunity to cultivate comparisons that are as deep as they are broad, and to appreciate the indispensability of cultural history to practically all aspects of imperial regime making and unmaking across this particular swath of the global past.

Such a purposeful focus on culture at this juncture in the history of the historiography of empire is worth remarking on. As an object of historical inquiry, culture is arguably the carrier of a number of historical forces that attention to politics or economics alone cannot capture. Though embedded in and constitutive of every aspect of imperial geopolitics, race, gender and sexuality were long invisible to the historians' eye because they were considered trivial, or at best inconsequential, to the workings of real power. Cultural history practices, which bring new forms of seeing and reading as well as new subjects to our sightline, open up the imperial archive to aspects of the past which, in turn, shed new light on old paradigms. Thinking with and through culture also reorients our gaze, pulling us toward sources—diaries, images, discursive motifs—in a diverse array of formations and spaces that illuminate dimensions of hegemony and power otherwise invisible: dismiss-able, even, as immaterial because they are ostensibly "only cultural." What the collective example of this series accomplishes is to suggest how, why, and under what conditions culture has been a maker of imperial history—indeed, that empires have been done and undone by the cultural forces they sought to control but which were not always completely in their grasp. As twenty-first-century forms of imperial power emerge, claiming historical newness and relying on past models of conquest and occupation all at once, we need narratives that insist on the power of histories attuned to the ideological and material work of culture more than ever.

Culture is at the dynamic heart of all imperial histories. It operates in spaces of high command and conjugal intimacy; in ceremony and in ordinary life; in military documents and botanists' texts; at court and on the plantation; through trade routes and refugee settlements; in the pronouncements of empresses and the movements of the lowly beetle; in the signing of treaties and the violence of the battlefield and the inner workings of the household. Thinking through cultures of empire, in turn, throws us back on the protocols and presumptions of the discipline by encouraging us to be ever vigilant about where—in what spaces and through what repertoires—history happens. Empire is not, perhaps, unique in this regard. The irony is that while imperial ambition and self-regard have often been steeped in convictions about the power of culture to conquer and colonize, imperial narratives on a grand scale are often the most impervious to the argument that culture matters. What follows is a wide-ranging and lively set of arguments about how and why that has been incontrovertibly so from antiquity to modern times.

Introduction

ANIA LOOMBA

For most people "the Renaissance" marks one of the highest points of Western culture and civilization. Generations of scholars, film-makers, artists, and others have celebrated the global voyaging and discoveries of daring "explorers" such as Vasco da Gama, Amerigo Vespucci, Christofero Colombo, Ferdinand Magellan, Hernan Cortés, and Walter Raleigh as exemplifying the spirit of "Renaissance Man." However, even though it is common knowledge that their ventures were part of Spanish, Portuguese, English, and Dutch colonization of various parts of the world, Renaissance *culture* is still not sufficiently connected to the birth of Western empires in this period. The novelist Michelle Cliff writes that she completed a dissertation on the Italian Renaissance in the 1970s without "dealing with the fact that the slave trade began in the Renaissance and that there were slaves in Europe even as Michelangelo was painting the Sistine ceiling. I was not even aware of it. . . . We were studying—now you'd have thought the slave trade would have come into this—the explorations of the Renaissance into the New World and how they influenced art" (Raiskin 1993: 62).

Today, thanks to the work of many scholars over the past three decades, it is less possible to sweep the history of colonization and slavery behind the arras while thinking about Renaissance art, literature, social mores, and habits of thought. This volume explores the different ways in which the cultures of the Renaissance were shaped by Renaissance empires. As it does so, it traces the ways in which Renaissance empires foreshadowed later imperial dynamics, but also how they differed from those that followed. In this Introduction, I will chart some of the major questions that have confronted scholars as they have attended to the organic connections between Renaissance cultures and the histories of Western empire.

WHOSE RENAISSANCE?

The terms "Renaissance" and "the West" are still tightly linked together in scholarship, education, and popular culture. The Renaissance (from the Italian word *rinascita* meaning "rebirth") is commonly understood to be a period between the thirteenth and the seventeenth centuries when Europeans began to value individualism, and developed self-reflection and personal ambition to a degree unprecedented earlier. As a result, they produced unparalleled new art, literature, philosophy, medicine, and science; went adventuring and discovered new parts of the world; reformed institutions such as the family, the church, and the state; and developed sophisticated commercial systems that eventually ensured that they dominated the rest of the world. All of these achievements together laid the foundations of the modern West, by which is meant Christian and Western Europe. The West, according to this view, was reborn by discovering its own "classical" past—ancient Greece and Rome—after having "died" during the medieval period, which was a barbarous time characterized by hierarchal oppression at every level. This view of the Renaissance was shaped in the nineteenth century, by scholars such as Jules Michelet, Jakob Burkhardt, and Walter Pater, and it depended upon positing a cultural break between the Renaissance and the medieval period, *and* by establishing a continuity between the Renaissance and a European classical past that lay in ancient Greece and Rome.

Many Renaissance thinkers and artists *did* self-consciously return to Greek and Roman pasts, in order to indicate that their world was qualitatively different from what went earlier. Indeed, it was the painter Giorgio Vasari who, in 1550, suggested that the artistic achievements of his own day represented a "rebirth" of classical arts after a fallow middle period, a view that still circulates today. Francis Bacon suggested that contemporary inventions such as the compass, gunpowder, and the printing press had led to this new age of progress. Consider Figure 0.1, the title page of Theodoor Galle's *Nova Reperta* (New Inventions of Modern Times) a print series published in the 1580s cataloging great discoveries and inventions understood as "modern." The series was designed in Florence by the Flemish artist Jan van der Straet, or Stradanus, and the plates were engraved in Antwerp at the workshop of Philips Galle. As Anthony Grafton observes, "this [picture] is a celebration of discoveries both geographical and technological. The latter includes gunpowder, the compass, the clock, printing, silk weaving, distillation, and the saddle with stirrups. Such devices and discoveries were considered by many as evidence of progress and the superiority of contemporary European civilization to that of the ancients" (1992: 203). These objects were of course also read as evidence of progress and the superiority of European civilization to that of rest of the world. There are ironies operating in Grafton's choice of examples; he does not note that most of the devices in this picture were invented in China, and in much earlier periods: printing in the eighth century, and gunpowder and the compass in the eleventh. The saddle with stirrups was widely used there by the fifth century and as for silk weaving, it originated much earlier around 4000 BC and was brought to Europe during the Crusades. Patricia Seed points out that "Islamic and Jewish science lay behind the Portuguese pioneering efforts in nautical astronomy that eventually became the basis of all of Europe's technical and scientific approach to high-seas navigation and domination of the seas" (1995: 186). As she notes, many of the instruments essential to Western colonial expansion—the astrolabe, the compass, the science of global latitude markings—were themselves appropriated from the non-western world.

Thus, both the geographical and temporal coordinates of what is celebrated as the Renaissance need to be questioned, even if these ideas were subscribed to by some thinkers during that period. A growing body of work has shown the idea of the Renaissance as a purely European movement to be a moribund myth, demonstrating the contributions of Muslim Spain, Mamluk Egypt, Ottoman Turkey, Persia, and the Silk Road to European artistic and intellectual history. Classical Greek learning, particularly in the realms of medicine, astronomy, mathematics, and philosophy was studied by Muslim and Jewish scholars and brought to Europe during the very period understood as barbaric and culture-

FIGURE 0.1: Title page of print series Theodoor Galle's *Nova Reperta* (New Inventions of Modern Times), 1600. Credit: Bettmann/Contributor/Getty Images.

less. Many medieval cities in Sicily, Spain, Italy, and Turkey were places where Muslims, Christians, and Jews developed syncretic cultures and were conduits through which classical as well as Eastern learning filtered into Europe. Arab, Ottoman, Indian, and Chinese knowledge about the decimal system, numerals, ship designs, bills of exchange, dyes, paper money, architectural designs, and prose romances (to take just a few examples), shaped the artistic and scientific achievements associated with the Renaissance (see Brotton 2006).

In short, "Renaissance culture" would not have been possible without the exchange of ideas as well as material goods between the "West" and "non-Western" people and places, including in the so-called Dark Ages. As Maria Rosa Menocal puts it, "the segregation of European . . . from Arabic when we are discussing many important aspects of the Middle Ages and its cultural history is an anachronistic and a misleading one" (1985: 61). There were other problems too with the Burkhardtian understanding of the Renaissance—for example, most of the culture it celebrated was not just European, but the exclusive domain of upper-class men, provoking early feminist historians to ask if women ever had a "Renaissance" (see Kelly 1986). The lower classes too were left out of the celebrations of this period, begging the question whether they too were imbued with the spirit, the curiosity, and the creativity that were being extolled as new and special. Even though a lot of what I have outlined above is widely known, it does not disturb the commonplace view of the Renaissance as signaling the inauguration of an exclusively European modernity, perhaps because this view is repeatedly re-inscribed in most scholarship and popular culture, in art museums, in theatrical performances, and in the ways universities organize their disciplines of study.

Why does this re-inscription happen? Perhaps it has to do with the fact "the Renaissance," as a construction about and by Europe, draws upon and confirms ideas of Western uniqueness and superiority that took shape and were entrenched during the long centuries of later European imperial domination of the world. Because "the Renaissance" is absolutely central to the very idea of a white and superior "Western culture," it is not surprising that its debt to non-European cultures has been systematically ignored and marginalized. In actual fact, as I have suggested, the Europe of both the medieval periods and the Renaissance was never neatly divided from the world outside, and particularly from Asia and North Africa, as the cultural and material history of the period testifies. The fact that a thirteenth century German romance like Wolfram von Eschenbach's *Parzival* features a white Christian knight who is first in the service of the Caliph of Baghdad, and then in love with a Moorish queen, tells us something about the border crossings that were prevalent in that period. Such border crossings continued over the next few centuries. Roberto M. Dainotto points out that exactly in the same period which Burkhardt and John Hale identify as one in which a self-consciousness about being European arose, a zealous humanist by the name of Giammaria Barbieri ... complicate[d] such a secure sense and assumption about European identity by electing Arab literature as the exogenous origin of modern European poetic tradition—a poetic tradition, needless to say, that was meant to represent one of the most stunning achievements of European humanitas in contrast to the rest of the "barbarous" world. (Dainotto 2006: 275)

At the height of the Renaissance, Ottoman courts welcomed, even employed, Italian scholars and artists, with Sultan Mehmet II commissioning the famous Italian painter Gentile Bellini (Figure 0.2), and the map-maker Francesco Berlinghieri dedicating his book *Geographia* (which updated Roman geographer Ptolemy's maps) to Mehmet. Apart from such connections, it is important to note that the contours and attributes of the continents or regions have varied

FIGURE 0.2: Portrait of Sultan Mehmet II, 1480, by Gentile Bellini (1429–1507), oil on canvas. Credit: De Agostini Picture Library/Getty Images.

over time (Lewis and Wigen 1997). Ancient Greeks understood the Aegean Sea as the dividing line between Asia and Europe; Romans used Europe and Asia to designate the eastern and western portions of their own empire; in the medieval period, Europe indicated the Frankish lands of Latin Christendom. The modern demarcations between Asia and Europe that we are used to, and particularly the identification of disparate nations as a collectivity called Europe, were partly the *result* of colonial ventures that took shape in the Renaissance.

COLONIALISM, HUMANISM, AND MODERNITY

Conservative scholarship of Renaissance culture has painted its rosy and self-contained picture by neglecting both the histories of intellectual and material exchange and the colonial ventures of the period. *Both* are central to Renaissance culture. If on the one hand, Renaissance science, art, and politics drew upon non-European materials, on the other, Renaissance thinkers and writers extolled the imperial ventures of their day. Abraham Ortelius's *Theatrum Orbis Terrarum* (1570), the most popular world atlas of the time, suggested European superiority over all other peoples through its descriptions of various lands and the arrangement of maps and images: its famous title page showed Europa seated above Africa, Asia and America (Figure 0.3). Thousands of copies of this image circulated as the atlas was produced in various editions and translations. If we revisit the title page of Theodoor Galle's *Nova Reperta* (see Figure 0.1), we notice that it appropriates objects such as gunpowder and the compass in order to celebrate their contemporary use by European colonists. The top left-hand corner of the picture shows a naked woman pointing to a roundel which contains a map of America and is inscribed with the names of Christopher Columbus and Amerigo Vespucci. The very first print in the collection underlines this imperial celebration: entitled "America," it depicts Amerigo Vespucci who holds an astrolabe in one hand and a staff with a banner of the cross in the other, and looks at naked woman wearing a feathered headdress and half rising from a hammock (Figure 0.4). In the background are a sailing ship, naked cannibals roasting human flesh, and wild animals. The text appended to the print read: "America. Americus rediscovers America—he called her but once and thenceforth she was always awake."

This picture has been analysed by many scholars as emblematic of the power of colonial ventures to shape European self-conceptions. In one of the first essays on the subject, Peter Hulme pointed out that while Europe is represented by an individual, historically identifiable, fully clothed man carrying emblems of both religious faith and technological progress, America is a naked woman who is brought to new consciousness by him: she "lies there, very definitely discovered" (1985: 17). Thus, the European male and upper-class subject achieves individuation precisely in and through his power over non-Europeans, a power

FIGURE 0.3: *Theatrum Orbis Terrarum*, 1570 by Abraham Ortelius, Title Page. Credit: Holmes Garden Photos/Alamy Stock Photo.

that is represented in highly gendered and sexualized terms. An analogous expression of imperial power is to be found in Sir Walter Raleigh's *The Discoverie of the large, rich and bewtiful empire of Guiana* which describes the Spanish emperor Charles V as taking "the maidenhead of Peru," and advertises Guiana as a country that "hath yet her maidenhead, never sacked, turned, nor wrought" (Loomba and Burton 2007: 138–9). In such inscriptions of colonial ambition, we see how closely its vocabularies draw upon those of patriarchal power. The reverse was also true, as poets and writers described sexual desire and female beauty in terms of conquests of fertile and desirable lands.

Commentaries on early modern travel repeated over and over again Charles Eliot's celebration of Raleigh as "a thorough representative of the great adventurers who laid the foundations of the British Empire," (2005: 310. [It is

FIGURE 0.4: Vespucci "Discovering America" 1492 (c. 1600). Plate 2 from *Nova Reperta*, c. 1600. Artist Theodoor Galle. Credit: Historica Graphica Collection/Heritage Images/Getty Images.

worth noting that Eliot's collection of travels has remained in print till today.]). Beginning in the 1980s, scholars began to analyse what exactly "adventure" meant, both for the conquered and the conquerors, and to explore the central place of colonialism and slavery in shaping Western cultures during this period. This scholarship was concerned not just with laying out the facts about Western empires in the Renaissance, but with tracing their centrality to Renaissance culture. As Felipe Fernandez-Armesto observes, when Michelet celebrated the Renaissance as a period of the discovery of man, he referred to the "individuality of man" and a "vague, collective narcissism" of the celebration of man; instead, Fernandez-Armesto argues, it is more apt to understand the way in which geographical discoveries of the period prompted "anthropological revelations as well as adjustments in the self-awareness of the philosophically inclined" (1987: 223).

Perhaps the most well-known of the philosophical "adjustments" are encapsulated in the debates about the unity of humankind prompted by the "discovery" of American Indians. For centuries, Christians had understood the peoples of the world to be part of God's plan. However different from one another, the peoples of Asia, Africa, and Europe were all descended from Noah's sons Shem, Ham, and Japhet. Assertions about which peoples had descended from which son varied over time—in medieval texts, such as Mandeville's widely disseminated *Travels*, Ham is the father of the Great Khan and the ancestor of the Mongols, Shem the progenitor of Africans, and Japhet of Europeans and "the people of Israel." From the fifteenth century on, in tandem with the growing slave trade, this division of the world was reordered, with Ham being assigned Africa, and Shem Asia (see Braude 1997). But how were American natives to be fitted into this older schema? How could the older maps of the world be reconciled with the knowledge that there were four parts of the earth and not three? In the late seventeenth century, many people still argued that

> it is apparent that America hath been very long inhabited, ... and since it is ... agreed that the supposed common parents of the rest of mankind, Adam, Noah and his three sons, had their habitations in some parts of Asia, and since we have no probable evidence that any of their descendants traduced the first colonies of the American plantations into America, being so divided from the rest of the world, ... that consequently the Americans derive not their original either from Adam, or at least not from Noah; but either had an eternal succession, or if they had a beginning, they were aborigines, and multiplied from other common stocks than what the Mosaical history imports ... (Hale 1677: 182–5).

Citing this argument, Sir Matthew Hale, chief Justice of England, conjectured that such people must have migrated earlier from one of the other parts of the world and were sons of Noah. More than a century earlier, the Dominican priest Bartolomé de las Casas had already argued that native Americans were children of God, imbued with reason and sense: "They are innocent and pure in mind and have a lively intelligence, all of which makes them particularly receptive to learning and understanding the truths of our Catholic faith and to being instructed in virtue; indeed God has invested them with fewer impediments in this regard than any other people on earth" (1992: 10). He was countering arguments that these "newly discovered" people lacked the human attributes of rationality. Las Casas also contended that "God made these people ... as innocent as can be imagined. The simplest people in the world—unassuming, long suffering, unassertive, and submissive—they are without malice or guile ..." (9). But these attributes could also be used to justify their necessary subjugation; as Francisco de Vitoria argued: "It would seem that for these barbarians the same applies as to the feebleminded, for they cannot govern themselves better than simpleminded idiots. They are not even better than beasts and wild animals, because they take neither more dainty nor better food than these. Their stupidity is much greater than that of the children or feebleminded of other peoples" (cited Todorov 1984: 181).

The debate went on for hundreds of years; toward the end of the sixteenth century, the humanist Michel de Montaigne meditated upon the difference between Europeans and the inhabitants of "that other world which has been discovered in our century," whom he also portrayed, much as Las Casas had done, as simple, unworldly, and egalitarian. He famously concluded that "each man calls barbarism whatever is not his own practice; for indeed it seems we have no other test of truth and reason that the example and pattern of the opinions and customs of the country we live in" (Montaigne 1957: 150, 152). From a different perspective, he suggested it was Europeans with their greed for material wealth and their ossified social hierarchies, rather than the people they called cannibals, who should be seen as uncivilized. Shakespeare's *The Tempest* drew directly upon Montaigne's work, but it complicated the debate by depicting the non-European "savage" Caliban as neither innocent nor gentle. What, then, was the play trying to say in pitting Caliban against Prospero, the learned European duke who colonizes the island, and seeks, with his daughter Miranda, to both "civilize" and exploit Caliban?

Peter Hulme, Stephen Greenblatt, and Walter Mignolo were among the prominent scholars who pondered such questions by turning to the European colonization of the Americas to delineate "the darker side of the Renaissance" (the title of Mignolo's 1995 book). Renaissance culture, in their work, was Western imperial culture. Much of this scholarship came in the wake of post-structuralist theory and postcolonial studies. In his path-breaking and controversial work, *Orientalism*, Edward Said had drawn upon the work of Michel Foucault to suggest that during imperial rule in the nineteenth century, Europeans constructed themselves as superior, rational, efficient, forward-looking, and masculine, precisely by positing non-European societies and cultures as the opposite—irrational, decadent, and decaying, effeminate, and altogether inferior. Stephen Greenblatt drew upon these insights to argue that Renaissance aristocratic "self-fashioning"—so long celebrated as is the quintessence of the period's creative individualism, rebellion against establish authority, and self-discovery—took place against the real or imagined image of an alien figure: "Self-fashioning," he wrote, "is achieved in relation to something perceived as alien, strange, or hostile. This threatening Other—heretic, savage, witch, adulteress, traitor, Antichrist—must be discovered or invented in order to be attacked and destroyed . . ." (1980: 9). As Hulme too had argued, the Renaissance man fashioned himself at least partly against the image of the newly discovered "natives" of the New World. Walter Mignolo also regarded "the rebirth of the classical tradition [in the Renaissance] as a justification of colonial expansion" (1995: vii). While it is difficult to summarize the nuances of their arguments here, these scholars showed how the colonial experience informed individuality, the break with traditions, new attitudes toward religion, and new forms of creativity—in short, all the attributes that had previously been celebrated as the achievements of "Renaissance Man."

Some of these scholars did not question Burkhardt's suggestion that this was a period when a new kind of consciousness emerged in Europe. Rather they suggested that in fact European colonialism facilitated the birth of a new European subject and laid the foundation of the modern world as we know it. This work was part of a larger shift, a move to re-conceptualizing, and even renaming the period as "early modern." As Leah Marcus put it, the Renaissance was better seen not "as a time of re-naissance, cultural rebirth, the reawakening of an earlier era conceived of as (in some sense) classic" but

> more in terms of elements repeated thereafter, those features of the age that appear to us precursors of our own twentieth century, the modern, the postmodern. . . . *Early modern* carries a distinct agenda for historians, who have adopted the name quite consciously as a sign of disaffiliation from what they perceive as the elitism and cultural myopia of an older 'Renaissance' history. (1992: 41–2)

In the years that followed, many early modern scholars argued that the period was "an early modern period" precisely because it germinated the seeds of what became full-blown imperialism. They were joining scholars in other fields who contended that modernity had been ushered in by colonialism. Thus, the "early modern" was, in fact, an "early colonial" period.

As Renaissance studies began to pay new and systematic attention to the Spanish, Portuguese, and English in the New World, and to examine how the histories of conquest shaped European culture itself, the paintings, literature, religion, and philosophy of the period could no longer be read in isolation from these developments. Thus, to return to the example of Shakespeare's *The Tempest*, the play, once celebrated as the Bard's final statement on art, was now analysed as drawing heavily upon contemporary accounts of colonial journeys to the New World, as well as to French humanist Michel de Montaigne's reflections upon civility and barbarism provoked by the discovery of Amerindians. Thus, its reflections on art could not be compartmentalized from its meditations on cross-cultural encounters. However, this revisionist way of understanding Renaissance culture came under open attack during the culture wars of the 1980s and 1990s. Precisely because Renaissance literature has been understood as synonymous with "Western civilization," to re-locate it in the context of imperial history is to somehow discredit it. Thus, the columnist George Will was outraged that a play like William Shakespeare's *The Tempest* could be read as connected to imperial history: for him such an approach "aims at delegitimizing Western civilization by discrediting the books and ideas that gave birth to it" (1981: n.p.). His view was not idiosyncratic or unique—in

1996 the American Council of Trustees and Alumni published a report called "The Shakespeare File," which suggested that reading Shakespeare "properly" would inculcate the right "American" and "Western" values; lamenting that Shakespeare had lost ground to, or was being contaminated by, topics such as "AIDS activism," "people of color," "insurgent nationalism," "homophobia," "third world liberation struggles," "urban poor," and "vagrancy" it concluded that "This country cannot expect a generation raised on gangster films and sex studies to maintain its leadership in the world. Or even its unity as a nation. . . . Shakespeare's works provide a common frame of reference that helps unite us into a single community of discourse" (Martin 1996: 6, 10).

Other, more serious critiques of the revisionist scholarship on Renaissance colonialism also emerged. These contended that, contrary to what was being suggested or implied by some of this scholarship, there was no singular or primal encounter between Europeans and non-Europeans during the Renaissance. Europeans reached the New World after centuries of contact with non-Europeans in Asia and Africa, and these previous histories shaped their vocabularies and attitudes in the Americas. Not only did Columbus think he was traveling to Asia when he reached America, but he continued to believe that the places he had landed in were part of the Old World. Columbus was part of the network of Genoese merchants and financiers who had long competed with their Venetian counterparts in importing Eastern goods; his voyage was not to discover new worlds but to gain a strategic advantage in a very old quest (even as his patrons, King Ferdinand and Queen Isabella of Spain, were more invested in the possibility of finding new islands in the Atlantic). Such a perspective, to be sure, had informed some of the early work on Renaissance colonialism. Peter Hulme (1986) for example, had traced how Columbus's *Journal* records his experiences in two distinct registers—one invokes images of the wealth of Cathay and its powerful rulers such as were used by Marco Polo—"gold," "Cathay," "Grand Khan," "intelligent soldiers," "large buildings," "merchant ships." But because Columbus cannot quite fit the people and lands he sees to these images, in order to describe them he also turns to an older vocabulary of "savagery," "monstrosity," "anthropophagy," that had come down to Europeans from Herodotus. In other words, previous histories of contact are crucial for unraveling the complicated cultural dynamics of colonialism in the New World.

One such history is that of the conquest of the Canary Islands, which lie off the northwest coast of Africa, and where Columbus replenished his fleets as he set out on each of his journeys. Indeed, as Columbus viewed the inhabitants of San Salvador, he explicitly recalled the Canary Islanders. But because the history of the Canary Islands has been marginalized, scholars of the New World have often mistakenly understood some contemporary discussions to be about native Americans when they were actually about the Canarians (see Hulme

1999: 221). The original inhabitants of the Canary Islands, the Guanches, were descended from the Berbers of North Africa, and they were "discovered" by the Portuguese and the Spanish in the fourteenth century. Their contemporary, Arab historian Ibn Khaldoun, described the battles between the Genoese and the islanders, noting that the European fought the islanders, "plundered them, captured some of them, and sold them as captives" (cited Wallace 2004: 202). From then on, Canarians were regularly sold in Mediterranean slave markets. They were understood to be different from black Africans because of their nakedness and their apparent ignorance of money and individual property. These attributes provoked a debate about the nature of humanity and the legitimacy of European rule that foreshadowed the one that took place in relation to American Indians (Fernandez-Armesto 1987: 7). Giovanni Boccaccio, who compiled an account of the Genoese voyages to these "Fortunate Islands," described the islanders as naked and beautifully formed, naturally modest, inclined to sharing communally, and indifferent to gold and jewels. As David Wallace notes, even as such accounts hark back to a tradition of writing about a mythical Golden Age,

> we are queasily aware of another textual tradition at work here, that of those slaving deeds of sale ... with their careful observation of physical virtues and identifying traits (such as circumcision). These handsome boys, so full of domestic sense and natural virtue (and so lacking in avaricious instincts) will fetch a good price in Lisbon (2004: 211).

For the humanist poet Francesco Petrarch, however, the islanders' nakedness and remoteness signified beastliness, incivility, and lack of the human capacity for sociability. Wallace makes an important point in arguing that the European "discovery" of the islands "forms a perfect physical complement to the recuperative labors of humanist philology" for, even as he was commenting on the islanders, and their plunder, Petrarch was discovering the work of Roman historian Titus Livius (Wallace 2004: 203).

At the same time, Pope Clement VI employed terms for Canary Islanders that harked back to another older history—they overlapped with those that were used for Muslims during the Crusades. The islanders were "enemies of the Christian faith" and were a threat to "neighbouring Christian peoples." The Pope, and the Iberian conquerors of the islands, both invoked a medieval argument that a people's sins against natural law, as well as blasphemy and idolatry, could deprive them of sovereignty. Of course, despite the Pope's rhetoric, the situation in the Canary Islands was quite different from that obtaining during the Crusades or in the ongoing battles with the Ottomans. The islanders were not old enemies with elaborate power structures of their own, but the very fact that this older anti-Muslim vocabulary could be repurposed underlines the fact that each encounter between Europeans and non-Europeans was necessarily filtered through the memories and perceptions of previous ones. Columbus, although primarily concerned with the quest of gold, also saw his mission as a sort of reconquest of the Holy Land, writing that "In this voyage to the Indies Our Lord wished to perform a very evident miracle in order to console me and the others in the matter of this other voyage to the Holy Sepulchre" (cited Watts 1985: 96). Las Casas describes how Spanish soldiers butchered Mexicans shouting "For Saint James, and at 'em, men!" (1992a: 50). According to legend, Saint James of Compostela (known as Santiago) had fought against the Moors in the battle of Clavijo in 822.

Thus, it is no coincidence that King Ferdinand and Queen Isabella of Spain oversaw the conquest of the Guanches at the same time as they funded Columbus's New World ventures, and also embarked on the *Reconquista* (the Christian movement to repossess Spain from the Moors). Later in 1492, the monarchs ordered the expulsion of Jews from the country and ordered Moors either to convert to Christianity or leave. The drive to overseas expansion and the desire to create "pure" national, religious, and racial identities were two sides of the same coin. The *Reconquista* was a manifestation of a long history of conflict between Christians and Muslims. A deep-seated hostility to Islam had been shaped by the long legacy of the Crusades, which was complicated by the Muslim invasions of Spain, and these were, in turn, revived in the Renaissance by growing fears of Ottoman expansion.

The Ottoman empire, which was, along with China, the most powerful empire in the world, controlled the Mediterranean trade, had conquered parts of North Africa, and had reached Vienna in 1529. In 1575, *The Notable History of Saracens* warned readers that Christian unity was necessary to face the renewed threat they posed:

> They were (indeed) at first very far off from our Clime and region, and therefore the less to be feared, but now they are even at our doors and ready to come into our houses, if our penitent hearts do not the sooner procure at the merciful hands of God, an united peace and concord among the Princes, Potentates and People of that little portion of Christendom yet left, which through division, discord and civil dissention hath from time to time enticed and brought this Babylonian Nabugadnezar and Turkish Pharao so near under our noses. (Curione 1575: Epistle Dedicatory)

By the seventeenth century, even as Europeans were trying to trade with various Muslim kingdoms, Islam was widely viewed as a "uncleane Bird" that had been bred in Arabia, a "poison" and a "pestilence" that had "infected" a large part of Asia, as well as Africa, and would overrun Europe if it was not checked (Purchas 1905: 316–19).

Ottoman domination catalyzed European voyages of "discovery." It is because Europeans had no easy terrestrial access to the riches of Asia that they had to search for sea routes to the East, a quest that led them to the West. It was both competition with Eastern empires and among themselves that fueled European nations' voyages in every direction. In May 1493, a Papal Bull split the world in half, awarding the eastern hemisphere to Portugal, and the western to Spain. The Treaty of Tordesillas that followed did not stop the two kingdoms from squabbling over some areas, such as the Moluccas, but each half included many areas that as yet neither had reached. Iberian appropriation of the world was unacceptable to other nations, and the Italians, French, English, and the Dutch eagerly joined the scramble for non-European goods, markets, lands, and people.

Several historians have warned against seeing the beginnings of several Western empires in the Renaissance as "a single-minded conquest by a securely organized Europe" suggesting that it is better viewed as "a multifaceted transformation ... born out of imperial rivalries with each other to a large extent" (Burbank and Cooper, 2010, 184). Such rivalries influenced, and were shaped by, trade and diplomacy between European courts and Asian ones. For example, even though the French were the most active in Crusades, King François I allied with Ottoman Sultan Suleyman I in his effort to shore up his defenses against the Habsburgs. And, to gain an edge over Spain, Queen Elizabeth I of England entered into trading agreements with the rulers of Morocco and Turkey, and she also tried to do the same with Mughal India. She even suggested to the Ottoman monarch that Protestants and Muslims had much in common with each other because both, unlike Catholic Spain, eschewed idolatry. In making treaties and alliances with non-Christians, Christian rulers were breaking Canon law, but all such alliances could be short lived: in 1571 different Christian powers had come together to clash with—and defeat—the Ottoman empire at the battle of Lepanto, and the battle was commemorated in paintings, tapestries, and literature for centuries after (see Hite 2012) (Figure 0.5). European nations were forged partly in and through their colonial endeavors, and such endeavors both pitted different Europeans against each other but also sharpened the rhetorical and material divisions between Europeans and non-Europeans, thus modifying rather than entirely dispensing with the idea of a Christian, pan-European race.

IMPERIAL CULTURES AND GLOBAL RELATIONS

Beginning in the 1990s, Renaissance scholars turned to these histories of rivalry and exchange to argue that an exclusive focus on the New World was in danger of presenting a distorted picture of global relations in the sixteenth and seventeenth centuries, when, instead of dominating the East, Europe feared the

FIGURE 0.5: Paolo Veronese, Allegory of the Battle of Lepanto, 1572. Saints implore the Virgin to grant victory to the Christian fleet; in answer an angel hurls burning arrows at the Turkish vessels. Credit: Leemage/Corbis via Getty Images.

mighty Turkish empire, but also desired to trade with it and with other Muslim powers such as Morocco and India. For some scholars, the import of postcolonial theory into precolonial periods was responsible for this skewered picture. Said's *Orientalism* had suggested that an opposition between "the familiar (Europe, the West, 'us') and the strange (the Orient, the East, 'them')" has animated "European imaginative geography" from the Greek times till the present (1978: 43, 57). As Su Fang Ng put it,

> [a] model of history based on the idea of a "first contact" or "discovery" ... has led to an anachronistic mapping of modern colonial structures onto the past. As such, they distort our view of the early—and even the not-so-early—encounters between Europeans and Asians. Sometimes, because of its

particular European orientation, conventional history gets even its facts wrong. While such histories tell us that Vasco da Gama was the first to round the Cape of Good Hope, in 1497, in fact he was preceded in the mid-fifteenth century by Shihab al-Din Ahmad Ibn Majid, an Arab navigator, who sailed westward to the Cape, up the west African coast, and into them Mediterranean through the Straits of Gibraltar, in essence rounding the Cape from the other direction. (2006: 295)

How could the asymmetry of European and non-European relations in the New World be the key factor European self-definition when, at the same time, Europeans desired to enter the powerful economic networks of the Mediterranean, Levant, North Africa, India, and China, feared the military might of the Turks, and were dazzled by the wealth and sophistication of many Asian kingdoms? As evidence to the contrary, some scholars showed that the early English fascination with Muslim worlds is born not out of a confident superiority and will-to-power, but a consciousness of marginality, or even of "the Christian West's inferiority complex."[1] Pointing out that a New World-centric New Historicism and a nineteenth-century Orientalism have *intersected* in early modern studies to produce the conception of an oversimplified opposition between Europe and its "others," Lisa Jardine and Jerry Brotton offer yet another model of contact, locating in the extensive material and artistic exchanges between Turkey and Europe, "a pragmatic engagement between East and West in which each fully acknowledged the participation of the other and negotiated workable relationships" (2000: 61).

At the same time, new economic histories of the period had begun to emphasize that at that time there were no signs of *inevitable* European hegemony in the future. Janet Abu-Lughod observed that Europe was but an aspiring new entrant or an "upstart" in the premodern global economy (1989: 12). Her view was extended by Andre Gunder Frank (1998), who suggested that right until the eighteenth century Europe was only a junior partner in Asian-dominated international trade. Throughout that period, it appeared, as Charles Davenant put it, that whoever controlled Asian trade would be in a position to "give law to all the commercial world" (quoted Arrighi 1994: 34). Kenneth Pomeranz (2000) also argued that until the eighteenth century there were no substantial differences in life expectancy, wages, consumption—of ordinary goods as well as luxuries—between core regions of Eurasia. Suraiya Faroqhi pointed out that there was greater traffic between the different "world economies" which Fernand Braudel had conceptualized as discrete systems: right until the eighteenth century, Europeans and Ottomans inhabited a shared context "that, for lack of a better term, we may call 'early modern'" (2006: 11). This body of scholarship also began to question the received narrative about Europe being the birthplace of capitalism. For example, Jack Goody's *The East in the West* contended that

European colonial-mercantile companies, regarded as forerunners of modern multinationals, were also successors to "the earlier forms of partnership such as the commenda found throughout Eurasia," obliging us to "modify the view that we are in the presence of a unique Western invention which others could not have achieved" (1996, 116).

Goody's work is part of scholarship on "connected histories" that challenges "internalist accounts of Europe" such as those which produced the conventional view of the Renaissance. While it is not possible for me to discuss the debates generated by such revisionary scholarship, it has been crucial in reorienting our perspectives on early modern global cultural relations, particularly in its emphasis on material and intellectual exchanges rather than binaries between Europe and its supposed "others." It also emphasized the simultaneity between economic and cultural developments in various parts of the world. For example, Sanjay Subrahmanyam traces the writing of "world histories" in widely disparate parts of the world (including Turkey, India, Russia, Mexico, China, and also England, Portugal, and Spain). He argues that in all these places the sixteenth century was "an explosive conjunctural moment in relation to the changing conventions of history-writing" (2005: 28). These changing conventions of historiography had to do with new geographical consciousness, a consciousness that was produced by the transfer of ideas and books and maps and travelogues between all these places. If historical consciousness is emblematic of modernity, then these books show, according to Subrahmanyam, that "history of modernity is itself global and conjunctural, not a history in which Europe alone first produces and then exports modernity to the world at large" (28).

As Subrahmanyam traces ideas and practices shared across continental boundaries, he underlines a massive historical shift in the sixteenth century, one that expands the geographies of the Renaissance but does not challenge the conventional periodization upon which it rests. He makes the passing suggestion, moreover, that this shared new self-consciousness may have something to do with the imperial ambitions of different societies of the time. And indeed, not only were some major Western and Eastern empires temporally coincident— Suleiman the Magnificent and Charles V both became rulers in 1520—they could also draw upon similar rhetoric and beliefs. Thus, the Ottomans and the Hapsburgs were both convinced that their dynasties would rule the world, and both drew upon the same models—those of the Roman empire, and of the Macedonian Alexander's conquests (see Burbank and Cooper: 2010, 117).

Understanding the histories of Europe as "connected" to the ones beyond is crucial to framing new perspectives on every aspect of European life and culture, from art, literature, and science to ideologies of gender, sexuality, and racial ideologies. For a later period, Ann Laura Stoler argues convincingly that "the history of sexuality simply cannot be charted in Europe alone" by showing how colonial cultures were crucial to shaping European sexual practices and fantasies (2002: 144). For the early modern world Valerie Traub traces how the European projection of deviance upon foreign peoples, in travelogues and medical accounts, was often designed for internal consumption, to control female sexuality at home (1995). But hostility and "othering" were not the only way of making sense of foreign sexual practices. Sahar Amer (2008) shows that French medieval literature borrowed from and imitated Arab literatures so that "the very notion of what constituted sex between women seems to have derived from cultural interstices."[2] Such work requires moving out of an exclusive focus on Europe, and engaging more seriously with scholarship on Africa, South Asia, the Ottoman empire, as well as the Americas.

ECONOMICS AND CULTURE

However, scholarship on "connected histories" does not pay attention to the particular forms of growth of Western empires in the period, which eventually *did* become hegemonic. What made Europe metamorphose into what Braudel calls "the monstrous shaper of world history" (quoted Arrighi 1994: 11)? Why did Europe manage to seize control and Asia fall behind? In economic terms the answer is clear—it was the colonization in the New World and the slave trade in Africa that started the ball rolling toward European global dominance. In *Capital*, Karl Marx famously identifies the sixteenth century as a period when the primitive accumulation of wealth necessary for capitalism involved *both* the alienation of European peasantry from the land, *and* European colonial adventurism. After describing the expropriation of the commons, he writes:

> The discovery of gold and silver in America, the extirpation, enslavement and entombment in mines of the aboriginal population, the beginning of the conquest and looting of the East Indies, the turning of Africa into a warren for the commercial hunting of black-skins, signaled the rosy dawn of the era of capitalist production. These idyllic proceedings are the chief momenta of primitive accumulation. Hard on their heels follows the commercial war of the European nations, which has the globe as its battlefield . . . (1997: 915–16).

Imperial silver connected the histories, economies, and futures of different areas of the world even as it engendered great asymmetry between them. Silver mines in Mexico and the Peruvian Andes produced eighty percent of the world's silver from the sixteenth century on, and these mines needed labor which was supplied in large measure by Amerindian and African slaves, sold by the Portuguese, as well as Dutch, Genoese, and British slavers. The silver trade and the slave trade fed one another (just as later, the slave and sugar trades were to do) and together catalyzed the enormous transatlantic movements of slaves, as well as the beginnings of a truly global economy. New World silver had an enormous effect on the economy of China which had long guzzled silver and gold from the rest of the world in exchange for goods that Europeans craved—V. Magalhaes Godinho describes China as a "suction pump" (*bomba aspirante*) for silver (quoted Flynn and Giraldez 2001: 144).

While the Spanish were the main exporters of silver to Europe, the Portuguese and later the Dutch were its main distributors into Asia—and Manila was one of the key places where it was transferred. China contained one-fourth of the world's population, and its huge demand for silver pushed up the price of, and profits from, the metal—in China its value was almost double the value outside. The colonial mines ensured Spanish wealth and power in Europe, and profits for the Portuguese and Dutch as well (the Portuguese also traded silver for slaves in Brazil). But eventually, with increasing supply, the prices crashed (the value of silver in relation to gold halved between the late sixteenth and middle of the seventeenth centuries), contributing to the eventual collapse of the Ming Dynasty.

But, as is evident even in this quick outline, the economic story is complicated by cultural attitudes. Colonization and slavery are not simply economic processes but are also enabled by, and in turn engender, particular ways of seeing or ideologies. From its earliest days, the European presence in the New World was marked by, as Las Casas also noted, violence and brutality toward the native populations. Moreover, not all empires of the period shared Europeans' expansionist ambitions, leading scholars to wonder if Europeans had a mind-set that was distinctive. The seven voyages of Zheng He (called Cheng Ho in Western writings) (Figure 0.6), the Muslim eunuch who commanded the Ming fleet, are often used to ponder the issue. Zheng He reached as far as the Somali coast and, some argue, as far as the Cape of Good Hope, establishing Chinese supremacy over sea lanes to as many as thirty countries before his emperors ordered a halt to such voyages, instead of taking the final steps to become truly hegemonic in the Eurasian world system. Europe, lagging far behind technologically and in terms of bullion accumulation, poised itself to fill the vacuum—the Portuguese journeys around the Good Hope followed shortly afterwards and have been described as an "analogue" to Zheng He's voyages (Robinson 1993: 99). Why did the Chinese abruptly pull back, creating the space for Portugal to forge ahead?

Giovanni Arrighi offers an economic argument. The "structural imbalance of European trade with the East," he writes, "created strong incentives for European governments and businesses to seek ways and means, through trade or conquest, to retrieve the purchasing power that relentlessly drained from West to East," whereas there was no such incentive for Zheng He "because there was no treasure to retrieve in the West" (1994: 35). But then Arrighi also suggests an ideological difference between "territorialist rulers [like the Ming emperors who] identify power with the extent and populousness of their

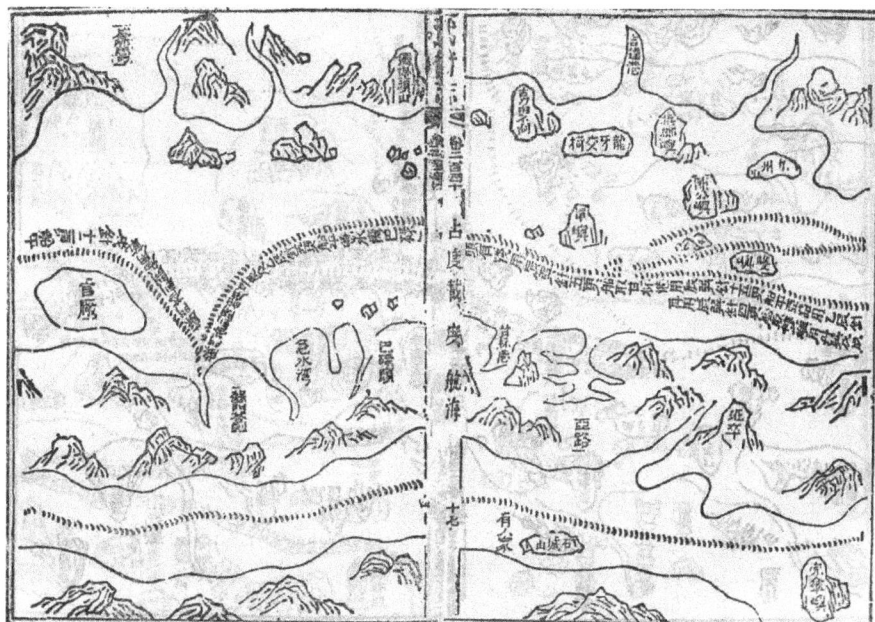

FIGURE 0.6: Zheng He's sailing charts. Public domain.

domains, and conceive of wealth/capital as a means or a by-product of the pursuit of territorial expansion" and "capitalist rulers, . . . [who] identify power with the extent of their command over scarce resources and consider territorial acquisitions as a means and a by-product of the accumulation of capital" (35). Here the suggestion is that the West *already* possessed capitalist ideologies as opposed to China, ideologies that facilitated the process of expansion.

Immanuel Wallerstein also discusses the case of Zheng He to consider differences between Portuguese and Chinese ideologies, which, in his view, stemmed from the fact that China was an "empire," whereas Portugal was part of a European "world-economy composed of many smaller states." An empire, he suggests, "conceives of itself as a whole, unlike a state in a 'world-economy.' . . . For an empire pretends to be the whole. It cannot enrich its economy by draining from other economies, since it is the only economy. (This was surely the Chinese ideology, and probably their belief)" (2011a: 60). It is unclear whether Wallerstein is suggesting that such empire-thinking is produced by an actual economic-political self-sufficiency, or whether it creates an *erroneous* belief in self-sufficiency, but in either case, it seems that for him too cultural differences are crucial. Others have suggested that Chinese world-views, including Confucianism, intersected with practical considerations, such as the fact that the Ming rulers were battling other enemies on their western borders (see for example Hing 2010; Chang 1974). As William Appleman Williams, notes, "The point is not to present the Chinese as immaculately disinterested, or whiter than white. It is simply to note that we now know that the *capacity* for empire does not lead irresistibly or inevitably to the *reality* of empire" (1980: 104; emphasis mine).

My argument here is that economic histories are not enough to explain differences in the development of the early modern world if unleavened with considerations of culture, and vice-versa. Even as Chinese world-views and ideologies caused them to pull back at a time when they could have enlarged their empire, Europeans displayed an aggression in areas where they did not yet possess power. There had been centuries of comparatively peaceful trade in the Indian Ocean between Indians, Arabs, Chinese, Armenians, Jews, and others, which the Portuguese and the Dutch disrupted with armed trading. J.H. Parry describes Vasco da Gama's ships, with their mounted guns, as heading "not . . . a voyage of discovery, but an armed commercial embassy" (1982: 79). Irfan Habib has suggested that the "European triumph over Indian (and Asian) merchants was not . . . one of size and techniques, of companies over peddlers, of joint stock over atomized capital, of seamen over landmen . . . [but] more a matter of men-of-war and gun and shot, to which arithmetic and brokerage could provide no answer" (1990: 399). K.N. Chaudhuri (1985) argues that the Dutch and English learned their methods of trade from the Portuguese, and were just as coercive, equally dependent upon military might. As one Dutch colonist wrote to the officials of the Dutch East India Company (VOC) in 1614, "Your Honors should know by experience that trade in Asia must be driven and maintained by the protection and favor of your Honors' own weapons, and that the weapons must be paid for by the profits from the trade; so that we cannot carry on trade without war nor war without trade" (quoted Corn 1998: 137).

The question of the slave trade in the Indian Ocean speaks eloquently to the cultural attitudes that permeated European voyages to the East and West, whether they were undertaken for "planting" or "colonization." In recent years, scholars have sought to break "the history of silence" that surrounded this issue partly because of the exclusive association of slavery with its Atlantic history, and partly because "Histories of the Portuguese empire in Asia, and the Dutch, English, and French charter companies that operated in this part of the world are equally reticent about the extent to which these nascent multinational corporations traded in and made use of slave labor" (Allen 2015: 9). African and Asian slaves were shipped by the Dutch VOC to work in their headquarters in Batavia, as well as in their plantations in the Moluccas, Ceylon, and the Cape of Good Hope. Wil O. Dijk writes that

> The first official data on the VOC's Bay of Bengal slave trade dates from 1621. This was also the year in which the Dutch, under Governor general

Jan Pietersz Coen, murdered practically the entire population of the Banda Islands in order to gain access to the nutmeg and mace trees that grew there so profusely and which the islanders were not prepared to simply hand over to foreign intruders. Having summarily dispatched the local population, the Dutch now needed to bring in slaves to take over the nutmeg cultivation. In June of that year, the first batch of 150 boys and girls were shipped from Coromandel to Batavia in the Schoonhoven. (2008: 16).

This is not unlike the dynamic of Atlantic slavery where slaves had to be shipped in to replace a decimated local workforce. As Markus Vink has shown, the

Dutch Indian Ocean slave system drew captive labor from three interlocking and overlapping circuits of subregions: the western most, African circuit of East Africa, Madagascar, and the Mascarene Islands (Mauritius and Reunion); the middle, South Asian circuit of the Indian subcontinent (Malabar, Coromandel, and the Bengal/Arakan coast); and the easternmost, Southeast Asian circuit of Malaysia, Indonesia, New Guinea (Irian Jaya), and the southern Philippines. (2003: 139)

Just as the European slave trade in the Atlantic intersected with earlier histories of African slavery, in the Indian Ocean too, as Vink shows, it took over pre-existing systems of servitude and bondage. Even the English were engaged in slave trade in India as early as 1622, six years before they openly participated in the Atlantic slave trade (Allen 2015: 22). Richard Allen rightly observes that although the numbers of slaves traded by Europeans in the Indian Ocean cannot compare with those exported across the Atlantic Ocean, "the significance of this traffic" lies in indicating "the global dimensions of European slave trading." Dutch, British, French, and Portuguese operations, "whether in the Atlantic or in the Indian Ocean world ... were dependent upon slave labor in varying degrees" (23). Allen argues that scholars of the Indian Ocean world need move beyond thinking of the area as an isolated unit; similar arguments have been made about the Atlantic. As Philip Stern has put it, the "real challenge facing the globalization of imperial history, has been that 'East' has been 'East' and 'West' has been 'West' not only in our imaginings of cross-cultural encounters but also within the historiography of empire itself . . ." (2009, 115). Broadening the scope of "connected histories," then, is one way to better understand the genesis and dynamic of modern Western empires, particularly in the period which marks their genesis. It is also, as I have suggested here, a way of thinking about the cultures of empire, an issue that is further illuminated by the histories of racial difference.

Vink points out that in the Indian Ocean world, just as in the Atlantic, Europeans often justified slavery by invoking the story of Ham, as well as writings of Greco-Roman authors that condoned slavery "within natural limits." As I have already mentioned, the story of Noah's curse upon Ham was a changeable one, and so his descendants, like the Amazons, or indeed the supposed Eastern Christian king Prester John could be assigned to Africa or India. I raise this point to return to the questions of imperial attitudes, and to suggest that we must take seriously the place of racial ideologies within them. Racial ideologies, with their deep roots in religious thought, class ideologies, as well as real and imagined cross-cultural encounters, do not simply follow upon already formed economic and social relationships, but also shape them. Racial ideologies, neglected in world-system analysis, can often illuminate the gap between imperial "capacity" and "desire," or between economics and culture.

Elsewhere Jonathan Burton and I have discussed at length why the wide-held supposition that the early modern period was free of race-thinking is erroneous (Loomba and Burton 2007). From the travel books of the period, to the atlases, scientific and medical books, encyclopedias, legal statutes, sermons, dictionaries, philosophical treatises as well as literary texts, we find expressions of somatic, ethnic, geographic, cultural, class, and religious differences that show how older ideas such as Oriental despotism, African lechery, Southern feebleness, or the Egyptian reversal of gender roles were invoked and transformed to demarcate white European Christians from others in the early modern period. It is impossible not to recognize the development of beliefs about skin color and religious identities that are recognizably racial. Tracing these changes, Burton and I suggest that racial ideologies and practices are not just engendered as a simple *consequence* of modern colonialism. Rather, many premodern ideologies and practices *shape* the particular forms taken by European colonialism and slavery. This insight does not preclude our ability to distinguish between different kinds of prejudice on the one hand and racism on the other, or to acknowledge how colonialism and capitalism also transformed the latter. But unless we attend to the long and protean histories of race, we simply cannot understand its relationship to colonialism.

Robert Bartlett's important book, *The Making of Europe: Conquest, Colonialism and Cultural Change, 950–1350* concludes that "the mental habits and institutions of European racism and colonialism were born out of the medieval world, the conquerors of Mexico knew the problem of the Mudejars: the planters of Virginia had already been planters in Ireland" (1993: 313). Work in medieval studies has further complicated the genealogies of race and colonialism by attending to the history of the Crusades as well as the relationships between Muslims, Jews, and Christians within Europe (see for example Metlitzki 1997; Nirenberg 1996; Heng 2003; Kinoshita 2006; Lampert 2010). This work, and related scholarship on early modern histories of race, reminds us that negative stereotyping can co-exist with relations of exchange and even reciprocity: thus, the stereotype of the raging Turk could take shape even as

Europeans desired to enter into business arrangements with Muslims, admired Ottoman learning and imported their literary and scientific texts. Moreover, racialized beliefs can also cross borders: thus as Robin Blackburn has shown, the belief that one should not enslave someone of one's own religion entered medieval Christian communities as they confronted the threat of Islam, which had long held such a prohibition; he observes that "[r]eligious adherence and religious imagery usually had the last word in justifications of enslavement, which is why the pagans of Lithuania, the Bogomil heretics of Bosnia, captives from the Caucasus, the Muslims of Andalusia, and the Jews had all been seen as potential slaves in Christian Europe of the later medieval period" (1997: 87). To understand why eventually blackness became a marker and a justification for slavery, we must engage with the long history of anti-black prejudice within Christianity, which could identify black skin with both an alien faith (hence Jews and Moors were seen as metaphorically and sometimes literally black) and with godlessness and bestiality. It is therefore not coincidental that, much before it became a rationalization of blackness, Noah's curse upon the descendants of his son Ham was popularly used to explain the servitude of European peasants, as is evident from writings such as Andrew Horn's 1290 text *The Mirrour of Justices* (Loomba and Burton 2007: 67–8). This is precisely the tradition made available by the biblical account of the story and it continues well into the seventeenth century in writings such as William Strachey's *The History of Travel into Virginia Britania* (1612) and Thomas Browne's *Pseudodoxia Epidemica* (1646).

CONCLUSION

Recent Renaissance scholarship has been at pains to underline the fact that the subsequent history of the Atlantic slave trade should not obscure the fact that Africans could occupy positions of power and learning in Renaissance Europe, and be respected and even glamourized there. Similarly, it has also been eager to contest the supposition that there has been an unbroken and unchanging history of hostility and alterity between Christians and Muslims, and Christians and Jews, suggesting that in contrast to the anachronistic import of colonial attitudes into this earlier period, what is needed now is a focus on the more equitable relationships between inhabitants of different parts of the early modern world, relationships that illuminate the long histories of trade, globalization, cosmopolitanism, and trans-nationalism (see, for example, the Introductions to MacLean 2005 and Singh 2009). The thrust of some of this work is exemplified by Myra Jehlen's argument that "Decolonization must begin at home with the recognition that the desire to recuperate the contingency of the European hegemony is not disinterested. We find ourselves, in the millennial twilight of the empire, with the urgent task of establishing that Europe's global dominion was not in the nature of things" (1993, 684).

It is indeed important to show that European domination was not an inevitable historical development. This has been precisely the burden of the scholarship on connected histories, premodern global histories, and economic histories of Asia that I have discussed. However, for reasons that I have also outlined in this Introduction, we cannot challenge a crude narrative of an endless clash of cultures by simplifying past histories of contact into a narrative of mutuality and equity. If we do so, we cannot explain why and how modern Western empires were born and shaped during the Renaissance, or indeed understand why so many of the cultural achievements of the Renaissance are overtly marked by imperial ambition (or question such ambition). As the essays in the present volume detail, the *cultures* of the Renaissance illuminate and are themselves the product of the *cultural history* of Western empires in the Renaissance.

CHAPTER ONE

War

THOMAS DANDELET

At the beginning of the twenty-first century, the Renaissance is at a crossroads both as a broad field of study encompassing the disciplines of history, literature, art, politics, and philosophy; and as a distinctive period in European history. As a mature field with roots in the nineteenth century and a particularly vibrant period of scholarly and institutional activity in the latter half of the twentieth century, the definition and direction of the Renaissance in the new century are open questions. A new essay on the theme of War in the Renaissance, as one example, immediately begs the question of why we need another treatment of a subject that, on the surface at least, has enjoyed considerable scholarly attention for many decades. Titles that include the terms war and Renaissance are many: John R. Hale, alone, almost made the theme a personal cottage industry with numerous titles including *The Art of War and Renaissance England* (1961); *War and Society in Renaissance Europe, 1450–1620* (1985); and *Artists and Warfare in the Renaissance* (1990). Hale's work and that of many others including Jeremy Black, Geoffrey Parker, James Tracy, and Michael Mallet, to name a few, remain foundational for understanding the narratives, mechanics, and metrics of war in the early modern period. The changing technologies of warfare; various causes, actors, battles, and logistics of war; and the impact of war on the economies, soldiers, and societies convulsed by the almost perpetual officially sanctioned violence of the state between 1400 and 1800 are all subjects that have been generally well studied.

What is missing in much of this literature, however, is a careful consideration of how all of these topics were related to the Renaissance itself and more specifically to the cultural history of the Renaissance. Most of the studies on warfare in the period use the term Renaissance as a simple chronological designator—as a convenient and shifting term to describe a historical period. The full and formal meaning of the Renaissance as a political, intellectual, and cultural movement that sought to revive and imitate the ancient Roman world in all of its literary, artistic, political, and military glory is largely absent in much of the literature. Hale's *War and Society in Renaissance Europe, 1450–1620,* to cite one example among many, lacks any mention of the Renaissance after the title page, and most military historians largely follow this example. Thus, there is still a basic need for historical analysis that connects the Renaissance as a cultural, political, and intellectual movement to the ideas, practices, and representations of warfare in the period from the fourteenth through the seventeenth century.

A related problem in the literature on warfare and the Renaissance is the often limited interpretation of the period and/or movement as focused on wars in Europe between republics, duchies, and national monarchies. How scholars choose to define the Renaissance is closely tied to the question of chronological and geographical boundaries. For much of the twentieth century, the Renaissance was treated as a predominantly Italian field of study that stretched from roughly 1350 to 1530. This was a largely Republican Renaissance with Florentine and Venetian studies dominating the field with Rome, Milan, Naples, and some of the smaller states such as Mantua, Ferrara, and Urbino receiving more limited attention as the "despotic" side of the Renaissance. By comparison, the Renaissance in Spain, Germany, France, and England, not to mention Poland and Portugal, received far less attention in twentieth-century scholarship. The use of the term as an organizing principle for the history of those territories was rare, and when used had a very short chronology that generally ended with the Reformation.

It follows that the political framing of Renaissance war has been largely confined to the European continent and Mediterranean in the late fifteenth and sixteenth centuries. Noticeably lacking in this view of the Renaissance is the central role that *empire* played as one of the primary causes and contexts for the transformation of warfare within Europe and on a global scale. More precisely, we lack a history of warfare that is rooted in the imperial Renaissance, or that distinctive Renaissance of ancient Roman ideals that sought to bring the Roman empire back to life in all of its cultural, intellectual, and military glory. It was this Renaissance that began in the mid-fourteenth century with Petrarch and extended to at least the late seventeenth century and the War of the Spanish Succession, which provided the most transformative ideas and ambitions that inspired and drove the rise of empires in western Europe, and that shaped the broad mentality toward war for the ruling class throughout the early modern period. In short, it was the desire for empire, inspired by the example of the ancient Roman empire, above all else, that drove European monarchs to war and conquest. It was the rebirth of imperial ambition and competition on the ancient Roman scale that militarized European society to an unprecedented level and made war a virtually permanent feature of European history from 1494 to 1715 and beyond.

A great deal of previous scholarship on warfare in the seventeenth century, and especially on the theme of the so-called "military revolution," has pointed to the rise of "absolutist" states in northern Europe as being behind the transformation of war in the period.[1] But the deepest and most expansive roots of the military revolution and transformation of warfare in this period are located in the fifteenth and sixteenth centuries in the fertile soil of the imperial Renaissance in Italy and Spain. The later absolutist states of the seventeenth and eighteenth century grew out of this tradition as they themselves sought empire. They were simply later branches of the earlier tree. Thus, the real military revolution came from the rise of global empires and the distinctive transformation of war, and the central ideas about war, that imperial conquest and contest produced. It is this Renaissance of Empire that provides the analytical frame for the essay that follows (Dandelet 2014).

PETRARCH AND THE REBIRTH OF THE ROMAN MILITARY IDEAL

As with so many other foundational aspects of the Renaissance, the dream of seeing Roman military glory reborn had its origins with Francesco Petrarch. When he first began to revive and imitate the epic poetry and discipline of history as practiced by the ancient Romans, warfare, broadly conceived, occupied an important role in his writings. Whether in the *Africa*, or in the collected biographies in his *Lives of Illustrious Men*, Petrarch's longest works focused on the great battles and military heroes of both the ancient Roman Republic and empire. While many of the central military figures and battles of antiquity such as Scipio Africanus and the Carthaginian wars, or Julius Caesar and the Gallic and Civil Wars, had never been forgotten in the medieval period, the texts most associated with them, namely Livy's *Punic Wars* and Caesar's *Commentaries on the Gallic and Civil Wars* were not widely read or owned, surviving in a relatively small number of manuscripts scattered around the monastery and cathedral libraries of Europe. Unlike the widespread chivalric literature of the late Middle Ages with its dominant ideal of the Christian knight, the ancient Roman texts and their distinctive literary style were largely unstudied and not imitated. Their military ideals and heroes were most often left in the shadows of pagan history.

But just as Petrarch's letters and poetry marked the true beginning of the related revival of Ciceronian Latinity, his epic poem, collected biographies, and large corpus of letters signaled the initial rebirth of knowledge of ancient Roman warfare and military ideals. This early humanist interest in ancient

Roman military history and accomplishments preceded by many decades conscious attempts to apply this knowledge to the practice and theory of war. But the ideals of Roman military culture increasingly shaped the political mentalities of the fifteenth-century Italian republics and principalities as they came under the influence of Petrarch and his disciples.

One of the most concise Petrarchan calls for the imitation of the ancient Roman military ideal came in a letter from February of 1362 written to the French monk and theologian, Pierre Bersuire, whom Petrarch had known decades earlier in Avignon and whom had been present at the French court when Petrarch visited the king of France on behalf of the Visconti in 1361 (Petrarch 2005, 240). The French military was weak at the time, and Petrarch wrote to Bersuire about the generally deplorable state of European soldiers including those of the Holy Roman Empire who had been fighting in Italy in his lifetime. They were more interested in drinking competitions than in fighting, he complained, and the needed remedy was a return to the military virtue of the ancient Romans. After noting that "my one purpose in initiating the present discourse was simply to discuss the Roman army," he goes on to state that no people or nation could equal them in the glory that came from their military skill (Petrarch 2005: 250). More specifically, he praised the power of their united valor, their courage, obedience, and dedication to military discipline on the part of both commanders and soldiers that they held to be "dearer than life and cultivated as something divine." The result for the Roman empire was that "With its valor and arms it overcame Italy, Europe and the entire world, and ordered it to be content with one ruler" (Petrarch 2005: 251).

Beyond the letters of Petrarch, and serving as a far more extensive and influential point of reference for the revival of the Roman imperial ideal of war and the warrior class, was the expansive biography of Julius Caesar written by Petrarch late in his life as the longest chapter in his *Lives of Illustrious Men*. As a model of humanist history following the ancient example of Suetonius, Petrarch's life of Caesar provided many examples of the skills, strategies, and virtues that led to military victories for the Roman legions fighting under the unparalleled leadership of the founder of the empire. Caesar was presented by Petrarch as "always great and exceptionally great when in great danger" (Petrarch 2007: 423), and it was his ability to inspire courage in his own men and fear in his enemies that distinguished his military valor. Put simply, "Caesar was the best both in war and in peace" (Petrarch 2007: 539), and it was this heroic and exalted literary portrait painted by Petrarch that made Julius Caesar, above all others, the model for aspiring emperors and military captains in their service throughout the Renaissance (Figure 1.1). Largely marginalized as a pagan tyrant in the medieval period, Petrarch's Caesar became instead a cultural touchstone and icon for proponents of warfare in the service of empire in the Renaissance.

FIGURE 1.1: Rubens, Peter Paul (1577–1640). Caesar. Oil on canvas. Credit: bpk Bildagentur/Art Resource, NY. ArtResource: ART428755.

Petrarch was a man with a mission to inspire the imitation of Roman military power in the ruling class of his own day, especially the Holy Roman Emperor Charles IV, but he was also happy to associate those whom he admired with the ancient Roman rulers. Such was the case with a contemporary member of the Colonna family, Stephano, the secular head of the clan in Rome and father of Petrarch's early patron, Cardinal Giovanni Colonna. A senator of Rome and warrior who hosted Petrarch when the poet visited Rome in 1343, Stephano was given the highest praise the poet could offer when he wrote back to Cardinal Colonna saying: "Good God! What a majestic personality ... I thought I was looking at Julius Caesar or Scipio Africano." (Coppi 1855: 125).

This was but one small example of the increasing praise of Julius Caesar as the pre-eminent ancient practitioner of war and example of military virtue in the northern Italian courts where Petrarch and his followers enjoyed much influence. The D'Este family in Ferrara and Gonzaga family in Mantua, above all others, cultivated an intellectual and artistic program in the fifteenth and sixteenth centuries that exalted Caesar and the Roman empire and tied their dynasties strongly to the ancient Roman empire. Sponsoring humanists like Guarino Guarini who produced new editions of Caesar's *Commentaries on the Gallic Wars*, and artists like Mantegna who painted bold new images of Caesar's ancient Roman triumphs, these princes acted as the first central protagonists of the images and ideas of ancient Roman war in its imperial phase.

By the late fifteenth century, this rebirth of interest in Julius Caesar had also spread to France, where humanist courtiers such as Robert Gaguin produced new editions of the *Commentaries* (1488) commissioned by the French monarch, Charles VIII. Inspired, in part by the example of the ancient Roman conqueror of France, this monarch pushed the revival of ancient imperial Roman war beyond the realm of images and ideas and into the realm of actual conquest when he invaded Italy in 1494. This was the real beginning of the Renaissance of war driven by dreams of imperial conquest and the example of the ancient Roman empire. For the next sixty-five years, the two dominant European powers, France and Spain, would fight for the first great prize of early modern imperial contest, namely domination of Italy.

THE ITALIAN WARS AND THE BEGINNING OF IMPERIAL CONTEST, 1494–1559

The central role that Italy played as the first principle theater of Renaissance war is well established. When Charles VIII invaded the peninsula in 1494 to press his claims to the kingdom of Naples as the heir of the earlier Angevin rulers, he led a large army of an estimated 25,000 men. The smaller powers of Italy including the duchy of Milan, the Florentine and Venetian Republics, and the papacy offered no initial resistance or actively collaborated with the French, and Charles VIII quickly took Naples from its much weaker Aragonese ruler, Alfonso. The king of Spain, Ferdinand, a cousin of the king of Naples, who was also the king of Sicily, had more direct and recent dynastic claims to the kingdom of Naples. War between the two most powerful kings of Europe was subsequently inevitable, and for more than half a century they and their successors fought repeated battles for control of the kingdom of Naples, the duchy of Milan, and more general political domination of the Italian peninsula (Guicciardini 1969; Zurita 1610; Mallet and Shaw 2012). Warfare between local powers had been common throughout the medieval period in Italy, and foreign interventions from the French, German, and Spanish monarchs were numerous as well with all of these powers claiming feudal rights at various periods over different parts of the peninsula. The Italian Wars that began in 1494 subsequently continued a familiar pattern initially but, as they progressed over the next sixty-five years, Italy and warfare were transformed by a new political reality, namely the rise of the world's first global power, the Spanish empire. In fact, the Italian Wars represent a perfect test case to measure the impact of empire on the development of warfare and vice versa, since the wars directly paralleled the rise of the Spanish empire first under Ferdinand of Spain and next under his grandson, Charles V (r. 1517–57) and his son, Philp II (r. 1557–98). At the same time, the Italian Wars represented the first major crucible from which emerged a distinctive new culture of war that was expressed and embodied in various forms of Renaissance intellectual, literary, and artistic production, and that spread throughout Europe in the sixteenth and seventeenth centuries. It was, above all else, a culture that increasingly strove to emulate and imitate the ancient Romans in their search for honor, fame, and glory through military victory, and saw war as an essential component of political legitimacy.

Briefly summarized, the period from 1492–1559 witnessed the following major expansions of the territories of the Spanish monarchs either through dynastic inheritance or direct military conquest, or some combination of the two: In 1492 Ferdinand and Isabella conquered the kingdom of Granada; 1492–1503 brought Isabella of Castile, the queen of Spain, the first New World territories of the Caribbean islands claimed by Columbus; 1504 marked Ferdinand's first victory over the French for control of Naples when Pope Julius II invested him with the feudal rights to rule that kingdom; in 1512, Ferdinand conquered the kingdom of Navarre; in 1517, the grandson of Ferdinand and Isabella, Charles V, joined their kingdoms with those of his father and grandfather, the Habsburgs, prince Philip and the Holy Roman Emperor, Maximilian; in 1520–1, Cortés conquered the empire of the Aztecs in Mexico for Charles V; in 1535, Charles V conquered the duchy of Milan in his second major victory over the French king Francis I; in 1535 Pizarro conquered the Inca empire in Peru for Charles V; in 1557, Philip II inherited from his father all of the New World kingdoms, the Spanish kingdoms, Franche-Comté, the Netherlands, and, in Italy, the kingdoms of Sicily and Naples and the duchy of Milan. This was the first global empire and one that in territory surpassed that of ancient Rome (Figure 1.2).

The French, by comparison in this period, won a number of short-lived victories in northern Italy up to 1535, but they were unable to hold any territories for more than a few years or to maintain a permanent military presence or government in the peninsula. In addition to the loss of Naples and Milan, the allegiance of important former allies such as Genoa with its bankers and naval forces and the Florentines, disappeared as both became allies of the Spanish monarchs by the late 1520s. Similarly, the critical military resource of Italian commanders and soldiers was lost as they entered into the service of the Spanish by the thousands. Although the French monarchs were repeatedly able to field large and often successful armies of over 20,000 men in the first decades of the wars, they were ultimately unable to hold the two major territories they

FIGURE 1.2: Rubens, Peter Paul (1577–1640). Emperor Charles V as Master of the World—allegory. Around 1607. Credit: Erich Lessing/Art Resource, NY. ArtResource: ART159759.

claimed a dynastic right to rule, Naples and Milan. This was directly related to the fact that the French claimed no victories or imperial acquisitions abroad in the period between 1494 and 1535, and subsequently had far less of the major resource needed to build and maintain a strong standing military, namely money.

By 1535, and increasingly thereafter for the rest of the sixteenth century, the Spanish empire enjoyed growing revenues from New World gold and silver mines, as well as from their new Italian territories. This was a major component of their military dominance in Europe and the Atlantic world at least until the middle of the seventeenth century, and its importance is first evident in the Italian Wars. During the early decades of the reign of Charles V in the critical years of the Italian Wars, an estimated 4,500,000 gold ducats came to the young emperor from the New World, an amount that was roughly twenty-five percent of his military budget. A similar amount and percentage of the war budget came from the Italian territories of Sicily and Naples underlining the comparable importance of both Old World and New World conquests and income to the funding of war. More generally, the unprecedented and consistent infusion of funding, especially after the discoveries of the silver mines in Potosi (1545) and Zacatecas (1546), were a critical aspect of the military revolution that had its origins in the rise of the Spanish empire. In the period from 1536–56, an additional 31,000,000 ducats came into Spain from the New World pointing to the growing importance of New World treasure for the war budget (Tracy 2002: 113). This model of filling the military treasury with the booty of conquest evoked the memory of the ancient Roman empire, and it went hand in hand with the rise of a permanent, professional, and stronger military force, one of the primary marks of military modernization first witnessed with the Spanish empire.

MACHIAVELLI AND THE ART OF WAR

A more permanent army was also desired in the Republican Florence of Machiavelli, who admired the example of the ancient Roman Republic with its citizen army. But his government never realized that objective and continued to rely upon hired foreign armies and generals to lead them, and to pay for war on an as-needed basis. There was no permanent army in Republican Florence in the age when Machiavelli was a member of the government from 1498 to 1512. Nonetheless, by the time Machiavelli was in exile and writing the only book that he published in his lifetime, *The Art of War* (1521), he had deep knowledge of the many famous battles of the Italian Wars that witnessed the clash of large armies of 10,000 to 25,000 men on each side including Cerignola (1503), Garigliano (1504), Agnadello (1509), and Ravenna (1512). He would also live to see the battle of Pavia (1525). Closer to home, he had deep knowledge of Florentine military affairs as a member of the government council in charge of war from 1498–1512. He had observed the many battles between the French and Spanish for control of Milan, and the emergence of the empire of Charles V, who was the de facto protector and political overlord of Florence when Machiavelli was writing (Machiavelli 2003).

With Fabrizio Colonna, a prominent Roman captain-general in the service of Charles V, used as his primary narrator in *The Art of War*, it was not surprising that Machiavelli, the great champion of republicanism, also drew on the example of the Roman empire as a source for examples for the waging and organizing of war together with the Republican traditions. His text, more than any other writing of the period, illustrated the importance of the ancient Roman example for Renaissance warfare including admiration for the most famous practitioner of war, Julius Caesar. Although two centuries separated Petrarch and Machiavelli, there was a direct line between Petrarch's letter cited earlier and *The Art of War*. Both saw the military power, discipline and organization of the ancient Rome military as a primary model and source of knowledge for rulers in their own day. But Machiavelli's lengthy elaboration on the earlier theme of Petrarch offered far more detail on how contemporary rulers ought to imitate ancient Roman warfare, and he did not limit himself to the Romans or to antiquity. The Italian Wars in which his main protagonist, Fabrizio Colonna, had played a central role for over twenty-five years, also provided a major point of reference for the reflections on the strategies and practices of war. The fact that Renaissance armies were using firearms and cannon meant that they had surpassed the ancients in terms of the technology of war, but for strategy and leadership the ancient Romans remained very much alive and relevant. Caesar's *Commentaries* accompanied many Renaissance captains into war to the extent that by the seventeenth century it was being called the "breviary of captains," and Machiavelli, the republican, did not hesitate to urge imitation of the founder of the Roman empire.

Machiavelli may have been a political leader and champion of the Florentine Republic until 1512, but in 1521, when he published *The Art of War*, the political tide had obviously turned. By then, Machiavelli was the political exile and outsider. Fabrizio Colonna, on the other hand, was the consummate insider and survivor who wielded great authority and status especially in the realm of waging war. By giving voice to the views of Fabrizio Colonna, Machiavelli was positioning himself for a political comeback in a context where the rising Spanish empire was casting an ever larger shadow over Florentine affairs.

This was simply political realism on Machiavelli's part. As *The Prince* most vividly demonstrated, by the time of his political exile in 1513, he had turned to providing advice for single rulers, and the model "new prince" was Fabrizio's patron, Ferdinand of Aragon. By the time that *The Art of War* was published in 1521, moreover, Charles V, Ferdinand's successor, had been crowned Holy Roman Emperor and also become ruler of the Aztec empire conquered by Cortés in 1521, thereby emerging as an even more powerful ruler than his grandfather. In this political context, *The Art of War* was a companion piece to *The Prince* since it provided pragmatic advice and reflection on the most important activity of any prince, monarch, or emperor—the waging of war. Moreover, both texts shared one additional political perspective that represented the most critical and persistent turn in the philosophy of war that marked Renaissance empires and imperial monarchs in the following centuries: the idea that war legitimized political power and brought honor, power, and glory to the ruler. This was a secular perspective derived from the example of ancient Rome, and largely divorced from any concern for Christian ethics. Increasingly, in actions, if not always in word, this Machiavellian perspective shaped the attitude toward power and war that drove the rising empires of Europe.

FIGURE 1.3: Anonymous, seventeenth century. Conquest of Mexico—The death of Montezuma at the hands of his own people on July 1, 1520. Spanish School, second half seventeenth century. Oil on canvas; 120 × 200 cm. This scene is considered to be part of the earliest of three complete cycles of paintings of the Conquest. Credit: Erich Lessing/Art Resource, NY. ArtResource: ART370950.

Like Petrarch 150 years earlier, Machiavelli provided a guide for imperial rule that drew upon ancient models such as the Caesars, but the persistent and thick experience of war in his own day, and the many examples provided by contemporary or near contemporary actors such as Fabrizio Colonna and other captains in the Italian Wars, made Machiavelli the more compelling and raw political muse and mirror for sixteenth-century conquerors whether they would admit it or not. Like Petrarch, his work was another critical cultural touchstone for imperial warfare and warriors, but the picture Machiavelli painted was of a more brutal and bloody contest informed by his own personal experience of war that Petrarch lacked (Figure 1.3).

THE SPANISH EMPIRE AND RENAISSANCE WAR

The theories about war and empire espoused by Machiavelli were only effective, of course, if there was the money and armies to put them into practice. Admiring the Roman legions and the victories of Caesar was one thing. Imitating them was another. While the French monarchs between 1494 and 1559, for example, were able to repeatedly raise armies for their Italian campaigns, they were not able to maintain a constant military presence in Italy. They had neither the necessary amount of money or men. The Spanish kings, however, did have the financial and human resources, and this allowed them to establish permanent armies and navies throughput their empire by the middle of the sixteenth century, a central mark of the Renaissance military revolution.

The most noticeable example developed first in Italy where the Spanish had a continuous presence by the middle of the sixteenth century of the famous Spanish *tercios*, or companies of roughly three thousand professional soldiers, in the kingdoms of Sicily, Naples, and Milan. The *tercios* first developed in Spain in the conquest of Granada by Ferdinand and Isabella in 1492, and it was a commander of those forces, Gonzalo Fernández de Cordoba, the "Great Captain," who also led the Spanish *tercios* in the conquest of Naples in 1504. Organized in the formation of a large block of men armed with pikes on the exterior guarding infantry armed with arquebuses on the interior, the *tercios* were a major factor that made the Spanish military the dominant fighting force in Europe in the period from roughly 1500 to 1650 (Quatrefages 1983a and 1983b; Thompson 1976).

With total numbers of Spanish troops in Italy ranging from ten to thirty thousand men throughout the period, the armies were commanded by the Spanish Viceroys of Sicily and Naples and the governor of Milan, all of whom also held the title of Captain General of the Spanish military forces. Spanish government in Italy was overwhelmingly focused on military affairs—on feeding, supplying, and housing the infantry and naval forces that guaranteed Spanish rule. Ultimately under the command of the king, the Spanish armies saw few battles in Italy after 1559 and the Peace of Cateau-Cambresis, when the French monarch acknowledged Spanish claims in Italy and withdrew for most of the next century. But Spanish armies in Italy were frequently called to serve other imperial needs: they fought in the Netherlands during the long decades of the Dutch revolts from the 1550s to the 1650s, for example, and they also joined other Spanish and Italian forces in the conquest of Portugal in 1580 (Parker, 2004) (Figure 1.4).

The transport of thousands of troops to Portugal in 1580 underlined the other critical component of the Spanish empire's war machine that came into its own as a permanent force in the latter half of the sixteenth century, namely the navy. Growing, but not yet well-organized or permanent, in the time of Ferdinand and Charles V, by the middle of the sixteenth century, Spanish ships circulated in small groups in the western Mediterranean between the major Iberian port cities and the Italian ports in Palermo, Messina, and Naples. Each of the Italian kingdoms were expected to pay for and maintain a number of ships for their defense, but in addition, Spanish ships and, after 1527, the fleet of Genoa, joined in the naval forces serving the Spanish monarchy. By the

FIGURE 1.4: Velazquez, Diego Rodriguez (1599–1660). The surrender of Breda, June 2, 1625. During the Dutch War of Independence, Justin of Nassau hands the keys of the city to Ambrosio Spinola, commander of the Spanish troops. Credit: Erich Lessing/Art Resource, NY.

1560's, a fleet of between 100 and 200 Spanish-allied ships sailed in the western Mediterranean.

While these forces enforced Spanish power in Italy, they also guarded the Italian coastlines from the Ottoman threat and the ships of their surrogates in North Africa who constantly raided both Italian and Spanish territories. The contest between the Ottoman and Spanish empires for dominance in the Mediterranean was another major cause of warfare in the period, and for the growing Spanish navy. The famous naval battle of Lepanto in 1571 between the Ottoman navy and an alliance of Spanish, Venetian, and Papal forces was an epic clash that involved combined forces of an estimated 160,000 men and 600 ships. It was the largest naval battle fought in the Mediterranean with oar-powered galleys since antiquity. (Parker 1988, 89; Beeching 1982). The victory of the Holy League led by Don Juan of Austria, illegitimate son of Charles V, and the king of Spain's half-brother, effectively ended Ottoman westward expansion in the Mediterranean. Comparisons with ancient Rome were not lost on contemporaries especially on the winning side, and the victory cemented Philip II's reputation as the new Constantine, or Roman emperor, of his time. War clearly brought honor and fame and glory to the most powerful imperial monarch of the age, Philip II, and the other victors. Moreover, the victory at Lepanto inspired a large wave of cultural production including poetry, theatrical reproductions of the battle, paintings, and sculpture to celebrate and commemorate the event.[2]

WAR AND IMPERIAL CONQUEST IN THE NEW WORLD

Beyond the Mediterranean, the simultaneous and interrelated growth of Spanish military and naval power in the Atlantic and Pacific worlds also deepened and solidified throughout the sixteenth and seventeenth century making the Spanish empire the first modern global power. War, again, played a decisive role in the expansion of empire. Superior military power in the form of soldiers fighting with armor, swords, horses, cannon, and firearms allowed relatively small numbers of Spanish soldiers to conquer and then rule over vastly larger numbers of indigenous peoples first in the Caribbean (1492–1510), then in Mexico (1520–1) and shortly thereafter in Peru (1532–5). The Spanish captains, Hernan Cortés and Francisco Pizarro in Mexico and Peru, conquered the Aztec and Inca empires with initial groups of roughly 600 and 200 Spanish soldiers respectively. Indigenous allies helped Cortés, but it was the technological superiority of Spanish weapons, together with political cunning and deception, that allowed him to impose political rule and quickly put down most rebellions with relatively small numbers of soldiers. Pizarro took a longer time to subdue the Inca empire in part because of internal rivalries and civil wars among the Spanish. But after Pizarro's death in 1541, the new Spanish military governors sent by Charles V imposed Spanish rule through the effective waging of limited wars so that within one generation Inca resistance was largely overcome.

The wars of conquest in the New World cannot be confused with war in Renaissance Italy. While there was an indisputable epic drama to the swift conquests of the Aztec and Inca empires, these were not great battles of well-trained Spanish *tercios* led by captains who had read Machiavelli's *Art of War*. No one confused the rough bands of Spanish soldiers for Roman legions. Rather, the unpolished and largely unprofessional soldiers that sought their fortune in the New World were fighting first and foremost for a chance at riches, or at least a piece of land with some indigenous people to work it for them. They had the advantages of horses, steel, and gunpowder, and a deep thirst for conquest, but little by way of noble political purpose.

What the conquistadors did share with their contemporaries who had conquered Granada, Naples, and Milan, was the militant culture of the

Reconquista in Spain and the humanist culture of Renaissance Italy that encouraged the imitation of ancient Rome martial values in pursuit of honor, glory, and power. It was a virulent combination that comprised the cultural foundations of the Spanish empire. For Spaniards who increasingly saw themselves as the early modern heirs of the ancient Roman empire, it was the rebirth of the imperial ideal and Roman ambition that served as an historical point of comparison and contrast. It was the Roman idea of empire that they appropriated as their own and sought to surpass. Cortés and his followers such as Bernal Díaz del Castillo saw themselves in a Roman mirror but judged themselves greater than Julius Caesar and the Romans. They had, after all, conquered vast empires with far fewer soldiers and resources than the Romans and much further from home (Lupher 2003).

Soldiers who doubled as authors were not limited to the few famous conquistadors like Hernan Cortés and Bernal Díaz, or the most famous of all soldier authors to fight at Lepanto, Miguel Cervantes. Rather, recent work has demonstrated that there was a veritable "Soldiers' Republic of Letters" made up of hundreds of soldiers who frequently migrated around the Spanish empire and wrote about their experiences in letters, poetry, and prose. They have been described as "not only the makers but also the partakers of an intense literary circulation and exchange" (Martínez 2016, 33). At the same time, these soldiers and their writings revealed how global empires, with rapidly growing institutions such as a navy, courier services, and a growing population of men who traveled the world, served as the vehicles for a distinct military literary culture (Martínez 2016: 33). Together with "high" humanists who wrote about war, attempting to imitate the style of Livy, Thucydides and Herodotus—men like the historians Machiavelli, Guicciardini, Zurita, Mariana, Giovio, Sepulveda, Morales, Herrera, and many others—these largely unknown authors make up another substantial layer of cultural production that was inextricably tied to the rise of Renaissance Empire.

What they shared with their more famous literary citizens in the Spanish Republic of Letters, at least, was a lofty sense of their place in history. By the end of the sixteenth century, royal historians like Antonio Herrera and Juan de Mariana agreed that the Spanish conquest of the New World was one of the greatest accomplishments in all of human history. The American conquests that built the Spanish empire had brought all of Spain the honor, glory, power, and riches that were the ultimate aim and promise of war. Spain was the heir of the Roman empire in all of these realms, and had indeed surpassed it in the geographical magnitude of its reach. With the conquest of Portugal in 1580, Philip II had added to the already vast Spanish empire all of the territories of the Portuguese empire including Brazil, the spice islands, the African and Indian trading fortresses, and the Atlantic islands. Combined with the Spanish conquest of the Philippine islands by Miguel Legazpi in 1565, and the quick growth of

Manila into the largest European settlement in Asia, these Pacific territories made Spain a truly global empire and the dominant military behemoth in Europe and the world (Parker 1988: 125).

The size and power of the Spanish empire made it the object of great envy, fear, and growing opposition among other European monarchs, especially the French and British, who in the sixteenth century had begun to entertain their own imperial ambitions. For both the French and the British, the pursuit of empire was stalled and stymied by internal religious wars as well as the stronger Spanish military. But by the late sixteenth century, both powers had at least begun to lay the cultural foundations of empire, and in the seventeenth century they would realize their own dreams of claiming Atlantic empires of their own.

WAR AND EMPIRE IN GREAT BRITAIN IN THE AGE OF ELIZABETH AND THE STUART MONARCHY

In the case of Great Britain, it was at an unlikely moment in the late sixteenth century, when its military power at sea was characterized more by pirates like Francis Drake than by any organized navy, that it managed to score a military victory against the Spanish that signaled its early entry into imperial contest in the Atlantic world. The planned Spanish invasion of England in 1588 by a large armada of Spanish ships, was yet another example of the military hubris and appetite of Philip II. Antagonized by the state-sponsored piracy of Drake and others against Spanish ports and ships in the Atlantic, angered by Queen Elizabeth's treatment of Catholics especially in Ireland, and tempted by the possibility of toppling the Protestant monarch and claiming further glory and reputation for himself as the new Constantine of his day, Philip sent a large fleet of ships against England to invade and possibly to conquer the island (Fernández-Armesto 1988: viii).

The largest naval operation since Lepanto, the Spanish Armada prepared in Spain counted an estimated 135 ships and 30,000 men. Another 16,000 men and the necessary transport ships were added in the Netherlands (Fernández-Armesto 1988: 8). While numbers of ships and men are difficult to calculate with precision, the number of Spanish war ships is estimated to have been between 35 and 50 (Fernández-Armesto 1988: 19). The English forces had roughly similar guns and cannon, but their ships were more agile in the North Sea, and they outmaneuvered the heavier Spanish ships. Bad weather further aided the English, and the Spanish Armada failed in its purpose losing many men and a few major ships to the British (Fernández-Armesto 1988: 162–3).

Elizabeth had her first major victory against the most powerful empire of her day, and she celebrated with a ritual triumph in the Roman style, parading through the streets of London in a "chariot throne." (Hopkins 2008: 1). The revival of the ancient triumph to celebrate victory in war was a well-practiced ritual in the Spanish empire by the late sixteenth century. Multiple triumphs were organized for Charles V in Palermo, Messina, Naples, and Rome after his victory in Tunis in 1535, and Philip II enjoyed a triumphal entry into Lisbon after the 1581 conquest complete with ephemeral arches and inscriptions celebrating his victory, just to name a few well-known examples. But the Elizabethan triumph of 1588 was a first for England, and it pointed to both rising imperial ambition and the accompanying celebration of war in a Renaissance style.

The early realization of global empire for the British, however, came not with Elizabeth but with her Stuart successors, James I (r. 1603–25), Charles I (r. 1625–49), and Charles II (r. 1660–85) (Figure 1.5). By the early seventeenth century, the ideas and aesthetics associated with Renaissance Empire had gained momentum in Great Britain as James I embraced the identity of an imperial monarch who sought to imitate none other than the emperor Augustus in both his attempts at home to make London the leading city of Europe, and in his attempts abroad to establish British colonies in North America (Leapman 2003: 184). The rising naval capabilities that the British demonstrated against the Spanish Armada also translated into an increased number of voyages to the coastline of North America for the purpose of establishing plantation colonies. During the reign of James I, five plantation companies were formed for Virginia, New England, Newfoundland, and Bermuda, and by the king's death in 1625, over 10,000 British settlers were living in British North American colonies (Macinnes 2007: 138–9). Unlike the Spanish conquests in the New World, early British colonization was not marked by any dramatic military actions like those of Cortés or Pizarro. With a more fragmented native population that had no equivalent to the Aztec or Inca empires, North America did not provide the stage for epic wars of conquest. The early

FIGURE 1.5: Struck gold medal of Charles II by John Roettier: the Increase of the Navy. London, England, AD 1667. D: 56 mm. The reverse of the medal shows "The Increase in the Navy" with the king's mistress, Frances Stuart, as Britannia. Copyright The Trustees of the British Museum/Art Resource, NY. ArtResource: ART307601.

warfare that did take place was largely defensive as the British attempted to protect their modest early plantations and settlements. Treaties with Spain in the reign of James I and Philip III that acknowledged the right of the English to settle the lands north of Florida also lifted the threat of Spanish opposition and war. British colonization subsequently continued, and in the reign of Charles I emigration to the New World increased to over 80,000. Of the early settlers, 53,700 were still alive in 1640 (Games 1999: 4).

By the latter half of the seventeenth century, the growing number of settlers led to increased conflict with the native tribes along the eastern coast of North America, and an escalation of warfare. The war with the Algonquians, or King Philip's War in 1675, to give one example, led to harsh retaliation on the part of the British colonists who forced the Indians onto reservations and out of New England. In the case of the Mohawk Valley in New York, the native population decreased by over ninety percent from an estimated 8,000 people to 440 by 1698. Like Spanish imperialism in South America, British empire building in North America led to a catastrophic impact on the population of the indigenous people who were killed by a lethal combination of violence, disease, and dislocation (Snow n.d.: 81). To make matters worse for Native Americans, by the middle of the seventeenth century, there was another European power seeking to build an empire on their land, and bringing their wars with the British to North America, namely the French.

FRENCH EMPIRE BUILDING IN THE SEVENTEENTH CENTURY AND THE APEX OF RENAISSANCE WAR

As the invasion of Italy by Charles VIII in 1494 so clearly demonstrated, the French monarchy from the late fifteenth century onward was motivated by imperial aspirations and the Renaissance dream of reviving the empire of the Caesars. Second perhaps only to Italian princes, the French monarchs identified deeply with the ancient Roman past, and especially with Julius Caesar whose *Commentaries on the Gallic Wars* played a central role in shaping French historical identity. More specifically, Caesar was a major military role model and "the best captain of his age" as the humanist and royal councilor, Jean Bodin, described him (Bodin 1606: 1610).

Like the British, however, the French monarchs of the sixteenth century were kept from realizing their larger political ambitions by a combination of superior Spanish power, a series of short-lived kings, and internal religious wars. But the lessons taught by successive generations of French humanists and monarchs were not in vain, and they found their realization in the age of Louis XIV (r. 1638–1715). Formally inheriting the crown upon his father's death in 1643, the young king was steeped in the ideas and images of empire and war from his youth as revealed by his first "scholarly" production: a translation of the first book of Caesar's *Commentaries on the Gallic Wars* done at the age of thirteen (Louis XIV 1651).

More concretely, Louis XIV benefited from the council and political direction of two of the most successful students and practitioners of Machiavelli's *Art of War* of the entire period, Cardinal Richelieu and Cardinal Mazarin, the de facto leaders of the French state in his youth.

In the case of Cardinal Richelieu, the prime minister for Louis XIII until his death in 1642, he was responsible for the rise of French military power to a level where its armies were able to score major victories against the Spanish troops that had been dominant for over a century. Governing throughout the first twenty-five years of the Thirty Years War (1618–48), Richelieu and Louis XIII began a military buildup that roughly doubled the size of French troops from an estimated 75,000 in the early seventeenth century to 150,000 by 1635, and they also expanded the navy to include two fleets, one for the Mediterranean and one for the Atlantic. To fund all of this, they imposed more taxes, sold more offices, and borrowed more money (Parrott 2001: 9).

Throughout the Thirty Years War, a central French goal was to undermine the power of the Spanish empire both through direct military engagement but also by funding rebellions in Italy, Portugal, and Catalonia. Their strategy met great success when Portugal regained its independence in 1640 from the Spanish king, Philip IV, the most serious reversal for the Spanish in over 150 years. Imperial contest was taking a toll on the Spanish who were stretched thin around the globe. The French had the benefit of a unified territory with an abundant population, but they also sought the riches and the reputation of empire, a fact that led Richelieu to more than triple the naval budget after he assumed power in 1624. The Atlantic fleet served, in part, to escort merchant convoys to the New World where the French established new settlements on the Caribbean islands of Guadeloupe, Martinique, Saint Croix, Saint Martin, and Grenada. Focused on growing tobacco and sugar using African slaves, these new colonies counted 3,000 French settlers and 1,200 African slaves by 1643 (Banks 2002: 16–18). Success in war and empire building clearly went hand in hand for the French, and an important victory over the Spanish at the Battle of Rocroi in 1643 further emboldened Cardinal Mazarin.

War and empire building were the major preoccupations of the century's most bellicose monarch, Louis XIV, and from the beginning of his reign, he used the language and imagery of the imperial Renaissance to promote this political project. Like his predecessors and contemporaries in France, Italy, Spain, and Britain, he followed the examples of the ancient Romans in their use of ritual pageantry, equestrian monuments, monumental palace architecture, and historical narrative paintings celebrating military victories to depict France as the new Roman empire of his time, and himself as the new Caesar (Dandelet

2014: 236–40). Spending as much as ten percent of his annual budget on art and architecture, the Sun King embraced the views of his minister Colbert that "the grandeur and spirit of Princes" was revealed by their building projects (Rabreau 1984: 127–30) (Figure 1.6).

But Louis XIV also recognized that what brought more glory and reputation to the monarch was military victories, and he built up the largest military of the

FIGURE 1.6: Warin, Jean III (1604–72). Statue of King Louis XIV at the Salon of Venus in the Grands Appartements. Credit: RMN-Grand Palais/Art Resource, NY. ArtResource: ART387347.

period during his reign. Doubling the size of the navy and army, he had over 450,000 soldiers on land, and another 100,000 men served in a navy that counted 400 ships. He spent an estimated two-thirds of the entire state budget on this formidable war machine, and he used it often. France was at war for more than half of the years he was in power, or roughly thirty out of fifty-four years on the throne after he took full control of the government in 1661 (Banks 2002: 23–4).

Not surprisingly, increased naval power led to an expansion of French New World colonies. The king sponsored new voyages such as that of Alexander de Prouville in 1664 that took 1,300 men and six ships to the Caribbean and then to Canada to impose governors on the colonies and to fight against Iroquois resistance to the French. At the same time, French exploration in the Mississippi River Valley was claiming the vast Louisiana Territory for Louis XIV in the heart of the North American continent. By the end of the seventeenth century, the French subsequently had a far more substantial presence in North America that looked much more like the beginnings of a real Atlantic empire (Banks 2002: 25).

While larger territorial claims bolstered the king's reputation, what Louis XIV and his ministers additionally hoped for from their colonies was more revenue from the sugar and tobacco trade in the Caribbean. To this end, the West India Company was established in 1664 which gave the crown a full monopoly over Atlantic trade. Governance and administration of the colonies was reorganized with the monarchy taking more direct control in appointing governors and imposing uniform taxes. In addition, two new trading companies were established under royal control to supply slaves to the sugar plantations (Banks 2002: 24).

The slave trade, and New World trade more generally, was one of the most lucrative sources of income for European empires in the later seventeenth century, and Louis XIV recognized in a letter from 1709 that the trade of the Indies was the real cause of one of the most overt contests for empire that took place in the entire early modern period (Miquelon 2001: 653). The War of the Spanish Succession that consumed most of Europe from 1700 to 1713 was the last great war of Louis XIV's lifetime, and it can be seen as the culmination of the wars between Spain and France that began in 1494 in Italy, and as the war that would determine the fate of European empires for decades to come. In 1700, the Habsburg monarchy of Spain was literally dying since the last of that line, Charles II, had produced no heir. Competing dynastic claims from the Austrian Habsburgs and Louis XIV based upon marriages to Spanish princesses were the formal cause of the war that broke out in 1700, but the entry of the British, Dutch, and Portuguese into the contest at various times over the next thirteen years underlined that there was much more at stake than whether the new Spanish monarch was another Habsburg or a Bourbon.

The French king won the first round of the battle with the Austrian Habsburgs, and he successfully place his grandson, Philip V on the throne in Madrid. This aroused much resentment among the British and Dutch who feared a Bourbon monopoly on trade in the New World, and although Louis XIV promised that the French and Spanish thrones would remain separate, this was not the case and the French were soon given the lucrative slave trade (Miquelon 2001: 653–77). This was a major factor that led the Dutch and British into an alliance with the Habsburgs against the Bourbon monarchs, and for the following decade wars were fought in Europe, in the Atlantic and Mediterranean, and in the North American colonies. The contest for empire had brought war to a considerable part of the world. It also drained the coffers of the French king who ultimately had to settle for an unfavorable treaty in 1713. Philip V and the Bourbon dynasty remained in Spain, but it awarded the slave trade to the British for the next sixty years and paved the way for their rise in the Atlantic world and New World. Louis XIV had won the dynastic war against the Habsburgs, but left France exhausted. On his deathbed the old king admitted that perhaps he had loved war too much.

That was a fitting epitaph not just for the French but for all Renaissance empires. The dream of reviving the military strength of the Roman empire that Petrarch urged in the late fourteenth century had come to pass with the Renaissance empires of Spain, France, and Britain in the sixteenth and seventeenth centuries. The monarchs and ruling class of Europe were enchanted by the rewards of empire—power, honor, glory, and money—and they embraced the main vehicle toward those goals, war, with a passion that spread around the globe. This was a potent political script that was hard to depart from for European governments, and its power continued to shape the eighteenth and nineteenth century globe as well.

CHAPTER TWO

Trade

DANIEL VITKUS

The Western overseas empires that arose during the early modern period would never have come into existence without trade—and in particular, without a globalizing form of commerce called "capitalism." Trade is an ancient human activity, but capitalism is a historically specific, innovative form of trade, and it simultaneously altered both the domestic economies of western Europe and the transnational economies that linked Europe to the rest of the world. The globalizing system of emergent capitalism built on and mutated from the old, long-distance commerce in luxury goods, including the longstanding traffic of the Silk Road that connected Asia to Europe. Capitalist forms of trade transformed many parts of the world during the two centuries that followed Columbus's arrival in the Western Hemisphere, so that by the late seventeenth century, the Englishman John Evelyn could boast of the Western empires' global reach in terms that seem inspired by one of John Donne's metaphysical conceits:

> Whoever Commands the Ocean, Commands the Trade of the World, and whoever Commands the Trade of the World, Commands the Riches of the World, and whoever is Master of That, Commands the World itself .... We, and other Nations have driven the Trade of the *East-Indies*, with his Treasure of the *West*, and, uniting, as it were, Extreams, made the *Poles* to kiss. (1674: 15)

The sixteenth and seventeenth centuries were a highly dynamic period of improvisational interaction between the Western empires (by which I mean those of Spain, Portugal, Holland, and England) and other cultures around the globe. During this time, these rapidly developing empires, undertaking a robust expansion of commercial mobility and colonial activity, began their long effort to dominate and exploit the rest of the world. Whenever feasible and advantageous, these early Western empires conquered and then built colonies; where that was not possible but valuable commodities were to be acquired, they established commercial factories and negotiated trade agreements; and where other powers abroad prevented a more intrusive or dominating presence, they introduced diplomats and merchants who dealt with those foreign powers in a more submissive way, conforming to the rules of a game that they could not dictate themselves. So, for example, the European empires conquered in Mexico, Peru, and Virginia; they established factories in Bantam, Goa, and Japan; and they sent their merchants and diplomats to negotiate commercial terms at the seats of power in places like Marrakesh in Morocco, Constantinople in Turkey, Isfahan in Persia, and the Mughal court in India. As a direct result of these efforts, by 1700, one million Europeans were living outside of Europe. This circulation of people, goods, and commodities had tremendous cultural implications, and authors throughout western Europe were inspired by the transculturation that resulted from these new mobilities. Playwrights, poets, and prose writers eagerly engaged in their work with the realities and fantasies that took place within the global system of early modernity.

It is important to understand this European imperial and commercial expansion, not as something preordained or as carried out exclusively by aggressive Europeans who visited their Euro-capitalist essence on passive peoples and economies elsewhere. It was not merely an "outward thrust"—as some economic historians have described it—but the result of a complex, dynamical interaction between western European actors, states, and institutions and a variety of other complex socio-economic entities in other parts of the world with which those European traders and colonizers engaged.[1] In other words, Europeans did not simply export their Western, capitalist ways, imposing them wholesale on foreign peoples—rather, Europe and the Europeans were themselves radically altered by their exchanges, including their trade, with other cultures across the globe.

Capitalism arrived on the world stage as a transcultural system with strong roots in the financial innovations of the northern Italian cities whose traders had reached nearly all of Europe and spread throughout the Mediterranean by the fourteenth century. According to the economic historian Ralph Davis, Italian merchants and financiers "had been developing very elaborate commercial techniques; of credit trading; of money transfer (through bills of exchange and letters of credit) and banking; of commercial partnership and agency; of foreign exchange dealing over distance and time; of marine insurance; of book-keeping and general documentation" (1973: 27). The capitalist drive for profit was enabled by these novel strategies, which were put into action first in the Mediterranean and were eventually adopted by other European traders. These new financial techniques facilitated the collective acquisition of economic power by the rising merchant classes in the form of capital, a process that is sometimes called "primitive accumulation." In Italy, these innovations facilitated the accumulation of wealth in the northern cities where merchant, noble, and ecclesiastical elites used their disposable income to sponsor the cultural flowering that we call the Renaissance.

Changes in economic technique were accompanied by structural changes in the domestic economies of western Europe and in the land-based commercial system, but at the same time, during the sixteenth century, a genuine world-economy developed based primarily on long-distance maritime trade. The overseas enterprises that would increase the wealth and power of Western capitalist elites began with the ferocious endeavors of commodity-seeking voyagers and mercenary leaders like Vasco da Gama, Columbus, Cortés, Pizarro, Sir Walter Raleigh, Thomas Cavendish, and Francis Drake. These (Portuguese, Spanish, and English) men all gained crown sponsorship and support, but their expeditions could not have been mounted without additional backing from merchant-class creditors and investors. They may have represented themselves as the loyal, heroic servants of royal patrons, but their expeditions were "adventures" in a new, capitalist mode that depended on innovative mechanisms of credit and debt. In his extensive study of the ideology of adventure, Michael Nerlich urges us to understand early modern (ad)venturing dialectically: it is "emancipatory" in empowering the bourgeoisie while weakening the old feudal system; and at the same time, it functions increasingly as "an ideology of exploitation and oppression" that "from its beginnings . . . contains the dialectic of expansion, of the extension of power, of the increase of profit and security" (1988: 1.81). Nerlich points out how the Western empires' aggressive expansion through financial and physical risk-taking took place in correspondence with a culture and an ideology that reinforced, rationalized, and glorified that expansionist impulse.

The shift from a feudal economy to capitalist forms of trade in western Europe involved many changes in its domestic economies (most notably the expansion of private property), as well as new forms of investment in risky long-distance enterprises. Some cultural historians have claimed that these new forms of commerce were directly and causally linked to the cultural flowering known as "Renaissance humanism," which began in Italy during the fifteenth century and quickly spread to other parts of Europe. The historical period in western Europe that came to be called "the Renaissance" (c. 1450–1650) has traditionally been defined in terms of cultural developments, but many historians have pointed to other foundational changes that marked the new era, such as the rise of the state, or the commercialization of society in terms of the establishment of the market as the fundamental unit of economic life in western Europe. This "commercialization" involved, within and beyond Europe, an increasing monetarization of transactions, the rapid growth of cites, new forms of consumerism, and the rising power of the urban capitalist classes. A gradual transformation unfolded, one that weakened the old feudal order and ushered in a new kind of class system without serfdom and with a vitiated aristocracy. These economic transformations were accompanied by a change in outlook—a new mentality or "spirit" expressed in various cultural forms (Rabb 2006: 65). With the capitalists' new accumulation of wealth came an effort to acquire the status and trappings of upper-class culture, and to dignify trade with aggrandizing imagery. We see this in Figure 2.1, De Bry's depiction of a prosperous merchant striding the dock next to a tidy bale of commercial goods. It was published in a book offering images like this one, which incorporated blank spaces where names and mottos, along with heraldic shields or escutcheons, could be inserted, allowing the rising merchant-capitalist to assert his "gentle" status.

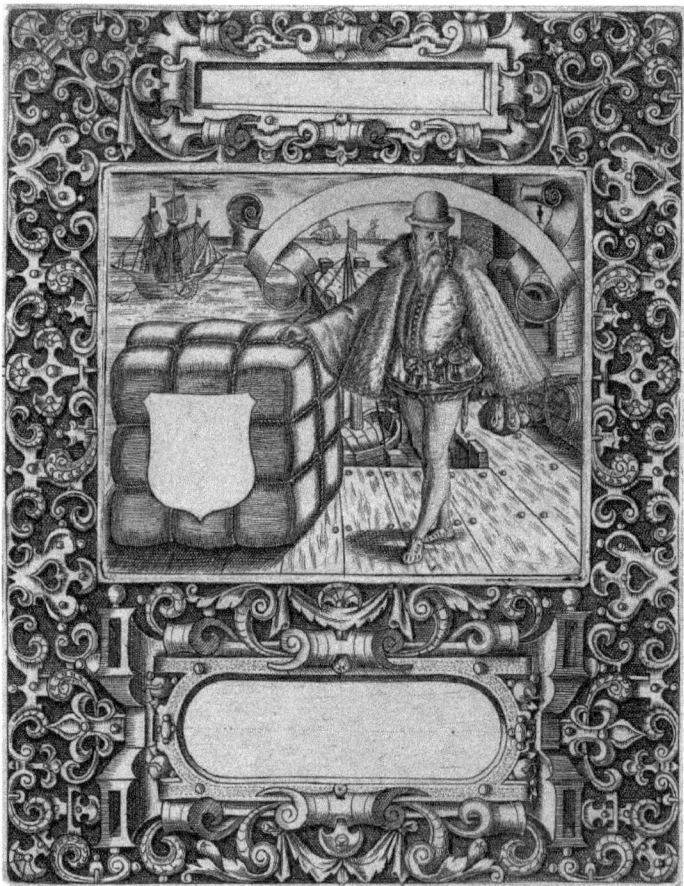

FIGURE 2.1: Engraving by Theodor de Bry in *Emblemata Nobilitati et vulgo scitu digna* (Frankfurt, 1592), p. 147 of 276 unnumbered pages. Credit: Getty Research Institute.

An important question, however, is whether our current understanding of the production of great works of art during the Renaissance, and the flourishing of artistic production under the patronage of new mercantile and imperial elites in western Europe, should be accompanied by an unqualified celebration of those same commercial energies and the aesthetic achievements they allegedly engendered. This is the approach taken by Lisa Jardine in *Worldly Goods*, where she boldly declares, "The seeds of our own exuberant multiculturalism and bravura consumerism were planted in the European Renaissance" (1998: 34). For Jardine and many other scholars who have written about the Renaissance, long-distance, cross-cultural trade and its attendant conspicuous consumption were part and parcel of the productive, creative energies that produced Renaissance humanism and its great works of art. Economic exchange, for them, is almost always a positive force in the "world" because it generates artistic achievement and the making of luxurious, beautiful "goods." They are particularly fixated on the art *object* as an exchangeable commodity that travels between cultures, producing a rich commercial and symbolic exchange between merchants and their cultures. But what about those works of art produced during the Renaissance that were sharply critical of the new consumerism and the new economic practices of the time? Or questioned and problematized the new forms of exchange, including those between "East and West"? This article will go on to examine these questions and will reach a conclusion that is at odds with the generally celebratory interpretations of Jardine, Jerry Brotton, and other scholars in the fields of literary studies, art history, and cultural history who tend to downplay or ignore the elitism, violence, and exploitation that enabled global trade and therefore accompanied high art production, multiculturalism, and consumerism during the "global Renaissance."[2]

The early modern phase of European overseas expansion (through increased long-distance mobility, through the creation of many new trade connections abroad, and through the establishment of permanent settlements and colonies by means of force and dispossession) was motivated by a desire for profit. Its initial impetus involved efforts to gain access to Eastern luxury goods, and to the gold and silver that could be used to purchase those goods. For centuries, Europe had been exporting gold and silver to Asia because Europeans produced very few commodities that were in high demand among their Asian trade partners. Traders from Europe were therefore obliged to pay for spices, silks, and other imports in specie. Though the exchange of goods between Europe and Asia tended to be asymmetrical (not goods traded for goods, but precious metals in the form of money in exchange for Asian goods) and therefore gave Asian economies a kind of advantage initially, there was one area in which western Europeans held the upper hand: they possessed highly developed practices and technologies for maritime violence, long-distance voyaging, and gunpowder-based warfare. The Chinese were the only Asian power who wielded anything like this kind of technology on a large scale (their naval power was demonstrated in the series of expeditionary voyages led by Admiral Zheng He between 1405 and 1455). Had the Ming rulers continued those efforts, China might have gained the potential to block the expansion of the Western empires; but by the end of the fifteenth century, Ming imperial policy shifted significantly to a more closed and self-sufficient posture toward the global economy. Just at the moment that the Chinese turned away from the enterprise of long-distance maritime expansion, the Western empires and their high-tech vessels arrived in Asia.

PORTUGUESE INNOVATION AND SPANISH CONQUEST

During the fifteenth century, the Portuguese (soon followed by others) used their advanced technologies (including lightweight guns, navigational tools, and tall ships) to move aggressively down the western coast of Africa, and then eventually sail around the cape to India. When Vasco da Gama's expedition reached India in 1498, it disrupted a relatively peaceful trade zone, and the Portuguese began using bombardment (and the threat of bombardment) to extort advantageous trade concessions from ports in the region. This success in reaching the source of the spices by sea and in making huge profits from venturing in that manner opened the way for others and also inspired various European "explorers" to seek a western passage to the Indies. Among those seeking a new route to the Indies was a Genoese navigator and business agent, one Cristoforo Colombo, who had been based in Lisbon from 1477 to 1485 and who traded along the West African coast during the early 1480s. At the Portuguese court, Columbus sought support to seek a western route to the Indies, one which would be easier than the long journey around the southern cape of Africa; but when Bartolomeu Dias returned to Portugal in 1488 with the news that he had successfully rounded the Cape of Good Hope, Columbus was forced to seek other patrons to invest in his attempt to cross the Atlantic.

During the years that followed, Columbus engaged in extended negotiations to secure the backing of Ferdinand II of Aragon and Isabella I of Castile, the rulers of Spain, but initially he was not successful. In January of 1492, however, just after they had conquered Granada, the last Muslim-ruled kingdom in Iberia, the Catholic monarchs agreed to grant Columbus the financial support and royal sponsorship that he had been seeking. In August he sailed west and made landfall on the other side of the Atlantic—but failed to achieve his primary objective, the discovery of a western route to the Indies. Instead, he arrived in the Western Hemisphere, landing first at what is today part of the Bahamas, which he mistook for East Asia. It was Columbus's "mistake" that opened the way for the Spanish and Portuguese to establish a truly global system, launching voyages into this so-called "New World" in order to plunder the civilizations they found there while continuing to pursue trade in Asia and Africa. In Asia, they faced a group of powerful empires they could not hope to defeat on the mainland, but in the Americas, they were able to overpower empires like those of the Aztecs and Incas because of the epidemics that afflicted the indigenous people there and weakened their resistance to conquest, domination, and enslavement. Mines were quickly developed in Mexico and Peru, and local peoples were forced to work in them. At the same time, Portuguese trade with West Africa had rapidly established a form of chattel slavery that soon filled Lisbon with African slaves (the first Christian-ruled city to adopt large-scale slavery in Europe since ancient times). The importation of slaves to Portugal was rapidly followed by the enslavement of indigenous peoples by Spanish and Portuguese colonizers in the New World, and when those indigenous populations grew thin in many places, the transportation of African slaves to the New World was then undertaken to supply needed labor there. At the same time, Spain and Portugal, then the British and the Dutch, built a web of trade relations and outposts that stretched across the globe, from Europe to the New World to Asia and Africa along newly extended and intensified oceanic trade routes. So when we look at trade and Western empire in the early modern period, we see a web of connections built on warfare, conquest, colonization, slavery, and new forms of overseas trade that funneled profits back to an emerging capitalist system in Europe.

This emerging capitalist system, especially in its overseas manifestations, established a pattern of uneven development that produced wealth for the merchant classes and their aristocratic allies while impoverishing both European and non-European laborers. The leading agents of the Western empires carried out exchange, negotiation, persuasion, or intimidation when these were feasible. But when they judged it to be justified or thought it might be effective, these proto-imperial powers employed violence, directly and literally, in the form of warfare, conquest, and slaughter. Sometimes, this violence was undertaken simply to spread fear and to preempt resistance. At the same time, the European colonizers inflicted systematic aggression through the dehumanization and social death that were part of a system based on slave labor and other forms of unfree labor. Many of the sea captains and government agents who sailed forth were ready and willing to use violence. They experienced and represented their brutal competition with other groups as a heroic endeavor that could earn them profit and reputation through bold, even unprincipled, action. Conquistadors like Cortés and sea-dogs like Drake succeeded in accomplishing crucial acts of conquest and appropriation, and they were to become larger-than-life heroes who served as important figures in the construction of imperialist discourse.

But swashbuckling derring-do was not enough to build an empire or bring home the goods. It required much more tedious, disciplined forms of calculation and obligation that could function to restrain or limit bold adventurers (or drive them to venture outside the sphere of legitimate, state-sponsored violence). As the important work of anthropologist David Graeber has shown, the new capitalist system and its Western empires were so restless and ruthless in their search for profit because these empires were founded on debt. There was a circular relationship between, on the one hand, the debts resulting from the loans required to mount overseas expeditions, found colonies, or wage wars; and on the other hand, the on-going need to invest in additional costly overseas ventures to obtain valuable commodities or better yet, gold and silver, in order to pay those debts. In fact, Graeber has observed that the founders of the Western empires in the New World were themselves debtors for whom "the world is reduced to a collection of potential dangers, potential tools, and potential merchandise" (2014: 319). To illustrate this point, he recounts how Cortés was already deep in debt when he obtained new loans on the promise of his appointment as Captain General commanding an expedition to Mexico. When the governor of Hispaniola canceled the voyage just before it was to depart, Cortés defied that order and left for Mexico where, on landing, he burned his ships so that his followers could not return, gambling everything on a victory there. Even after his successful conquest of Mexico, Cortés and his followers continued to have serious problems keeping out of debt. They were pursued by creditors, a situation that urged Cortés on to other enterprises and schemes. And when those failed to restore his good credit, he returned to Spain to petition Charles V for assistance. Ironically, Charles V was himself deep in debt to financial institutions in Naples, Florence, and Genoa. Charles's share of the treasure coming from Mexico and the other New World mines was desperately needed to pay off his own debts.

VIOLENT TECHNOLOGIES

Why was overseas trade prosecuted with such energy by the territorial states of early modern Europe? Why did they pursue the difficult enterprises of conquest, colonization, and trade in faraway places, despite the tremendous cost, in men, materials, and capital? Would it not be easier to remain closer to home to develop and protect economic interests there? Medieval merchants had already learned that long-distance trade in certain valuable commodities offered opportunities for profit that exceeded the limits of the domestic market or of mere agricultural productivity. Economic elites in western Europe were necessarily building on the networks and methods of late medieval exchange, but they pushed their pursuit of profit further, in the new spirit of capitalism, into newly acquired overseas territories, and they did so using new technologies and new economic devices.

One of these new technologies was the "tall ship" bearing lightweight, swiveling guns and other advanced forms of gunpowder weaponry (Figure 2.2). As Paul Virilio has observed, "history moves at the speed of its weapons

FIGURE 2.2: Frans Huys, Armed Four-Master Putting Out to Sea from *The Sailing Vessels (After Pieter Bruegel the Elder)* (Hieronymus Cock: Antwerp, c. 1555–6). Credit: Metropolitan Museum.

systems," and the new maritime technologies—navigational, and for ship design, gun-bearing long-distance sailing vessels—moved history forward (2006: 10). Intra-European warfare was almost incessant during the period leading up to the sixteenth century and led to the rise of a class of skilled mercenaries and military technicians, including those who were knowledgeable in maritime warfare and transportation. Maritime labor was a precious commodity for early modern merchant-investors and their navies. Trained sailors were targeted under impressment and strict rules of service while working on board during long-distance voyages. Trade and the profit derived therefrom could only take place on the backs of the mariners whose lives and health were at great risk. Mortality rates were very high due to shipwreck, disease, and ocean-going violence. The early joint-stock companies quickly developed strict rules for controlling crews. Of course, the chief investors in foreign trade, and those who profited most, rarely traveled on long-distance voyages. They preferred to stay home and exploit the labor of those who risked their lives on the open sea and in foreign ports, including the captains, masters, and factors who served their interests abroad.

Long-distance trade in this period cannot be properly considered or accurately understood without acknowledging the violence, coercion, danger, and exploitation that defined that trade, but a by-product of such systemic violence was the forced opening of a greater field of interaction and exchange, that could, for those who were privileged to enjoy such benefits, encourage a more open, tolerant, and cosmopolitan mentality. Trade brought more Europeans into contact with other cultures across the globe. In some cases, this produced a curiosity and a desire for knowledge, or even a respect for and attraction to other cultures and their ways. At the same time, cross-cultural exchange through trade provoked new forms of xenophobia, racism, and fears of cultural contamination or of "going native" while abroad.

In hindsight, we can see that the competition between the Western empires of the early modern period was slowly constructing a world-system that did not require a single imperial hegemony or a cultural homogeneity. But there was much cultural and ideological work that had to be performed in order to support, justify, and process the new experiences, new identities, and new forms of commodity consumption that Europeans encountered (and at times adopted) as they voyaged afar for trade, profit, and the appropriation of other peoples' lands and labor. The Western empires and their home cultures would increasingly absorb and contain cultural differentiation, while simultaneously trying to make sense of the novelty and diversity that they encountered abroad. Competing impulses of attraction and desire, on the one hand, and repulsion and fear, on the other, coexisted. Cultural productions in the homeland increasingly included representations of foreign cultures and peoples, and exchanges with them. This new cultural production functioned in a variety of ways: some texts worked to demonize foreigners while others endorsed contact and exchange with foreigners and their ways—if only to obtain knowledge, commodities, and profits. Some writers promoted travel, exchange, and knowledge-gathering as beneficial, while others warned against the dangers of cultural contamination by means of sexual, alimentary, religious, and other forms of intercourse. For instance, Bishop Joseph Hall published his anti-travel tract, *Quo Vadis? A Just Censure of Travel as It Is Commonly Undertaken by the Gentlemen of Our Nation* (1617), in the hope that he could warn English readers against the "dangerous issue of their curiositie" (sig. A4v). Conversely, there were travel writers who indulged their curiosity, exhibited their powers of observation regarding what was "strange" and "wonderful," and celebrated the pleasures of travel and their own accomplishments along the way. They include the Italian Pietro della Valle, who journeyed throughout Asia, Thomas Coryate who walked all the way from England to India, and Sir Henry Blount, whose *Voyage into the Levant* (1636) employed a Baconian empiricist lens through which he saw the Ottoman empire and other Levantine places.

CULTURAL RESPONSES TO NEW ECONOMIC PRACTICES

Many of the cultural productions that today we might label as "literary" (including discovery and travel narratives, ethnographic writings, poems, plays, and prose fiction) contended with conflicted feelings about how commercial expansion and circulation were changing the European homeland. Many such texts functioned to model both proper and improper forms of interaction with people who spoke other languages, dressed differently, followed other religions, and so on. How far should a virtuous, god-fearing European merchant or traveler go in his or her interactions and exchanges with foreigners? What should be the cultural, moral, or religious limits of such journeying? These questions are tied to a long tradition in western European societies that placed trade and merchants in a critical light. Given the basic ascetic and anti-materialist principles of Christian teaching, which advocate not the accumulation of worldly goods but rather their renunciation, it was quite common to see the figure of the urban merchant or the wealthy trader attacked as a sinful usurer or a greedy Mammon-worshiper. To seek worldly gain, to hoard wealth, and to engage in usurious practices were all seen as sinful and as antithetical to basic Christian virtues like poverty, charity, and abstinence. From the medieval period through the early modern period, those who enriched themselves by trade became the targets of satirical criticism. While it is true that there was also an image of the virtuous merchant, the fair dealer who offers a fair bargain and treats his fellow citizens charitably, the satirical portrait of the merchant as avaricious sinner or usurer was more prevalent. From Dante's hoarders and wasters in *The Inferno* to Chaucer's *The Canterbury Tales*—which includes the Pardoner's ironic dictum *radix malorem est cupiditas* ("the love of money is the root of all evil")—medieval authors in western Europe warned their readers against greed and the accumulation of wealth. With the arrival of capitalism, it was not only the notion of avarice as a sin, but the very structure of exchange itself—the new forms of usury that systematically bred money from money and moved the economy from mere "trade" into an increasingly financialized economy based on speculation—that provoked a variety of cultural responses. Many conservative writers saw the new capitalist class as an unethical group who threatened the social order, and these same authors sometimes upheld an idealized image of the generous aristocrat or gentleman whose charity and virtue contrasted with the new class of voracious economic parasites. Thomas Nashe, for example, wrote in 1593, "It is now grown a proverb that there is no merchandise but usury" (cited in Tilley 1950: 457). Other writers, by contrast, celebrated the energy of the new economic order and the wealth that it could generate. And there were those who expressed a wary or ambiguous view of a phenomenon that was not recognizable then as we see it today from our historical perspective. For instance, a popular emblem book included this image of a castaway merchant (Figure 2.3), washing up on shore with a pack of goods on his back; the Latin tag reads, *"Auri sacra fames quid non?"* (To what lengths will men not go for the cursed love of gold?).

FIGURE 2.3: Castaway merchant in Geoffrey Whitney, *A Choice of Emblemes* (Leiden, 1586). Credit: Huntington Library, San Marino, California.

Because the new economic power was understood, at the time of its emergence, in terms of preexisting ideologies, it was frequently labeled as usury, as Mammon worship, or as the sin of avarice. David Hawkes, in his work on early modern usury, argues that the vast majority of people in early modern Europe believed that usury was evil. Authors throughout western Europe attacked usury in print, and one of these anti-usury tracts featured this frontispiece (Figure 2.4). Here, the usurer, with a demonic spirit whispering in

FIGURE 2.4: From John Blaxton, *The English Usurer* (London, 1634). Credit: Folger Shakespeare Library.

his ear, declares, "I say I will have all, both use and principal," which refers to the collection of interest on loans. This image was accompanied by verses implying that the only good usurer is a dead usurer and comparing him to a ravenous pig: "The covetous wretch, to what may we compare,/better than swine: both of one nature are,/One grumbles, th'other grunts: both gross and dull,/hungry, still feeding, and yet never full . . . . Like him the Usurer, howsoever fed,/Profits none the living, till himself be dead."

Hawkes shows how the new monetization and commodification were seen as a form of idolatry that allowed mere representation to trump the solid material realities of work, subsistence, and the older forms of local exchange that were practiced under feudalism. Early modern people often reacted to the novel economic practices and to those who drew their power from them with horror: they recognized these as something unprecedented and frightening, as a threat to what they sometimes called "the commonwealth" (i.e., the common good). Hawkes argues that they were able to perceive quite clearly the fundamental harmfulness of capitalism because it was new and had not yet been naturalized, but they understood and condemned its unethical nature within a traditional framework. The (more-or-less conservative) attacks on usury and the new economic system often relied on Christian ideology, and sometimes drew on the longstanding Christian tradition of anti-Semitism. For example, we see this when Christopher Marlowe opens his 1591 play, *The Jew of Malta*, with the title character, Barabas, dealing transnationally in luxury goods and counting his wealth. Barabas is wheeling and dealing, describing the kind of transactions that allow him to grow rich; and in doing so, he reveals to the audience that his goal is to abstract, concentrate, and hoard his wealth in the most spatially efficient form possible. The following lines position the new merchant-usurer within a global matrix that has its center everywhere and circumference nowhere because wealth consists in capital and credit, not in any specifically locatable commodity or transaction. Instead, all is flow, flux, and exchange:

> This is the ware wherein consists my wealth:
> And thus methinks should men of judgement frame
> Their means of traffic from the vulgar trade,
> And as their wealth increaseth, so enclose
> Infinite riches in a little room. (1.1.33–8)

In the character of Barabas, Marlowe took the old stock character of the miserly Jew, based on a medieval anti-Semitic stereotype, and produced a new capitalist super-villain who was completely remorseless. Following Marlowe, in citizen comedies like those of Ben Jonson, Thomas Middleton, or Philip Massinger, the ancient figure of the miser from Roman comedy was adapted and rebooted as a parasitic contemporary villain, and this humanist adaptation was mixed with traditional elements from the medieval Christian drama. I will return to the theater of the English Renaissance in the final section of this article, where my discussion of that specific cultural context will provide a more detailed view of one area within a vast body of cultural production that represented and sought to understand how trade was changing Europe and the world in profound ways.

EPIC REPRESENTATIONS OF EMPIRE

Merchants and capitalists were not always represented negatively in early modern texts: the emergence of capitalism and the rise of the Western empires as long-distance networks were exciting, stimulating phenomena that inspired new forms of culture that sometimes celebrated the energy and power of the rising merchant classes and romanticized their "adventures." In writings about the earliest of the Western overseas empires, that of the Portuguese, we can already see a tense ambivalence about trade in various representations of imperial adventuring, along with an anxiety about the inevitable intensification of contact and exchange with foreigners. This is very clear even in the most nationalistic literary celebrations of a providential, post-*Reconquista* empire, such as the Portuguese national epic, Luís Vaz de Camões's *The Lusiads* (*Os Lusíadas*), first printed in 1572. Many sections of that poem glorify the Portuguese imperial enterprise by retelling the story of Vasco da Gama's historic voyage (1497–9) from Lisbon to India and back, via the Cape of Good Hope, as the main plot and by presenting the later imperial successes of the Portuguese in the form of a prophecy about future glory, predestined by God (Figure 2.5). Da Gama's first voyage to India becomes a heroic, epic journey that brought glory and wealth to the Portuguese homeland by establishing a direct maritime trade route to "India, with its various/Peoples who prosper and grow rich// From gold and sweet perfumes and peppercorns,/Cardamoms, hot chilies, and precious stones" (Camões 2008: 7.31). Camões repeatedly emphasizes the importance of seeking a noble glory first, of pursuing a Christian mission with virtuous motives that serve, not personal aggrandizement or ambition, but the greater cause of Portugal and her rulers as the vanguard of Christendom; and he warns against too much desire for wealth, profit, rich commodities, and condemns "Vile self-interest and the sordid thirst/For gold" (Camões 2008: 8.96). In a striking counterpoint to the poem's frequent expression of imperialist zeal, as Da Gama's fleet is about to depart from the port, a character known as the Old Man of Restelo delivers a diatribe against imperialism and its motives, cursing such voyages for their alleged pride and folly:

> O pride of power! O futile lust
> For that vanity known as fame!
> That hollow conceit which puffs itself up

And which popular cant calls honour!
... To what deaths, what miseries you condemn
Your heroes! What pains you inflict on them!

... To what new catastrophes do you plan
To drag this kingdom and these people?

[. . .] Already in this vainglorious business
Delusions are possessing you,
Already, ferocity and brute force
Are labeled strength and valour,
The heresy, "Long live Death!" is already
Current among you, when life should always
Be cherished. . . . (Camões 2008: 4.95–9)

FIGURE 2.5: Portraits of King Henry the Navigator and Vasco da Gama from Richard Fanshawe's translation of *Camões's Lusiads* (London, 1655). Credit: Huntington Library, San Marino, California.

Although the Portuguese head for home from India without an agreement with the Samorin (the ruler of Calicut), their consolation is that they leave with "hot peppers [Da Gama] had purchased/ . . . mace from the Banda Islands;/Then nutmeg and black cloves, pride/Of the new-found Moluccas, and cinnamon,/ The wealth, the fame, the beauty of Ceylon" (Camões 2008: 9.14). This list of commodities represents the low-weight, high-value spices that commanded such high prices back in Europe and therefore facilitated huge profits for a developing commercial network that would soon be incorporated in the maritime world system under capitalism.

While Camões celebrates Da Gama's voyage as a successful epic accomplishment, in fact the voyage was something of a failure, and not only in Da Gama's leaving India without sealing a trade pact: the journey led to the deaths of 105 of the 160 original crew members and the loss of two ships. Nonetheless, in his 1666 chronicle account of the voyage, the Portuguese writer Manuel de Faria y Sousa looked back to Da Gama's voyage, providing this rosy view when describing the reaction to Da Gama's homecoming:

> There were Public Thanksgivings throughout the Kingdom for the good success of this Voyage . . . And all men's expectation being raised with the glory of the Action and hope of ensuing Profit, it was now consulted how to prosecute what had begun, and resolved, that according to the disposition they had found in the People of those Countries there was more need of Force than Intreaty, in order whereunto thirteen Vesse[l]s of several sizes were fitted, and Peter Alvarez Cabral was named Admiral. (Faria y Sousa 1695: 53)

Indeed, the Portuguese voyages that followed employed violence in the Indian Ocean zone whenever necessary in order to gain the trade concessions that the Portuguese desired. Trade was imposed by force and the threat of force, and by doing so the Portuguese broke the Arab-Venetian monopoly on the spice trade connecting India to western Europe. After consolidating their position in India through subsequent voyages, the Portuguese captured and fortified the commercial ports at Goa, Melaka, Hormuz, and Colombo between 1510 and 1515.

The Portuguese experience was foundational to Western imperial discourse (as well as to the Atlantic slave trade). But as Josiah Blackmore and others have shown, early modern Portuguese authors did not universally or blindly support the imperial project. Empire, its "civilizing" and Christianizing purposes, and the economic benefits said to ensue for the home nation were all questioned. In fact, some Portuguese writings turned from epic to tragedy, offering in their writings a melancholy strain that emphasized shipwreck narratives and diminished aspirations in the wake of the disastrous defeat of the Portuguese army and the death of its leader, King Sebastiao I, at the battle of Alcazar

Al-Kabir in 1578 and the consequent seizure of the Portuguese throne by the Spanish king, Philip II, in 1580. As for the Spanish empire, its murderous treatment of indigenous people in its American plantations and mines was harshly criticized by authors like Bartolomé de las Casas who, in his *Short Account of the Destruction of the Indies* (1542), appealed to his readers to support a kinder, gentler colonial regime that did not rely on torture, murder, or the enslavement of native peoples.

Just as Camões' epic drew directly on the experience of voyaging and economic expansion, there were Spanish epic poems that took their central story from specific events in the recent history of imperialist adventuring. Alonso de Ercilla's *La Araucana* (1589) and Gaspar Perez de Villagra's *Historia de la Nueva Mexico* (1610), for example, drew on the firsthand experiences of these two poets who both participated in colonizing efforts—one at the northern perimeter of Spanish New World conquest in New Mexico, and the other at the southern edge of the Spanish American colonies in Chile. England also produced imperialist epics during the early modern period, but in the case of Edmund Spenser's *Faerie Queene* (1596) the epic narrative followed the pattern of Italian Renaissance humanist authors like Ariosto and Tasso who conceal the economic motives and objectives of empire beneath a façade of chivalric heroism set in the past or in a romance fantasy-land. In contrast, Camões, Ercilla, and Villagra based their poetic narratives much more closely on real-world events. But all of these epic poets used the classical humanist mode to ennoble their imperial theme, to connect the exploits of the ancients to the imperial endeavors of their own day, and in doing so, to both glorify and question real-world colonial exploits. In their epic poems, the raw economic forces that drove imperial expansion were repressed—hidden beneath the veneer of a chivalric code touting martial valor, self-sacrifice, glory in the service of the country, and other heroic virtues—all wrapped in beautiful poetic language.

FROM TRAVEL NARRATIVE TO THE STAGING OF TRADE

Overseas ventures were also described in the travel narratives and ethnographic writings that proliferated, some of them collected and disseminated in compilations like those assembled by Giovanni Battista Ramusio, Richard Hakluyt, Samuel Purchas, or Melchisédech Thévenot. For the Victorian historian J.A. Froude, Richard Hakluyt's *Principal Navigations, Voyages and Discoveries of the English Nation* (1598–1600) formed "the Prose Epic of the Modern English Nation."[3] While these disparate tales of "true travels" may have served a nationalist agenda not unlike that seen in national epic poetry, they also functioned in highly unpoetic ways, offering a rich source of practical information for merchants planning investments in long-distance trade who were seeking to develop a global commercial network that was connected to the world system. They included exciting stories about shipwreck, battles at sea, the "discovery" of new lands, first encounters with indigenous peoples, the wealth and luxury of foreign courts; but also they offered specific information about foreign lands and foreign peoples—their customs, language, food, clothing, political systems—in short, their way of living. Travel narratives provided reports detailing the lay of the land in those places, the challenges provided by the sea, the coasts and harbors, the maritime traffic, and so on, along the way. This geographic, ethnographic, and commercial data was usually organized around the figure of the bold, virtuous traveler who narrates and comments on his experiences abroad. This was one place that merchants and potential voyagers could go to find models for action and behavior as well as practical information. As we will see, the theater was another, where audiences attended many plays that staged cross-cultural exchange.

The English and Dutch merchant-adventurers were particularly well organized at an early stage of the Western empires' expansion: after the Portuguese and the Spanish, they became the leading pioneers of a globally ranging proto-capitalism. The two earliest forms of the capitalist joint-stock corporation in England were both established in London during the sixteenth century—the long-distance trade companies (The Merchant Adventurers, The Muscovy Company, then later The Levant Company, The East India Company) and the theater companies (such as The Lord Chamberlain's Men who established a corporation in 1599 that included Shakespeare and a group of other investors).[4] Both the trade and the theater companies were founded on a structure of shared risk, meted out between investors who received profits or incurred losses in proportion to the shares they held. This was the capitalist scheme that made Shakespeare a rich man and permitted him to retire to his hometown as a wealthy landowner who had purchased an entailed estate there. The permanent playhouses in London, including the famous Globe Theatre, were profoundly commercial in nature, though the leading companies retained links to the residual feudal economy when they performed at court in return for payments provided by the royal household. The Globe Theatre, as its name indicates, was a site for the performance of a transnational drama— one that brought all the exotic interest of other cultures, religions, and places home to the London stage. Most of the plays performed there were set in the Mediterranean world, in the distant past, or in places even further away. It was a theater of mobility and cross-cultural exchange: travel and cultural mixture were constantly at the center of its action. It was an imaginary nexus for the coming together, processing, and modeling of information, objects, and behavior from all over the world. And it was also a theater that relentlessly represented what we would now call "economic life." Especially in comedy, a genre organized around the acquisition of spouse and property for those who enjoyed the fruits of the happy ending, economic transactions and exchanges, including the marriage contract, were central. In other words, what Gayle Rubin (1975) has termed "the traffic in women" or "the political economy of sex" was frequently staged in the London theater of the early modern period.

Let me return then to the English theater, where the medieval morality play tradition lived on, but was altered to suit the new commercial spirit of early modern times. What had been an allegorical religious drama focusing on the question of Everyman's temptation and potential salvation was adapted to more secularized or particularized moral questions that arose in new socio-economic situations. We see this, for instance, in an Elizabethan morality play like Robert Wilson's *The Three Ladies of London* (1582). Employing the conventional device of personification allegory from the morality play tradition, *The Three Ladies* presents, in contemporary London, a steep decline in the fortunes of Lady Love and Lady Conscience—a reduction in their status that is caused by the rise of a new capitalist class represented by Lady Lucre and her allies Usury, Dissimulation, and Fraud. In the first scene, Lady Love and Lady Conscience are concerned that Usury and Lucre will bring on their "fall" (1.4), but Fame assures them that if they stay away from "Lucre's lust lascivious,/ Then Fame a triple crown will give" (1.24–5). And yet the two initially virtuous Ladies are unable to escape the sway of Lady Lucre—Lucre and her allies quickly force Love and Conscience to submit to their greater power. In the next scene, Lady Lucre is approached by Fraud, Usury, Simony, and Dissimulation, who quickly become her eager, unprincipled clients. Upon meeting Usury, Lucre notes their connection through a transnational network:

> **LADY LUCRE** Usury, didst thou never know my grandmother, the old Lady Lucre of Venice?
> **USURY** Yes, Madam, I was servant unto her and lived there in bliss.
> **LADY LUCRE** But why camest thou into England, seeing Venice is a city Where Usury by Lucre may live in great glory?
> **USURY** I have often heard your good grandmother tell
> That she had in England a daughter, which her far did excel,
> And that England was such a place for Lucre to bide,
> As was not in Europe and the whole world beside.
> Then, lusting greatly to see you and the country, she being dead,
> I made haste to come over to serve you in her stead. . . . (2. 216–25)

Usury is immediately welcomed to Lucre's service, and in the scene that follows, we encounter an Italian merchant who has just arrived from Venice, Mercadorus, who asks to be introduced by Dissimulation to Lady Lucre. Mercadorus is then brought before Lucre, who asks him if he will "dare . . . secretly to convey good commodities out of this country for my sake" (3.31). He answers,

> Madonna, me do for love of you tink no pain too mush,
> And to do anyting for you me will not grush
> Me will-a forsake-a my fader, moder, king, country, and more dan dat;
> Me will lie and forswear meself for a quarter so much as my hat.
> What is dat for love of Lucre me dare, or will not do?
> Me care not for all the world, the great devil, nay, make my God angry for you. (3. 32–7)

Lucre likes what Mercadorus has to say, and she instructs him to import worthless "trifles" (43) and "baubles" (44), which he must market in England by means of "lying, flattering and glozing" (51). In return for these trifles, England will export valuable grain, meat, leather, and precious metals. At the end of the play, Lady Lucre is punished, but so are Lady Conscience and Lady Love. Conscience and Love become culpable and must be disciplined because they were corrupted and willing to serve Lucre. Wilson's topical allegory links domestic unemployment and poverty to the increased importance of English trade with foreigners in the Mediterranean and to the new forms of usury that were practiced by wealthy proto-capitalists. *Three Ladies* employs a traditional form of drama and traditional moral values to target the new trade and the rising class of merchant-usurers as an un-Christian force bringing economic disruption, exploitation of laborers, and a parasitical class of people who would place the love of money above all other values.

As the London theater developed and changed, the traditional form of personification allegory was employed less frequently over time. Instead of a character called "Mankind," "Lady Lucre" or "Lady Conscience," we meet more naturalistically individuated figures, but in many cases they retain, in names like "Sir Bounteous Progress," or "Justice Greedy," an affiliation with a moral type or stock character. These changes in how dramatic character was presented correspond to a shift in European culture from a stronger sense of community and commonality toward an increasingly individuated subjectivity marked by the ideology of emergent capitalism with its new forms of possessive individualism and commodity fetishism. In the work of the London playwrights who followed Wilson (including Marlowe, Jonson, Shakespeare, and Middleton), the commercial life of the city continued to be a focus. This was especially the case for a new form of comedy, called "city" or "citizen" comedy, that represented urban life and the vigorous energies of commerce in its traditional center and marketplace, the City of London. The critical, satirical note is very strong in these plays; their plots were structured around commercial and marital transactions, and the main male characters were shown in the pursuit of wealth, with the goal of securing a lucrative marriage to an heiress.

Shakespeare's *Merchant of Venice* (1597) is an important early version of the city comedy genre. The setting is shifted from London to the commercial city of Venice, a place that represented, for many English subjects, an open polity founded on cross-cultural and inter-religious exchange. Nonetheless, *The Merchant of Venice* is typical of the city comedy form in the way that it combines and conflates the erotic and the commercial. Debt and credit define the characters in this play and drive the action. The young gallant Bassanio's effort to obtain the hand of Portia (and in doing so, to take control of her wealth and property) is dependent on a strained and dubious system of credit and debt that has already rendered him desperate. He confesses to Antonio:

'Tis not unknown to you, Antonio,
How much I have disabled mine estate
By something showing a more swelling port
Than my faint means would grant continuance. (1.1.122–5)

His "chief care" is "to come fairly off from the great debts/ Wherein my time, something too prodigal,/ Hath left me gaged" (1.1.127–9). All of Bassanio's "plots and purposes" involve "How to get clear of all the debts [he] owe[s]" (1.1.133–4) so that he can continue his excessive and parasitical way of life. In his need to raise cash, Bassanio manipulates his homosocial network, obtaining the leverage of Antonio's credit in order to raise a stake from the usurious Jew Shylock. Based on the credit pledged by his merchant friend Antonio, Bassanio is able to purchase the appearance of a worthy suitor of means, though he is in fact an insolvent debtor. The play demonstrates the truth of the adage that Portia's companion Nerissa invokes to admonish Portia for complaining that she, like Antonio, is unhappy despite her prosperity: "they are as sick that surfeit with too much as they that starve with nothing" (1.25–6). Here, Shakespeare hints at the connection between the excesses of those who enjoy great wealth by exploiting others and the deprivations suffered by members of the lower classes who must serve the elites for low wages or else starve. To be a "merchant" engaged in trade in this text is to be a part of the new capitalist system in which capital is raised and increased, not by the honest sale of goods for a fair price, but by means of a "trade" that is really speculation and usury made possible by the underhanded manipulation of debt and credit networks. In fact, the play takes as one of its central themes the commodification of human beings, and of human flesh, which is the consequence of the radical new capitalist system that relies on investment, risk, credit, and debt to increase the wealth and power of the merchant class.

The play's pattern of trade and transaction as a swindle is quite clear. As in other city comedies, *The Merchant of Venice* features the triumph of witty, clever characters who prevail through deceptive and improvisational performances, through the tactic of disguise, and through timely unveiling and unscrupulous seizing of opportunity, as well as by means of verbal play that exploits the slipperiness of law and language in order to pull the wool over the eyes and ears of their victims. Honest bargain, firm contract, and fair and equal enforcement of the law all must give way to a moral malleability that is laced with sadistic laughter. We see a pattern unfold as a series of cruel swindles take place in the comedy: in the trick pulled on Shylock when his property and daughter are stolen; when a legal game of bait-and-switch deprives Shylock of his religion and wealth at the end of the trial; when Bassanio plays the casket game and wins because Portia bends the rules of the game by providing him with strong hints and clues that give away the correct casket (something she does not do for the other suitors, who she mocks and humiliates); and finally, when Bassanio presents himself as a wealthy young man of means and then later has to confess to Portia (after he has won her) that he is "worse than nothing" (3.2.259), a financial zero. All the while, the interanimation of erotic and commercial language is fundamental to the structure of this play, as it was to other comedies like it. Portia herself speaks eloquently of how her intrinsic worth as a human being must become an itemized quantity of fungible commodities for Bassanio's sake—"to stand high" in Bassanio's "account," she must become a "sum of something" (3.2.158). The wordplay here suggests that she must be reduced from her power and autonomy as an unmarried heiress and "lord" (3.2.167) of Belmont to become a mere part of a possessed thing. Her transformation speaks to the reifying power of capitalism.

The uneasiness produced by Shakespeare's *Merchant of Venice* is indicative of a strong ambivalence about the new economic practices of the day. For the audience, there is an excitement to be had in identification with the romantic heroes who win out and claim the prizes that come with comic closure, but at the same time there is an uncomfortable sense that a distasteful fraud, theft, and trickery are essential elements of economic life in these imaginary cities. There is a strong tension in the text between, on the one hand, a comic celebration of the energies and possibilities of the new economic system and, on the other hand, the satirical exposure of a moral malaise or commercial corruption.

As time went on, the city comedy genre continued to enjoy popularity on the London stage and expanded with the economy. It came to incorporate a range of variations: these include what Jean Howard (2007) has termed "chronicle comedy" or "London city drama." This type of city comedy is based on actual events that were recorded in the chronicles of the time. An example is Thomas Heywood's *If You Know Not Me, Part II* (1605), a play that looks back to the Elizabethan era, the defeat of the Spanish Armada in 1588, and the construction of the new Royal Exchange, which was opened in 1571 by its founder Sir Thomas Gresham, as a venue where merchants, trading internationally in commodities and bills of exchange, could meet and make deals.

If You Know Not Me begins with a big business deal—a trade agreement is in the midst of its final negotiation. One of Gresham's "Factors" meets a "Barbary Merchant" to discuss the final details of a trade pact that Gresham is hoping to make with the sultan of Morocco for the monopoly on sugar, a valuable luxury import. In the opening lines of the play, Gresham is praised by both men: the Barbary Merchant characterizes him as "a man of heedful providence,/And one that by innative courtesie/Winnes love from strangers" (251). His factor, employing a rhetoric of humility, then says Gresham is "a Merchant of good estimate:/Care how to get, and forecast to increase/(If so they be accounted) be his faults" (251). Here, both assessments of Gresham's virtue as a merchant dedicated to trade with foreigners retain hints of unease, including implications of "fault": "innative" signifies as "innate," but also hints at "unnatural"; and these lines also imply that he is perhaps going too far, not only in his excessive love of "strangers," but also in his capitalist "care" for getting and increasing profits above all. The play expends a great deal of effort to create an imagination resolution of the tensions between Gresham's dependence on foreigners and his role as a heroic supporter of queen and country. Nonetheless, his reckless spending and international deal-making serve as a demonstration of his power and as a sign of his excess. Gresham's reliance on foreign commodities is clearly in tension with chauvinistic notions of domestic English-Christian virtue. And when the sultan of Morocco dies suddenly and his heir refuses to honor the sugar monopoly agreement, Gresham has to shrug off a loss of 60,000 pounds. And yet, it is part of the cultural work of a play like *You Know Not Me, Part II*, to draw on the exciting new energy of high-stakes, overseas capitalist trade while exploring a new national post-Armada identity and a new sense of England's place in an expanding, global trade matrix. At the same time, doubts and problems about trade and its risks, and about the dangers of debt and rampant commodification, sometimes show themselves to the audience. For instance, a petty peddler named Tawneycoat and Gresham's wastrel nephew, John Gresham, are both bankrupted by their debts, and they rely on Gresham to relieve them from insolvency and disgrace. These plot threads are parallel to the episodes involving Gresham's relationship with the queen and her reliance on Gresham and other city merchants to provide the subsidies and loans that she needed to keep her throne. Ceri Sullivan has gone so far as to declare the play "a pantomime of commercial disaster" (2002: 87).

The overall effect of the play is conflicted and complex: it is not simply an unambiguous celebration of Gresham as a kind of merchant-hero or model of commercial virtue. A character called Old Hobson, who represents the traditional virtuous merchant, is mocked and taken advantage of, but when he hears that a man in his employ is to be hanged for embezzling a hundred pounds, he rushes to save his life, declaring,

> A hundred thousand pounds cannot make a man;
> A hundred shall not hang one by my means:
> Men are worth more than money.... (321)

As Hobson rushes off to save this man from execution, Alexander Nowell, the Dean of St. Paul's, remarks that Hobson "is plain and honest," but laments,

> ... how many great professors
> Live in this populous city, that make shew
> Of greater zeal, yet would not pay so deare
> For a transgressors life. But few are found
> To save a man would lose a hundred pound. (321)

Another act of charity is shown by the recently widowed Lady Ramsey, whose husband had been Lord Mayor. When the trickster John Gresham, Gresham's nephew, rudely asks for her hand in marriage in the street, she declines his offer but then agrees to pay all of his debts. This resolves the trickster subplot but without the traditional marriage, and the rest of the play turns to the attempted assassination of the queen followed by the war with Spain and the defeat of the Armada. Despite a bawdy trickster subplot, lots of festive jollity, and a happy ending featuring the English victory over the Armada, the play makes clear that the queen herself must rely on City capital to ensure that she is capable of defending England against foreign invasion. The celebration of the Armada's defeat and the stirring patriotic tone of Heywood's conclusion paper over the deeper structure of an economy that is threatened, not only by war or foreign invasion, but by a powerful, rising class of risk-taking merchants who live off credit, debt, and other usurious forms of commerce, who have powerful allies at court and a web of agents abroad, but neglect the poor that live all around them.

City comedies like *You Know Not Me* were London-based, but as London grew, quadrupling in population during the sixteenth century, from 50,000 to 200,000 souls, and continuing to increase rapidly during the Early Stuart period, the capitol was becoming a world-city. The connections between London's commercial "city" and the world economic system grew stronger, and with that came a rising ambition and competition with the other Western empires. The London theater dramatized these changes in travel plays like Thomas Heywood's *The Fair Maid of the West*, Part I (*c.* 1600) and Part II (*c.* 1625); John Fletcher's *The Island Princess* (1620); John Fletcher and Philip

Massinger's *The Sea Voyage* (1622); and Philip Massinger's *The Renegado* (1624)—penned by the same London playwrights who were writing city comedies. In these travel and adventure plays, European, Christian characters follow the trade routes to overseas Muslim territories, matching their venturing spirit against the power of "infidel" empires in North Africa or the Spice Islands, or (in *The Sea Voyage*) to the New World.

CONCLUSION: CIVILIZATION, BARBARISM, AND EMPIRE

In the persistence of the morality play tradition, and in the rise of the city comedy genre and its extension into travel and adventure drama, we observe a clear cultural pattern that is symptomatic of the changes and tensions produced by emergent capitalism as it disrupted the old aristocratic order and turned "trade" into something less submissive to noble privilege, more politically powerful, and more global. Taken as a group, these English plays offer a kind of cultural barometer showing the changes in economic pressure and expressing many of the anxieties that accompanied those changes. I hope that all of the examples cited and discussed here from the literary production of the early modern period have helped to demonstrate the many connections between, on the one hand, the economic changes, occurring both domestically and globally, that enabled and transformed the Western empires and, on the other, the way that various cultural productions reacted and responded to economic change in ways that were often critical but sometimes celebrated the energy and transformation that new forms of trade brought to the early modern society. Of course, early modern people in England and other parts of Europe did not understand or describe their own economic situation as "emergent capitalism," but that did not stop their culture from registering the shock, anxiety, and exhilarating promise that the new economic system generated. They may not have had our vocabulary or analytic framework at their disposal, but their writings express both the attraction and the repulsion offered by the new economic order and its avatars.

This essay has focused on the relationship between the new commercial practices of the early modern period and the cultural productions that represented, celebrated, and criticized those practices. I have tried to demonstrate that trade was not simply an engine of economic, cultural, or moral "progress," but also brought on many cruel and destructive activities throughout the world. The long history of exploitation and conquest that came with global trade under capitalism must be an important part of our story when we recount the artistic and cultural achievements of the European Renaissance. This is especially important to keep in mind when we are talking about highly profitable commercial activities that benefited the few, not the masses—and the works of art that were carried out for the sake of the upper classes and their wealthy patronage cultures. As Walter Benjamin famously declared in his *Theses on the Philosophy of History*,

> Whoever has emerged victorious participates to this day in the triumphal procession in which the present rulers step over those who are lying prostrate. According to traditional practice, the spoils are carried along in the procession. They are called cultural treasures, and a historical materialist views them with cautious detachment. For without exception the cultural treasures he surveys have an origin which he cannot contemplate without horror. They owe their existence not only to the efforts of the great minds and talents who have created them, but also to the anonymous toil of their contemporaries. There is no document of civilization which is not at the same time a document of barbarism. (1969: 256)

That "anonymous" toil is the labor of the workers who made early modern trade possible. Their toil produced a surplus value that was appropriated by the rulers of the Western empires. Trade, especially in its new global, capitalist forms, allowed for the building of the Western empires, and for the emergence of a powerful new capitalist class. While Europe's upper-class elites and merchants competed with each other to sponsor or acquire works of art, violent commercial battles were being fought to control the centers for trade around the world. All of this is not to say that all forms of commercial activity during the early modern period were pure exploitation, or that all Renaissance art and culture should be condemned and shunned for its complicity with the new capitalists and the imperial victors. But the celebratory approach to the relationship between trade and early modern culture must be replaced by a much more critical view that does not occlude or understate the troubling aspects of early modern political economy, so that we might arrive at a more complex, balanced picture of Renaissance art and humanism, and of the global exchanges that informed these transformative cultural phenomena. Many of the texts that I have cited here, including poetry and drama, do just that: they show how the new humanism and the spirit of Renaissance individualism were closely tied to trade and emergent capitalism, and they ask readers and playgoers to confront the dark side of the Renaissance and the fundamental problems of class privilege, exploitation, social injustice, commercial swindling, and greed. We must not fetishize the art objects and literary texts that were produced during the age of emergent capitalism, placing them in a separate aesthetic sphere. And if we do seek to place artistic and intellectual production within an economic context, we must not be too quick to define and accept those commercial energies as unproblematic forces for empowering or enabling a wonderful symbiosis of talented artists and wealthy patrons. Nor should we laud the avatars of empire and the commercial elites because of their refined aesthetic taste and transnational "cosmopolitanism" or admire their sponsorship of a "global Renaissance" without understanding and acknowledging that Renaissance art and literature could also instigate questioning and even resistance to the new forms of trade.[5]

CHAPTER THREE

Natural Worlds

VINITA DAMODARAN AND RICHARD GROVE

The colonial encounter with the tropics and the global hunt for resources between 1450 and 1650 under the mercantile capitalism of European empires transformed the natural worlds of the Renaissance leading to a cultural and intellectual efflorescence. This was a period when, as the historian Donald Worster puts it, "capitalism became the pioneering, and ... most important, architect of that new integrated world economy," the environmental impact of European colonial expansion on so much of the world territory became apparent and humans as environmental agents begin to dominate over nature. The idea of a threshold or turning point is key to the debate on changing human nature interactions in the early modern period and defining that moment is a major problem both in terms of the dating and also in terms of a new culture of valuation of the landscape when people became aware of the importance of human agency and its possible damaging effects.

Empires historically have tended to possess the resource demands, the urban needs, the capital and the information networks, command of trade routes on land and at sea, enabling them to increase their carrying capacity and further augment their command of surpluses by landscape-transforming colonizations. They also transform the disease environment and create the conditions through their urban and network characteristics for periodic mass mortalities during extreme climate events, introducing an element of great instability as well as transition in populations. The advent of the more seaborne empires in the Renaissance beginning with Venice imposed new demands on timber resources, for example in the Balkans as well as novel patterns of forest administration, early conservation, resource organization and classification, analysis of soil types and soil erosion. With the development of sugar, in the fifteenth century a step change occurred in the speed of landscape transformation in the

Mediterranean, followed by the East Atlantic, the West Atlantic, the Caribbean, South America, and finally the South Atlantic. Plantation agriculture and the rapid developments of markets in high-value sugar and other addictive drugs (tea, coffee, tobacco, opium, cocaine) as well as urban foodstuffs from the sixteenth to the eighteenth century further created the conditions for profitable capital investment in the commodity frontier (Grove 1995; Richards 2003). We begin to see the transformation of the Canaries, Madeira, and Cape Verdes, but these are a logical development of the colonization and transformation of many of the Mediterranean islands especially by the Genoese in an earlier period. At the same time, one can see the emergence of a nascent environmental consciousness and an emerging culture of "environmentalism" (Grove 1995).

For environmental historians, the recent preoccupation with human-induced climate change designated by some earth system scientists as the Anthropocene comes as a surprise as the concept of human nature interactions over time has long been a central object of their study.[1] Since the 1950s, the *Annales* school had emphasized the importance of geography and climate in understanding history over what it called "the longue durée." Other environmental historians followed such as John F. Richards, Donald Worster, and Richard Grove who examined the resource demands of early empires. As the eminent historian Worster noted, environmental historians had long recognized the cultural history of nature as being as important as the ecological history of culture. For Worster, then, the purpose of environmental history was "to put nature back into historical studies, or, defined more elaborately, to explore the ways in which the biophysical world has influenced the course of human history and the ways in which people have thought about their natural surroundings" (Worster 1994: 5). Grove further argued that to understand the interactions between the natural environment and social structures over the last few millennia in a global frame we need, as a first step, to understand the conjuncture between extreme climate events, the dynamics and features of empires, and their organized responses to the environment, especially to anomalous or unusual events. This does not constitute crude environmental determinism but is a recognition of the role that the environment plays in human affairs and the cultural response of societies to environmental change. This was a view that resulted in the Integrated History and People of the World project (IHOPE) in 2005 when an interdisciplinary group of social scientists, historians, sociologists and scientists came together on a project to integrate socio-environmental interactions over centennial time scales (Costanza, Graumlich and Steffan 2006).

ENVIRONMENTAL HISTORY AND EMPIRE

It is now an accepted premise that global environmental history must deal with capitalism as cornerstone of the world economy. At the same time, as John

McNeill notes, "all global history should take account of local conditions whether it is environmental history or any other variety. It requires what natural scientists, especially those who work with satellite imagery, call ground truthing" (Corona 2008). Environmental history has been described as the interdisciplinary study of the relations of culture, technology, and nature through time and as the historically documented part of the story of the life and death, not of human individuals but of societies and species in terms of their relationship with the world around them. Some environmental historians argue from a materialist/structuralist perspective while others argue from a much more cultural perspective. There is some disagreement about whether the natural world constitutes any kind of order or pattern that we can know and, if it does, whether that order can be apprehended by means of science or not. There is also a debate about what is natural and what is not, about whether indigenous people managed the whole environment or only some part of it, and how much was wilderness and how much was mythical. There are also divergent opinions over the extent to which nature influences human affairs, some scholars taking the position of limited environmental determinism, and others insisting that culture determines all. As Caroline Ford has argued, many of the studies in environmental history stress the blurred aspect of the nature-culture divide (Ford 2007).

Environmental history therefore seeks to address the absence of nature in many forms of historical writing. In histories of empire, this absence is particularly marked considering the fact, as Richard Grove argues, that the development of an environmental sensibility among Europeans can be traced to the encounter of European travelers, surgeons, naturalists, medical officers, and administrators with environments of the tropics from 1500 and with the recognition of the damage done to these environments by them. Grove's work revises this "unnatural history" of the empire, and indeed the growing domain of environmental history has taken root in studies of empire. He argued convincingly that from the fifteenth century the global network of trade and travel transformed European understandings of nature. The plethora of information that travelers, surgeons, and later scientists of the British, Dutch, and French empires gathered from the wider world helped them to build up an understanding of the fragility of nature. The botanic gardens they established on remote islands such as the Canaries and on St. Helena became important centers for scientific networking rooted in the knowledge on medicine, climatology, and agriculture. The process of botanical garden-making in the period of the Renaissance was both about science and culture underlining the garden as an environmental text and a metaphor of mind defining the wellbeing and health of man. It further signaled a new aesthetic valuing of the environment. While the ruling agendas continued to be medical and therapeutic, garden making was highly imitative. The pattern and influence of the Renaissance gardens in Padua, Leiden, and Amsterdam in the sixteenth century exercised organizing power over the gardens in Paris, Cape, St. Vincent, and at Calcutta. As Grove notes, "The garden defined modes of perceiving, assessing and classifying the world in terms of a Hippocratic agenda" (1995: 13). Grove's work voluminously documents and convincingly argues for the originality, vitality, and effervescence of colonial science in the colonies from the sixteenth to the nineteenth centuries and the new cultures of knowledge that made possible the emergence of a truly global environmental awareness. It depended on a new empirical knowledge of the scale of the world and actual observations of human ability to change the natural environment on a global basis (Grove 1995).

THE RESOURCE FRONTIER OF THE EARLY MODERN WORLD

The extension of what Immanuel Wallerstein has called the capitalist "world system" on a global scale between 1200 and 1788 had a critically important dimension in terms of resource exploitation (Wallerstein 2011a; Abu-Lughod 1989). During the early modern period, when imperial expansion was becoming a characteristic of state building, humans established new links, primarily by sea, around the entire world and due to maritime improvements a truly global economy emerged (Figure 3.1). Constitutive of this early modernity was the collections of plants, animals, peoples, and voyaging (Winterbottom 2016: 5). Worster has highlighted the maximizing culture of early capitalism in terms of consumption patterns and resource use and in the process the destruction and transformation of indigenous societies and cultures. European merchants and companies found that they could exploit the trade goods, markets, and resources of almost every land, in what became an expanding commodity frontier, the "unending frontier" in the title of John Richards important book on the environmental history of the early modern world (Richards 2003). According to Richards, "increased human mobility encouraged the rapid growth of the "'world hunt' . . . commercial hunters and gatherers killed off species of wild fish, mammals and birds as well as trees and bushes whose carcasses possessed value in the early modern world economy. Humans voraciously and systematically located, extracted, processed, packaged, shipped, priced, sold and consumed wild animals in ever greater quantities over ever greater distances" (2003: 9). The rapidly growing economy put traders in contact with indigenous peoples to procure timber, furs, and medicinal plants often with devastating impact on these peoples. The world hunt also affected the oceans. After about 1400, fisheries extended to an oceanic scale as seals and whales were hunted from pole to pole. New seafaring abilities allowed humans beings an expanded access to the resources of the ocean. Mariners outside the

Mediterranean ventured outside their coastal waters and covered long distances to hunt fish, whales, seals, and walruses. Western Europe became the primary beneficiary of the capitalist world economy controlling interregional maritime trade. Markets centered in that region directed the exploitation of natural resources on a world scale (Richards 2003: 9). As Richards notes, "Capital investment moved readily from one world region to another. Prices for commodities quoted in the urban centres of the new world economy sent signals to producers round the globe. New commodities in increasing quantities and variety flowed to world markets. Monetary systems based on metallic forms of money—copper, gold and silver—expanded and interlinked in new ways. Aggressive trade, war and settlement challenged and shocked isolated and insular local cultures and societies" (2003: 1–2).

The argument presented by John F. Richards and Richard Grove about the expanding resource frontier of Europe has also been replicated by other environmental historians notably by Alfred Crosby in *Ecological Imperialism* where he argues that the process of imperial expansion, whether in terms of direct conquest in what Crosby calls the creation of neo-Europes in the temperate world with the colonization of the Americas, Australia, and New

FIGURE 3.1: Baldaeus Phillipus, English Fort of Bombay 1672. Credit: The Biodiversity Heritage Library.

Zealand, or through indirect disruptions as a consequences of trading patterns and military actions, fundamentally changed many ecological processes. The introduction of horses to the Americas in 1519 by Spanish conquistadors, the humble potato from the Americas to Europe in the 1580s, and rabbits to Australia in the eighteenth century transformed the environments of these places (Crosby 2004). This is not the first time such changes had altered the planet's ecology; the emergence of agriculture and the domestication of animals has meant that the Holocene, the geological period since the last glacial episode, has been a period which saw accelerated anthropogenic-induced changes in most places, but the speed and scale of change in the last half millennium particularly after 1500 is what is most important. The ecological dimension of such imperialism is what needs much more attention than it has received until relatively recently. Crosby focuses exclusively on the white settler colonies and omits any discussion of the extensive regions of the colonial tropics. When we turn to the tropics we see, for example, that almost every part of Africa was gradually drawn into a world economy dominated by Europe between the fifteenth and nineteenth century. The period after 1500 which saw the enmeshing of the slave trade and the ivory trade capitalized by Europeans and Indian merchants effectively drew Africa into global networks of trade and exchange.[2]

Tropical environmental history is still a growing field. The focus on the political and administrative aspects of empire has occluded the material impacts of colonization on people's lives and cultures. One of the first symptoms of the early phases of globalization was the marginalization, enslavement, and then extinction of small indigenous cultures, especially those of island peoples; the indigenes of the Canary Islands are a classic example. However, it was on uninhabited islands such as St. Helena and Mauritius that the full effects of highly capitalized plantations, forest clearance, and import of alien animals (especially pigs, goats, and rats) were first observed. The extinction of the dodo in Mauritius in the mid-seventeenth century made a great impression on contemporary naturalists. The fact that oceanic islands were perceived as highly desirable "Edenic" locations in long-running European cultural traditions served to emphasize the shock of their manifest and rapid degradation. Moreover, their degradation threatened their role as watering and supply stations for company ships. In these circumstances, the colonial governments of many small islands became environmentalist, if only to ensure their own survival and that of their agricultural settlers and slaves (Grove 1995). Grove has examined at some length the cultural meanings of the "Edenic" both in Europe and the newly discovered non-European world from 1600 and the ways in which British, Dutch, and French scientists drew on their knowledge of remote islands to build up an understanding of the potential fragility and exhaustibility of nature. Concentrating on deforestation and the phenomenon of desiccation they operated within an intellectual framework of the Renaissance informed by new, dynamic and empirically-rooted ideas in medicine, climatology, agriculture, and botany.

Indeed, even before the advent of large continental-based European empires in Asia, Africa, and the Americas, the scale of artificially caused environmental change was already being realized as European maritime countries started to exploit new kinds of natural resources on a global scale. As early as the 1670s, the catastrophic consequences of European capital- and labor-intensive activities became clear as the early island colonies experienced drought due to the drying up of perennial streams, soil erosion, dust storms, and the disappearance of animal and plant species (Grove 1995). A hesitantly emerging global consciousness was one of the most profound consequences of the speeded up early modern circulation of peoples. Identifying, naming, and classifying of climates, minerals, human groups, animals, and plants originated in the taxonomic impulses of enthusiastic observers.[3] The New World had a strong impact on Renaissance man and "discovery" in a global sense transforming their cultural sensibilities and, as Grove notes, gave them the opportunity to locate Gardens of Eden in an emerging geographical context with oceanic islands first to be seen as "Edenic."

INDIGENOUS CAPITAL ACCUMULATION

Capitalist accumulation and regional trade developed quite autonomously from Europe in South and East Asia in the early modern period. Here too, major transformations of the natural landscape took place under empires whose cultures of consumption and accumulation compared favorably to Europe. Some developments, like the deforestation of the Ganga basin, by early Indian empires had already been long in progress, but they quickly accelerated after 1400 as powerful empires developed. As Richards notes, two dissimilar early modern states, the Mughal empire in India and the Dutch republic in western Europe, successfully powered economies of prodigious productivity (Richards 2003: 24–6). The Mughal empire in Asia was an agrarian, not a maritime economy.[4] By the mid-seventeenth century, with a large centralized empire of sub-continental proportions and with over 100 million people, Mughal India and in particular the region of Bengal had become a vast granary producing immense surpluses of rice and clarified butter. Cheap, abundant food stuffs encouraged rising artisanal output as Bengal's cotton and silk textiles found a ready and growing market in Asia and Europe. In comparison with the Mughal empire, the Dutch republic was small, with a population of 1.9 million living in an area of 42,000 square km. Due to a combination of institutional circumstances the Dutch republic came to dominate the shipping and commerce of the early modern world. Dutch shipping had become the most technically advanced in

Europe and between 1570 and 1620 Dutch traders cornered the trade in the worldwide rich trades, sugar, furs, slaves, precious metals, diamonds, spices, and textile developing new links with the Caribbean, Brazil, West Africa, Northern Russia, and the East Indies (Richards 2003: 24). The Dutch East India Company became the primary conduit for European trade with Japan, South East Asia, China, and India. As great maritime powers, the European mercantile empires quickly outstripped its Asian competitors.

For Immanuel Wallerstein, the rise of Europe was the result of a unique combination of relatively free labor, large and productive urban populations, and merchants and governments that facilitated long-distance trade and the reinvestment of profits. However, Kenneth Pomeranz has argued that there is little to suggest that western Europe had economic advantages either in capital stock or institutional advantages in 1600 (Pomeranz 2000). He suggests that European domination of Atlantic trade did not make Europe dominant in terms of financial profits and capital accumulation but it did relieve the strain on Europe's land, energy, and resources. For Pomeranz then, Europe's overseas extraction was a crucial factor leading it out of a world of Malthusian constraints. It is not surprising that the great divergence debate emphasizes the advantage of western Europe in terms of resource extraction from the colonies. It was this advantage that was critical to the different trajectories of growth between Europe and Asia, leading to the decline of Asia in economic terms. The historian Parthasarthi Prasannan also has put paid to Smithian, Weberian, and Malthusian arguments with regard to the development of capitalism in Asian societies from the sixteenth century arguing for claim of economic and cultural equivalence with Europe in pre-industrial standards of living, technological capacity, and institutional efficiency. Furthermore, like Grove he examines the ways in which western science was actually global science in which Indian knowledge participated from the outset, until British intervention dismantled the court patronage that undergirded scientific inquiry (Prasannan 2011). It was colonization of India and extraction from the seventeenth century that accounted for the rise of Britain and the decline of India, not cultural stagnation or religion.

BOTANIC GARDENS AND PLANT EXCHANGE

When we focus on some case studies of overseas extraction in the context of Renaissance-era imperial expansion, the importance of exotic plants cannot be underestimated. Indeed, as noted by David Mackay, the economic importance of plant interchange buttressed the philosophy of empire (Mackay 1985). Between 1415 and 1487 the Portuguese built on even older patterns of pharmacological trade in the Indian Ocean region. The study of networks following long-distance oceanic trade from the fifteenth century demonstrated the shared roots of Indian, Middle Eastern, and European medicine and the transformation of European science by indigenous technical knowledge (Grove 1995). In August 1487 Bartholomew Dias had traversed the southern tip of Africa and in 1521 Magellan's fleet had crossed the Pacific and circumnavigated the globe. With the arrival of Vasco da Gama in Malabar in 1498 the scene was set for a rapid exchange of biological and botanical material particularly among Asia, Europe, and the Caribbean (1995: 24). The joy of discovery of the minutiae of the tropical world in late-sixteenth-century travelers' accounts was paralleled by the rise of botanical science and natural history in Europe. The rise of botanical gardens in Renaissance northern Italy in Pisa and Padua was one result of these interconnected developments, resulting in the first major book on Asian botany by Gracia da Orta, a Portuguese physician who lived in Goa, published in 1563. The book was translated into Latin by Charles D. Ecluse (Clusius) a Flemish doctor and botanist based in Leiden establishing connections between the Dutch botanical establishment and India and leading to the diffusion of knowledge between South West India and the Leiden botanical garden and resulting in the famous *Hortus Malabaricus* of Van Reede in 1678 (Figure 3.2). Grove has argued that both Orta's text and Van Reede's

FIGURE 3.2: Henrick Van Reede *Hortus Malabaricus* (1678–93). Credit: The Biodiversity Heritage Library.

texts privileged Malayali Ayurvedic medical botanical and zoological knowledge and are based on indigenous knowledge. Grove notes the diffusion of medico-botanical knowledge that tended to privilege non-brahmanical epistemologies and impose an indigenous logic. By the seventeenth century this relationship was changing as "the practices of collecting and transplanting plants, gardening and practicing medicine as well as publishing natural histories were directly linked to the colonial exploitation of resources"(Winterbottom 2016: 115). Surgeons of the East India Company such as Samuel Browne and Edward Buckley were embedded in networks that involved different European companies, private interests, and missionary interests building up a lucrative business of buying and supplying drugs. Both of these men, for example, spent time looking at Indian practices in Madras and reporting them back to their European counterparts in the 1680s. The process of comparison of plants was carried out in botanical gardens which became critical to new ways of thinking about nature and modes of perceiving, classifying, and assessing the world, globally and in terms of a Hippocratic agenda (Grove 1995: 13; Winterbottom 2016: 126). The search for *materia medica* was matched by a surge of interests in other crops such as pepper and cardamom.

As Deepak Kumar argues, colonial developments cannot be solely understood in terms of politics or trade. There was he notes "a strong cultural context to all that was happening on the eve of colonisation.... Formidable Asiatic empires from the Ottomans to the Manchus had begun to show signs of decline. The old order was crumbling and the new was yet to emerge and when it did it came via new routes and new knowledge" (Kumar 2015). By the seventeenth century, the Dutch and the Portuguese found themselves embroiled in a war along the coastal hinterlands of the Indian Ocean trading world. In 1663, the Dutch gained exclusive access to the pepper trading rights on the Malabar Coast through a treaty they signed with the Raja of Cochin (Chaudhuri 1985). The Malabar Coast shifted from Portuguese to Dutch control and the everyday resources of the indigenous people became highly sought after by a European elite. With trading houses or factories built by the Dutch, pepper, cinnamon, and cardamom trade proceeded at a more sophisticated rate. By the end of the seventeenth century the English East India Company's choice for the location of its main factory on the Malabar Coast was Tellicherry because of its proximity to the pepper producing areas. With the British takeover of the subcontinent a number of the territories of the Mughal empire became British territories (Wallerstein 2011a; Prasannan 2011: 21–51). Losing its American colonies had significantly damaged the British shipping industry. However, in the newly won colonies of the Indian Ocean, namely Java, and the Malabar Coast, the dense teak forests provided an excellent substitute. By the 1800s, the British Empire's modes of resource use, well developed trading network and factory system, and new technologies to shorten seafaring travel contributed to the next great epoch in the history of globalization. Richard Tucker, describes Malabar as almost entirely domesticated by global capitalism under the most complex system of resource extraction which any European empire ever established in the developing world (Tucker 1989). This colonization had a strong cultural dimension. New knowledges downgraded Indian religious and cultural traditions and knowledge practices (Mitter 1992). Those of its science were beginning to be condemned as unscientific and primitive with oriental learning being seen as belonging to the realm of the senses and imagination (Inden 2000). The cultural downgrading of other societies was linked to earlier environmental understandings in the sixteenth and seventeenth centuries.

EARLY ENVIRONMENTAL ENQUIRY AND CULTURES OF SAVAGERY

Early environmental ideas were driven by the need of empire builders to understand and acclimatize themselves to foreign environments. Europeans regarded the tropical environment with a mixture of promise and terror. The promise, presumed the exuberance of nature in the tropics while the terror derived from the high risk of death that European sojourners faced. We have argued that the great expansion of European maritime travel and settlement after 1400 stimulated new ways of viewing the relationship between man and nature. As early as the fifteenth century, the newly discovered islands in the Atlantic—the Canaries and Madeira—were seen as sites of redemption. For Grove, the island metaphor of the Renaissance constituted a vital part of the discourse and culture of early colonialism. As he noted, "the new world had a strong attraction for renaissance man" and "discovery" gave an opportunity "to locate gardens of Edens, Arcadias, Elysian fields and Golden ages in a geographical reality" (Grove 1995). The new world conceived of in island terms was both desirable for example, as reflected in Columbus's writings in 1492; "the songs of the little birds are such that one would never desire to part hence" and redemptive freeing one from the constraints of European society.

The reverberations of these imperial mentalities in the realm of Renaissance literary and cultural are well known. For Shakespeare, the location of *The Tempest* provided the setting for speculation about the Edenic qualities of the island and the vision it offered to create an alternative utopian society. Accounts of a shipwreck on the Bermudas prompted Shakespeare to conceive of an island as a meeting place between the indigenous inhabitant and the European colonist. *The Tempest* was also a play about the European response to a new physical environment as well as to an indigenous inhabitant. Caliban was probably inspired by Montaigne's writings which built on real stories of travel. For Grove, *The Tempest* debated a whole range of social options and the contradiction between the projection of Edenic or paradisiacal properties on to the island and the empirical complexity of the island in terms of its flora and fauna (Grove 1995: 35). The Renaissance had promoted a renewed interest in the value and portrayal of the natural world, as reflected in *The Tempest* which focused on allegedly civilized Europeans as they attempted to relocate themselves in a "wilderness."

The Renaissance-era accounts of many of the earliest encounters between Europeans and Amerindians contain reactions toward New World peoples that implied or more directly offered praise for what was perceived to be their "natural" manner of living. Idealized portrayals of Amerindians in these writings reflect the varied, and at times conflicting, fables about faraway lands and peoples across the sea that shaped the experiences and expectations of late-fifteenth-century and early-sixteenth-century explorers, missionaries, and soldiers who traveled to the Americas (Marshall and Williams 1972). Imagined visions of distant lands occupied by magical creatures, instantiations of mythological "wild men" or inhabitants of a golden age who were celebrated in song and poetry seems to have helped to create the archive of the idea of the noble savage. Michel de Montaigne's essay "Of Cannibals" in 1580 drew upon such earlier descriptions but set them in the context of an ongoing discourse about the corruption of European societies and the superior excellence of nature's treasures, which included for him most of the indigenous inhabitants of the New World who had hardly strayed from their original naturalness. Montaigne's essay is often interpreted as an ingenious attempt at complicating the idea of savagery, for he directly challenges the view that Amerindians are savage in any pejorative sense. A proper understanding of the term savage, in his view, shows that Europeans who have altered themselves and their environments are in fact savagely artificial, rather than naturally pure. As Montaigne argues,

> These people are wild (sauvage), just as we call wild (sauvage) the fruits that nature has produced by herself and in her normal course; whereas really it is those that we have challenged artificially and led astray from the common order, that we should rather call wild (sauvage). The former retain alive and vigorous their genuine, their most useful and natural, virtues and properties, which we have debased in the latter in adapting them to gratify our own corrupted taste. (Montaigne 1685 [2002]: 153)

What animates the behavior of savage peoples given that they lack "culture" as understood by Europeans? The role of climate was central to Montaigne's understanding of the role of fortune in helping to bring about and maintain savage societies. New World peoples were blessed by an abundance of natural resources: "They live in a country with a very pleasant and temperate climate … they have a great abundance of fish and flesh and they eat them with no other artifice than cooking" (Montaigne, 153). The infantilization of New World peoples by noble savage writers was meant primarily as an attack upon the decrepitude of European civilization which they generally viewed as well past its prime. For example, John Locke would assert with confidence in 1680s "that in the beginning all the world was America" (Marshall and Williams 1972: 190).

Shankar Muthu underlines the irony of treating the New World people in these accounts as the earliest, least artificial, and most natural humans—the very attempt to humanize them or to turn their presumed savagery into a badge of honor ultimately cast them as lacking the cultural attributes which would have made them human (Muthu 2009). It is important to note that many of these ideas and representations in real accounts was reflected in fictional accounts and the disillusionment with existing, political, social, and religious forms can be seen in the utopian literature in the seventeenth century which described imaginary voyages to imaginary lands (Ellingson 2001). Writers often had access to "real accounts" due to the extensive voyaging in the period and the boundary between travelers' fictional accounts and fictional "voyages" was not absolute (Lovejoy 1936). In Defoe's *Robinson Crusoe*, a solitary man is able to live a virtuous existence and bereft of all mechanical aids and sophistications of civilization. Both Defoe's *Crusoe* and Jonathan Swift's *Gulliver's Travels* made references to contemporary knowledge shown in travelers' maps. Historical maps were an aspect of the new textualism of the Renaissance and as exploration shifted attention from the Mediterranean to the Oceanic, historical atlases reflected a growing interest in and understanding of cartography (Black 1997: 18). Understanding the role of climate was part of this quest for new knowledge and the links between culture and climate were beginning to be formulated by the seventeenth century.

EARLY ENVIRONMENTAL LEGISLATION

The empirical observation of the damage caused by European empires resulted in a sense of nascent environmental consciousness from a relatively early period. From 1500, the European impact on oceanic islands was documented both as watering holes for ships and due to the fact that practical survival on oceanic islands was difficult. This encouraged wider questions about the sustainability of a confined settlement. Islands soon became symbolic of the explored world and encouraged ideas about limited resources and the need for conservation or sustainability. These early colonial responses to environmental crisis thus allow us to understand global networks of knowledge.

Grove argues for example, that the Caribbean and its littoral, along with Bermuda, has been a very important area for working out the processes going on in world environmental history in the context of European economic expansion and globalization in the early modern period and for an early transition in attitudes to nature that predate eighteenth-century debates. Some of the early travelers like Columbus had been genuinely sustained by their conviction of the locations of discoverable Edens, Indic or otherwise. By the late sixteenth century, as we have seen, growing volumes of capital in connection with agricultural, urban, and proto industrial transitions was transforming the world. By the mid-seventeenth century colonial plantation investments by European trading companies, (Dutch, English, and French) were bringing out rates of soil erosion and deforestation which were marked and commented on by these early naturalists. Indigenous cultures and societies particularly on oceanic islands, such as the Canaries, Madeira, and the Caribbean were under attack.

It is no accident that the earliest writers to comment specifically on rapid environmental change in the context of empires were naturalists who were themselves often actors in the process of colonially stimulated environmental change. Grove and Damodaran have argued that the early pioneers of an environmental critique of the European and American empires depended on having an historical perception of rapid rates of ecological change, and access to evidence for rapid change (Grove 1995; Grove and Damodaran 2006). Between 1500 and 1800 the colonial environment presented a different set of problems to the early colonialists compared to metropolitan Europe as ecological pressures were felt much more catastrophically in the colonial margins, especially the degradational impact of new settlement and plantation agricultures. The cultural impetus independent of the economic motive had also resulted in the widespread clearing of forests in the Caribbean, to enable these landscapes to resemble Europe and the idea of the links between forests, climate, and disease had resulted in extensive forest clearance. The ecological deterioration that followed made an impact on European observers resulting in environmental enquiry and some early legislation which must be seen in the context of an emergent culture of environmental intervention.

Some of the first comprehensive forest-protection legislation on such colonies was introduced after 1620, in Bermuda and a little later in the Caribbean Leeward Islands. In Montserrat, the mountain forests of the island were protected from felling after 1702 by a rigid ordinance, with the knowledge that unrestricted logging caused soil erosion and flooding on lower grounds and in towns (Grove 1995). The Caribbean islands, with their large settler and slave populations, came under sustained ecological pressure at an early date and, as on Mauritius and St. Helena, awareness quickly grew of the physical changes and extinctions brought about by commercial clearance. As early as 1616, measures had been taken to protect the indigenous edible sea birds in Bermuda. Other legislation followed making conservation an integral part of colonial landscape control.

The earliest environmental historians then were these early naturalists and scientists of empire. As early as the mid-seventeenth century we find that intellectuals and natural philosophers such as Richard Norwood and William Sayle in Bermuda, Thomas Tryon in Barbados, and Edmond Halley and Isaac Pyke on St. Helena were all already well aware of characteristically high rates of soil erosion and deforestation in the colonial tropics, and of the urgent need for conservationist intervention, especially to protect forests and threatened species (Grove 1995: 114; Lefroy 1879; Tryon 1684). Halley, for his part, made the first accurate estimates of the global volume of the oceans and the varying quantities of different elements in marine-land-atmosphere cycling over time (Halley 1694: 468–73; Macpike 1932; Thrower and Glacken 1968). On St. Helena and Bermuda this early conservationism led, by 1715, to the gazetting of the first colonial forest reserves and forest-protection laws. In the ensuing century, forest-reserve legislation responding to fears of deforestation-induced climate change slowly began to spread around the world, especially throughout the French, British, and Dutch empires.

The rise of imperial networks of information from 1500 enabled the emergence of a new global environmental awareness as well as the first accurate accounts of global change bringing about an early environmentalism which highlight the older and far more complex antecedents of contemporary conservationist attitudes. The gradual emergence of a complex European epistemology of the global environment should be linked to the cultural dynamics and the pervasive and creative impact of the tropical and colonial experience that challenged European attitudes to nature and transformed the western and scientific mind after 1500. As Grove argues "early environmental concerns emerged as a corollary and in some senses as a contradiction to the history of the mental and material colonization of the world by Europeans" (Grove 1995).

The dynamics of imperial systems are thus central to understanding transformations in world environmental history. Equally important to us, as historians, as the next section of the paper shows is the need to develop an understanding of the conjuncture between extreme climate events, the features of empires and their impacts and organized responses to the environment, especially to events such as the seventeenth century crisis.

CLIMATE ANOMALIES, CULTURE AND THE SEVENTEENTH CENTURY CRISIS

The seventeenth century crisis and its climatic basis has had significant impact on recent historiography. Using new research in climate history, historians such as Geoffrey Parker, Richard Grove, David Clingingsmith, and Jeffrey Williamson have been able to assess the impact of climatic events on historical change and rebellions in the seventeenth and eighteenth century. For Geoffrey Parker and Sam White there is robust evidence that global cooling occurred in the seventeenth century and that it had a dramatic effect on European society, culture, and historical events in the period (Parker 2013; White 2011). The idea of a global crisis is here to stay and the fact that climate formed an integral part of it is accepted by these historians. A central premise of these seventeenth-century historians is that the synchronicity of the many political disorders of mid-seventeenth-century Eurasia was no accident but was dependent on climatic factors. The term seventeenth-century crisis was first coined by English Marxist historian Hobsbawm in 1954 and later taken up by Trevor-Roper (Hobsbawm 1954, Trevor-Roper 1959). Climate, which was mentioned regularly by historians of the *Annales* school, but rarely elsewhere, came to be seen as perhaps the most significant driving force behind those upheavals gathered under the term "crisis." How do we see the role of climate versus culture in history and how do we avoid crude environmental determinism? By exploring the arguments on the seventeenth-century crisis in the context of Mughal India we hope to answer some of these questions.

For the longer part of its history, and in the overwhelming majority of texts produced that addressed the issue of the seventeenth century, the "General Crisis" focus has been on Europe. In 1975, Jonathan Israel began to extend the geographical boundaries of the debate in his work to Mexico and the General Crisis of the seventeenth century (Israel 1975). Further territorial extension was slow to materialize—suffering no doubt from the general move away from structuralist thinking—indeed, it was more than a decade before the Ming/Qing transition in China was first considered in this connection by Frederick Wakeman and not until 1990 that a special edition of *Modern Asian Studies,* presenting four articles—all economic histories—on "The General Crisis in East Asia," introduced to General Crisis theory the study of highly developed economies such as Japan, Indonesia, and India (Wakeman 1986). Contributions to this volume from Anthony Reid and William Atwell looked at South East and East Asia respectively, John Richards considered the period in Mughal India, while Neils Steensgaard discussed "unity in Eurasian history."[5] Two key communalities can be drawn out of this phase of the historiography in which the debate moved into Asia; firstly the notion of the Crisis as a fundamental transformation between epochs, era, or *epistemes*, between old and new, which dominates the historiography of the crisis in Europe faded as identification becomes more a matter of noting the coincidence of a sufficient number of negative incidents encompassing a broad enough geography and sufficiently diverse areas of human life and, secondly, climate began to be seen as quite a significant factor in bringing about the crisis first highlighted by the *Annales* school. Here we examine the evidence for a cooling climate and the impact of the seventeenth century crisis on India in the context of the political, military, and administrative culture of the Mughal empire.

The Little Ice Age coincided with two periods of unusually low sunspot activity, the Spörer Minimum (1450–1540) and the Maunder Minimum (1645–1715). Both solar minimums coincided with the coldest years of the Little Ice Age (LIA) in parts of Europe. In the mid-fourteenth century, a combination of violent climate oscillation halved Europe's population and caused severe depopulation in Asia. A period of global warming followed and then a very cold period peaking in the mid-seventeenth century. Climatologists refer to the period as one of cooler average temperature prevailing at the end of the medieval warming to the beginning of our contemporary era of global warming. The historian Geoffrey Parker does not engage in this debate but simply appropriates the term to refer to the crisis and the LIA referring to climatic conditions between 1610 and the winter of 1708–9. Parker notes that three natural forces combine in this period to generate cooler temperatures and greater climatic variability: reduced solar energy; increased volcanic activity; and a greater frequency of El Niño (Parker 2013).

For Parker, the period was seen to coincide with the El Niño Southern Oscillation current (ENSO) in the oceans which operates in two distinct phases, alternating over a period of roughly two to seven years. These phases are characterized by warming in the tropical Pacific and the Indian Ocean, often suppressing rainfall in the western Pacific in the case of El Niño and converse in the case of La Nina. ENSO events vary widely in their manner of expression, "centers of action," duration and depth, but are typically accompanied by extreme weather events. The links of El Niño with Asian Monsoon is important here and the structure of Sea Surface Temperatures (SSTs) in the Indian Ocean is linked to more familiar pattern of SSTs in the Pacific Ocean (Damodaran, Allan and Hamilton, forthcoming). The mid-seventeenth century saw the weakest period of monsoons on record and in the seventeenth century ENSO events happened twice as often. In fact, the period saw the weakest East Asian monsoons of the past two millennia. It was believed that ENSO events also triggered volcanic eruptions and that the global footprint of El Niño events included three regions besides the land adjoining the Pacific, with the Caribbean suffering floods, Ethiopia and North West India experiencing drought, and Europe suffering hard winters.

The years of the LIA coincide well with the Mughal empire in India. Parker argued convincingly that "although Europe and East Asia formed the heartland of the General Crisis, the Mughal Empire . . . also experienced episodes of severe political disruption in the mid-seventeenth century" resulting in widespread violence. The Mughal empire can be seen as having "come close to revolution . . . in the 1650s," while the seventeenth century as a whole is described as a period in which wars were fought "almost continuously" (Parker

2013). Droughts, floods, and famines, particularly in the late 1620s and early 1630s in Gujarat and the Deccan are also cited as examples of upheaval. However, the main event by which Parker attempts to bring Mughal India into the fold of the "General Crisis" is the 1658–62 war of succession. This is interesting as much of the violence of the wars of succession should be seen as part of the culture of Mughal rule. Parker notes this but puts it down to climate rather than culture and politics noting that yet even this rich empire could not overcome the weaknesses caused by "bloody tanistry"[6] (Parker 2013: 410). The ruthless wars of succession were indeed built into the very nature of the Mughal system of power transfer—tanistry rather than primogeniture which meant that wars of succession were inevitable and, indeed, occurred with every transfer of power in the period. The Mughals in the seventeenth century enjoyed exceptionally long reigns—Shah Jahan ruled for some thirty years, Aurangzeb for nearer fifty—and serious battles for control of the empire erupted always toward the end of emperor's lives as their ability to assert their authority began to wane as it did in the case of Shah Jahan in the late 1650s. In the period 1658–62, Mughal wars of succession caused widespread hardship and death in a ruinous civil war between brothers Aurangzeb and Dara Shikoh, successors of the emperor Shah Jahan. The crisis of succession in Mughal India and the movement of the armies coincided with another great drought where in Gujerat in 1659, famine and plague once again became apparent creating particularly difficult conditions for the Indian population in the late 1650s and early 1660s. Contemporary reports noted that "people [are] dying daily [. . .] the living hardly able to bury the dead" (Agarwal 1983: 41).

What was the environmental impact on the Mughal empire? Historically the Mughals were great tank and canal builders to combat the frequent droughts in their empires. The construction and maintenance of reservoirs was encouraged by rulers (Hardiman 1998). Their impact on the forests of North India, however, had been enormously destructive with increasing agricultural settlement and inroads into the forest frontier at frequent intervals (Gommans 2002). Their introduction of goats had increased soil erosion and their hunting practices had had a negative impact on the wildlife populations of the country. As one writer notes, Mughal painters recorded with minute accuracy their landscape through their miniature paintings of animals, birds, plants, and hunting practices (Divyabhanusinh 2012: 275). The emperors all practiced hunting, especially Jahangir who killed wildlife indiscriminately including tigers and lions (Figure 3.3) At the same time their love of gardens and their penchant for tree planting was a very significant part of Mughal culture. During his reign, the emperor Akbar encouraged trees of every description to be planted resembling the trees of paradise and giving shade to tired travelers.

The destruction of forests, the push of the agrarian frontier, the spread of commercial crops and complex systems of tax collection made agricultural

FIGURE 3.3: Anonymous. Emperor Jahangir on a lion hunt, 1615. From the collection of the Aga Khan Museum.

communities more vulnerable to famine. As Mughal ruler, Akbar's reign was dominated by two major famines in Gujarat in 1556 and 1595 lasting three years. Abul Fazl the court historian describing the horrors of this famine noted that the mortality was great "Man ate their own kin and the streets were blocked with corpses" (Agarwal 1983: 24). Abdul Qadit Badauni, another contemporary historian, noted that the whole country was deserted and no husbandmen remained to till the ground (Agarwal 1983: 23). In 1595 another famine caused by the failure of rains affected North India especially Kashmir and Lahore. Jesuit missionaries reported that the streets of Lahore were blocked up with human corpses. In 1618–19 there was famine in the Deccan and on the Coromandal coast. The traveler, Methwald who left the east coast in 1622 wrote about the ravages of the famine in Vijaynagara. In the reign of Shahjahan, during the protracted La Nina episode in 1630–1 a severe famine occurred which affected Golconda, Ahmednagar, and parts of Malwa. According to the contemporary historian Abdul Hamid Lahori, there was no rainfall in the Mughal territories of the Deccan and Gujerat. The drought was followed by severe floods. The middle of the seventeenth century, as noted, had seen the weakest period of monsoons on record and the rains failed in 1646 and 1647. Heavy mortality was reported from Pulicat and Madras, and the traveler William Foster recorded that half the people in the area of Nagapatnam were dead and the stench of the dead bodies and the dying people was terrifying. The first year of Aurangzeb's reign was likewise marked by a famine of intense suffering causing unspeakable suffering in Northern and Central India. Col. James Tod noted that caste distinctions broke down and that the famine was a great leveler of social divisions, "there was no longer distinction of caste, Sudra and Brahmin were indistinguishable. Men ate men." Cities were depopulated and Bihar had a severe famine in 1671 which encouraged the slave trade. In 1687 there was another severe famine that broke out in Golconda. June 1687 saw floods and the city of Hyderabad was depopulated with houses, rivers, and plains filled with corpses. From 1704–7 another great famine hit the Deccan but this famine caused by drought was not so severe as that during the reign of Shah Jahan.

On the face of it then, while Parker's interpretation of famine events in Mughal India as being a result of climatic uncertainty can be justified from contemporary descriptions, Parker's claim of "exceptional violence" in the seventeenth century as a whole is questionable, as we suggested earlier, for tanistry and wars of succession were part of Mughal politics and culture. Furthermore, his overall argument sits in some contrast to the historiography, for example, of John F. Richards and Irfan Habib and others, who have described the seventeenth century as a period of relative calm and stability (Richards 1990; Habib 1963). Lack of comparative and contextual data on monsoon failure also leaves Parker's argument somewhat open—details of how common these were, their geographic extent, how long they lasted, what traditional coping mechanisms existed, and what social and administrative contingencies were in place are needed in order to form any accurate idea of the meaning and significance of monsoon failure in general, and of specific droughts for Indian society. Furthermore, that Parker can point to near continuous warfare is not in itself proof of exceptionalism in a rapidly expanding and militaristic early modern empire, which, throughout its existence, failed to define solid boundaries and was always involved either in expansion or suppression of rebellion somewhere in its vast territory (Edwards and Garrett 1974; Gommans 2002).

John F. Richards saw no evidence of a seventeenth century crisis in India, identifying instead, continuity and prosperity which endured well into the following century when the region experienced a distinct and unrelated eighteenth-century crisis as the Mughal emperors lost power to local lords and later the East India Company. Richards' conclusions are not very different from those reached some thirty years earlier by the distinguished economic historian of early modern India, Irfan Habib in his work *The Agrarian System of Mughal India*. For Habib, it was the strength of the Mughal empire as an administrative unit which was its most remarkable feature; the revolt of 1580 and the Rajput revolt a century later being practically the only points at which the elite or the theocracy made any play of contesting the power of the semi-divine monarch. Moreover, Habib holds—contrary to Parker—that in the light of the refusal of contesting parties to ever discuss or consider partition, the wars of succession beginning in 1628, 1658, and 1707, should be viewed not as moments of weakness or near collapse, but as markers of the remarkable durability and cohesion of the empire (Habib 1963).

Habib emphasizes the stability and security afforded by Mughal military supremacy—albeit accompanied by violent suppression and coercion of the masses of peasants and workers—and the extreme—if impermanent—power afforded to the emperor via the *Jagirdari* system of delegated revenue collection.

This system rendered the *Mansabdars* "completely dependent on the will of the Emperor," and allowed for the collection of taxes which reduced the populace to bare subsistence, producing enormous and highly concentrated wealth for a small elite (Habib 1963: 360). The system was, however, fundamentally flawed: multiple layers of delegation in tax collection, the regular relocation of regional administrators, and a lack of central control over these *Zamindars* who were seen as the primary threat to order in the empire, left the system open to exploitation whereby the masses suffered enormously at the expense of the various layers of the elite (Habib 1963: 317–22). In time, some local lords, particularly in Hindustan began to rebel against centralized power, refusing to pass on revenue. Poor and subjugated elements were dawn to rebellious regions by more tolerable and equitable conditions and thus the power of rebellious elements grew (Habib 1963: 366). By the mid-late seventeenth century, the Jat, and later the Maratha revolts had become a significant threat to imperial order—they would eventually be its undoing—yet these were slowly developing and evolving states of confrontation, which spread gradually, slowly eroding centralized power, rather than a well-defined crisis prompting its collapse (Habib 1963: 329–46).

For Clingingsmith and Williamson, it was the eighteenth century which witnessed the most significant upheavals in India's economic and political structure (Clingingsmith and Williamson 2009). Herein, it was seen that the turmoil accompanying the dissolution of the Mughal empire, into a constellation of smaller states and their forced regrouping under the East India Company, frustrated commerce and industry, leading to economic decline. Even here, however, the notion of crisis, and even of economic decline itself remains controversial and is far from settled as an historic fact. Work by Bayly, Alam, and Marshall lays emphasis on continuity rather than disruption, with Mughal administrative units are seen to remain largely intact, pre-existing growth trajectories are maintained, and the only major change is in the amount of money passed on by local powers to central Mughal administration (Clingingsmith and Williamson 2009, 2011). It was, furthermore, in the latter part of this era, the years 1700 to 1760, that India reached its peak as a manufacturing center (2009: 223).

Parker's extension of the General Crisis to India then is on much shakier ground than it was in regard to China where at least upheaval—whatever its cause—is beyond contention. In light of the historiographical consensus that the seventeenth century was a time of relative calm in the Mughal empire and that major upheaval did not occur until the early to mid-eighteenth century, the attempts to extend the crisis into the subcontinent are considered, at present, in need of more evidence. Parker's arguments, in the case of India, appear to be open to exactly those criticisms which were leveled at those of Hobsbawm, Trevor-Roper, and others beyond the 1960s; that levels of upheaval were simply not that exceptional and continuity in systems of power was more marked than transformation. What makes these weather anomalies different from say a century earlier or a century later? Parker asserts that "the seventeenth century experienced extremes of weather seldom witnessed before or after and never so far since" (Parker 2013). In his analysis the LIA possesses a decisive agency revealing itself in striking weather events that intervened in historical processes influencing the outcome of battles, destroying empires. The claim requires comparative and quantitative evidence, more detailed work on documentary and paleo sources. Furthermore, in terms of climate it is important to note that impacts are always asymmetric, simplistic notions such as weak or strong monsoons or intense El Niño episodes do no justice for the possibilities of variation in mode of expression and centers of action of these climate events. A more useful approach then, is one that focuses on cultural, regional, and national differences and the resilience of agricultural communities and their production strategies in the face of population pressure, exogenous shocks, and environmental change. Famine causation is complex and links between drought and famine needs to be re-assessed in the early modern period. Despite these caveats, there is a strong need to develop a database that will help us put together a clear famine series, climate series, disease series, wage series, and price series for South Asia and the Indian Ocean world from 1500 to 1900 which is currently woefully inadequate.

This chapter has shown the ways in which history of the early modern imperial world can be enriched by these recent trends in historiography in terms of a global environmental and climate history. In brief, early colonialism brought about step changes in rates of environmental and landscape change with early island plantation agriculture, hunting, and fishing and also in terms of environmental information collection, storage, and transmission. Colonialism of this kind enabled new cultural imaginings and the collection of systematic data on oceanic islands through the establishment of colonial botanic gardens with the employment of scientists as surveyors and naturalists from 1500. By actively promoting and enabling the journeys of travelers and artists, European colonial empires encouraged the systematic organization and cultures of natural history and global botany. By the beginning of the seventeenth century as we have shown, this had resulted in some nascent conservation legislation. Studying imperial systems is thus central to understanding transformations in world environmental history. Equally important to us, as historians, as the second section of the paper shows, is the need to develop an understanding of the conjuncture between extreme climate events, the dynamics of empires, their military and administrative cultures and in turn their environmental impacts and their organized responses to anomalous events such as the seventeenth-century crisis.

CHAPTER FOUR

Labor

MICHAEL GUASCO

The story of early modern empires (c. 1450—c. 1650) is largely a story of the dawning of an era of long-distance, transoceanic navigation, new trade networks, and territorial appropriation. It is also, crucially, an era of dramatic transformations in the realm of labor as massive numbers of often unwilling people from Europe, Africa, and the Americas were corralled into service to suit the goals and ambitions of incipient imperial powers. Spain, Portugal, England, France, and the Netherlands competed against each other (and sometimes cooperated together) to corral and control manpower in order to harvest the mineral wealth and agricultural resources—most notably in the Americas—that fueled the rise and expansion of new transoceanic empires. It was an age of adaptation and innovation that redefined the nature of work and the meaning of labor (and laborers) for centuries to come. Work cultures evolved in dramatic and previously unimagined ways for those who performed it and those who controlled it. Indeed, while seventeenth-century maps vividly recount the rapid aggrandizement of territories across the globe, and the imposition of reimagined terrestrial spaces, the transformations in culture of labor may have been the most dramatic—or, perhaps, traumatic—consequence of what might easily be called "Renaissance imperialism."

NEW LANDS, NEW PEOPLE, NEW LABOR

There is certainly no more familiar image of the dawning of a new era of global expansion than the three small ships of Christopher Columbus's flotilla cresting the western horizon. Columbus, as a man of vision (or just plain lucky, depending on how the story is told) portends a dramatic break in the historical timeline—the moment that seemingly marks a rupture between "the Old" and "the New." With Columbus, scholars and the general public at large can imagine a world transformed by discovery, encounter, cross-cultural exchange, invasion, and perhaps even conquest. All of these interpretive paradigms, individually and in combination with each other, have much to recommend. But it is also arguably the case that an emphasis on the adaptations and innovations in labor—as something that rationalized the movement of peoples and something that was reconceived in the context in the emerging plantation complex—was the defining experience of the early modern Atlantic world.

Consider the familiar story of Christopher Columbus and his four voyages of "discovery" (1492, 1493, 1498, and 1503). These expeditions are routinely memorialized as lines on a map, documenting the range of new places encountered by the man who would become Spain's Admiral of the Ocean Sea. The voyages are a celebration of European expansion and movement from East to West. Less familiar, however, is what moved in the other direction: Indian slaves. Upon the successful completion of his first voyage, Columbus returned in force to the Caribbean with an invasion force numbering seventeen ships and perhaps 1,500 colonists. Even as the Spanish set about trying to identify the sources of valuable commodities, Columbus initiated a scheme to generate revenue from a transatlantic slave trade—something he could easily be credited with inventing. European mariners had previously kidnapped twelve Indian natives and sent them to Europe when the first expedition sailed home. The game changed, however, in early 1495 when Columbus's second expeditionary force dispatched 550 Indians to be sold as slaves in Spain. Hundreds of native men and women died en route while the survivors proceeded to the auction block. From this opening gambit, Columbus dreamed of the fabulous wealth he could generate from his share of this early transatlantic slave trade (Reséndez 2016: 7–25).

In the wake of Columbus's effort to profit from slavery in the early 1490s, the Spanish enslaved Indians in massive numbers throughout the Americas, largely for two reasons. First, many entrepreneurial people imagined that they could profit from the buying and selling of commodified bodies. Second, and more importantly, Spanish invaders recognized that there was a great deal of work to be done in these new lands and compelling Indians to labor as slaves was clearly the easiest way to extract wealth out of American soil. Recent estimates of the number of Indians who may have been subjected to slavery (and related practices that some scholars might count as slavery) suggest the full scope of the system. The historian Andrés Reséndez has estimated, for example, that the total number of Indian slaves in the Americas before 1650 ranged somewhere between 1.25 and 2.5 million people. By way of comparison, fewer than 1 million Africans were enslaved and transported to the Americas during this same period. Thus, even if Reséndez's lower-end estimate is closer to the mark, Indian slavery was a significantly more common and widespread phenomenon than scholars typically appreciate (2016: 324).

Indian slavery was one of the most immediate consequences of this era of mutual discovery, but it did not proceed without complications. From the moment early Spanish settlers became aware of the presence of mineral wealth in the form of gold and silver, a struggle ensued between the forces of greed and those who would rather see natives treated with a bit more care. On the one hand, Spanish prospectors worked to control Indian labor, initially exploiting the nearby Indians on the island of Hispaniola where the Spanish established their first permanent settlements and, soon, discovered the Cibao goldfields in the island's mountainous interior. As the indigenous population declined precipitously during the first decades, Spanish slave traders began raiding nearby islands and the North and South American mainland for more slaves. Once silver lodes were discovered later in the century—most famously in Potosí in the South American Andes in 1545 and Zacatecas in central Mexico in 1546—additional pressures mounted to control as much labor as possible to sustain the production, refining, and transportation of the commodities that would make Spain the envy of Europe during the sixteenth century (Elliott 2006: 93–4, 97–9).

On the other hand, Indian slavery was not without its critics. Whereas Ferdinand and Isabella had momentarily tolerated Columbus's effort to import Indian slaves into Spain, Isabella quickly reversed course. Official crown policy from the late 1490s forward would be that Indians were free vassals who were entitled to compensation for their labor. This was Isabella's stance when she asked in 1498, "What power of mine" does Columbus possess "to give my vassals to anyone?" Certainly, there were exceptions to the rule that Indians should not be enslaved. In 1503, Isabella allowed that cannibals and Indians captured in a "just war" could be taken. But the Laws of Burgos, which served as the first comprehensive legal code for Spanish America in 1512, reiterated the view that Indians were, by nature, free people. Several decades later, the New Laws of 1542 would once again assert that the Spanish should not enslave Indians. And, in this last case, the prohibition was sweeping. Even if they were captured in a "just war" they could not be enslaved (Abulafia 2008: 293–4; Elliott 2006: 68, 97–8; van Deusen 2015).

There were reasons why the crown was repeatedly forced to clarify its opinion on the subject of Indian slavery. The main issue, of course, is that during the frontier stage of Spanish colonialism (*c.* 1492—*c.* 1519), Spanish settlers had ranged widely and in a largely unregulated fashion to aggrandize human capital to sustain their colonial enterprises. Traditionally, the Iberian world (and much of Western Europe) had operated under the assumption that when and if someone fell into a state of slavery, it was a deserved fate. Slavery was a characteristic feature of the Mediterranean world during the fifteenth

FIGURE 4.1: Title page depicting Atahualpa and numerous scenes of Native Americans mining for silver. From Theodor de Bry, *America*, pt. 6 (Frankfurt, 1596). Credit: John Carter Brown Library, Brown University.

FIGURE 4.2: Native Americans search for gold in a stream. Illustration derived from Gonzalo Fernandez de Oviedo y Valdés, *Historia general de las Indias* (Seville, 1535). From Giovanni Battista Ramusio, *Navigazioni e viaggi*, vol. 3 (Venice, 1556). Credit: John Carter Brown Library, Brown University.

century, but enslaved peoples, whether they were North African Moors, sub-Saharan Africans, Greeks, Tartars, or Slavs were traditionally understood as being in that condition because they could be thought of as either enemies of the church or victims of a "just war." But that was not how things played out in the immediate aftermath of the arrival of the Spanish in America. Rather, it was something of a feeding frenzy. It was for this reason that the Spanish government dispatched a new Spanish administrator, Nicolás de Ovando, to Hispaniola in 1502 to restore order to an island that was being torn apart from within by the Spanish invaders as they scrambled and fought with each other to control the goldfields and acquire Indian slaves. To improve local conditions and push back against slavery, Ovando famously instituted the *encomienda* system, which involved granting control over a discrete population of Indians to an *encomendero*, who possessed the authority to make use of the Indians as laborers in various endeavors (not least, mining gold) (Abulafia 2008: 237–8).

In theory, the encomienda system offered Indians greater protections and shielded them from rapacious slave traders. Indians would continue to live in their local communities and would be governed on a day-to-day basis by their own *caciques*. In reality, the encomienda system became a cultural practice that allowed invaders to generate wealth in the Americas. Although the glint of filthy lucre spurred thousands of Spanish invaders to risk ocean voyages, endure privations, and put their lives at risk in military campaigns, it eventually became less gold and silver itself and more the ability to control large numbers of dependents as laborers that sustained Spanish colonialism in the sixteenth century. In the aftermath of the conquest (post 1519), Hernan Cortés followed Ovando's pattern of establishing order out of chaos by rewarding hundreds of his followers with *encomiendas*. Although it worked through many names indicative of subtle variations (such as *repartimiento* and *depósito*), the encomienda system served to satisfy the hunger of conquerors by giving them access to tribute and the labor of Indians (Elliott 2006: 39–40). In theory (again), the encomienda system constituted an exchange that obligated both parties to serve each other—Indians by performing services and *encomenderos* by offering instruction in the Christian faith. In practice, of course, the system largely facilitated imperialism by encouraging restless conquerors to settle down and reap the rewards of territorial acquisition by lording over a population that could be compelled to labor in agriculture, mining, manufacturing, or any of a number of profitable activities. Ibero-American society and culture, such as it was in its formative years, was rooted in the belief that the indigenous inhabitants of the Americas could, and should, be forced to labor.

The cultural consequences of the exploitation of Indians by the Spanish, particularly in the realm of new labor demands, are demonstrated in interesting ways by considerations of gender. On the one hand, indigenous women bore a greater economic burden and were forced to perform new and sometimes onerous tasks as a result of Spanish innovations. Women often became the primary producers of goods in their local communities, often for tribute payments, as men were drawn away by the labor demands imposed on them by both the state and individual *encomenderos*. Women and children, however, were also preyed upon as workers and compelled to labor in places like Potosí, where they toiled in the dangerous silver mining industry, or in the *obrajes* of central Mexico where they might be even be chained to a loom or locked in a room so that they could weave cloth (Jefferson and Lokken 2011: 94–6, 119–22). On the other hand, some women found new opportunities. European women, for example, sometimes rose to extraordinary positions of power as *encomenderas*, typically when they inherited rights upon the death of a spouse (Powers 2005: 160–5). Some women also played critical roles as independent producers in urban economies, such as Potosí, where Spanish, indigenous, and African women supplied many of the goods and credit that sustained the local economy (Mangan 2005: 134–60). The new Spanish economic order created a range of new burdens and, occasionally, a few opportunities that fundamentally altered the roles that women played in early colonial societies.

Thus, from an early date, it was clear that Indian slavery and its subsequent legalistic modifications posed some serious challenges to colonists and natives alike. For one thing, as much as Spain attempted to impose rules and restrictions, Indian slavery never really disappeared. Between 1515 and 1542, as many as 200,000 Indians were captured and enslaved in Nicaragua alone. Other estimates of the scale of the ongoing slave trade in Spanish America between 1550 and 1650 (after it was largely outlawed), indicate that there may have been more than 100,000 Indians enslaved in the Caribbean, another 200,000 in Mexico and Central America, and 500,000 in Spanish South America (Blackburn 1997: 133; Reséndez 2016: 324). This was the system that religious figures like the Dominican friar Bartolomé de las Casas tried to stifle when they railed against the abuses endured by native peoples.

The example of Las Casas is instructive of the distance between the laws of the land and actual practice on the ground and the way an emerging political culture of American labor regimes routinely honored Iberian precepts in the breach. Las Casas famously debated Juan Ginés de Supúlveda in Valladolid in 1550 and 1551 on the justice of the conquest and nature of Indians. By all accounts, Las Casas advanced the more compelling argument in Spain. The idea that Indians needed to be protected was formally extended in 1563 when they were classified as *miserabiles*, which promised them formal protections and legal rights within the empire. Further protections were issued in 1573 when the crown endorsed ordinances drawn up by the Council of the Indies to regulate imperial expansion and limit what could be done with Indians (Elliott 2006: 76–7). Yet, virtually every new moral victory and legal protection drafted by royal officials in Spain was met with opposition in the Americas. Under the best of circumstances, colonial officials responded to the new rules with a deferential *"obredezco pero no cumplo"* ("I obey but cannot comply"). At worst, Spanish officials met resistance when they did try to enforce new regulations. When the newly appointed viceroy of Peru Blasco Núñez Vela appeared in 1544 and attempted to implement the New Laws, he prompted a civil war that led to his death on the battlefield just two years later. Indian slaves were valuable commodities and the Spanish in America saw imperial efforts to limit slave holding as a threat to their bottom line—taking captives and making slaves was an important avenue to wealth and power in the New World (Bryant 2014: 24–9).

Although the indigenous people of the Americas introduced new challenges, the problem of integrating conquered, non-native peoples into the cultural and political community had been encountered previously on the Iberian Peninsula. After 1492, for example, Spanish Christians had to decide what to do about the recently conquered Moors of Granada. Christians and Muslims had lived in close proximity to each other for centuries and the two groups had intermingled somewhat seamlessly during the medieval period. But toleration and integration (such as they were) largely existed more as a matter of necessity. At the conclusion of the *Reconquista*, Spanish Christians deported, enslaved, or demanded the wholesale conversion of Spanish Muslims. Medieval notions of difference, such as *limpieza de sangre* ("purity of blood"), made it virtually impossible for Spanish elites to accept the idea that Moors or Jews or anyone else could ever become fully "Spanish." Given the chance, then, Spanish officials defaulted to discriminatory policies, most infamously in the realm of religious persecution (Nirenberg 1996).

A similar story unfolded in the Americas. Although colonial officials tried to establish order by maintaining separation between Europeans and indigenous peoples, Spanish settlers and natives mixed with each other—biologically and culturally. Spanish America soon came to be the home of large numbers of *mestizos*, which facilitated the development of distinctive *mestizo* cultures in different parts of Latin America that were shaped to varying degrees by European, Indigenous, and (eventually) regionally-specific African cultural norms. As had been the case in the Iberian world, a tension between segregation and integration necessarily shaped the daily lives of the inhabitants of these new, multi-cultural community. Many colonists, particularly the *encomenderos* and other elites, treated Indians with impunity based on the popular idea that Indians deserved their fate as a conquered people, but also because they were fundamentally different sorts of people. Indian slavery and related forced labor systems could not have persisted without such an underlying ideological foundation. In spite of this bit of imperial fiction, however, cultural convergence and racial intermixture—*mestizaje*—were much more common during the sixteenth and seventeenth centuries than many people preferred to acknowledge (Elliott 2006: 79–87).

The Spanish were hardly the only European power to embrace Indian slavery. Every European nation either tolerated or actively promoted Indian slavery as a necessary aspect of their American endeavors (Gallay 2002; Rushforth 2012). The Portuguese were arguably the most intensive practitioners of Indian slavery for a time (particularly during the second half of the sixteenth century) and they expressed even fewer qualms about the subject than the Spanish. As quickly as they arrived on the scene in coastal Brazil in 1500, Portuguese colonizers followed in the footsteps of their Iberian neighbors by preying on Indians. In 1503, Portuguese ships returned from a Brazilian expedition with a mixed cargo of what would prove to be the basis of the early Luso-American economy: brazilwood and Indian slaves. Historian Stuart Schwartz has argued that the characterization of Indians as *negros da terra* is a stark indication that the Portuguese immediately valued Indians for their role as laborers who would serve European masters. During the initial decades of Portuguese efforts to establish control over Brazil, the number of Indian slaves under European control was probably small. By the second half of the century, however, Indian slaves fueled the massive expansion of the brazilwood trade and, more importantly, the development of a new sugar plantation economy that would ultimately redraw the American landscape and go a long way toward defining American slavery (Schwartz 1985: 52).

Indian slavery persisted much longer in Portuguese America as a legal institution but it was not without its critics either. Like some Spanish rulers and members of the clergy, the Portuguese crown attempted to protect Indians with vague declarations that Brazil's natives should be treated well. Again, the governing rationale for this concern was largely spiritual. To achieve the goal of facilitating the wholesale conversion of Brazil's Indian peoples, the Portuguese brought in Jesuit priests who turned out to be powerful opponents of Indian slavery. And like the *reducciones* in Spanish America, the Jesuits rounded up Indians and placed them in supervised settlements, known in Brazil as *aldeias*, to promote conversion and protect vulnerable natives from predatory slave raiders. The tension between the clerical mission to harvest souls and the colonial imperative to harvest sugar put Europeans at odds with each other— and not just metropolitan officials with colonists but also people divided by their primary commitment to sacred and secular gains. The Jesuits, however, could only do so much. As long as there were available Indians nearby, and as long as labor demands continued to escalate to service the sugar *engenhos*, Indian slavery continued to be tolerated (Eisenberg 2003; Hemming 1978).

Predictably, no matter how many voices were raised in protest and how many restraints were placed on the abuse of Indian slavery, the Portuguese devastated the natives in their midst. The church and the demands of an industrializing plantation economy were not the same thing, but they both compelled Indians to alter their lives dramatically. And then there was the

FIGURE 4.3: Slaves process sugar cane and make sugar. Illustration derived from Girolamo Benzoni, *Historia del mondo nuovo*, pt. 5 (Venice, 1565). From Theodor de Bry, *America*, pt. 5 (Frankfurt, 1595). Credit: John Carter Brown Library, Brown University.

all-too-familiar spread of epidemic diseases, which had not greatly impacted Brazil's native peoples initially but struck with a vengeance in 1562. By some estimates, the coastal Indian population was cut by half, which only increased the pressure Portuguese predators placed on Indian communities as they sought to keep sugar plantations fully manned. In 1570, the Portuguese king finally intervened on behalf of the natives, decreeing that Indians could only be enslaved as a result of a "just war" or because they had engaged in cannibalism. Like the Spanish before them, Portuguese slave traders had kept the number of their slave retinues up with fictional devices, such as the practice of *resgate* or ransoming Indian slaves from their enemies in the wake of indigenous conflicts. But with new pressures from above and declining numbers as a result of years of slaving and new epidemic diseases, Indian slavery became difficult to maintain (Schwartz 1985: 51–72).

Between 1492 and the mid-seventeenth century, Indian lives were reshaped by the forces of conquest, slavery, and epidemic diseases. Any one of these would have been bad enough, but most native groups had to deal with all three. In the case of slavery, there were efforts on the part of some Spanish and clerical officials to ameliorate conditions, but forced rotational labor drafts like the *repartimiento*, *encomienda*, and *mita* (in the Andes) did not always lead to a meaningful reprieve from back-breaking labors, forced relocation, or separation from family and friends. Only as their numbers dwindled over time were the Spanish and Portuguese compelled to look elsewhere for new pools of labor. Indians would continue to be impacted by the extractive demands of European colonialism well into, and beyond, the early seventeenth century, but they would increasingly find themselves working alongside and nearby other people whose labor was an exploitable resource.

AFRICAN SLAVERY AND THE TRANSATLANTIC SLAVE TRADE

Columbus's decision to enslave Indians was unsurprising on more than one level. As someone with intimate ties to the Portuguese Atlantic world, and especially the Madeira Islands, he was familiar with what had already become standard practice in Portuguese expeditions along the African coastline: the African slave trade. Portuguese mariners began returning with shiploads of African captives during the 1440s. Initially, the numbers were relatively small but by the final decades of the fifteenth century, Portuguese ships were returning every year with hundreds of Africans with the intention of funneling them into the labor markets of coastal cities on the Iberian Peninsula. Beginning in the second half of the fifteenth century, then, Iberian seafaring towns began accumulating African slaves. By the early sixteenth century, five to ten percent of the population of cities like Seville and Lisbon consisted of enslaved Africans. Other times, African slaves were transshipped to the expanding economies of the Atlantic islands. There, they were put to work on sugar plantations and related enterprises in the Madeira Islands, Azores, and Cape Verdes. African slavery was an expanding institution before Columbus set sail across the Atlantic (Phillips 1985: 149–53, 160–3; Northrup 2002: 6–10).

During the entire history of the transatlantic slave trade some number well in excess of 12 million African men, women, and children endured the dehumanizing experience of captivity, enslavement, and forced transportation across the Atlantic. The largest numbers were transported during the height of the trade during the eighteenth century. In fact, approximately eighty percent of all of the human beings shipped against their will by British, Portuguese, French, and other slave traders, endured the indignities of the trade during the eighteenth and nineteenth centuries. Even so, African peoples, largely from Senegambia, West Central Africa and various ports in between were sold into slavery and transported in massive numbers to labor in American mines and plantations before the 1650s. Scholars estimate that 950,000 people were reduced to slavery before the mid-seventeenth century and shipped out to serve European masters in Portuguese Brazil, the Spanish American colonies, and incipient Dutch, French, and English outposts throughout the Americas. Many men, women, and children would die in the process—nearly twenty-four percent of the Africans who were crammed into the dank holds of European slave ships died as a result of systematic abuses and harsh conditions, shortages of food and water, diseases, and the other perils of transoceanic navigation. Thus, although nearly 1 million people were entombed in the holds of slave ships before 1650, no more than about 750,000 survived the months-long journey across the Atlantic to take up the implements of labor on American soil (*Voyages*; Smallwood 2007; Rediker 2007; Mustakeem 2016).

The enslavement of African peoples is typically imagined as something that was centered in Portuguese Brazil, the British Caribbean, mainland North America, and French sugar islands like Saint Domingue. Certainly, there is good reason for the persistence of this popular assumption—probably more than 10 million enslaved Africans ended up in one of these places during the entire history of the trade. Before 1650, however, the majority of captive Africans were shipped to Spanish America. Indeed, recent scholarly work has added significantly to the authoritative online resource, *Voyages: The Trans-Atlantic Slave Trade Database*, suggesting that before 1640 about 530,000 Africans arrived in Spanish America while the number arriving in Brazil was only about 266,000 (Borucki *et al.* 2015: 433–46; Bryant *et al.* 2012). Slavery, before it became enduringly focused in Brazil, Barbados, and other places where crops like sugar, tobacco, coffee, and cotton defined the institution, expressed itself differently when the realities of Spanish America shaped the institution.

African slavery as both a labor practice and a system of commodification was not the same thing before 1650 as it would become after. The first thing to note is that the transition to the use of enslaved Africans as a replacement force for the dwindling number of bound Indians took place in Spanish America before it occurred elsewhere. Before 1580, bound African slaves were relatively rare in the Americas, with fewer than 85,000 anywhere in the Spanish colonies and perhaps only 4,000 in Brazil. At the same time, African slaves were already an important part of a mixed labor force in Madeira and predominated in the Canaries (Vieira 2004). When they did appear in Spain's transatlantic world, they often came from Spain, where they could also be found in large numbers in Iberian port cities. Additionally, they performed a surprisingly wide range of tasks, on land and at sea, and had sometimes even begun operating as free members of local communities. African slaves were also transported along the African coast, from one place to another. Between 1475 and 1540, for example, perhaps 12,000 African slaves were imported into the Gold Coast from other coastal regions of Africa (Garofalo 2012; Smallwood 2007: 15).

During the final decades of the sixteenth century, the slave trade changed in ways that began to redirect enslaved Africans in much larger numbers and in a more precise fashion toward Spain's American colonies. It also began to take shape as a system that was almost wholly devoted to fueling the expansion of a colonial economy based on extractive practices. First, Europe extended its presence in Africa after 1570 when Portugal established a permanent foothold in the kingdom of Kongo. Europeans, and the Portuguese in particular, had been working their way up and down the coast for more than a century by this time, but their slave trading efforts had been somewhat intermittent and unsystematic. Moreover, many of the slaves they acquired came from the more northern regions, especially in and around Senegambia. Once they were able to entrench themselves in West Central Africa, they began to ship out much larger numbers of African captives. For example, between 1500 and 1580, the Portuguese acquired around 114,000 African slaves in the Senegambian region. Only about 16,000 seem to have been taken in West Central Africa. During the final two decades of the century, however, 31,000 slaves were exported out of Senegambia while 102,000 were snatched away from West Central Africa (*Voyages*; Eltis 2001).

Second, Africans became much more widely available for use as slaves in Spanish America after 1580 when Spain and Portugal were consolidated under King Philip II. Before this time, Spain had not been able to access significant numbers of African slaves directly from African ports because the Treaty of Tordesillas of 1494 had defined Africa as a Portuguese sphere of influence. If Spanish colonists wanted to purchase African slaves, they had to go through the Portuguese (or northern European interlopers) which was not easy to do. With the union of the two crowns, however, the Portuguese slave trading system was thrown open to the Spanish colonial world, or precisely those people who had the greatest demand for bound labor. Between 1580 and 1640 (when Portugal regained its independence) 445,000 slaves were sold into slavery in the Spanish colonies and another 261,000 were sold in Brazil. And, unlike the earlier period when slaves from Upper Guinea predominated, the majority of the new arrivals were from Angola and Kongo in West Central Africa, especially after 1620 (Borucki *et al.* 2015: 440; Wheat 2011).

The demand for African slaves had a profound impact on the development of regional subcultures in the Americas. Because new arrivals came from different parts of Africa, the articulation of new African American identities and new cultures of slavery varied from place to place and changed over time as trading patterns evolved and shifted. Much of this process played out slowly over the course of centuries, but certain patterns were already in evidence in the period before the mid-seventeenth century. In Central America, for example, most of the Africans who arrived during the sixteenth century came from Senegambia and West Africa but by the seventeenth century they were overwhelmingly coming from West Central Africa (Lokken 2013). As the sources of slaves changed, new cultural communities emerged that were often grounded in the specific point of origin of enslaved peoples. In Peru, enslaved men and women from disparate communities in Guinea-Bissau constructed a new identity as *brans* that allowed them to distinguish themselves from other enslaved Africans who traced their origins back to West Central Africa (O'Toole 2007). Different African backgrounds and the circumstances that fed enslaved Africans into different regions where they might labor to produce sugar or mine gold created the circumstances that allowed for people of African descent to create new and meaningful cultural communities (Lovejoy 2004).

By the seventeenth century, as the Iberian powers had almost thoroughly dismissed the legitimacy of Indian slavery, African slavery emerged as a viable and desirable alternative. Demographic and local political realities in the Americas helped shape the emerging consensus that the enslavement of African peoples was a more legitimate practice than the exploitation of indigenous Americans. Las Casas famously, and to his later regret, advanced this position early in the sixteenth century. At the same time, however, African slavery and the transatlantic slave trade were conditioned by incipient racial ideology in the early modern Atlantic world. Some scholars have argued that the language of race emerged at an early date in the Iberian world and was deployed to buttress the social, economic, and legal dislocation of sub-Saharan Africans, Moors, and other non-Christian and non-European peoples (Sweet 1997). While Africans were utilized as slaves in parts of Europe from an early date, however, they were not initially accorded as either natural slaves or the only group suited for enslavement. Phenotypical differences, most notably skin color, became a frequent point of conversation during the fifteenth and sixteenth centuries and, as it wormed its way into western European society and culture, blackness became an outward indicator of a whole range of shortcomings that would slowly blossom into a whole catalog of derogatory stereotypes (Guasco 2014: 60–77, 102–9; Kendi 2016: 15–30). European slavers did not conduct their affairs because of anti-black racism, but racial discourse certainly facilitated the ease with which labor-hungry American *conquistadores*, planters and settlers looked to both Africa and the institution of slavery to serve their needs (see also Burton's chapter on Race, this volume).

Most of the newly arriving African captives entered Spanish America at Cartagena, Veracruz, Buenos Aires, and Hispaniola. From there, they were often reshipped to further off places, such as Lima and Mexico City. Roughly sixty percent of newly enslaved Africans were men. More than twenty percent were children. To the Spanish who purchased the newly enslaved, however, these individual characteristics mattered less than the ability of African men and women, boys and girls, to produce wealth and demonstrate mastery. Slavery, although more famously associated with the countryside, was a vibrant urban institution during this early period. Africans typically constituted between ten and twenty-five percent of the population in colonial American cities, where they were employed as domestic servants and as both skilled and unskilled laborers. Slaves were both adornments designed to emphasize the social status of their owners as well as workers who filled important roles in the labor market. Thomas Gage, an English Jesuit who spent time in Mexico and Guatemala during the 1620s and 1630s, saw African slaves performing every possible labor. Gentlemen marked their station in life by outfitting "train[s] of blackamoor slaves . . . in brave and gallant liveries." Yet, slaves and free blacks alike were also important craft workers, they produced and distributed goods from nearby gardens and orchards, and were a significant presence in the entire range of commercial enterprises (Bennett 2003: 14–32; Guasco 2014: 229–30; Elliott 2006: 99–101).

Rural areas were even more thoroughly populated with enslaved Africans. Gage took notice of the wheat fields and sugar plantations in the vicinity of central Mexico, including one in particular that was owned by the Dominicans that employed "above two hundred blackamoor slaves, men, and women, besides little children." The religious orders routinely possessed and made use of enslaved Africans to work in a wide range of agricultural enterprises, including sugar and grapes for winemaking. The Jesuits, in particular, became large-scale slave owners in Peru. The case of the religious orders as slave owners is an instructive reminder that just as Indians were protected, and many Spanish were fully aware that the native population had plummeted in the century after the Spanish conquest, Africans found few benefactors. To the Spanish, Africans promised some relief from their labor problems, but Peru's distance from the main channels of the African slave trade led to constant complaining throughout the period that there were not enough workers to go around (O'Toole 2012: 25–7).

Gold mining was one industry closely identified with enslaved African workers. Partly, this was because gold deposits were often found at some distance from concentrated populations of Indians. Thus, while Indians continued to predominate in the silver mines of places like Potosí, sometimes as

FIGURE 4.4: "How the Negro Slaves Work and Look for Gold in the Mines of the Region called Veragua" [Panama]. From the *Histoire naturelle des Indes*, manuscript, c. 1586, fol. 100r. The Pierpont Morgan Library, New York. MA 3900. Bequest of Clara S. Peck, 1983. Credit: Pierpont Morgan Library, New York.

conscripted laborers but many times as free workers, enslaved Africans worked the goldfields, especially in New Granada (modern-day Colombia). There, beginning in the late sixteenth century, Africans were divided into labor gangs called *cuadrillas*, given a small plot of land to grow their own food, but otherwise tasked with panning for gold. The value of Africans was recognized at an early date in regions that were gold-rich and Indian poor. For this reason, Francisco Auncibay, a member of the *audiencia* of Quito, petitioned the king of Spain to subsidize the importation of 2,000 African slaves. Calculating the costs of bringing in labor—indigenous or African, free or enslaved—was a constant pressure on would-be employers (Klein and Vinson 2007: 24–5; Blackburn 1997: 147; Bryant 2014: 1).

As important as slavery was to the work that was performed in Spanish America, it is worth emphasizing that there was not always a direct correlation between labor and slavery, or between race and slavery. Slavery was equally important in governing social relations, shaping colonial relationships, and defining race as it was simply a matter of production, economy, and trade (Bryant 2014: 5–6). Moreover, many "slavish" tasks were actually performed by wage labors who were of indigenous, African, or mixed descent. Free blacks made up a steadily growing part of the population in Spanish America, especially in urban areas, yet continued to play a vital economic role in a range of skilled trades. In Peru, free blacks could be found in such significant numbers that they founded numerous social organizations, or *confraternities*. In New Spain, the free black population exceeded the enslaved population by the mid-seventeenth century, numbering more than 110,000 people. As Thomas Gage recognized, slavery was vital and widespread in Spanish America, but social and economic relations were also quite fluid. Many of the free people he encountered were "mestizos, and mulattoes, who live in thatched houses." At the same time, he remarked on the presence of more well-to-do individuals, like "a Blackamoor in an estancia of his own, who is held to be very rich." A wide range of possibilities existed for people of African descent in seventeenth-century Spanish America (Elliott 2006: 108; Bennett 2003: 19–20; Guasco 2014: 230).

The transition to African slavery in Brazil was much more squarely connected to the expanding demands of the sugar industry. During the second half of the seventeenth century, Brazil and the West Indies would develop as the central arenas in the full articulation of the New World plantation complex. Sugar was already a familiar and important crop in the Mediterranean and Atlantic worlds by the sixteenth century, where it was typically grown using a mixed force of free and, increasingly, enslaved workers. Sugar plantations began to appear in Brazil at mid-century, especially in the northeastern coastal region, and sugar quickly replaced brazilwood as the primary economic activity. By the 1570s, new sugar plantations and mills appeared with remarkable frequency. Unfortunately, the expansion of plantation agriculture largely coincided with the tragic decline in the indigenous population from the combined effects of decades-long slave raiding and new epidemic diseases. Portuguese planters had never been completely enamored of Indian slaves at the mills, accusing Indians of being bad workers. A combination of factors therefore encouraged the *senhores de engenho* to look across the Atlantic at about the same time that their Spanish neighbors were doing the same thing (Schwartz 2004: 187–90; Curtin 1990).

The Portuguese slave trading numbers tell the demographic story with startling clarity. In the thirty years before 1580, Brazil imported approximately 28,000 enslaved Africans. In the thirty years after 1580, that number was closer to 114,000. During the next thirty-year period (1611–40), Portuguese sugar planters received something in the range of 286,000 Africans, a tenfold increase on average of the number of Africans who were arriving on an annual basis just a half century earlier. Like the Africans who were being transported and sold into slavery in Spanish America during this period, a majority of people were increasingly from West Central Africa.

What the numbers don't reveal is just how much labor changed beginning in the final decades of the sixteenth century. One important transition was the shift from a labor force consisting primarily of Indian slaves to one consisting of African slaves. A second related transition, however, was equally important. Just as Africans could be said to have replaced Indians, African slaves and free people of color also gradually took the place of skilled whites in the more specialized tasks associated with the sugar mill. These included blacksmiths, carpenters, stonemasons, sugar masters, and more (Schwartz 2004: 187–90). Portuguese production techniques and a willingness to take advantage of African workers not simply as cutters of cane in the fields but as artisans, craftsmen, and knowledgeable producers in the critical work of refining sugar led to massive growth in Brazil during the early seventeenth century. Virtually overnight, Brazil became the dominant sugar producer in the world (Klein and Vinson 2007:43–7).

African slavery was a growth industry in Latin American and the Caribbean. European empires and new cultural communities were shaped by the interactions of Europeans, Indians, and Africans and the entrenchment of slave labor. Its most expansive period was yet to come, with the British, French, and Dutch seemingly waiting in the wings in the middle of the seventeenth century. In Spanish and Portuguese America, however, slavery's versatility and adaptability revealed itself, especially during the late sixteenth century. Africans appeared— to Europeans—extraordinarily suitable to labor in mines, on plantations, and in a whole host of rural and urban activities. But just as slavery adapted itself to New World exigencies, so too did people of African descent engage in creative cultural adaptations to sustain themselves and their descendants throughout the centuries-long ordeal of New World slavery. Importantly, however, just as

Africans were preyed upon with escalating frequency during this era, the situation that would define the lives of millions of future Africans—a likely short and difficult life as a slave on sugar, tobacco, coffee, or cotton plantation as the normative experience—was not yet the order of the day. Only in Brazil could this eventuality be perceived on the horizon. Elsewhere, slavery was characterized much more by its variety, fluidity, and adaptability.

SERVANTS AND SERVITUDE

The establishment of European overseas colonies, the discovery of gold and silver, and the development of a transatlantic plantation complex dramatically altered the culture and meaning of labor throughout the Atlantic world. For Indians and Africans, it meant new compulsory systems of exploitation and inaugurated an era of massive forced relocation and tragically high mortality rates. But it also served as the impetus for the creation of new communities of individuals who were either forced or chose to craft innovative New World cultures in the face of considerable adversity. For Europeans, labor was an equally important issue. Sixteenth-century Europe—England in particular—endured a labor crisis that promoted colonial enterprises during the seventeenth century. After England began establishing colonies, especially in the Chesapeake region of North America and throughout the Caribbean, the need for labor led to structural and cultural innovations that changed the way people had traditionally performed and thought about work. Nowhere was this more true than in the case of the English laboring class, which transported itself to the Americas in large numbers beginning in the early seventeenth century. With the invention of indentured servitude during the second and third decades of the seventeenth century, a new way of facilitating the movement of people across the Atlantic and compelling them to labor was born.

Perhaps the most well-worn narrative of the nature of labor in late medieval and early modern Europe begins with the so-called "Black Death." In the aftermath of the massive epidemic that reached the Italian Peninsula in 1348 and rapidly spread throughout Europe, perhaps one-third of the population perished. A consequence in some parts of Europe, particularly areas bordering the Mediterranean, was an increase in demand for non-Christian slaves. Muslim and other African slaves became commonplace in the Italian city-states and the Iberian Peninsula. Legal slavery had once been widespread in the British Isles, France, Germany, and Eastern Europe, but it had largely evaporated during the medieval period for political, religious, and economic reasons. Serfdom arose in some parts of western Europe as another way of maintaining control of what would be an otherwise mobile laboring population. Thus, the late medieval period witnessed the emergence of serfdom, which went by a number of different names but basically involved two forms: serfs who were bound to another person (personal serfs) and serfs who were bound to an estate (tenurial serfs). The distinction between the two groups were subtle, but the significant issue was that some people were categorized as bondmen and bondwomen by virtue of their lineage alone while many others—quite likely many more in western Europe—were bound by virtue of the land they occupied (Bush 1996: 200–6). From a strictly legal perspective, as well as the conditions of life, serfdom routinely had more in common with freedom than slavery. Even so, serfs clearly resented the implication that they might not be at liberty to conduct their lives as they saw fit and bitterly—indeed, violently—resisted the efforts of lords and masters to impose their will on enserfed peoples.

Most of the work that was performed in Renaissance Europe, however, was performed by wage laborers and servants. Much of that work consisted of domestic service, apprenticeships and craftwork in the skilled professions, and agricultural work. Wage labor was also increasingly common. Agricultural labor, animal husbandry, and the apprenticeship system were all governed by labor contracts that defined the mutual obligations of the master and servant. This system had been detailed in medieval England when the English government had acknowledged the importance of having a reliable and smoothly running system by enacting a legal framework for managing employer-laborer relations in the Statute of Laborers (1351). For the next 200 years, the Statute of Laborers provided the rules that defined the nature of contracts that governed agricultural laborers and apprentices, established wage rates, and delineated the punishments for breaking agreements.

By the sixteenth century, however, new issues arose that revealed problems in the English labor system. As Robert Steinfeld has observed, the underlying assumption in early modern England was that labor was "a common resource to which the community had rights, and the laborer . . . had legal obligations to make that resource available to community members on terms and conditions the community prescribed." The nature of work, or rather the perception among elites that it was growing more difficult to govern workers, prompted new legislation early in the reign of Queen Elizabeth. English society appeared to many social commentators to be disordered by excessive mobility rates and laborers who either refused to work or who left work without cause. In truth, England had changed since the mid-fourteenth century, with an escalating population, high rates of unemployment, rising food prices, and the enclosure movement put many would-be workers in difficult straights. Thus, Parliament enacted the Statute of Artificers (1562) to limit the mobility and independence of the independent working class (day and wage laborers and artificers). What this parliamentary legislation revealed most clearly, however, was that that labor was both a problem in need of managing and an interest that divided potential employers based on a variety of considerations (Steinfeld 1991: 60–6; Newman 2013: 17–24).

The perceived problem of an unruly and too often unwilling labor force prompted Tudor officials to take even more drastic steps to bring the supposedly idling masses to heel. In 1547, Parliament even passed legislation that promised to impose slavery on individuals who refused to work. Although it was apparently never imposed and was removed from the books after only two years, the willingness to address vagabondage with actual bondage suggests the nature of the crisis Tudor elites perceived. This use of state power to compel labor did not occur in isolation. Earlier in the century, Sir Thomas More had imagined a world where slavery would take men, break and tame them, and then free them once they had cultivated the ability to work properly. Later in the century and into the early Stuart era, similar proposals were bandied about to reduce crime by reducing offenders to slavery in order, as Sir William Monson put the issue, to "terrify and deter" or simply "make men avoid sloth and pilfering and apply themselves to labor and pains" (Guasco 2014: 33–8).

One important response to the labor problems faced by sixteenth-century England was penned by the editor, translator, and colonial promoter Richard

FIGURE 4.5: A vagabond or criminal being whipped through the streets of town (c. sixteenth century). Woodcut engraving. From Raphael Holinshed, The first volume of the Chronicles of England, Scotlande, and Irelande (London, 1577). Credit: Houghton Library, Harvard University.

Hakluyt. In 1584, Hakluyt authored "A Discourse on Western Planting," which he intended to be read as a policy piece by Queen Elizabeth and her advisors on the virtues of colonization. The twenty-one-chapter document ranged widely, but among the issues raised by Hakluyt was the domestic labor crisis that currently plagued England. Unlike social critics who bemoaned "idle beggars and sturdy vagabonds," he recognized that the island nation was overpopulated and it was difficult for well-intentioned, able-bodied men to find work. He also argued that bleak economic prospects had led many good souls to give up. The solution? England could prosper and English men and women could find gainful employment with the emergence of new places to work and new work to perform as a result of transatlantic colonialism (Mancall 2007: 145; Guasco 2014: 35). Imperialism could solve the early modern labor crisis.

Hakluyt's vision of a colonial empire did not take shape immediately, but by the early seventeenth century new American enterprises began to emerge in the Chesapeake (1607), the Caribbean (*c.* 1620s), and New England (especially after 1630). What many of these colonial ventures had in common was a desperate need for labor, especially in those places where new, intensive cash-crop agriculture became the order of the day. In some cases, the English looked to their Iberian predecessors for examples of ways to exploit Indians as workers. But whereas Indians were preyed upon in massive numbers by the Spanish and Portuguese to serve their imperial designs, the English did not have that option available to them. Native population densities were much lower in coastal North America than in the Caribbean, the central valley of Mexico, or the Andes (Hatfield 2004: 15–18). Similarly, although the English clearly hoped to get a hold of as many enslaved Africans as they could, that goal was impossible to facilitate as a result of the distance of North America from standard slave trading routes and the absence of a regular supply. Only in Barbados were English planters able to acquire significant numbers of enslaved Africans during this early period and even there it was not until the 1640s (when perhaps 25,000 Africans disembarked on the island) that measurable numbers of slaves began arriving (Coombs 2011; Newman 2013: 189–215).

Because there were few alternatives, the English typically chose (where labor and colonists were most desperately needed) to exploit white indentured servants as their primary way of peopling the colonies and providing adequate labor throughout the first half of the seventeenth century. Indentured servitude was theoretically a mutually advantageous exchange between a servant who was willing to barter his or her labor for a period of four to seven years in exchange for the cost of passage to one of England's American colonies. Servants hoped merely to endure the demands placed on them by their masters and held out for the promise of perhaps owning their own plot of land and even becoming a master themselves when their time expired. Masters, however, recognized in the system the chance to acquire a labor force over which they exercised extraordinary control. As a result of the assumptions of the two groups, the population/employment crisis in England, and the need for labor in the colonies, the servant trade was robust during the early and middle decades of the seventeenth century. Servants were the single most important migrant group in English America. This was particularly true in the Chesapeake, where approximately eighty percent of migrants before 1650 (roughly 16,700 out of 21,200) came in bondage. Barbados was equally disproportionately populated by bound servants. Thus, although there were about 8,000 planters on the island in the mid-1640s, there were an additional 20,000 white servants even though the island had not yet fully converted to sugar monoculture (Morgan 2001: 8–25; Tomlins 2010: 35–42, 78–82; Beckles 1989: 18).

The main problem with indentured servitude was that it represented an innovation in the labor relationship that seemed, to servants in particular, potentially threatening to the rights and privileges that governed their lives as English men and women. For example, the line between indentured servitude and slavery was perilously thin and it did not take long for servants to complain that they were being used, and being bought and sold as, slaves. One colonial promoter, writing in 1649, attempted to discourage such a view when he observed that "servants serve no longer than the time they themselves agreed for in England." In making this argument, William Bullock advanced the argument that servitude in the colonies was grounded in traditional English labor relationships, such as the use of annual, mutually-agreed-upon labor contracts. But the reality of the American colonies was quite different from life in England. Indeed, a widespread culture of bound service distinguished the American colonies from England from the outset.

Servitude in the English colonies represented a creative and innovative effort on the part of would-be masters to achieve maximum control over the servile population. Thus, although indentured servitude was not slavery, scholars routinely assert that indentured servitude was an institution that was notable for the liberty it offered masters to treat their servants both harshly and as disposable property. In this way, it has been argued, they prepared the ground for the eventual transition to racial slavery (Newman 2013: 77; Swingen 2015: 11–31; Handler and Reilly 2017; Donoghue 2013). The reverse of that formulation, however, may be closer to the mark. While it may have been structurally rooted in English forms, indentured servitude seems to have been conceptually crafted to replicate the realities of an Atlantic world in which the most desirable laborers were slaves (Guasco 2014: 164).

Certainly, law and custom allowed that laborers occupied the lowest rung on the English hierarchical ladder and it was a common view that laborers existed to satisfy the larger needs of the community. Whether or not they were property, however, was the source of ongoing disputes. In the colonies, servants expressed the view that they could not, or should not, be bought and sold. As early as

1618, John Rolfe commented on the large number of complaints against colonial leaders for "buying and selling men and bois." Rolfe never doubted that servitude was useful and necessary, but he sympathized with the view expressed by John Smith a few years later when he lambasted "the old Planters" for selling men, women, and children for whoever "will give the most." Few doubted the injustice of working servants hard, but that they might be sold in order to turn a profit turned the stomachs of critics who perceived some rather un-English innovations in the disposition of English labor (Guasco 2014: 166–7).

There were those, however, who did comment on just how bad the day-to-day life of a servant could be in the colonies. Richard Ligon, who arrived in Barbados in 1647 just as it was rapidly transitioning into a full-scale sugar plantation colony, claimed that English servants lived worse lives than African slaves because "they are put to very hard labour, ill lodging, and their dyet [is] very sleight" (Ligon 1673: 43–5; Wareing 2017). Barbados, perhaps more than any other place in the English Atlantic, desperately needed laborers, who were worked hard and often died quickly as a result of the work itself and the adverse climate. During the 1640s, more than 2,000 new servants reached the island every year, and not all of them completely voluntarily. In order to satisfy the demands of labor-starved planters, unscrupulous servant traders began figuring out that there was money to be made by rounding up the homeless, the desperate, vagrants, and prisoners and disposing of them across the ocean. It was hardly surprising, then, that planters felt little compunction about treating people they considered to be the dregs of English society with callous disregard. Unlike servants in England that might plausibly be imagined as part of their employers extended family, indentured servants in England were a sometimes criminalized and wholly commodified work force that was worked to the point of death (Newman 2013: 71–88).

Indentured servitude was a remarkably English phenomenon driven by the confluence of domestic problems rooted in an excess population and a singular commitment to settler colonialism. Still, there were some other examples of European nations employing temporary white bondage in order to get work done in the colonies. Many male emigrants to France's overseas colonies, for example, were servants known as *engages* who typically served three-year terms. These men went to France's Caribbean colonies, including Guadeloupe and Martinique (1630s), while a few others ended up in New France (Canada). Those who ended up in the islands invariably worked hard. Early reports from the French islands echoed those of English observers in Barbados: French servants were "worse treated than the slaves—they have to be forced to work, since they are so miserable and hungry" (Blackburn 1997: 286). Their lives were arguably slightly better in New France, where the climate was less than ideal but the work certainly less onerous. Still, the impression is hard to escape that white servants in the early French Caribbean and even New France chafed at the unexpected difficulties that faced them in their new surroundings (Boucher 2007: 304–5).

Ultimately, the difference between the expectations of European migrants—most of whom seem to have been contractually bound in the northern European colonies—and the realities of the worlds they came to inhabit created a great deal of tension, especially in the plantation colonies. A widespread culture of white servitude, including the emergence of a new class of local elites whose mastery was premised on the control of scarce labor resources, laid the groundwork for the eventual transition to racial plantation slavery in a number of colonies. Colonial promoters and unscrupulous merchants intent on rounding up colonists consistently emphasized that a life in temporary servitude in the Americas was little different from what people had known in Europe, except with the promise of great rewards after just a few short years. What indentured servants found, however, was that servitude meant something entirely new in a world where labor was being redefined by the indiscriminate exploitation of the indigenous inhabitants of the Americas and enslaved Africans. Indentured servitude was shaped as much by New World systems of forced labor, for labor's sake alone, as it was by old European notions of the way that labor helped organize an organic society. Indentured servitude was marvelously successful at helping the English establish territorial control of large swaths of North America and in parts of the Caribbean, but it was not without its costs.

CONCLUSION

The new world in which labor was exploited to serve the needs of would-be power brokers had important consequences in a number of related arenas. The idea of the nation gained traction as different European powers engaged in a contest not just for new lands, but also for control over scarce resources—not least labor. Gender was made meaningful in new ways in the context of the revolutionary transformations in labor, just as ideas about who could be compelled to work and what work they should perform changed the way Europeans thought about women, gender, and sexuality (see also Traub's chapter on Sexuality, this volume). Ideas of race, which had previously circulated in a somewhat inchoate fashion, became much more meaningfully connected to the imperial order as the Spanish, Portuguese, English, French, and Dutch tried to make sense of Indians and Africans as potential members of colonial societies, merchantable commodities, and exploitable laborers. Racial discourse provided a way of justifying measures that would not bear close scrutiny if enacted on other Europeans, just as slavery reinforced emerging notions of difference that increasingly advanced the argument that non-European peoples were bestial, subhuman, cursed, or otherwise deserving of their fate.

As the meaning and practice of labor changed during the early modern period, so too did the culture of labor. Notions of who should work, the nature of the relationship between masters/employers and laborers, how that work should be governed, and the meaning of labor in different societies were all largely reimagined and implemented in the context of colonialism. Even at the end of his life, Christopher Columbus could never have imagined how the Atlantic world would look by the middle of the seventeenth century. His "discovery," however, set in motion a series of transformations in labor that shaped the emerging culture of the broader Atlantic world. What happened with native peoples, enslaved Africans, and indentured servants represent remarkable cases of European innovation and adaptation to unforeseen and largely unimagined economic circumstances. The revolutionary transformations in labor that occurred throughout the Atlantic world forever changed how work and workers would be rationalized, routinized, and commodified to serve imperial power.

CHAPTER FIVE

Mobility

JONATHAN GIL HARRIS

In our day and age of get-rich-quick schemes, "mobility" is a term we might associate primarily with *upward* mobility, with the aspirational movement of the poorer sort into the moneyed classes. This kind of mobility was a much rarer phenomenon in the early centuries of the Western empires. That doesn't mean upward social mobility was absent from them: indeed, it was a persistent fantasy. Just think of Simon Eyre, the humble London shoemaker in Thomas Dekker's play *The Shoemaker's Holiday* (1599). Thanks to a fortuitous, shrewd investment in a shipload of foreign commodities that he resells at a considerable mark-up, Eyre acquires great wealth and eventually becomes mayor of London. Profit from the global mobility of goods, services, and capital, in Eyre's case, drives the local mobility of the entrepreneur-citizen. Expectations of profit similarly drove many of the architects of Western empire—joint-stock company investors, colonial settlers, pirates.

But the mobility with which this chapter is concerned is a world away from that of Dekker's venturing rags-to-riches shoemaker. It is of a different order, in the twin sense of being of a different type and emerging from different material foundations. Even though upward mobility may be one of its consequences, the mobility I examine here is what we might call a *fugitive* mobility. This mobility is the province of refugees who, through choice or circumstance, have fled their homes in other parts of the world. Though the instances I examine here belong to an age long past, fugitive mobility provides an uncanny mirror image of the refugee crisis of the current age, with the geographical direction of movement between Europe and Asia sometimes reversed.

We don't think of the early modern period as a time of refugees. This is largely for two reasons. First, the discourse of the refugee presumes national borders, immigration authorities, and the principle of asylum, phenomena that did not exist in the early modern world. But that doesn't mean that early modern people weren't uprooted from their homes or forced to relocate to new lands. England, for instance, was flooded with Protestant religious refugees from the Low Countries—among them, quite possibly, Thomas Dekker's family—due to the sectarian and economic tensions of late sixteenth-century Europe. Second, we tend to think that global mobility in this period was exemplified by the agents of Western empire: trading company representatives, ambassadors, conquistadors, evangelists. No matter whether we view their mobility as heroic or oppressive, we presume that the story of Western empire largely involves powerful Europeans acting upon subaltern natives. In the process, we forget that there were refugees who moved in the shadow of European imperialism, and whose lives traced forms of mobility that help us complicate as well as clarify aspects of early modern Western empire and its cultural histories.

Fugitive mobility therefore entails what may seem several paradoxes of agency. First, even as the conceptual syntax of Western empire denies agency to subalterns, fugitive mobility presumes subaltern agency in refugees' cross-border migration. Second, even as the logic of post-Enlightenment liberalism sees agency as voluntaristic rather than compelled, fugitive mobility presumes that agency can often be forced. And third, even as postcolonial studies makes of the subaltern a synonym for the disempowered yet agential non-European subject, fugitive mobility can equally be the province of the disempowered yet agential European. All these paradoxes, I will argue, help us better understand the cultural histories of the age of Western empire.

This chapter tells three stories of fugitive mobility. One is about a subaltern non-European—a woman of Armenian descent from Mughal India who accompanied her new English husband back to London. Another is about what we might call a subaltern European—a religious refugee to Portuguese and then Bahmani India from the Iberian Peninsula. But the story with which I begin this chapter is about a subaltern Moorish migrant who blurs the boundaries between European and non-European, and in ways that tell us something about the historical blind spots informing powerful distinctions of geography and religion that we take for granted in the present.

All three migrants, for very different reasons, were forced to leave their places of birth and pursue new lives in different locations. And all did very well for themselves, enjoying as the fruit of their geographical mobility a social mobility that placed them in proximity to local power—although in rather different ways from the upwardly mobile heroes of early modern capitalism such as Dekker's Simon Eyre. Yet the fugitive mobility we will see here is not confined to geographic and social mobility. It is, primarily, testimony to forms of *transculturalism*: which is to say, global networks of knowledge and practice that

1. extend across what we now tend to think of as insurmountable borders of geography and/or religion;
2. depend on cities with multilingual citizens engaged locally and globally in various forms of cultural exchange; and
3. allow certain migrants to move into, and operate advantageously within, the seemingly alien terrain of a new culture.

Transculturalism can operate in tandem with, and even buttress the interests of, imperial institutions. But it can also exist outside these, within other global networks.

Likewise, the three lives I examine here intersect with but also escape the orbit of Western empire. Carved out of the raw materials of global Islamic and Jewish cultural networks, the Spanish *Reconquista*, Mediterranean piracy, Central Asian trading routes, and diverse traditions of Christian and Muslim patronage, the three transcultural biographies illuminate the connected histories—to use Sanjay Subrahmanyam's term—that linked Europe, Africa, and Asia long before as well as during the age of Western empire (Subrahmanyam 1998, 2005a, 2005b, 2007). In the process, we can glimpse ways in which Venetian, Portuguese, and English imperial projects were uneasily superimposed over other, earlier forms of transculturalism. My objective in telling these three stories, following Dipesh Chakrabarty (Chakrabarty 2000), is to provincialize Europe in the age of empire—that is, to decentre it by relocating it within more capacious networks of early modern global cultural mobility, within which Western venturing was by no means the dominant practice.

THE TRANSCULTURALISM OF THE EXPELLED ANDALUSIAN

Shakespeare's play *Othello* tells the story of a Moor who, freed from slavery, becomes a Christian and rises to a position of prominence in Venice prior to his tragic fall, engineered by someone who resents the success of a foreigner. It has long been noted that *Othello* uncannily replays, and possibly draws on, the story of a sixteenth-century Muslim refugee to Europe who converted to Christianity. That man is known to us now as Leo Africanus; but he was born as al-Hasan ibn Muhammad al-Wazzan. Leo Africanus's story is well known to students of *Othello*. By contrast, the story of al-Hasan involves geopolitical complexities that unsettle the narrative of east to west migration at the core of Shakespeare's play.

On the surface, Leo Africanus's biography is an early sixteenth-century version of Othello's: an African childhood involving travel, redemption from slavery, and preferment by powerful Italian figures, but also xenophobic harangues by European enemies. A Berber Moor from Fez, al-Hasan ibn

Muhammad al-Wazzan journeyed extensively through northern and western Africa in his youth and early adulthood before his migration to Europe. These travels are partly documented in his well-known treatise, the *Description of Africa* (originally dictated in Arabic in 1526, subsequently translated and published in Italian by Giovanni Battista Ramunio in 1550 (Figure 5.1), and later translated into English by John Pory in 1600). In it he provides descriptions of the Berber and Arab parts of northern Africa and the sub-Saharan gold-trading kingdoms of western and central Africa. Shakespeare most likely read Pory's English translation of the *Description* and had it in the back of his mind as he wrote Othello's famous speech about his African travails (Shakespeare 2006: 1.3.128–70); Shakespeare also may have been influenced in his characterization of Othello by the *Description*'s assertion, with regard to Berber Moors, that "No nation in the world is so subject unto jealousy; for they will rather lose their lives, then put up any disgrace in the behalf of their women" (Africanus 1896: I.183).

Most readers who encounter Leo Africanus through Shakespeare know too that he was taken prisoner by pirates—Spanish corsairs—in the Mediterranean in 1518. European piracy, despite its illegality, was a significant aid to early modern imperialism: Sir Francis Drake may have been lionized as an English hero, but his good deeds for the state consisted of acts of piracy that allowed him to capture shiploads of Spanish gold, a significant source of bullion for English coffers in an emerging mercantile economy that increasingly understood wealth as treasure rather than land. But Mediterranean and Atlantic pirate crews devoted to the plunder of African shores sought out capital in the form not just of bullion but also of human labor: that is, Muslim slaves, and of a rather different kind from those who populated the mamluk economies of Islamic sultanates in Central Asia and India.

Like many Muslims captured by pirates at this time, al-Hasan (as he was still called) was in all likelihood initially destined for sale in the slave markets of Europe. But he somehow managed to win the favor of his captors, and was eventually presented to Pope Leo X. Two years later, in 1520, al-Hasan had converted to Christianity, assuming the Latin name of Johannes Leo de Medici—the last being the family name of the Pope. Although the reasons for al-Hasan's preferment are unclear, it is quite likely that Leo X was interested in cultivating him as a native Muslim informant to help combat the expected invasion of Sicily and South Italy by the Ottoman empire, increasingly the major power in the Mediterranean. The Ottoman empire's chief European adversary was Venice; although a republic rather than an empire in the literal sense, the Italian city represented one of the bulwarks of European imperialist ambition, with maritime colonies in the Adriatic Dalmatian coast, Greece, Crete, and Cyprus. It is no surprise that Leo Africanus's *Description of Africa* was first published in Venice. His treatise became in this context less an anthropological description

FIGURE 5.1: Title page of the second Italian edition, translated by Giovanni Battista Ramuno, of Leo Africanus, *La Descrittione dell'Africa* (Venice, 1554). Credit: Universitätsbibliothek Heidelberg.

and more a repository of useful travel knowledge for a would-be expansionist power embroiled in conflict with the Ottomans, whose territories now extended over much of northern Africa.

The newly baptized Leo Africanus was to suffer a significant setback in 1521 upon the death of Leo XI and the appointment of his successor, Adrian VI, who was opposed to an African enjoying such a prominent position in the Papal court. In the face of Adrian's overt hostility, Leo Africanus moved from Rome to Bologna; but after dictating his treatise there in 1526, he faded more or less completely from the historical record. We do not know exactly when he died, or where.

Reading Leo Africanus's story as a real-life counterpart to that of Shakespeare's Moor might help us illuminate aspects of *Othello*. But it also commits a certain amount of violence against the complexities of al-Hasan's pre-conversion biography and, indeed, against the larger historical formations through which he moved. If we see his mobility through the lens of *Othello*, it is easy to regard Leo Africanus simply as an African tennis ball, swatted around by various European imperial agents—Spanish corsairs, Roman popes, Venetian publishers. This ignores the other global, non-imperial networks that helped form al-Hasan, and that provided him with invaluable skills for negotiating the vicissitudes of his new European home as much as Africa. His *Description* may provide us with a proleptic glimpse of imperialist European travel knowledge. But his treatise is the product of other political economies and networks of cosmopolitan exchange that long predate Western empire.

What is most forgotten in Leo Africanus's story is al-Hasan's story (Davis 2007; Masonen 2001; Loomba and Burton 2007: 153–7). Leo Africanus's kinship with Othello as much as his second name might serve to univocally Africanize him. Indeed, al-Hasan's Arab name is in at least one document supplemented by the title al-Fasi, meaning "of Fez." Yet, though ethnically a Berber, al-Hasan was not a native of the Maghreb region of north-western Africa. Instead he was European by birth, born in Granada in 1494. Granada was, of course, the last Moorish emirate in the Muslim-ruled Spanish territory of Al-Andalus, reconquered by the Christian armies of Ferdinand and Isabella of Castile in 1492. But to call pre-*Reconquista* Granada a Moorish city is to erase its extraordinary ethnic and cultural diversity (Nash 2005). The Umayyad conquest of the eighth century had brought Islam to the Iberian Peninsula; Granada was set up as an independent kingdom by the Berber Zawa Ben Ziri in the eleventh century. Yet the city from the outset was highly plural. It had a large Jewish community: Granada's hill location, on top of which stands the stunning Moorish fort complex of the Alhambra, began as a Jewish colony called Gharnata, meaning "hill of strangers." The city also boasted Berber, Arab, and Christian quarters. Many languages were heard on its streets. Andalusi and Maghrebi Arabic, Castilian and Mozarabic Spanish, Latin, Ladino, and Hebrew were spoken by Granada's native inhabitants, and the tongues of many foreign visitors added to its linguistic soundscape. The Moroccan traveler Ibn Battuta visited Granada in the 1350s; it was here that his travel stories were first committed to pen and paper by the local jurist Ibn Juzayy. And these stories speak of an extraordinary web of multicultural connections that linked Granada diversely to Europe, Africa, the Middle East, India, and even China.

If al-Hasan had been born even twenty years earlier, he may have been remembered as an Andalusian Spaniard. But he was born just two years after Boabdil, the last Emir of Granada, was defeated by Ferdinand and Isabella. In the years immediately following the fall of Moorish Spain, hundreds of thousands of non-Christian residents were forced to migrate. Many Muslim and Jewish refugees from the Iberian Peninsula relocated to North Africa. Fez, a Moroccan city that already had something of the cosmopolitan character of its Andalusian cousins, received a large number of the refugees; to this day, the city is thought of as the custodian of Golden Age Andalusian culture. Among the migrants were al-Hasan and his family. He may have been only an infant at the time, but the new city to which he and his family had shifted—bursting with refugees from Spain—would have had something of the character of Granada, both culturally and linguistically.

Fez's multicultural, multilinguistic landscape represented everything that the emergent Christian Spanish empire sought to erase physically and intellectually at home. And the success of that erasure can be seen partly in the still-dominant narrative of the European Renaissance, which presents the latter largely in terms of an Italo-centric Christianity that, with the help of learning and imaginative liberation, rediscovered a lost pagan Latin and Greek past. Written out of this Renaissance narrative is the role played by Golden Age Spain, particularly Andalusia, and the generative power of startling cultural proximities that we have been trained to see as temporally and spatially remote—Latin, Arabic, and Hebrew. The transcultural conversations Andalusia witnessed were crucial to the European Renaissance. They helped create the extraordinarily syncretic systems of mathematical and medical knowledge that characterize early modern European thought, which drew as much on Arabic Avicenna and algebra as it did on Greek Galen and geometry. It also arguably engendered the powerful tradition of courtly love poetry, which can be traced back to Andalusian Sufi poets whose expressions of ecstatic longing for a distant beloved were communicated through trade routes to the troubadours of Provence and, under their influence, became a stock in trade of European literature from Petrarch to Shakespeare (al-Dabagh 2010: 49–68). This syncretism, almost completely banished from Spain, survived in locations like Fez's al-Qarawiyyin University, the madrasa where al-Hasan studied; its curriculum included not only religious texts but also legal treatises from a variety of cultural and linguistic traditions. And it provided al-Hasan with the tools he needed to negotiate a lifetime of crossing cultural and linguistic borders.

At an early age, al-Hasan seems to have accompanied his uncle on a diplomatic mission to Timbuktu in West Africa. In 1517, when still in his early twenties, he was part of another mission to Constantinople; his route back to Fez took him through Cairo, at the turbulent time of its invasion by the Ottomans, and then via the Mediterranean to Tunis, where he was captured by the Spanish corsairs. His travels to Cairo and its environs provide the basis of some of his anthropological descriptions of Africa; these accounts, remarkable for their understanding and sensitivity to multiple cultural forms, demand to be seen less as stories told by an Othello-like migrant from the Muslim to the Christian worlds than as expressions of a transcultural mobility constitutive of Granada's distinctive syncretism.

But the most enduring legacy of al-Hasan's Granada-influenced upbringing is to be seen in another piece of his writing. It is less famous, partly because it hasn't survived in its entirety, but also because it doesn't quite fit the *Othello* narrative of east-west migration and redemption. I am referring here to a remarkable document that he prepared in the 1520s for the Jewish Paduan physician Dr. Jacob Mantino.[1] It is a glossary of medical terms, written in three languages: Arabic, Latin, and Hebrew—the languages of Granada. Something of this multilingualism survives also in the signature that he left on the one surviving fragment of the text. There he signed his name, not as the Latinate Leo Africanus—the African Lion—but, rather, as Yuhanna al-Asad al-Gharnati. Yuhanna is the Arabic rendering of the Latin Johannes, his Christian baptismal name; al-Asad is Arabic for Lion ("Leo" in Latin); al-Gharnati is not just the Arabic name for Granada, but also for the Jewish colony that had been on its hills. This name condenses all the cultures that conspired to shape "Leo Africanus," before as much as after his migration to Europe.

The multilingual name may have also been a playful joke for the benefit of his intellectual partner, Dr. Jacob Mantino. The doctor had been trained in Padua. But he was not Italian; like al-Hasan, he was a refugee from the violence of the *Reconquista*—a Spanish Jew who had escaped in 1492. Their bond suggests a mutual Andalusian camaraderie and, perhaps, a shared homesickness. Perhaps it was something like homesickness that made Leo Africanus disappear from the record. There are hints that he went back to Africa and reconverted; it is tempting to think that, although Leo Africanus—a short-lived figment of the Christian imperialist imagination—may have died, the altogether more transcultural Andalusian Yuhanna al-Asad al-Gharnati survived and was resurrected in Fez. That transculturalism had previously allowed al-Hasan the mobility to migrate to Europe and become Leo Africanus. But it also gave him potential escape routes into other non-European networks. In other words, the multicultural legacy of Granada both facilitated and resisted forms of Western empire.

Other refugees from pre-*Reconquista* Spain—the kin of Dr. Jacob Mantino ben Samuel as much as of al-Hasan ibn Muhammad al-Wazzan—similarly deployed their transcultural skills to trace paths of fugitive mobility through various parts of the world, weaving their way between Western empire and non-European locations outside its orbit. Let us turn, now, to India, to follow one such path.

THE TRANSCULTURALISM OF THE ARABOPHONE RELIGIOUS REFUGEE

It is easy to think of sixteenth-century Goa, the Estado da Índia's capital, simply as a Portuguese colonial city. A quick tour of Old Goa reveals a cityscape seemingly in thrall to Lisbon and Rome, dominated by the Basilica of Bom Jesus and the Se Cathedral of Saint Catherine as well as the Church of San Caetano and the ruins of the Saint Augustine Church Tower. Yet these remains tell only a selective story. The Goa that emerged in the wake of Afonso de Albuquerque's conquest of the city in 1510 may have been a possession of Portugal. But the sixteenth-century city was a transcultural palimpsest: its many layers included not just old Bahmani physical structures but also certain modes of transnational kinship and intimacy that predated the Portuguese conquest but also continued after it, if only in underground form (Desouza 1989; Lach and Van Kley 1998: 833–70).

In the fifteenth century, when it was still part of the Bijapur sultanate, Goa was a port of call within the mostly Arabic-speaking trading web that extended from Al-Andalus in Spain, via North Africa and Aden, to Ahmadnagar in India, where Arabic was one of the tongues of the sultan's court. Many of the people who plied the highways and seaways of this network were Andalusian and northern African Muslims. Others were Sephardic Jews from the Iberian Peninsula who had a strong affinity with Andalusian Muslims such as Leo Africanus. They spoke, wrote, and dreamed in Arabic; their cultural reference points were Arabic; and their gastronomic preferences were also profoundly influenced by their Moorish neighbors. Even in Christian-ruled areas such as Castile and Portugal, Sephardic Jews were speakers of Ladino—a vernacular mixture of Spanish, Hebrew, Aramaic, and Arabic. In Ladino, for instance, Sunday is not "domingo" (as it is in both Spanish and Portuguese) but "alhad," derived from the Arabic "alhat." And the Ladino word for freedom is not the Spanish "liberdad," but "alforria"—derived from the Arabic "hurriya." Make what you will of that, but clearly Sephardic Jews did not associate the idea of liberty with Christian rule.

Despite the final *reconquista* of 1492 which drove Jews and Muslims out of Spain and Portugal, and the Portuguese conquest of Goa in 1510 which created a European Christian bulwark in India, the Judeo-Muslim network linking the Iberian Peninsula to India did not disappear. Portugal, like Spain, may have expelled or forcibly converted its Jews. But King Manuel of Portugal practiced an early version of the policy of "don't ask, don't tell": in 1504, he promised the country's New Christians—Jews who had supposedly converted to Christianity—that he would not inquire into their private religious observances for a grace period of thirty years. This was less because of any profound religious tolerance on his part than because the Portuguese interest in India depended in no small way on the Andalusian Judeo-Muslim network of trading and political connections as well as the local knowledges these had engendered. After all, Portugal's growing maritime power was dependent not just on skilled Jewish labor—Vasco da Gama's navigator-astronomer Abraão Zacuto, for example, was a Jew—but also on wealthy New Christian merchant families with international connections. These connections were often Judeo-Muslim, tracing the trajectory of old affiliations from the dispersed culture of Al-Andalus, extending through North Africa and the Ottoman empire to the Arabian Peninsula and the Indian Ocean (Harris 2015).

If anything, the transnational Judeo-Muslim network was revitalized by the Portuguese imposition in 1534 of the Inquisition, when King Manuel's grace period lapsed. As a result, a number of Iberian "New Christians" of Sephardic origin, many of them still covertly practicing Judaism, relocated to Goa to flee the reach of the Inquisition. There they often passed as true Christians. For those New Christians who still secretly professed Judaism, Goa had much to recommend it. The city already had a Jewish population prior to its conquest by Albuquerque in 1510. Some of the Bijapuri Jews appear to have been Spanish speakers and therefore part of the larger transnational Judeo-Muslim networks that connected the Iberian Peninsula and North Africa to South Asia via the Ottoman empire and the Arabian Peninsula. There is no reason to believe that these original Jews left after the Portuguese conquest: Albuquerque gained the support of local Hindus and some Muslims by granting them their religious freedom, and it is likely that the Bijapuri Jews would have been given a similar promise. Indeed, their polyglot skills would have made them useful to the fledgling Portuguese Indian state as go-betweens with local Konkani, Marathi, and Arabic-speaking rulers. In the years after 1534, Goa remained a multicultural city where people of many ethnicities, tongues, and faiths mingled. For the New Christians of the Iberian Peninsula, it may even have seemed a little like the pre-expulsion multicultural communities of Andalusia.

Because 1534 was the year the Inquisition was instituted in Portugal, it was in some ways a more decisive year for its Jewish population than 1492. 1534 also happens to be the year in which a man known as Garcia da Orta migrated to Goa (Boxer 1963; Carvalho 1934). Orta is now celebrated as a Portuguese hero and patriot, largely because he wrote what is commonly regarded as the first treatise on tropical medicine, *Colloquies on the Simples and Drugs of India*, published in Goa in 1561 (Figure 5.2). His image appeared on the Portuguese 200-escudo coin in the 1990s; many municipal sites in Portugal—hospitals and

FIGURE 5.2: Title page of Garcia da Orta, *Colóquio dos Simples* (Lisbon, 1578). Public domain. Accessed via Wikimedia Commons: https://upload.wikimedia.org/wikipedia/commons/5/5d/Garcia_de_Orta_book_cover.jpg

parks—are named for him; even a garden in modern-day Panaji, the capital of Goa, bears his name. Orta had relinquished a prestigious chair of medicine at the University of Lisbon to accompany the newly appointed viceroy, Martim Afonso da Sousa, to Goa as his personal physician. Orta's decision to give up the post has often been narrated by the Portuguese as an exemplary act of patriotism; the epic poet Luis Vaz de Camoes, who stayed with Orta briefly in Goa, praised him as such (Orta 1913: x). But when Orta's master da Sousa's term as viceroy expired in 1538, the doctor did not return to Lisbon. And that was because he had a secret: he was an undercover Jew and had almost certainly come to Goa in 1534 to flee the specter of the Inquisition, wagering that it wouldn't chase him to India. He was joined there by his mother Lenore and sister Catarina, and he married a New Christian cousin of his, Briana de Solis, whose family too had also migrated to Goa.

The Inquisition was finally set up in Goa in the 1550s, partly at the urging of the future St. Francis Xavier. Around this time, Orta mysteriously relocated to the Ahmadnagar sultanate. And here Orta joined the medical retinue of the Nizam as a *hakeem* or traditional Arabic doctor. The retinue was very much in thrall to the medical theories of the Uzbeki-Persian writer, Avicenna, known in Arabic as Ibn Sina, and Orta too became an acolyte (Goodman 2005). Orta had a distinct advantage in Ahmadnagar inasmuch as he was conversant in Arabic, the lingua franca of the Nizam's court. During his period of service in Ahmadnagar, Orta dispensed a prescription in Arabic for the Sultan of Bidar's brother, Hamjam. Here we can witness the extraordinary multiculturalism of the Arabic-speaking Indian world. Hamjam was descended from a Turkish slave in Christian Georgia; yet in Muslim Bidar, he could converse in Arabic with a Sephardic Jew from Portugal.

Orta returned to Goa and published his *Colloquies*, which won him fame and perhaps some respite from the Inquisition. How much, if at all, can we read Orta's Jewishness back into the *Colloquies*? Like the eponymous letter in Edgar Allan Poe's *The Purloined Letter*, Orta's Jewishness is an open secret throughout the *Colloquies*: not immediately visible to us precisely because it is there in front of us, the last place we would look for it. Yet once we become aware of it, it's hard not to see it everywhere.

On the one hand, Orta goes through the motions of sounding like a dutiful, if not particularly religious, Roman Catholic. He refers to a Dominican friar as a member of "our faith," welcomes the mass conversions of Tamil pearl fishermen undertaken by Miguel Vaz and Francis Xavier in south India, and refers critically to Lutheran Protestantism (Orta 1913: 406, 297). On the other hand, Jews from all over the world make repeated cameo appearances in Orta's narrative as reliable first-hand sources of medical knowledge. His colloquy about the aloe is partly influenced by a conversation with some Jews from Jerusalem, his understanding of cardamom's etymological link to the Arabic hamama is derived from a Spanish-speaking Jewish apothecary, and his knowledge of other medical materials is indebted to a Jewish trader from Turkey (Orta 1913: 107). These divergent tendencies in the *Colloquies* suggest three things: Orta, like his fellow New Christians in Portugal, felt compelled to pass as a Catholic; despite the pressure to pass, there were many travelers and migrants in India at this time who self-identified as Jewish; and whatever pressure to hide their identities these Jews may or may not have felt in other Portuguese company, they didn't feel any such pressure when talking with Orta.

The *Colloquies* also hints at Orta's deep cultural affinity with Andalusian Muslim culture. Near the beginning of the treatise, Orta notes the recent degeneration of medical education in Spain, lamenting that "now you have neither masters nor preceptors in Salamanca or Alcalá, for all are either dead or banished" (Orta 1913: 4). Orta's reference to the "banished" masters implicitly acknowledges how, in the wake of the 1492 expulsion, Spain had lost a rich Judeo-Muslim corpus of medical knowledge with deep roots in Andalusian Arabic culture. This corpus derived not only from Averroës, author of the influential medical treatise *Kitab al-Kulliyat fi al-Tibb* (Book of Generalities), but also from Arab-speaking Jewish physicians such as Hasdai ibn Shaprut of Córdoba, Abraham ben David of Catalonia, and Joshua ben Joseph of Lorca (Lowney 2005; Anidjar 2002; Alfonso 2008). Rather than performing a radical break with Iberian medical tradition, then, Orta's embrace of Avicenna in Ahmadnagar in fact marked a conscious return to it, at least in its Judeo-Muslim form. Indeed, like his Sephardic medical forbears, Orta wrote with an Arabic-language edition of Avicenna on his desk in his Goan study.

In other words, Orta could operate successfully within a variety of cultural locations. As a New Christian who had diligently leveraged the support of his Portuguese political patrons, he was awarded the quit-rent of Bombay, then a new Portuguese possession. But as a Sephardic physician deeply immersed in Judeo-Muslim cultural networks that extended from the Iberian Peninsula to India, he also found it easy to enter the Indo-Islamic world of the Ahmadnagar court as an Arabic-speaking colleague of Muslim physicians. The turnstile between his Portuguese and Indian worlds swung both ways, and in a fashion that perhaps typifies the experiences of actors within stateless transnational networks of the kind I have outlined here.

Orta died a Portuguese celebrity of sorts, and was buried in a principal Goan cathedral—quite possibly the first version of the Se Cathedral. But the Inquisition was to catch up with him. A year after Orta's death in 1568, his sister Catarina was burned at the stake in Goa as "an impenitent Jewess" (Carvalho 1934: 65).[2] And Orta's remains were dug up, incinerated, and flung into the Mandovi River. This shows how the cityscape of Old Goa that we now see conceals violently suppressed non-Christian histories. It shows too, more specifically, how Garcia da Orta and other crypto-Jewish refugees to Goa shouldn't be thought of simply as sometime residents of a Christian colonial city. Hounded and dispossessed by the Portuguese state (Priolkar 1961) and seeking new lives in the Bahmani sultanates, these Goan men—like their ancestors—were more at home in Judeo-Muslim than Judeo-Christian worlds.

THE TRANSCULTURALISM OF THE MUGHAL HAREM LADY

The two biographies I have sketched so far might create the impression that only early modern men typify the kind of fugitive mobility I have been examining in this chapter. We do glimpse women in the story of Garcia da Orta's migration to the subcontinent—his mother, his sister, and his wife—like him, New Christian refugees attempting to escape the horrors of the Inquisition. But despite the da Orta women's migration from Portugal, it is notable that they experienced considerably less opportunity for mobility than Garcia did. No escape for them into the Bahmani heartland; they remained in the colonial European space of Goa, confined to conventional patriarchal roles.

Women who migrated to India in the early years of Western empire did not end up only in colonial locations, however. The Mughal court was an unusually multicultural place, comprised of lords from many locations across the subcontinent, Persia, Central Asia, and even Europe. If the court was multicultural, the royal Mughal harem—never quite the sexual wonderland of the western imagination but, rather, a large multi-generational women's quarters—was even more so (Lal 2005; Anjum 2011; Mukherjee 2001). In addition to its Mongolian, Uzbek, Rumi Turk, Persian, and Rajput royal wives and family members, the harem also included the wives of foreign men retained in the court. Humayun's harem, for example, briefly housed the wife and children of a visitor from Poland. Later harems featured female Ethiopian, Russian, and Circassian slave-guards. Also living in the royal harems of Akbar and Jahangir, in the late sixteenth and early seventeenth centuries, were several high-ranking Armenian Christian women. One of them was named Mariam Khan. The daughter of a migrant who served in Akbar's and Jahangir's courts, Mariam herself became the first Indian-born woman to migrate, in 1614, to England.

Mariam Khan's story unfolds in exactly the same decade as that of a more famous non-European woman migrant to England, the Native American "princess," Pocahontas. Despite the saccharine-sweet modern Disney treatment of her, Pocahontas's experience of migration was a grim one (Fuller 1995: 120–2; Hulme 1986, 143–7; Linton 2006). After being taken captive during hostilities in 1614 between English settlers in the Virginia colony of Jamestown and local tribes loyal to her father, the Algonquin chief Powhatan, she was married to the English tobacco planter, John Rolfe. She was also made to convert to Christianity. In 1616, Pocahontas and her husband sailed to England. Her brief time there saw her become an actor in a drama that she hadn't scripted. Displayed in London as a civilized savage, an advertisement for the good effects of the English colony in Jamestown, she was given a new name and identity—Rebecca Rolfe—which underlined how much she was the property of her European masters: not just her husband but also the Virginia Company, the joint-stock company that bankrolled the first sustained English experiment in

FIGURE 5.3: Copper engraving of Pocahontas wearing a tall hat. Engraving by Simon van de Passe, 1616. Credit: National Portrait Gallery.

New World colonization (Figure 5.3). Pocahontas died, in the suitably named Gravesend, as she was about to sail back home in December, 1617. Enforced migration in the service of Empire could be a deadly business for a woman.

On paper, Mariam Khan's story is similar to Pocahontas's: a trophy non-European aristocratic wife of an English trading company official, taken back to England as an advertisement for a colonial project (Malieckal 2011; Fisher 2004: 22–9). Her first husband, Captain William Hawkins, was an English East India Company officer who had been dispatched to India in 1608 to present King James's request to Jahangir that an English trading post be established in

Surat; Jahangir, favorably impressed with Hawkins, awarded him the title of "Khan" (lord) and had him married to Mariam, his fellow Christian and Khan. Hawkins was quite keen to convey to his countrymen the status he had acquired in India, and he arranged to take Mariam—and the money and slaves that came with her—back with him to London as part of a drama of triumphal return. This drama was not to eventuate, however; Hawkins died at sea in 1613. Within a year, Mariam had married another East India Company employee, Gabriel Towerson, who sailed with her to England in 1614–15. Like Hawkins, Towerson seemed particularly interested in Mariam for her wealth and status; he was no doubt taken by the fact that the worth of her jewelry alone was more than twice that of his annual income. Towerson lived with Mariam for two years in England, but abandoned her after bringing her back to her native Agra in 1619. At least she survived, unlike Pocahontas, to return home from England. But her tale had an equally grim ending. Mariam sued Towerson, and the East India Company, for alimony; when he died in the Amboyna Massacre of 1623, however, his estate was divided among his brothers, and Mariam never saw a penny of it. She disappears from the record after this.

We can, of course, read Mariam Khan's story, like Pocahontas's, as yet another instance of a non-European woman becoming a pawn in a game played by powerful European men. But there are also stark differences between the circumstances of Mariam and Pocahontas, particularly Mariam's migrant family background and the culture of the royal harem in which she had lived. When read in light of these differences, Mariam's tale of fugitive mobility also becomes rather different from Pocahontas's. No longer just mute testimony to patriarchal and imperial power, it also serves as a reminder of different, non-western constellations of identity formation and cultural mobility.

We don't know precisely when and where Mariam Khan was born. Her father, Mubarak Khan, was a wealthy Armenian Christian merchant who served in the courts of the Mughal emperors Akbar and his son Jahangir. Mubarak was one of many Armenians who found favor with the Mughals. One record reports that, after meeting an Armenian merchant named Hakobjan in Kashmir in the 1560s, Akbar encouraged him and his fellows to settle in Agra (Seth 2005). This was partly a humanitarian invitation: the Armenian Christian communities of Persia had been racked by years of war with the Ottomans. But Akbar's strong support for the émigré community had much to do with the transnational web of trading connections that Armenian merchants had established from the Levant through Persia to Portuguese India. Akbar tapped into this web with enthusiasm, promoting Armenian Christians to positions of power in his court. The Armenian Abdul Hai Firangi ("Hai" was a common name for Armenians in Persia), for example, served as the qazi or judge of the Imperial Camp—in effect, Akbar's chief justice. Abdul Hai's grandson, Sikander Zul-Qarnain, was made faujdar (commander) of Sambhar, a lake-town in Rajasthan, with the approval of Jahangir; he inherited his command from his father, Iskander, Abdul Hai's son-in-law, who had likewise served Akbar faithfully (Beveridge 1989: 194).

Abdul Hai Firangi's full name suggests how Armenian migrants occupied an intriguing liminal position in the Mughal world. They were Christians, but assumed Muslim names; yet they weren't allowed to blend seamlessly, as Abdul Hai's sobriquet "Firangi"—a term normally applied to foreign Christians—makes clear (Fazl 1927: I. 373n1). This liminality was by no means disempowering; indeed, Armenians were allowed to practice their own religion without restriction, and churches were built for them in Agra, Lahore, and elsewhere. In other words, Mughal Armenian migrants enjoyed an experience of transculturalism not unlike what we have witnessed in Fez, with Leo Africanus/al-Hasan ibn Muhammad al-Wazzan, or in Goa, with Garcia da Orta.

As the daughter of a powerful Armenian merchant who had found favor in the court, Mariam Khan would have grown up in the royal harem or *zenana* of Agra Fort (Figure 5.4), where she would have enjoyed unusual privileges. The daughter of Akbar's Armenian qazi Abdul Hai Firangi, Bibi Juliana, had been accorded a special status in the harem; Akbar had requested that Bibi Juliana's sons, including Sikander Zul-Qarnain, be raised there alongside Jahangir's son

FIGURE 5.4: The Harem court of the Khas Mahal, Agra Fort. Mariam Khan would have lived here in the 1610s when Jahangir had her married to Captain William Hawkins. Credit: Biswarup Ganguly. Accessed via Wikimedia Commons: https://commons.wikimedia.org/wiki/File:Harem_Court_-_Khas_Mahal_Complex_-_Agra_Fort_-_Agra_2014-05-14_4140.JPG

Khurram, the future Mughal emperor Shah Jahan, and share the same wet-nurse (Harris 2014: 150–69). Contrary to western fantasy, most of the women in Akbar's zenana weren't the emperor's wives or concubines, let alone playthings. Rather, they were themselves players within larger networks of political as much as familial relations. As Ruby Lal has shown, the women in the royal zenana were part of a complex social fabric that blurred the boundary between the public and the private (Lal 2005). They played key roles in brokering familial bonds, generating state policy, mediating political conflicts, and even launching trading ventures. The Mughal harem also served as a laboratory for transculturalism: the 5,000 women in Akbar's zenana, where Mariam most likely lived as a child before Akbar's death in 1605, were comprehensively assimilated into a larger project of knitting together the multiple cultural strands of the Mughal empire.

This project is evident in the Mughal court's famed entertainments. The image of the harem as a pleasure-palace is doubtless enhanced by the fact that Mughal women danced, sang, and played musical instruments. Yet these pastimes weren't just pleasurable diversions. The Dhrupad classical music of Akbar's court, in the syncretic fashion so typical of Mughal culture, deliberately combined elements of local Hindu and foreign Turko-Persian musical traditions (Wade, 1998). The emergence of the Dhrupad style was connected to Akbar's larger project of forging shared transcultural bonds across an ethnically, religiously, and linguistically diverse territory. This project helped spawn a distinctively Hindustani musical identity: indeed, the late sixteenth century was when trademark Indian instruments such as the sitar and the sarod emerged into the musical mainstream. Yet these instruments were both cultural hybrids. The sitar is a fusion of long-necked lutes from Turkic Central Asia and the Indian veena; its name derives from the Persian sehtar, or thirty strings. The sarod also has a mixed lineage: loosely based on a Central Asian and Afghan instrument called the rubab, the sarod's name is the Persian word for "beautiful sound" or "melody."

Musical performances at court were also accompanied by dancing girls from the zenana. Although some of the Mughal dancers were concubines and slave-girls, royals and high-status women of the harem, such as Jahanara Begum, the daughter of Shah Jahan, also took part in them. The dominant style was the Mughal version of the Kathak dance tradition. Kathak's roots date back to ancient performances by Hindu storytellers (Kathak is related to the Sanskrit "katha," meaning "story"). But the multiculturalism of the Mughal zenana prompted Kathak dancers to absorb elements of Persian and Central Asian forms (Massey 1999).[3] Indigenous Hindu techniques, including the tribhanga (thrice-bent) formations, remained part of the Mughal Kathak dancer's repertoire. But other foreign innovations were introduced. Whereas most Indian dance forms demand bended legs (or what ballet practitioners call the demi-plié stance), the Mughal form of Kathak appropriated the straight-legged position of Persian dancers. This enabled the dancer to devote more attention to her feet, with which she tapped out intricate percussive patterns—emphasized by scores of ankle-bells—in response to the rhythms of the tabla. Under the influence of Sufi dervishes, Kathak dancers also incorporated the *chakkar* (spin), which again required skillful footwork, including turning on the heel. We might see this footwork as a metaphor for the biography of the harem woman. Her feet were trained to move in ways that not only transformed her individual body but also integrated her into a larger entity—Mughal culture in all its syncopated diversity. The body of the zenana Kathak dancer, after all, was a transcultural palimpsest: it collated aptitudes from various parts of the world.

In sum: Mariam entered her marriage with Captain Hawkins as someone immersed in the ethos of transculturalism, and habituated to a certain freedom as a "player." When her father died in 1612, she experienced a crisis because other male relatives expropriated his property. The marriage to Hawkins, and the prospect of visiting England, may have appealed to someone used to crossing cultural boundaries in the Mughal harem. According to Hawkins, at least, she was "willing to goe where I went, and live as I lived" (Malieckal 2011, 112). That things unraveled so utterly for her after her English adventure doesn't mean she lost agency; it's simply that the playing field in which she operated had radically shrunk, diminished by Towerson's rejection of her. Mariam's legal suits for alimony and compensation from Towerson and the East India Company hint not only at a strong sense of injustice, but also an ability to cross borders and learn other systems—in this case, the legal system of the English—an ability no doubt cultivated in the environment of the harem.

Mariam's fugitive mobility is clearly different from those of the men I have examined here, including her father. It was aggressively circumscribed, as was Pocahontas's, by Englishmen and English patriarchal structures. But, as I have suggested, Hawkins' comments about her "willingness" to marry and travel with him hints at something other than docile submission to the will of her husband. She, like al-Hasan ibn Muhammad and Garcia da Orta before her, retained a measure of agency that was the product of the dynamically pluralist cultural environment in which she had grown up. This indicates how early modern encounters between Europeans and non-Europeans were enabled not just by the relatively new machinery of European empire but also by other local, older networks of trade, transculturalism, and patronage.

As a result, we can gain a better understanding of European imperial and commercial entities such as the Estado da Índia and the East India Company as not simply dominating forces in other hapless parts of the world. Interacting with earlier, cosmopolitan networks of cultural and commercial exchange, these entities encountered forms of knowledge and agency—foreign and subaltern European—that they sometimes tried to co-opt but also often found themselves excluded from. Further, we can recognize how the foreign landing points of western imperial and proto-imperial ventures were never pure, singular phenomena but always already a constellation of cosmopolitan milieus, populated in part by foreign refugees operating within largely Islamicate systems of patronage. "Fugitive mobility" might therefore describe not only the migratory lives of early modern European refugees in India as well as African, North American, and Indian refugees in Europe. It might also describe the process of moving our understandings of Western empire and its global locations in new, unexpected directions that allow us to expand the horizons of agency that attach to the very notion of mobility itself. If the current refugee crisis has increased Europe's sense of itself as a civilizational center, then the transcultural refugees of the early modern period can equally help us re-provincialize Europe.

CHAPTER SIX

Sexuality[1]

VALERIE TRAUB

Sexuality was a significant feature of early modern Europe's expansion across the globe. Insofar as empires are hierarchical enterprises of social as well as geopolitical incorporation, they seek to regulate sexual relations through both encouragement and sanctions. It has long been a critical commonplace that Europeans uniformly and systematically denigrated the bodies and sexual practices of those peoples they encountered, projecting excessive desire and "unnatural" practices onto them. Because sexuality was associated with relative degrees of "civility" and "barbarity," and sexual stereotypes circulated across national borders, sexuality frequently is credited as one of Western empire's prime strategies of "othering."

As this essay will argue, Europeans between 1450 and 1650 regularly used discourses of sexuality to denigrate and control those they encountered; in addition, European sexual (and racial) identities developed by defining Latin Christendom against the perceived sexual practices of "heathens" and "infidels." This essay also argues, however, that a binary framework does not fully describe Europeans' sexual imaginaries or contacts around the world during the early years of empire. Over this 200-year period, European discourses did not reflect a codified set of beliefs, and both alterities and commensurabilities were promoted for reasons of morality and strategy. Subject to local conditions, contingent relations, and pragmatic motives, sexuality presents to the phenomenon of empire a number of contradictions.

These contradictions are in part a function of sexuality itself. "Sexuality"—by which I mean erotic desires and intimate bodily acts—operates, on both an individual and cultural level, through processes of connection as well as differentiation; it is expressed through deeply felt physical urges, circulated through highly symbolic systems of representation, and institutionalized in concert with economic and political imperatives. Both at the individual and collective levels, sexuality can be unsettling, informed by the twin energies of desire and anxiety (Traub 1992). Subject to both incitement and prohibition, sexuality is often a site of simultaneous allure and danger, inviting identifications with and disavowals of "others" in complex and ambivalent ways. Sex can involve genuine appreciation, curiosity, and vulnerability, the acceptance of someone who appears different from the self. It can also involve individual and structural forms of coercion, exploitation, and domination, including projecting onto others one's own disavowed desires. Moreover, erotic intimacies across races, ethnicities, religions, and cultures are necessarily qualified by the thorny question of what constitutes consent within asymmetrical relations of power.

Given this psychological and political complexity, generalizing about sexual attitudes and practices is perilous for any period. What people said and, perhaps more importantly, *did* with their bodies and the bodies of others were not always in lockstep with European aspirations of rule. Divergence between official and local attitudes was common, and individual practices were sometimes at odds with those condoned by the community. Various forms of intimacy developed on the ground, under the radar of official regulation. Key to the conjunction of sexuality and empire is the disjunction between prescription and practice, and thus the significance of what Anna Clark calls "twilight moments"—illicit sex occurring at the threshold of social awareness (Clark 2008). Compounding the difficulty of accessing past sexualities is the fact that documentation comes almost exclusively from European sources, many of which were penned at some temporal distance. As they traveled around the globe, Europeans encountered sexual cultures that sometimes seemed wholly unfamiliar and sometimes uncomfortably (or seductively) close to home. While it would be a mistake to take European descriptions of non-European sexualities at face value, some of the practices they describe were indeed indigenous to local cultures—even if their meanings were often misinterpreted. Travelers' interpretations of sexual cultures involved a mix of fact and fantasy; their responses ranged from incomprehension, misunderstanding, and projection to curiosity, admiration, and, at times, emulation and adoption.

Further complicating an assessment of sexuality is that this period witnessed a number of ideological struggles *within* Europe regarding the nature and meanings of sex, including the moral campaigns of the Spanish Inquisition; the Protestant emphasis on companionate, erotic "domestic heterosexuality" (Traub 2002); changing regulations of brothels; and the emergence of urban subcultures of sodomites and "mollies" (Bray 1982). Several questions thus guide my inquiry: How did discourses of sexuality come to signify in cross-racial and cross-religious contexts? What ideas about sexuality did Europeans carry with them as they confronted different sexual cultures? What continuities existed between European and non-European attitudes and practices? Where did sexual contact occur across race and religion? How did these encounters, both discursive and actual, inform subsequent ideas about sex for both colonizer and colonized? How did discourses of sexuality advance or hinder the repertoires of imperial rule? And what changes and continuities in the conjunction of empire and sex can be traced over the course of this period?

This essay focuses on sexual discourses and practices generated primarily out of two major empires-in-the-making.

While Catholic Spain and Portugal competed for resources and territory until they were formally united in 1580, their policies on sex were often aligned. The Iberians conducted anti-Semitic pogroms during the late fourteenth-century *Reconquista*, mass conversion of Jews and Muslims throughout the fifteenth century, and mass conversion of Amerindians by the sixteenth century. Each of these efforts of conversion and expulsion was informed by the notion of blood purity (*limpieza de sangre*), a discourse of heredity wherein sexual reproduction figured centrally. Despite these concerns, by the sixteenth century both conquistadors in the Americas and Portuguese soldiers and "factors" in the East regularly entered into sexual relationships with native women. Whereas in the Americas Iberians quickly moved from forging alliances to open warfare followed by settlement, in the fortified trading enclaves in the East they used sexual arrangements to negotiate their relative geopolitical dependency.

Although England expelled its Jewish populace before the Iberians and took active part in the Crusades, its imperial ambitions on a global scale were belated: it took the English almost two centuries to follow the Spanish example, and even then, private rather than state investment underwrote settlement. Throughout the period, the English struggled to subdue the Irish, ultimately developing a system of settler plantations that consolidated their power over the archipelago. In 1600, encouraged by the success of Iberians and the Dutch East India Company (VOC), English merchants began sending factors to the East Indies and Japan, exploiting sexual arrangements with native women to strengthen their tentative toehold. The Portuguese, Spanish, and English carried with them in their travels prior experience of the transnational Mediterranean and diplomatic and mercantile experiences with the Ottomans, Mughals, and Savafids. They almost always represented their ventures as evangelical, and the ministers and missionaries who accompanied them had a tremendous impact on indigenous sexual systems. By the end of the period, the Dutch also composed a formidable mercantile and naval power with trading outposts in the East Indies, whose factors likewise developed improvisational sexualities attuned to their new environs.

Crucial to understanding the imbrication of sexuality with empire in this period is that both phenomena were only emerging as modes of identification. With the exception of Spain, whose rapid conquest of the Aztecs and Incas vastly extended its territorial rule, the idea of a "western" empire until the seventeenth century was more aspiration than reality, more a matter of claiming *imperium* as a title and pursuing dynastic marriage to acquire territory than it was military conquest. For Europeans, the most consequential empire at the time was that of the Ottoman Turks, which was conceived as a decidedly "eastern" phenomenon. If two of the primary goals of empire are to turn conquest into governing and to balance "incorporation of people into the polity" with "sustaining distinctions among them" (Burbank and Cooper 2010: 11), the empires that are my focus follow different timelines for doing so. They also operate in competitive relationship to one another, as well as with other European powers.

The concept of "sexual identity" was no less incipient than that of empire. The idea of a sexual identity—an inner force that is constitutive of the self and that in modernity has taken the form of "gay" and "straight"—probably was experienced only by a very few. Sexual practices were regulated in Europe by means of religion, which, until late in the period, oversaw laws regarding marriage, reproduction, and sex conducted outside of marriage. Protestants and Catholics alike viewed sex through a Christian framework of sin, wherein erotic desire is a "natural" appetite that, while inherently sinful, is necessary for the propagation of humankind. Like all natural appetites, sex was thought to require moderation and regulation, and to be satisfied in a legitimate manner: either in pursuit of marital reproduction or, for men, with prostitutes who served as "outlets" for concupiscence (Clark 2008; Wiesner-Hanks 2008). Guided by the medieval differentiation between the natural and the unnatural, laws were developed (or revised) in this period to punish a host of sexual acts: a) regarding the proper use of body parts (sodomy and tribadism), b) across species (bestiality), c) that challenged patriarchal and Christian imperatives (fornication, adultery, and rape), and d) confuted emerging ideas of race (interracial and inter-religious sex).

Lust rendered all humans prone to committing sodomy—which referred, throughout this period, to any non-reproductive sexual act, including oral and anal sex, bestiality, and mutual masturbation. As a "crime against nature," sodomy (or colloquially, "buggery") was by the mid-sixteenth century accorded the legal status of treason in most European states. Various theologians and legal writers, however, minimized the existence and gravity of female-female sex—as long as it did not involve an "instrument" or dildo. Accordingly, it was prosecuted far less frequently than male-male sex (Traub 2002). The conceptual capaciousness and indeterminacy of sodomy rendered it a versatile ideological weapon, but also rendered its meanings confused. This confusion is exacerbated by two paradigms that governed understandings of same-sex desire: the "cognitive dissonance" with which male-male sex was subject, whereby intimate male friendships were exalted rather than condemned (Bray 1982, 2003); and the difficulty that men had envisioning how women might erotically enjoy one another (Traub 2002; Velasco 2011; Lanser 2014). The incidence of sodomy and tribadism tended to be projected onto other nations and faiths in a disavowal of its presence at home. In sixteenth century Germany, the verb *florenzen* or "to Florence" linked male-male sex to Italy (Puff 2003), while Spaniards considered it a trait of Muslims, Turks, and North Africans. Accusations of sodomy tended to target men who abused a youth, were "aliens," or suspect on religious or political grounds. With the exception of Florence's Office of the Night, which institutionalized prosecutions of male-male sex from 1432 to 1502 (Rocke 1996), Lucca's *Offizio sopra l'Onestà*, which sought to eradicate both male and female sodomy from 1448 to 1647 (Hewlett 2005), and Inquisition Spain, which prosecuted all manner of sexual offenses to ensure Catholic orthodoxy (Monter 1990; Garza Carvajal 2003), prosecutions of sodomites tended to sporadically erupt in Europe during moments of social crisis (Bray 1982, 2003). Given the conceptual capaciousness and instability of sodomy, Jonathan Goldberg's formulation—that "any inquiry into" sodomy "will never deliver the sodomite per se, but only ... sodometries, relational structures precariously available to prevailing discourses" (Goldberg 1992: 20)—is a theoretical and historical premise of what follows.

Concepts of sexuality depended on expectations regarding gender. Considerations of gender in this period tend to focus on the extent to which figures accord with dominant ideals of masculine and feminine roles. But gender is "also an administrative ... structure for the management of sexual difference and reproductive capacity" (Stryker and Azuria 2013: 8), as well as a source of socially resonant metaphor. Sexuality intersects with gender when masculinity is correlated with sexual virility or weakness, and femininity with chastity or promiscuity. The concept of two genders was fixed in social, legal, and medical practice, and the near-universal presence of patriarchal systems across the globe means that gender inequalities remained a constant (Bennett 1997). Yet, gender, like sexuality, was rife with contradictions, and agency as well as domination was built into the social fabric. On the one hand, God-given distinctions between male and female were intended to ensure that women were viewed as inferior (even as their laboring, affective, even intellectual capabilities were depended upon); on the other hand, the humoral theories that governed medical practice imagined gender differences on a continuum, whereby some women could be more "manly" than "effeminate" men. Those persons whose gender presentation challenged binaries were also often interpreted as challenging the gendering of sexual roles such as penetrative and receptive.

Concepts of sexuality and gender were intimately entwined with ideas about cultural, geographical, religious, racial, and bodily differences (and similarities). On a conceptual as well as material level, race was linked to gender and sexuality because "all racial ideologies depend on the careful regulation of lineage and sexual contact" (Loomba 2016: 231). Categorical notions of racial difference, however, were not yet fully formed, nor did they evolve during the period in a linear way; they were local, regional, created to address issues at hand (Heng 2003, 2011a, 2011b). One of the most important aspects of race in the period is that labels such as "Christian," "Turk," "Jew," and "Moor" were used to refer to both religion and race. The presence of religion-based race, combined with various etiological theories—geohumoral, climactic, astrological, theological—ensured that "no single idea about race dominated early modern European thinking" (Burton 2013: 505). Indeed, given that race (even in modernity) *"has no singular or stable referent … race is a structural relationship for the articulation and management of human differences, rather than a substantive content"* (Heng 2011a: 262, emphases in original), we are better able to understand the conceptual flexibility and social utility of race as it intersects historically with sex. Like "sodometries," race is relational, its meanings contingent; moreover, its instrumentality is enhanced precisely because it can be construed as either lodged in the body (nature) or in culture (Loomba 2009).

With the extension of European enclaves and settlements to the east and west, prior tactics of xenophobia and social exclusion based on religious justifications of inferiority were selectively repurposed to address new cultural and political imperatives (Kaplan 2016, 2018; Loomba 2016): increased trade across national boundaries, greater numbers of religious converts, the transatlantic slave trade. Within these shifting conditions, sexuality gained signifying power by means of the following conceptual rubrics and discourses:

- geospatial imagining, in which grand territorial ambitions are figured through representations of gendered bodies;
- bodily morphology, whereby the size and shape of body parts, genital ornamentation, and relative bodily positions proffer physical confirmation of erotic practices;
- contamination and disease, whereby aberrant or excessive sexuality circulates throughout the body politic, threatening its purity and integrity;
- two conceptual strategies through which specific bodily practices are imagined, represented, and regulated: the natural and unnatural, and the licit and the illicit.
- the sexual (re)production of race, which operated by means of slavery, interracial sex, and discourses of racial (im)purity and religious conversion.

GEOSPATIAL FIGURATIONS

Sexuality was a powerful symbolic means for representing issues having little or nothing to do with sex. Sexual rhetorics, for instance, played a prominent role in the repertoire of European xenophobia. The Dutch besmirched French men as effeminate; the French derided the English as sexually sluggish; the English assumed Irish desires were bestial. These nations collectively impugned the Italians and Spanish, characterizing them as sodomites and whores. During times of social crisis, sexual scapegoating could lead to executions of resident aliens and foreigners.

Perhaps the most pervasive way that fear of foreigners informed sexual representations was through the Plinean repertoire of the monstrous races, which included hermaphrodites, Amazons, and wild men and women with bodies covered with hair. They populated medieval travel narratives and chivalric romances that celebrated the deeds of Alexander the Great, who offered rulers from England to the Malay Archipelago a compelling model of imperial conquest (Ng 2006) (Figure 6.1). Because the monstrous races adorned the borders of early manuscripts, maps, church columns, and friezes, their influence extended far beyond the ranks of the literate (Friedman 1981).

The most persistent monstrous race, supposedly appearing in Africa, India, eastern Europe, and the Americas, was that of the Amazons. So convinced were the Spaniards that Amazons would be found in the New World that contracts of exploration included instructions to search for them (Fuchs 2001), and Amazon tribes accordingly were "discovered" by Columbus, Vespucci, Carvajal,

FIGURE 6.1: Detail of hermaphrodite, Monstrous Races, woodcut by Michael Wolgemut, Wilhelm Pleydenwurff, and workshop, in Hartmanm Schedel, *Liber Chronicarum* (Nuremberg Chronicle) (Nuremberg: 1493). Credit: Courtesy of the Hatcher Library, University of Michigan.

de Orellana, and Thevet (Bleys 1996). As late as 1596, Sir Walter Raleigh relocated Amazons in Guiana, where they "do accompany with men but once in a year, and for the time of one month" (Loomba and Burton 2007: 137). Exploiting this fantasy to entice Queen Elizabeth to colonize America, Raleigh (who famously described Guiana as "a country that hath yet her maidenhead") urged Elizabeth to foil her Spanish enemy by invading "where the south border of Guiana reacheth to the dominion and empire of the Amazons," for "those women shall hereby hear the name of a virgin, which is not only able to defend her own territories and her neighbours, but also to invade and conquer so great empires and so far removed" (Loomba and Burton 2007: 138–9). As mythic figures of female valor and sexual abstinence, Amazons functioned as the limit case of both masculinity and empire (Lochrie 2005). By the late sixteenth century, the Amazon in Renaissance literature was represented precisely so that she might be domesticated (Schwarz 2000). The fact that Elizabeth herself could be figured as an Amazon suggests that this trope of female dominion was highly flexible, and that the ascription, adaptation, and assimilation of Europe's "others" was a strategic consideration (Figure 6.2). Geospatial tropes of gender and sexuality were continually reworked, as when the "virginity" of the New World was appropriated by Elizabeth to name her new colony, or by mapmakers to represent the continent of Europe itself as an inviolate virgin empress (Figure 6.3). Whether imagined as defending her chaste body, sexually open to imperial possession, or a willing agent of imperial might, the Amazonian "virgin" offered a geospatial trope of considerable plasticity.

BODILY MORPHOLOGIES

Various etiological stories regarding the cause of erotic desire circulated over the course of the early modern period. While literary discourses tended to privilege the heart and eyes as the site of desire's origin, the Galenic doctrine of the four humors posited that desire originates in the liver, while also granting considerable power to geographical location and climate (Floyd-Wilson 2003). Geohumoralism thus offered a powerful moral cartography and sexual etiology, whereby the "complexions" and behaviors of those who lived in temperate climatic zones were temperate, while those who lived in the equatorial or "torrid" zone were subject to greater intensity and fluctuation. Within this framework, inhabitants of southern climes generally were considered more prone to sexual "excess" of various sorts.

Geographical treatises and travel accounts reiterated geohumoral ideas. Jean Bodin (1566) opined that due to their cool, dry complexions, peoples of the south "are seized by frenzy more easily than northerners"; and "because self-control was difficult, particularly when plunging into lust, they gave themselves over to horrible excesses," including bestiality (Loomba and Burton 2007: 96).

FIGURE 6.2: "Elizabetha Angliae et Hiberniae Reginae, &c (Truth Presents the Queen with a Lance)," engraving by Thomas Cecil (c. 1625). © The Trustees of the British Museum.

Pieter de Marees (1602) describes the people of Sierra Leone as "very lecherous, and thievish, and much addicted to uncleanenesse: one man hath as many wives as hee is able to keepe and maintaine. The women also are much addicted to leacherie, specially, with strange Countrey people" (Morgan 2004: 30). Iberians viewed those Amerindians who lived along the humid coasts as more sinful than those in the interior; most Mexican natives were sodomites, opined Bernal Díaz del Castillo, but "especially those who live along the coasts and in hot lands." So, too, Pedro Cieza de Leon distinguished between the sodomitical Ecuadorian coast and the sexually moderate mainland (Trexler 1995).

From the Philippines to Goa to North Africa to the Americas, the scant or transparent clothing worn by peoples in hot and humid climates was interpreted as nudity, and it fostered European suspicions of sexual sin. Non-missionary bodily positions during sex were also, within a gendered Christian framework, considered unnatural. One reporter noted that Baja California natives "copulated

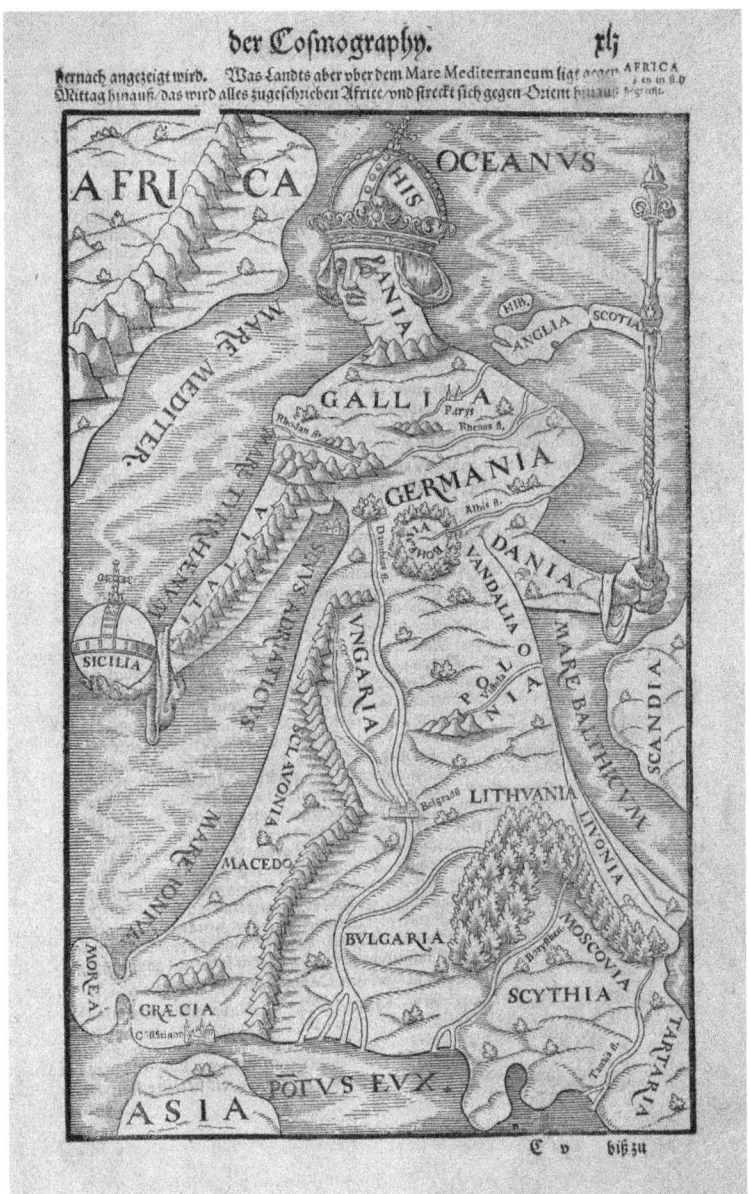

FIGURE 6.3: "Europa Regina," or "Europa Prima Pars Terrae in Forma Virginis," engraving by Johan Putsch, in Sebastian Münster, *Cosmographia Universalis* (Basel: 1544). Credit: Stephen S. Clark Library, University of Michigan.

like animals, the female placing herself publicly on all fours" (Trexler 1995: 123). Gonzalo Fernández de Oviedo (1526) described the talents of the wives of certain *caciques* who specialized in a form of "viper copulation" or fellatio (Trexler 1995: 133). The external appearance of native peoples, however, was as often described as pleasing as it was foul. Early descriptions of northern Amerindians, for instance, admired their "exceeding smooth and well proportioned" bodies (Godbeer 2002: 155) and their "perfect constitution" (Guasco 2014: 178).

Although the body was not always a reliable indicator of sexual virtue, certain body parts were accorded heightened sexual status, serving conclusively as indicators of inner traits. De Marees describes the "great privy member" of Guinean men, opining "whereof they make great account, therein they much surpass our countrymen" (Loomba and Burton 2007: 211). Conversely, Richard Jobson (1623) explains Mandingo men's reputed hypersexuality as the mark of Ham's curse, evident in their "burthensome," outsized "members" (Loomba and Burton 2007: 205–6). The breasts of Guinean women were described as "very foule and long, hanging downe low like the udder of a goate," and, under the conditions of New World slavery, would come to signify their supposedly innate savagery (Morgan 2004: 27). Edward Topsell (1607) went a step further in linking humans and animals, comparing the libidinous nature of "men that have low and flat nostrils" to that of "apes that attempt women" (Loomba and Burton 2007: 166).

Genital modification and ornamentation became a source of fascination after Antonio Pigafetta (1526) reported the practice of palang piercing in the Visayan Islands (Philippines). All boys and men, he reported, pierce their "members . . . from side to side with a rod of gold or tin, as thick as a goose quill" (Nocentelli 2013: 18–19). Such genital modification signaled to Europeans the unfortunate effeminacy of Asian men. Tales of Java, Siam, and Burma similarly fixate on men's insertion of round "yard balls" or bells under the skin of the penis, which ring during intercourse (Figure 6.4). As described by Niccolò de' Conti (1492),

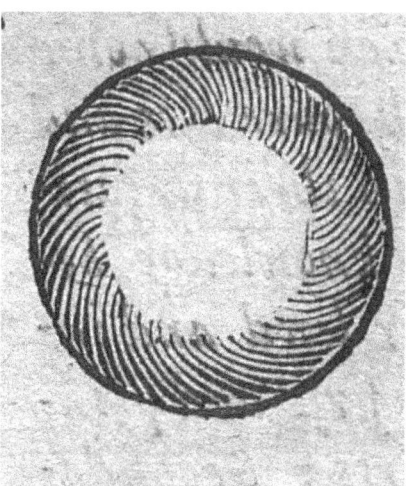

FIGURE 6.4: Southeast Asian yard ball, in John Bulwer, *Anthropometamorphosis* (London: 1654). Credit: Hatcher Library, University of Michigan.

"This they do to satisfy the lasciviousness of women, because these piercings and swelling of the member give women great pleasure" (Nocentelli 2013: 28). Jan Huygen van Linschoten (1598) and John Bulwer (1650) claimed that the practice had been introduced to prevent sodomy, for which reason Bulwer recommended the technique be "severely imposed upon the *Persians* and other Nations of the *Levant*" (Nocentelli 2013: 35, 37).

Perhaps because it was a pervasive practice related to religious observance, circumcision of the penis particularly fascinated Europeans. Then, as now, observant Jews and Muslims considered male circumcision a religious covenant. In tales of conversion to Islam, circumcision was often treated as conversion's most distinctive material sign. To Christians, for whom Saint Paul had enjoined a "circumcision of the heart" that bound them in spiritual rather than corporeal covenant, the loss of the foreskin was viewed with horror. Within the transnational Mediterranean, where piracy was an everyday occurrence, men and boys were often taken as captives, whether for ransom or to staff posts within the Ottoman empire. In exchange for their freedom—or in order to move up the Ottoman hierarchy—many turned "apostate" and, in the European imaginary, their change in bodily morphology functioned as a metonym for the loss of faith. The fantasy of forced adult circumcision loomed so large that in numerous travel accounts and stage plays, circumcision "was conflated and confused with the idea of castration" (Vitkus 2003: 5). Conversion narratives harnessed the body's signifying capacities to the aspiration that religious faith be made legible—visible for all to see.

The hope that sexual status be visibilized on (or in) the body was both projected onto and thwarted by the hymen, whose reputed presence functioned as a controversial signifier of female chastity (Traub 2002). Some travelers to Burma and Siam suspected the existence of hymenotomy rituals (Nocentelli 2013: 41), but otherwise, the discourse of the hymen was primarily focused on Europeans. In tales of threatened religious conversion, the intact hymen of Christian women who resist apostasy served as a sign of women's heroic religious constancy (Degenhardt 2010).

The discourse of the clitoris, in contrast, was implicitly racialized. Drawing on Greek, Arabic, and Latin sources, medieval anatomists recognized that the labia and clitoris—their anatomy was not terribly precise—were a source of erotic pleasure that could be satisfied independently of men (Lochrie 2005). Although the functional physiology of the clitoris remained confused throughout the period, sixteenth century anatomists promulgated detailed descriptions of the clitoris as the "seat of women's delight," without which women would be unable to conceive children. In addition to authorizing female erotic pleasure, these treatises proffered designations of medical pathology and sexual crime (Park 1997). Within this discourse, the allegedly enlarged clitoris of Mediterranean and African women played an especially prominent role. Leo Africanus had explained that Egyptians excised the "nymphae" or clitoris because it grew too long. Considered an essential rite of girlhood, clitoral circumcision was widely practiced in the Muslim world. But in the early modern period, the collision of travel and medical knowledges produced a "psychomorphology," whereby the hypertrophic clitoris, presumably more frequent in hotter climes, heralded the presence of the "tribade" who pleasured both herself and other women by rubbing and penetration (Traub 2002).

CONTAMINATION AND DISEASE

That medical treatises are a source of information about alleged sexual practices is unsurprising, for early modern Europeans believed lust itself—whether considered an infection of the eye, heart, or liver—to be contagious. Their theories of the origin and transmission of diseases included humoral imbalance, astrological forces, environmental miasmas, body-to-body contamination, and divine punishment for sin. Thus, sexual acts, as well as sexually transmitted diseases and genital ailments, were thought to travel easily from body to body. According to Girolamo Fracastoro, whose Latin poem depicting the suffering shepherd "Sifilo" gave syphilis its modern name (1530), contagion could occur only after a prior corruption of the body or soul. Even non-sexual diseases were implicated in this nexus of associations: throughout the period, leprosy, "perhaps the most dreaded, the most symbolically saturated, and certainly the most socially stigmatized disease of the Middle Ages" (Solomon 1999: 283), was widely believed to be transmitted through illicit sex (Jacquart and Thomasset 1988).

Like leprosy, syphilis left marks on the body—suppurating sores, aching bones, nasal decay, blindness—that figured not only individual suffering but social ills. Present among the European peasantry by the mid-fifteenth century, syphilis reached epidemic proportions in 1494 in Naples and quickly made its deadly way to England by 1498 and Japan twenty years later. Its origin was a matter of dispute, as evidenced in the national character of its names: it was known variously as the French, German, Neapolitan, Spanish, Portuguese, and Castilian disease. The Turks considered syphilis the *male dei cristiani*, while Africans blamed Jews who had been driven out of Spain. In 1538, Diaz de Isla influentially argued that sailors who had sex with Haitian women in Hispaniola introduced the disease to Europe in the 1490s, while others blamed prostitutes who serviced soldiers during the siege of Naples in 1494–5. Although early on physicians linked the disease to genitals, they were divided about the role of sexual intercourse in transmission, in part because moderate sexual emission was considered essential for health. By the early sixteenth century, however, the disease became known as *lues venerea* and *morbus venereus*, attesting to the causal link between coitus and infection. Partly due to humoral theories, partly due to the less visible symptomology on female genitalia, and partly because of garden-variety misogyny, women were figured as more likely than men to transmit the disease (Arrizabalaga 2005; Siena 2005).

The most significant diseases of sixteenth- and seventeenth-century America, of course, were those brought by the Europeans, whose foreign microbes (especially small pox and measles) decimated native populations. Given the astronomical number of deaths caused by pandemic infections as well as by harsh labor, the opining of Oviedo that syphilis was divine retribution for sodomy—"See how just is God, to give them [syphilis] where [sodomy] is practiced" (Trexler 1995: 141)—is particularly chilling. Slaves in the Americas also experienced high rates of infertility (often due to malaria), miscarriage, and infant death. In addition, natives and enslaved Africans engaged in reproductive resistance, employing emmenagogues and abortifacients to terminate pregnancy. Iberians at the time were divided on the cause of the rapid decline of the Mexican population. Around 1611, Reginaldo de Lizárraga averred that the decline of population along the Pacific coast was divine retribution for sodomy. In the mid-sixteenth century, A. de Zorita attributed to Mexican men active avoidance of intercourse with women (Trexler 1995) in a strategic circumvention of reproductive futurity. Among slave populations it is known that "prolonged breast-feeding accompanied by sexual abstinence was one of the few cultural practices transportable from West Africa to the Americas." Europeans typically misconstrued these practices, interpreting African women's infrequent pregnancies "as a consequence of sexual promiscuity and its attendant diseases and disorders" (Morgan 2004: 66).

SODOMY

The conflation of hygienic, medical, gendered, racial, and moral imperatives informed not only discourses of disease, but of sodomy. Iberians referred to sodomy as *la lacra*—an infestation, disease, or plague (Garza Carvajal 2003), and vehicles of sodomitical contagion were variously described as the devil, humid climates, unhealthy vapors, or Jews, Moors, and foreigners (Solomon 1999). In *Reconquista* Iberia, clerics and rulers used fears of sodomitical contamination to revive Christian piety and embark on expulsions of Muslims and Jews (Nirenberg 1996). For their part, some indigenous peoples of Brazil assert to this day that sodomy arrived with the conquistadors (Trexler 1995).

All Western states agreed that sodomy, most often interpreted as male-male sex, was a grievous sin against God and king and must be stopped. The only question was whether it was endemic and why it was tolerated. As it was in Europe, sodomy was associated with a panoply of vices, but in the Americas this specifically included castration and cannibalism. The first report of sodomy in the New World states: "on capturing young boys from the islands," the

Caribs "first castrated them, then used them sexually until they grew to adulthood, at which point they were killed and eaten" (Trexler 1995: 65). Writing from Mexico in 1519, Hernán Cortés made the sweeping claim to Emperor Charles V that "we have come to know, for certain, that they are all sodomites" (Garza Carvajal 2003: 138).

Because of the pivotal role it played in justifying conquest, the extent of sodomy in the New World was hotly debated. Bartolomé de Las Casas famously denied that any American tribes condoned sodomy, while Cieza argued of the Incas that "only single individuals, from one to ten in any village, practiced this 'evil,' 'just as sinners did everywhere.'" One Dominican theologian rejected the idea that indigenous sodomy justified conquest because "it would follow that the French king could make war on the Italians because they commit sins against nature" (Trexler 1995: 5). Defending Inca rule, Cieza argued that the Incas themselves sought to suppress sodomy, demanding that those besmirching their reputation apologize (Trexler 1995; Garza Carvajal 2003). Garcilaso de la Vega—himself a Peruvian mestizo, illegitimate son of a conquistador and Inca princess—likewise maintained that Inca rulers punished sodomy by public burnings (Trexler 1995). Whether Amerindians were described as condoning or condemning sodomy often seems to correspond to the chroniclers' larger political designs and ethical positions (Bleys 1996).

Of particular interest to conquistadors was the gender-variant figure designated by anthropologists as the "berdache" or by today's native communities as "Two-Spirit" people—a man who dressed and performed the domestic duties, including sexual duties, of women for the duration of his life. Unlike eunuchs, berdaches were not castrated, nor were they believed impotent. With typical imprecision, Europeans generally referred to them as "hermaphrodites" and read their activities through the lens of sodomy. The extent to which these figures should be considered a third gender or transgender remains subject to debate, as are the varying sexual roles they are thought to have fulfilled across different tribes (Sigal 2003). All early modern commentators agree that certain males passed as women, including wearing women's jewelry, using cosmetics, pitching their voices, and performing feminine gestures. According to Lopez de Gómara, these men "lacked only breasts and childbirth to be totally women" (Trexler 1995: 127).

Although gender-variant persons lived throughout the Americas, their cultural status varied considerably by tribe. When Jacques Le Moyne de Morgues drew "hermaphrodites" among the Tumucua of northeastern Florida, his captions describe their function as that of military load-bearers, transporting the injured and carrying the dead to burial (Figure 6.5). Whatever their function during times of war, these people seem to have played important roles in pre-conquest religious institutions, in the domestic retinues of native elites, and in commercial sex (Sigal 2003). Particularly in Mexico, sex between older and younger males appears to have been a typical feature of temple life, with young

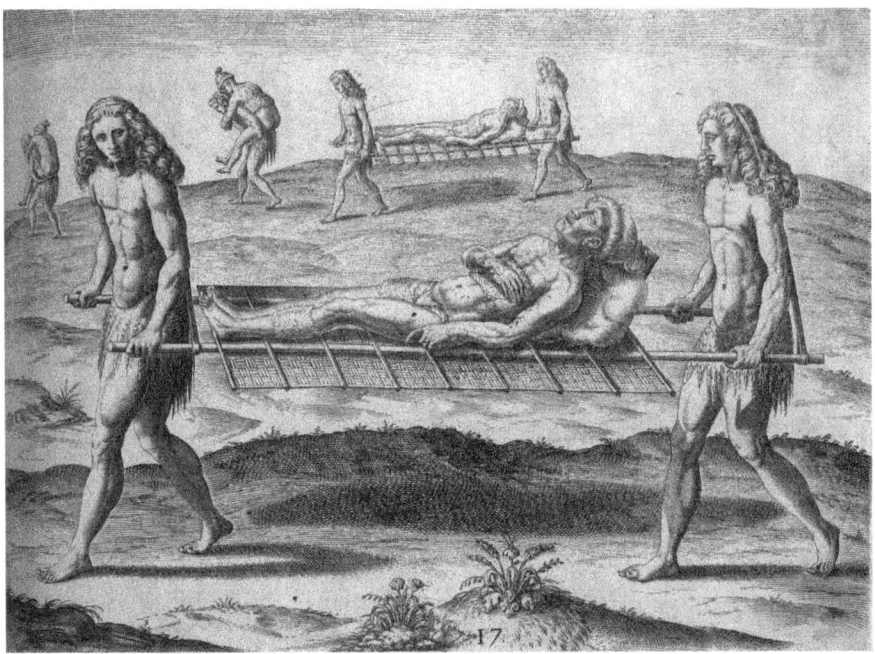

FIGURE 6.5: "Hermaphroditorum officia," engraving by Le Moyne de Morgues, in Theodore de Bry, *Brevis narration eorum quae in Florida Americae* (Frankfurt am Main: 1591, xvii-r). Credit: Clements Library, University of Michigan.

men receiving religious instruction by priests and older youths who routinely sodomized them, especially during religious festivals.

Lords of the Ecuador and Peruvian coasts apparently kept adolescent boys to be used for sexual purposes. The line between the elite use of berdaches and prostitution was a thin one. In 1541, Hernando de Alarcón related the tale of a Yuma chief, whose son, he explained, was one such boy: "when one died, a search was made for all the pregnant women in the land, and the first male born was chosen to exercise the function of women. . . . These men could not have carnal relations with women at all, but they themselves could be used by all marriageable youths of the land" (Trexler 1995: 87). When, prior to his execution by the Spaniards, Chichimeca was asked "why he wore a woman's clothes" he "confessed that he had done so from childhood and earned his living off of men in the office [of women]" (Trexler 1995: 90). Brothels populated by berdaches existed in at least three sites in Central and South America, but some Two-Spirit people lived with their husbands, performing a wife's domestic duties (Trexler 1995).

Native views of Two-Spirit people varied across the Americas, ranging from acceptance of their role as an essential religious resource, tolerance of the rights of nobles, and condemnation of the abuse of boys. Iberian reactions, in contrast, were overwhelmingly negative: conquistadors and missionaries interpreted them as "pathics" (sexually passive effeminates), sodomites, and whores. (Catholic clerics also were outraged by the "active" partner, who, while manly, committed unnatural, "filthy" acts.) Accordingly, European reactions were harshly punitive, including individual and group executions. The first recorded European punishment of gender variance and sodomy in the Americas occurred when the conquistador Vasco Núñez de Balboa discovered the brother of the *cacique* of Quaraca, Panama, as well as some of his courtiers, dressed as women and engaged in sex in 1516. The conquistador immediately threw forty of them to his mastiffs. According to Peter Martyr d'Anghiera, the native community applauded Balboa's actions "for the contagion was confined to the courtiers and had not yet spread to the people" (Trexler 1995: 82). More likely, the community realized that its survival depended upon demonstration of acquiescence of the destruction of a group that may have already been viewed with ambivalence (Miranda 2013: 354). In Puerto Viejo, Ecuador, Captain Francisco Pacheco and Chief Justice Juan de Olmos "burned great numbers of these perverse Indians." Later colonialists approvingly noted that swift punishment upon first encounter had diminished the incidence of sodomy. Continued repression of sodomy was the policy of both the Spanish and Portuguese, with the most extensive prosecution occurring between 1657 and 1658, when the Mexican High Court arrested and interrogated 123 "effeminate" men, executing fourteen of them (Garza Carvajal 2003; Gruzinski 2003).

Allegations of gender variance, crossdressing, and sodomy among Amerindians in this period overwhelmingly involve men. Mention of female-female sex is rare, but such women were sufficiently recognizable to be referred to in indigenous languages. According to Torquemanda, Mexicans called such women *patlache* (Trexler 1995), while a 1560 dictionary of the language of Peru defined *yanachani* as "one woman embraces another naked" (Horswell 2003: 32). The languages of the Dutch Caribbean likewise contain words for women who love women, some of which date back to the fellowship of enslaved women during the Middle Passage—suggesting that the "imperial experiment" produced a greater range of erotic modalities than generally acknowledged (Tinsley 2010: 41). Although Moche ceramics include representations of female-female sex, it suited some Europeans to perceive it as a "newfound evil," a sign of the cultural degeneration of noble tribes since the conquest (Trexler 1995: 139). Seventeenth-century confessional manuals included questions to be directed to women such as, "Have you sinned with another woman . . . ? When you engaged in this abominable sin, were you thinking about married men? unmarried men? the priest? the friars? your male kinfolk?" (Stavig 2003; 144), exhibiting the difficulty men had in conceiving of women's erotic interest in other women.

One notorious European who today is described as both lesbian and transgender is the Spanish "Nun-Lieutenant" (*la Monja Alférez*), whose given name at birth (1592) was Catalina de Erauso. Over the course of his transatlantic career, Erauso assumed the names of Alonso Díaz Ramírez de Guzmán (while serving as a soldier to the crown in colonial Peru) and Alonso de Erauso (after resuming his residence in Spain). An autobiography, a published letter, a play performed in 1626, and news pamphlets published in Madrid, Seville, and Mexico recount his transition from unwilling nun to masculine adventurer. Erauso enjoyed physical caresses with several Spanish and mestiza ladies in Chile, Peru, and Mexico, only narrowly escaping their designs for marriage. Unique among European cross-dressers, Erauso successfully parlayed his transgender performance into social acceptance and considerable celebrity. He did so, in part, by claiming the privilege of elite, white masculinity, as well as his unequivocal support for Catholicism, militant nationalism, and service to empire (Perry 1999; Stepto and Stepto 1996; Velasco 2000 and 2011; Garza Carvajal 2003) (Figure 6.6). Erauso's success raises the question of how many other people used migration to far-flung colonies as an opportunity for self-reinvention.

European travelers to the Ottoman empire were similarly obsessed with sodomy, and horrified to witness men walking the streets with their adolescent paramours. William Lithgow's (1640) enumeration of Turkish vices is a typical wholesale denunciation of Ottoman "luxury": Turks "are extremely inclined to all sorts of lascivious luxury, and generally addicted, besides all their sensual and incestuous lusts, unto sodomy, which they account as a dainty to digest all their other libidinous pleasures" (Loomba and Burton 2007: 219). The Portuguese Tomé Pire (1513–15) described everyone in Hormuz (Persian Gulf) enjoying the "abominable vice," serviced by male prostitutes who "are beardless and always dress as women," alleging that the Persians ridiculed the Portuguese for being horrified by this practice (Trexler 1995: 61).

The understanding of Turkish sodomy as a sophisticated, urbane pleasure informs Europeans' fascination with the sultan's seraglio, both in terms of the alleged practices of depraved eunuchs responsible for serving the sultan (Guasco 2014) and of the women enclosed therein. The Muslim practices of claustrating women within the home and covering female bodies when in public were conflated with the mysterious space of the harem. Despite the fact that Europeans were prohibited entrance to the inner spaces of the palace, travelers detail the "unnatural" acts of women pleasuring one another with cucumbers and gourds within its confines. Narratives of female-female intimacies extended to other homosocial spaces, such as the Turkish *hamam* (bathhouse), which in the European imagination became a watery hotbed of female lust (Traub 2002). Although such tales are mainly restricted to the Ottoman empire, François Pyrard describes the investigation of thirty

FIGURE 6.6: "Doña Catalina de Erauso," Francisco Pacheco, *Historia de la monja alférez* by Joaquin Maria de Ferrer (Paris: 1829). Credit: Northwestern University Library.

women's alleged use of bananas for sexual purposes in the Maldives (Nocentelli 2013).

African men were only rarely associated with sodomy, whether in the Old World or the New. When travelers to Angola, Bacongo, and Madagascar described isolated cases, they also did so in terms of sexual passivity and cross-gender roles (Bleys 1996). Leo Africanus described "[t]he innkeepers of Fez being all of one familie called Elcheva, goe apparelled like women, and shave their beards, and are so delighted to imitate women, that they will not only counterfeite their speech, but will sometimes also sit down and spin. Each one of these [degenerate innkeepers] hath his [male] concubine, whom he accompanieth as if [he] were his owne lawfull wife" (Smith 2009). Much of Africa remained unknown to Europeans; and the growing association of male effeminacy with sodomy probably was incompatible with the requirements of the transatlantic slave trade, for which virile masculinity was a *sine qua non* (Bleys 1996). Leo Africanus also provided a description of female fortune-tellers in Fez, whom he termed *fricatrices* and *Sahacat*, who tricked women into having sex with them (Traub 2002). Once transported to the New World, Africans accused of sodomy were largely subject to the harsh anti-sodomy laws that governed their settlements. In 1646 Jan Creoli, a "negro," was burned at the pillory in New Amsterdam for allegedly sodomizing the ten-year-old Manuel Congo (Bleys 1996: 34).

In the Far East, male-male sex was a common practice within Buddhist convents, the theaters, the Japanese caste of *samurai*, and the imperial Chinese court. The Jesuit missionary Francis Xavier harangued against the ephebophile Buddhist *bonzes* of Japan, and the failure of Christianization was attributed to the Japanese elite's habit of sending sons to Buddhist convents, where they would "serve the lust" of pederastic priests. In Ming China the Jesuits attempted to suppress sodomy, likewise an integral part of certain cultural institutions, in part through religious teachings: when translating the Ten Commandments in the late sixteenth century, Matteo Ricci changed "Thou shalt not commit adultery" to "Thou shalt not do depraved, unnatural, or filthy things" (Bleys 1996: 29).

PROSTITUTION, CONCUBINAGE, MARRIAGE, POLYGYNY, AND CONVERSION

Male prostitution, both in Europe and beyond, was incorporated into discourses of sodomy, and as such, was roundly condemned (if often tacitly tolerated). Female prostitution was less uniformly censured, riven as it was with the contradictions of patriarchy. As an endemic feature of Europe's own sexual cultures, female prostitution was seen as a necessary evil: it discouraged men's pre-marital fornication with "virtuous" women, thereby protecting other women's chastity, and it reduced the incidence of rape and male-male sex (Karras 1996). Approval of India's courtesans is voiced by the Venetian Nicolò de' Conti (1493), who "all but recommended the skills of India's public prostitutes to his European readers: these women . . . were marvelously skilled at caressing men each according to his age" (Trexler 1995: 61). Iberians described brothels populated by indigenous women in Nicaragua and the Yucatan and, like de' Conti, noted their utility in reducing male-male sex.

The medieval Catholic Church forbade Christians from sexual contact with Jews and Muslims. Popes even debated the legal status of marriage between Christians and Christian converts (Kruger 1997). Interfaith marriage was a sexual crime equivalent to adultery; it was associated with other unnatural acts, and, like them, could be subject to capital punishment (Clark 2008). Punishments were differentiated by gender and religion: female Christians were punished more rigorously than men, and Christian men were punished more for marrying a Muslim than a Jew. Despite such edicts, Spanish and Portuguese men frequented Muslim and Jewish prostitutes at home while engaging in sex with African and Amerindian women abroad. Paradoxically, most brothel prostitutes in the Spanish New World were Spanish, since men assumed their right to nonwhite women's sexual services without payment (Powers 2005).

The seemingly universal access of men to commercial sex was accompanied by ideas about the proper conduct of women. By the early 1500s, European travelers were obsessively narrating the devotion, submissiveness, chastity, and erotic attractiveness of women in the East (Loomba 2002). Such stories often contrasted Turkish and Indian women to their European counterparts, who were seen as lacking in proper obedience. Proof of the highly refined nature of female submission, many travelers opined, was the Hindu practice of *sati* (the burning of widows on their husbands' funeral pyres). Although the tradition was denounced as evidence of Hindu savagery, the actions of the widows themselves were applauded as the epitome of heroic chastity and devotion (Banerjee 2003). Similarly, the Chinese practice of foot binding (*chanzu*) was judged a savage custom, yet nonetheless upheld by the Dominican friar Domingo Fernández Navarrete (1659) as "very good for keeping females at home. It were no small benefit to them and their menfolk if it were also practiced everywhere else too" (Nocentelli 2013: 83).

Ideas about Eastern sexual practices were influenced by medieval romance, which promulgated visions of virtuous and alluring Saracen princesses who convert to Christianity after falling in love with Christian adventurers (Britton 2014; Heng 2003). The fear that Muslim women might seduce Christian men and cause them to "turn Turk" was assuaged by such women's conversion to Christianity (Degenhardt 2010). This topos gained new life in sixteenth- and seventeenth-century stage plays (Nocentelli 2013), civic pageants, and court masques. In such texts, Sultans were often depicted as driven by cruel lusts for the Christian captives they acquired by war, a depiction influenced by the shift in Ottoman practice from dynastic marriage to marriage and concubinage with kidnapped Christians. Converted consorts could rise in status (Peirce 1993), a reality that led literature and travel narratives to impute sexual alongside materialistic motives to those male "renegades" who voluntarily converted (Vitkus 2003; Burton 2005; Nocentelli 2013). Captive boys were thought to be especially vulnerable to conversion (Games 2008; Smith 2009), and the abduction, conversion, and circumcision of the eroticized male adolescent circulated throughout the imperial imaginaries of both western powers and the Ottomans (Boone 2014; Arvas 2016).

Many Amerindian cultures permitted youthful sexual experimentation, practiced some form of polygyny, and did not perceive marriage as necessarily permanent. So, too, in the Philippines, native women seemed unconcerned with virginity and exited unhappy marriages without negative consequences (Nocentelli 2013: 24). European observers of polygyny and serial monogamy tended to misinterpret them as evidence of promiscuity: polygyny was adultery, they maintained, and serial monogamy a form of desertion (Morgan 2004). Dissenting voices defended the chastity of Amerindian women and "the high and honourable esteem" their cultures held for "the marriage bed" by asserting that polygyny was the custom only of elites (Godbeer 2002: 157).

Practiced in the Americas, the Ottoman realms, India, China, and the Moluccas, polygyny attracted as much admiration as horror. In the case of the Ottomans, it was seen as a viable basis of population growth, believed to be "the foundation of all great empires" (Games 2008: 59). In addition, the gendered double standard it enforced was thought an appropriate tool of patriarchal control. English "women would be more dutiful and faithful to their husbands," wrote William Biddulph (1608), if the English would only imitate the Turks: "for there if a man have a hundred women, if any one of them prostitute herself to any man but her own husband, he hath authority to bind her, hands and feet, and cast her unto a river, with a stone about her neck, and drown her" (Biddulph 1608: 792). Indeed, Martin Luther (1524) and Philip Melanchthon (1531) both declared plural marriage to be compatible with Scripture, and Christian sects experimented with polygyny in Münster, Westphalia, and the Netherlands. In response, a papal bull of 1537 made monogamous marriage a prerequisite for baptism. The Portuguese followed suit, banning polygyny and concubinage in its holdings in India (Nocentelli 2013).

INDIGENOUS AND TRAVELING WOMEN

In the Americas, white endogamy was unusual during the early years of empire, and interracial sex, including concubinage and marriage, was often promoted as a helpful tool of settlement. Between 1509–38 over one thousand Iberian women settled in the Americas (Poska 2016). Nonetheless, with the exception of Puritan New England—which encouraged family migration (Amussen and Poska 2014)—the first generations of colonists across the Americas experienced severely skewed gender ratios. In the 1550s, the ratio of Spanish men to women in Lima was eight to one (Powers 2005). In 1619, Sir Edwin Sandys asked the Virginia Company to send one hundred women to Virginia to encourage colonial men to settle into orderly family life (Brown 1996; Godbeer 2002). While most female migrants were indentured servants, schemes to entice elite women to the colonies were pursued by the English and Spanish crowns. Still, in 1624, fewer than 230 of the 1,250 Europeans living in Virginia were adult women (Brown 1996). In 1635, only six percent of immigrants from London to Barbados were women (Amussen 2007). But by the mid-seventeenth century, the response to officials calling for "loose wenches" to replenish the white population led to more women making the transatlantic journey. The presence of white women was thought to discourage men from engaging in cross-race liaisons, and they served as race breeders, maximizing the potential for whites' future security and dominance.

Recognizing that marriage could cement political alliances and lead to the transfer of territory, the Spanish monarchy had advised early conquistadors to marry daughters of *caciques*. Spaniards found common cause with Indian practices of elite polygyny and the "donation of women," using marital alliance with indigenous princesses to gain territory and authority (Carrasco 1997). Tecuichpotzin (renamed Doña Isabel), the daughter of Moctezuma II, was married by Cortés to five different men to bolster Spanish authority over Aztec realms (Games 2008). While some Iberians feared such alliances might damage their racial honor and preferred to take native women as slaves and concubines, many others benefited from legal marriages. The dowry of a wealthy Indian woman, who enjoyed local influence and prestige, could enable an impoverished Spanish migrant to find his footing in the New World. Conversely, for non-elite native women, whose fathers valued alliance with powerful local Spaniards, liaisons with colonists could secure upward mobility. By 1534 in one pueblo, a third of Spaniards had native wives (Clark 2008). Given differences in marriage rituals, however, the status of many cross-race marriages proved a source of cultural conflict. After the increased migration of Spanish women in the second half of the sixteenth century, men frequently abandoned their native "wives," despite the fact that those women (and their families) considered themselves to be legally married, and their children legitimate (Powers 2005).

English settlers were less eager to partner with native Americans. Religious and legal prohibitions, communal insecurity, fears of "going native," and, in the north, a more balanced gender ratio all contributed to a relative lack of interracial sex. William Symonds' sermon (1609) urged planters leaving for Virginia to refrain from cultural apostasy by eschewing marriage to "the heathen," articulating anxieties about "the challenge of retaining a civilized identity while living in a far-flung wilderness" (Godbeer 2002: 160, 158). A 1610 Jamestown law instituted the death penalty for any man who raped a native or deserted the colony to live with neighboring tribes. Nonetheless, when Englishmen abandoned struggling colonies to live in native communities, they married Indian women, as did many colonists who were captured during raids.

Two Amerindian women who became notorious for their sexual unions with Europeans exemplify the difficulties of straddling two cultures. Pocahontas, the adolescent daughter of the Algonkian chief Powhatan, married John Rolfe, a Jamestown colonist, in 1614. The young girl had first visited the colony as a ten-year-old envoy, seeking the release of one of her father's men, and she continued to visit the colony until her marriage to a native man. Later kidnapped by the English, she was converted during her captivity and, apparently voluntarily, married Rolfe. Rolfe's petition to the governor of Jamestown evinces the ambivalence of a man who has fallen in love with a "barbarous" woman (Townsend 2004). Denying that he is motivated by "any hungry appetite" or "incontinency," he argues that their alliance would be "for the good of this plantation, for the honour of our country," and also "for the converting to the true knowledge of God and Jesus Christ an unbelieving creature" (Godbeer 2002: 161–2). Both Powhatan and the English viewed the marriage as a form of détente, and Pocahontas and her father considered her an ambassador to the crown. Invited by the Virginia Company to visit London in 1615, Pocahontas, with her young son in tow, had a formal audience with King James, attended a court masque, and sat for the painting of her portrait (Robertson 1996) (see Figure 5.3 in Mobility chapter). Pocahontas's diplomatic endeavors resulted in disappointment, and she died before her ship's return to Virginia. William Alexander, Earl of Stirling, "traced the beginning of success in Virginia to Pocahontas's marriage," ironically praising it "as a precedent because it calmed the Indians' natural and realistic fears of being overrun." As long as Amerindians converted, "'the promiscuous offspring' of those marriages, 'extinguishing the distinction of persons,' would create a new mixed American reality." Others, however, continued to fear the "corruption of language or blood" involved in racial mixing (Kupperman 2000: 193).

Malintzin (aka Doña Marina or Malinche), another captive who functioned as cultural intermediary, became an interpreter to the Spanish commander Cortés during his conquest of the Aztecs. Most likely a noble Nahua, she was enslaved as a child by the Mayas and given as a peace offering to Cortés, who then "gifted" her to Alonso Hernández Puertocarrero. Already fluent in Nahua and Chontal and Yucatec Maya, Malintzin quickly learned Spanish. Employing her linguistic versatility and social acumen to traverse three distinct cultures, she negotiated between Cortés and Moctezuma (Motēucçoma), while eventually giving birth to Cortés' son, Martín. She repeatedly saved the Spanish from disaster, and when Malintzin exposed an Aztec plot, the capital of Tenochtitlan was razed. Within ten years of her transfer to the Spaniards, she died. As a cultural go-between whose efforts led to the destruction of the Aztec empire, Malintzin's legacy has been deeply divided: initially honored in Spanish historical records for her assistance and accorded respect for her power in Nahuatl documents, she was harshly condemned in postcolonial Mexico as *la chingada*, "the fucked one," a traitor to her race. But the very idea of a pan-Indian identity is a post-conquest phenomenon and being "fucked" is no longer something for which the victim can reasonably be blamed (Townsend 2006). Moreover, her actions embody self-preservation within a gendered political system in which she had no cultural alliances to protect (Karttunen 1997: 310–11).

The lives of less elite women are difficult to discern in the historical record. Two such women, both intended as gifts to Queen Elizabeth I, are a case in point. During his search in 1577 for a northwest passage, Martin Frobisher abducted an Inuit, along with her infant, to serve as companion to an already captive Inuit man. Despite the designs of the English, these two captives "did they neuer vse as man and wife, though the woman spared not to do all necessarie things that apperteyned to a good huswife" (Andrea 2016: 146). Along with her baby, this anonymous woman died soon after her arrival in England. A similar situation was faced by the Nogai "Tartar girl" whom the Muscovy merchant Anthony Jenkinson acquired in Astrakhan in Central Asia. This Muslim captive became known as "Ippolyta the Tartarian," "surviv[ing] her ordeal of war, starvation, slavery, and forced transportation to find herself in a position of some comfort" (Andrea 2016: 142) while serving in Elizabeth's court. Nonetheless, we know very little about her.

The importation of captives as gifts to ruling elites was a form of political currency shared by many nations for whom the exchange of women oiled the gears of commerce and diplomacy. Dynastic marriages within Europe had long bolstered political alliances across confessional and territorial rivalries. From the beginning of their contacts with Europeans, Powhatan and Moctezuma had sought security through the gift of daughters. That the English considered, but then rejected, the use of dynastic marriage to forge alliances with non-Europeans is clear from an East India Company record (1614) regarding a marriage proposal for Iskendar Muda, the Sultan of Aceh: "The King of Sumatra having desired one of His Majesty's subjects for a wife with sundry proffers of privileges to the issue, a gentleman of honorable parentage proposes his daughter, of most excellent parts for music, her needle and good discourse, as also very beautiful and personable." While the Company did not pursue this offer, it took the view that "if the King consent it . . . would prove a very honourable action" (Ng 2006: 307; Games 2008).

Where joint stock companies rather than the state remained the main engine of empire—as they did in Southeast Asia—factors enjoyed considerable liberty to arrange their domestic lives according to local conditions. Whereas the VOC permitted employees to marry and their wives to accompany them, most Portuguese and English companies forbid wives to travel with their husbands (Games 2008). This led, not surprisingly, to "greate disorder," as one merchant complained in Bantam, where few of the factors were willing to live "without the companie of women." In Japan, "every one of the East India Company employees who lived there for more than a few months quickly established long-term liaisons with Japanese women," a phenomenon fostered by the prior conversion of many Japanese to Christianity (Games 2008: 104, 105).

In Portuguese India and the Philippines, cross-racial marriage was a deliberate strategy of colonization. Like the western conquistadors, European men in the East were encouraged to wed local women, for the future of the Portuguese empire was thought to rest on those *casados* (married men) whose marriages would dispossess natives of their territory (Nocentelli 2013). In Asia as in South America, Europeans depended on local women to navigate unfamiliar cultural terrain, and they believed that, like converted Jewesses, native women would absorb the status of their husbands and their mixed-race children would identify as European Christians (Nocentelli 2013; Kaplan 2016). That Asian and American women were relatively unencumbered by discourses of strange bodily morphologies contributed to their presumed racial assimilability. Nonetheless, the women recommended for the *política dos casamentos* were to be "white and chaste" Muslim and upper-caste Hindu women, rather than low-caste women who were deemed "black and corrupted." But insofar as the majority of men marrying were those judged by their superiors to be of "low birth and dubious worth" or apostate Portuguese "tak[ing] refuge among the Moors," the Crown withdrew its financial support, deciding instead to ship Portuguese orphan girls to its outposts by the mid-sixteenth century (Nocentelli 2013: 62–3). When in 1620 the VOC eliminated legal concubinage for its Dutch settlers, one apparent result was that those that "keeptt a blacke base whore," in the racist language of English observers, "have marryed them" (Nocentelli 2013: 100–1). Unions between Europeans and local women were not necessarily permanent or monogamous, and many such women were enslaved. Even when their domestic practices might mimic marriage, men often abandoned their "wives" when ordered back home. While this was done with impunity, it did not go uncensored by certain Europeans.

Interracial sex was not restricted to that between men and women. Portuguese Inquisition records mention Baltazar da Lomba, who had sexual relations with Indian men (Mott 2003). And in the mid-sixteenth century, the Jesuit M. de Nóbrega found Portuguese men in coastal Brazil marrying male berdaches "according to the custom of the land" (Trexler 1995: 135).

SLAVERY AND THE SEXUAL (RE)PRODUCTION OF RACE

As the high incidence of cross-race sex suggests, racialization by means of sexuality was a complex and contradictory process. In part this is because the meanings of blackness—used to refer indifferently to Africans, Amerindians, and South Asians—were unstable. In medieval theology and popular culture, blackness was associated with sin and the devil, both of which were linked with sex through the Fall. Whiteness, conversely, was allied with nobility, purity, sexual innocence, and chastity—and increasingly, to the "unmarked" category of European. Perhaps the most influential association of blackness with race and sex was the biblical legend of the sons of Noah (Genesis 9–10). When Ham (also known as Cham) sees his drunken father sleeping nude, he mockingly relates this incident to his brothers; when Noah awakes, he retaliates by cursing Ham's progeny. Amplifying the import of sexuality to this legend is Ham's defiance of an edict of sexual abstinence during the flood. While earlier commentators located Ham's descendants in Asia (Braude 1997), by the 1620s the English were using the legend of "the cursed race of Cham" to justify African slavery in the Americas (Amussen 2007; Guasco 2014). Providing an origin story linking black skin, perpetual servitude, and sexual promiscuity, this story contributed to beliefs in Africans' moral and physical degeneracy that were used to legitimate racial slavery.

England's discriminatory treatment of Jews prior to their expulsion in 1290 (including mandating the wearing of physical signs, fantasizing biomarkers such as male menstruation, condoning mob violence, and establishing apparatuses to track Jews' activities) set the stage for future racial thinking (Heng 2011a, 2011b). Spain's blood purity laws further developed a concept of biological race by defining Jewishness not as "a statement of faith or even a series of ethnic practices but a biological consideration" (Friedman 1987: 16). By the early fifteenth century, the terms "raza," "linaje," and their cognates in other languages "were already embedded in identifiably biological ideas about breeding and reproduction" (Nirenberg 2007: 79). Within early modern debates about relations among bloodlines, skin color, environment, behavior, and inferiority, ideas about sex exerted considerable influence. Contesting earlier geohumoral paradigms, George Best (1578) influentially offered his "eyewitness" description of "an Ethiopian as black as coal brought into England, who taking a fair English woman to wife, begat a son in all respects as black as the father was" as evidence that "this blackness proceedeth rather of some natural infection of that man, which was so strong, that neither the nature of the clime, neither the good complexion of the mother concurring, could any thing alter" (Loomba and Burton 2007: 108). Imagining race as both inheritable through blood and a product of infection, Best doubles down on interracial intimacy as a site in which race is produced—and to some extent, logically confuted. Within this matrix of sex and race, religious conversion and slavery played constitutive roles. Conversion to another religion and enslavement to a foreign polity licensed various forms of racial crossing, in which sex was often instrumental. By raising the specter of a world in which racial and religious identities were unstable and malleable, conversion and slavery provided contradictory if potent crucibles in which sex was racialized and race was sexualized.

During the early years of colonization, slavers attempted to balance the number of men and women brought from Africa and devised prohibitions against interracial sex; nonetheless, sexual contact among white colonists, Africans, and native Americans occurred regularly. The social worlds of indentured servants and slaves, in particular, were not fully distinct, and colonial trials for fornication suggest the extent to which some of this sex was mutually desired. In punishing these misdemeanors, North American magistrates did not initially discriminate between interracial and intraracial couples (Godbeer 2002; Guasco 2014). Far more prevalent, however, was the systematic sexual exploitation of slave women by white men. As an institution, slavery was structurally dependent upon sexual coercion and violence. The condition of enslavement precluded the ability to withhold sexual consent, and rape was a routine experience of many slave women's lives. Recent scholarship suggests that it may also have been part of some male slaves' experience as well (Aidoo 2018). In addition, in most locales, slave women's reproductive capacities underwrote the entire enterprise of racial slavery. By the 1650s, North American planters had begun to refer to slave women as "increasers" and their children as "produce," and, when calculating their property, they "supplemented the present value of enslaved person with the speculative value of a woman's reproductive potential" (Morgan 2004: 91, 82). In the West Indies, the policy of working slaves to death rather than allowing for gestational pauses in labor meant that few women had the opportunity to give birth (Tinsley 2010).

How slave women in the early colonial period experienced sex with the masters, sons, and laborers who laid claim to their bodies is largely unknown. We can surmise that the majority of such contacts were experienced as brutal expressions of domination, meant not only to enforce whites' claim of possession, but to terrorize the entire slave community—including other men (or women) with whom a woman might be intimate. Cross-race sex within slavery was a weapon of white supremacy. At the same time, scholars of North America have brought forth evidence for later eras in which complex experiences of mutual desire and need may have moderated the experience of non-consent. Enslaved (and free) women of color in Gulf ports not uncommonly cohabited voluntarily with white men, and often gained their freedom, property, and status by doing so (Gould 1997). In areas where few European women migrated, such as the Caribbean, women of color often served as housekeepers who provided sexual services as well (Tinsley 2010). Furthermore, in certain areas of the antebellum South, consensual sex between white women and black men not only occurred, but was tolerated (Hodes 1997 and 1999).

All cross-race liaisons, within and without slavery, took place within a broad framework of asymmetrical power. While most were the result of sexual assault and exploitation, others were born of mutual desire, opportunism, accommodation, and/or creative "survivance" (Andrea 2016). Their cultural and demographic impact was profound, as the offspring resulting from such relationships cultivated new cultures of *mestizaje*. The growing significance of multi-racial children was one of the "tensions of empire" (Stoler 2002), to which one response was the development of ranked systems of racial classification: *creoles*, referring to those of Spanish descent born in America; *mestiços*, born of European father and native mother; *castiços*, born of European father and mestiço mother; *mulattos*, born of Spaniards and Africans; and *zambos* (born of Africans and natives). For the first half of the sixteenth century, in urban areas mestizas born of Spanish fathers and native women were often taken from their mothers and raised in Spanish households or *casas de recogimiento*, in the hope of ensuring Hispanicization and marriage to Spaniards or Hispanicized mestizos (Powers 2005).

Regulation was imposed unevenly across different sites, occurring less forcefully in the East than in the Americas, where legal experiments became intent on fabricating ideals of racial constancy. By the end of the sixteenth century, Spain had legally limited the privileges of its racially mixed population in the Americas, including forbidding Africans, mestizos, and mulattos from residing in Indian villages. In the seventeenth century, marriage patterns became more endogamous, with Spaniards marrying Spaniards, Indians marrying Indians, while mestizas and mulattas tended to marry Spaniards, and male *castas* married Indian and African women. Nonetheless, interracial extramarital unions, especially between white men and nonwhite women, continued to proliferate (Powers 2005).

In 1662, the Virginian assembly enacted a law "that all children borne in the country shalbe held bond or free only according to the condition of the mother. *And* that if any christian shall commit fornication with a negro man or woman, hee or shee soe offending shall pay double the ffines imposed by the former act." In 1664, Maryland legislated the obverse: "all Children born of any Negro or other slave shall be Slaves as their fathers were for the terme of their lives," further mandating "That whatsoever free borne woman shall intermarry with any slave . . . shall Serve the Master of such slave dureing the life of her husband. And that all the Issue of such freeborne woemen, soe marryed shall be Slaves as their fathers were" (Cott 1996: 29–30). The imposition of these opposed injunctions demonstrates not only increased methods of sexual regulation of free and enslaved populations, and incoherent attempts to fix concepts of racial identity, but the tight interweaving of sex and race. By suturing sexual practices to racial formations, and birth status to naturalized servitude, such laws contributed to a more systematic typology of hierarchically-defined, racialized difference that was enacted through, and bolstered by, sex.

CONCLUSIONS

Despite confessional differences and uneven imperial timelines, the Portuguese, Spanish, and English shared many ideas about sex. They feared sexual diseases, associating them with women and lust, and officially condemned sodomy while condoning male-male intimacies. Especially in the early years of contact, Europeans were as inclined to express admiration as denigration of indigenous sexual practices. Particularly when the patriarchal control of women was involved, an almost universal ambivalence, admitting of both admiration and censure, limns their accounts. Across European nations, polygyny, widow immolation, and foot binding—while testament to cultural alterity—were periodically recommended to solve Europe's gender troubles. Intra-European differences, however, are evident as well. Due in part to Protestant investment in the "Black Legend," for instance, the English and Dutch were as likely to castigate Spaniards as indigenous peoples for sexual barbarism.

The uneven temporalities of different empires are crucial to assessing the sexual modes of European engagements with indigenous peoples. In the early days of imperial undertakings, colonial men of all ranks felt free to engage in informal and formal, long-term and short-term, sexual alliances across race and religion. With the exception of male-male sex, the extent to which such activity was considered "illicit" is worth considering, as male gender privilege tended to trump anxieties about racial purity. But as empire progressed, the blurring of boundaries between concubinage, prostitution, and marriage became the object of greater regulation, especially as more European women made their way to the colonies.

Cross-racial sexual contact in the early years of empire-making enabled colonists to gain a foothold in areas of precarity. In part this was possible because of commonalities among European and non-European sexual cultures, including the near-universal privileging of male-female marriage; efforts to regulate sex between those within and outside the community; the robust existence of commercial sex (including male prostitutes); reliance on dynastic marriage to forge alliances and gain territory; official horror, but tacit tolerance, of male-male sex; the idea that prostitution could minimize sodomy; belief in sexual contamination as both an individual and collective ill; and even concepts of the natural and the unnatural (although not universally articulated through the idiom of sin).

Yet, significant differences between European and non-European sexual practices are also clear. Mesoamerican ideals of gender parallelism and complementarity, as well as the presence of Two-Spirit people, struck Iberians as entirely foreign. So did practices of genital modification and ornamentation. While concubinage, eunuchs, and polygyny *seemed* alien, they in fact were familiar from the Old Testament, and numerous European men quickly procured concubines. Especially consequential for the majority of non-Christians was enforced religious conversion, with its imposition of the concept of sin, the intrusions of the Catholic confessional, and the outlawing of polygyny. In the Americas, the enforcement of monogamous marriage as a corollary to Christian baptism disrupted the indigenous marriage system, including its gender complementarity, with the effect of diminishing women's status. Native men objected to the loss of productivity that resulted from having only one wife, while native women no longer enjoyed the possibility of exiting an unhappy marriage, leaving them vulnerable to abuse and their actions in self-defense susceptible to punishment (Deeds 1997). By the end of the period, the frequency of concubinage between Spanish men with Indian or casta women "contributed to a decline in status for women in general" (Powers 2005).

Key to the sexualization of empire and the racialization of sex is the elasticity of interpretative practices, which could be highly opportunistic. Europeans' claims regarding a people's sexual immorality were often countered by other Europeans' assertions of their innocence, virtue, chastity, and fidelity. Sexual innocence, sexual primitivism, and sexual sophistication each could be attributed to a lack of civilization; scant or transparent clothing could signify either uncivilized behavior or sophisticated allure. To some extent, primitivism and innocence were more often linked to sexuality in the New World, whereas Asians were considered victims of their own urbanity. Resemblance of a given practice to that of one's own culture could be embraced or abhorred. Sodomy, bestiality, and prostitution were sometimes proposed as confirmation of the universally fallen nature of humankind and other times read as distinctive signs of a populace's barbarity. Sodomy and prostitution could be interpreted as both savage and sophisticated. The same interpretative flexibility inflects Western attitudes toward *sati*.

The repurposing of older sexual tropes, repertoires, and strategies—such as analogies between body and geopolitical space, the sexualized legend of Ham, and the reincarnation of the Muslim seductress from medieval romance to early modern drama—contributed to new effects of sex in imperial contexts. The recycling of conceptual repertoires in fresh circumstances has been shown to be a prime strategy of racialization, requiring historical methods that employ nonlinear temporalities (Heng 2011a; Loomba 2007, 2016). A view of sexual regimes over the longue durée reveals that they too are subject to nonlinear "cycles of salience," whereby certain perennial preoccupations regarding bodies and intimacies appear as trenchant, go dormant, and reappear according to specific political and social exigencies (Traub 2015).

This is not to suggest that the sexualization of empire reveals a static reiteration of familiar themes or that there was no change over time. Our period begins, after all, when the fourteenth-century *Travels of Sir John Mandeville*, with its depictions of hermaphrodites and Amazons, was still "regarded as the most authoritative and reliable account of the world" (Braude 1997: 116); it ends with the institutionalization of race-based slavery and race laws regulating sexual contact across the Americas, a racially-based caste system in Central and South America, and interracial concubinage poised to become standard practice in East and Southeast Asia. In various places around the globe, certain aspects of sexuality were in the process of acquiring "modern" contours: in addition to the passage and enforcement of sexual-racial laws, these include the emergence of robust religious and medical regulatory apparatuses; the development of "domestic heterosexuality," which locates erotic desire at the heart of conjugal relations; the public appearance of subcultures of sexually like-minded men; the ascription of sapphism onto previously uncontroversial female intimacies; the minoritization of specific erotic practices; the anatomical essentializing of desire into a semiotics of the genitalia; and, for a few early moderns, modes of identification of a sexual "self." The misattribution of these features as exclusively modern requires us to rethink the periodization of sex alongside that of race. In addition, the continual reformulation of these features can train our eye on the fact that the very categories by which sex is "known" (e.g., berdache, tribade, concubine, whore) is itself the product of contingent historical processes (Traub 2015; Spiess 2013). Who decides what counts as a category and which cultural understandings are occluded in that process (Loomba 2009)?

Such changes suggest the extent to which imperial activities and discourses about sex "elsewhere" altered the meanings and management of sex back "home." Texts detailing foreign sexual practices undoubtedly contributed to the erotic educations, imaginaries, and disciplines of countless Europeans. The European ideology of "domestic heterosexuality" emerged not only as a corollary, but partly in consequence of, new patterns of cross-race sex. Representations of Hindu widows, both those who immolated themselves and those who didn't, influenced European discourses on the attributes of a "good wife" (Banerjee 2003). Likewise, polygyny occasioned theological debates about Christian monogamy (Nocentelli 2013). Concerns about the transmission of racialized attributes focused medical attention on the nature and mechanics of conception in ways that would lead to new scientific paradigms (Loomba 2016). Furthermore, the "assessment of an entire people's position on a gradual scale of masculinity," underpinned by increasingly rigid beliefs in the sexual passivity and indolence of Asians and the hypermasculinity and virility of Africans, led to a geospatial mapping of sexual-racial types (Bleys 1996: 45). Of crucial import for Europeans was the gradual shift from a Christian paradigm of sin and metaphor, wherein sexual practices indexed an individual's location on a spectrum of fallenness, to a decontextualized and metonymic paradigm, whereby the sexual proclivities of a few could represent the endemic nature of entire populations (Bleys 1996; Garza Carvajal 2003).

At stake in such macro-level discourses are individual erotic practices, arrangements, and subjectivities. Although one can only speculate about what happened to the penis bells that were brought back by European travelers, numerous sexual "opportunities" were enhanced by global travel. Bigamy was so common in the early years of male migration to the Americas that it was considered the quintessential colonial crime (Brown 1996; Powers 2005). When the Dutch official Joost Schouten was prosecuted for sodomy in 1644, he "declared to have picked up the practice during his stay among the Siamese" (Nocentelli 2013: 39). Referring to the transvestite hoteliers of Fez, Burton speculates that "European notions of sexual identity may have ... formed through encounters with non-European cultures and then filtered back into the urban centres of Europe" (Burton 2013: 498). Although what comprises a sexual "identity" historically remains open to question (Traub 2015), reports about sodomites abroad may have "facilitated the institution of a discourse about same sex-praxis at home," with male cross-gender roles "conducive to identifications of sodomy with femininity on a social level, and with passivity on a sexual level" (Bleys 1996: 44). Perhaps for some European men, the American berdache or Moroccan transvestite made the idea of a public transgender existence more intelligible, contributing to the rise of molly houses. So, too, the image of women pleasuring one another, routinely projected onto Turkish and African women, may have popularized ideas about European sapphists by the late seventeenth century (Traub 2002).

Demographically, as well, the global movements of Europeans affected Europe's own sexual landscapes. Between 1500 and 1650, 100,000 Portuguese and 437,000 Spaniards migrated to the New World (Burbank and Cooper 2010); between 1607 and 1700, 400,000 settlers from the British Isles followed suit (Altman and Horn 1991). This unprecedented long-distance migration, dominated by men, "left hundreds of thousands of women ... in charge of households and family estates," while also limiting Europeans' fertility (Amussen and Poska 2014: 4–5). In addition to women bearing fewer children, the relative paucity of men contributed to higher rates of unmarried women; and as rates of female singleness rose, new affective and sexual possibilities, beyond those traditionally offered single women by the convent, became more available (Bennett and Froide 1999). Analysing the unprecedented number of representations of sapphism in the period around 1600, Susan Lanser observes that many of them crop up in the westernmost edges of Europe, positing that "it may not be accidental that the three major producers of sapphic discourse—England, France, and Spain—are also three of the most heavily expansionist European powers" (Lanser 2014: 73).

At the same time, the number of interracial relationships in Europe's cities grew as more migrants entered Europe. By the 1550s, almost 2,000 Africans were imported into Spain every year (Lawrence 2005; Amussen and Poska 2014), and African slaves were clustered as well in England's thriving ports (Amussen 2007).

As colonization progressed, some Europeans living in Peru, Jamaica, Virginia, the East Indies, and Japan sent their biracial children to be educated as Christians back "home," securing for their sons' legal status as denizens and ensuring that their daughters would not become slaves (Games 2008). The future of such mestizos typically depended on the dispossession of native mothers (Powers 2005). After the death of his mother, Martín, the son of Malintzin and Cortés, accompanied his father to Spain, was legally legitimized, became a knight of Santiago, and died fighting the Moors in the War of Granada (Karttunen 1997). Having spent much of his youth in England, Pocahontas' son Thomas returned to Virginia when he approached twenty years old. In 1641, he asked colonial officials for permission to visit the new ruler, Openchankeno, "to whom he was allied." Yet, after the English executed Openchankeno in 1644, Thomas participated in the ongoing war against his mother's tribe (Townsend 2004). The conflicting loyalties evident in these two cases only begin to suggest the diverse cultural competencies and resilience required of mixed-race people as they sought a sense of cultural belonging.

It has recently been argued that early modern literary critics have overinvested in the negative consequentiality of interracial sex while underestimating what must have been its pervasive, quotidian presence (Grady 2017). It is certainly true that literary critics, in particular, have generally assumed early moderns' attitudes toward interracial sex were uniformly condemnatory—an attitude belied by the thirty-nine interracial marriages officially conducted in London in the early to mid-seventeenth century (Habib 2008). The nearly global presence of mix-raced offspring demonstrates even more conclusively that interracialism was pervasive. While the category confusion posed by mixedness is not in itself subversive of empire (Stoler 2002), racial mixture was, by the end of our period, officially perceived as a threat to social order. Even as ever more stringent laws were devised to regulate it, it continued unabated, resulting in entire societies that, at their foundation, were culturally mixed by means of a complex interweaving of desire and domination, love and fear.

Conceptualizing sexuality *as* (rather than *in*) history, Lanser posits "that sexuality might be not only an effect but a stimulus and that sexual representations might thus have a kind of agency in organizing larger discursive frameworks and in fomenting or forestalling change" (Lanser 2014: 3). In the context of empire, sexuality was just such a stimulus. Engaging in quotidian acts of sexual pleasure, coercion, negotiation, and violence, people involved in the emerging "web of empire" (Games 2008) contributed to the destruction and creation of families, sexual subcultures, settlements, and, eventually, nations. Along with the massive disruption of indigenous sexual cultures, epistemic changes forged by the sexuality of empire ultimately led to new global formations of race, marriage, reproduction, inheritance, prostitution, sodomy, and slavery.

CHAPTER SEVEN

Resistance

SU FANG NG

In *The Wealth of Nations* (1766), Adam Smith identified colonial expansion as the source of European wealth: "The discovery of America, and that of a passage to the East Indies by the Cape of Good Hope, are the two greatest and most important events recorded in the history of mankind." But he also lamented the resulting oppression: "To the natives, however, both of the East and West Indies, all the commercial benefits which can have resulted from those events have been sunk and lost in the dreadful misfortunes which they have occasioned" (Smith 1776: IV.7.166). Early modern discoveries initiated Europe's first age of imperialism. By the late eighteenth century an ascendant Europe was poised to dominate most of the modern world. But this centuries-long shift was gradual and uncertain. Eastern Europe was itself under threat of colonization by an expanding Ottoman empire. For much of the period western Europe was an economic backwater. Colonial expansion proceeded in fits and starts. Neither European empire nor native resistance to it was unified. Different European groups competed for trade and territory even as equally factious native groups, whether in the Americas, Asia, or Africa, clashed with each other, sometimes working with Europeans and other times resisting them.

Cultures of resistance were quite various. Resistance could take overt forms of violence or be expressed in everyday acts. In response to bloody wars of conquests, like the ones the Spanish empire waged in the Americas, native resistance was violent and explosive, taking shape in armed conflicts, frontier wars, or slave rebellions. On the Malabar coast, Portuguese attempts to control the pepper trade faced continual armed resistance from Asians, especially in the guise of so-called "piracy" (Pearson 1979; Pearson 1988: 44–51). Indirect expressions of resistance, which James Scott calls everyday forms, the "ordinary weapons of relatively powerless groups: foot dragging, dissimulation, desertion, false compliance, pilfering, feigned ignorance, slander, arson, sabotage, and so on," were equally important cultural practices (Scott 1985: xvi). Natives contested European imperialism through legal channels as well, advancing counter-claims against European claims of possession and dominion in the contact zone, that interstitial third space of cultural hybridity and conflict (Adorno 1987; Pratt 1991; Belmessous 2012a).[1] This contestation extended to literary representations of Europeans, for instance in Indonesian chronicles, discussed later. Cultural forms of resistance thus manifested both in ordinary practices and in contested meanings of written productions, whether documentary, legal, or literary.

It is important to keep in mind that native resistance against Europeans was sometimes linked to or even originated with their resistance against local political authorities. Just as early modern western European "New Monarchies" consolidated power by curbing the feudal aristocracy to create national administrative, fiscal, military, and even religious institutions, outside Europe too similar processes of state centralization took place, even in small Southeast Asian states like Makassar (South Sulawesi, Indonesia) and Ayudhya (Thailand) (Slavin 1964; Goodman 1988; Caldwell 1995; Kulku 1986).[2] Monarchies from Europe to Southeast Asian polities to the Ottoman empire and elsewhere were internally riven by territorial disputes (Elliott 1992; Goffman and Stroop 2004). Territories peripheral to emerging national centers, whether Scotland or Catalonia or the Bugis kingdom of Luwuq in South Sulawesi, were vulnerable to secessionist movements. In these political conflicts, outsiders were often recruited to support the expansion of the state or the resistance of the peripheries, gaining trading privileges in exchange for their collaboration. Consequently, European conquistadors or merchants often found themselves embroiled in local conflicts. Whether it be the Spanish in the Americas or the Dutch in the East Indies, Europeans expanded their colonies with the help of native allies, while native groups became embroiled in intra-European competition.

Cultures of resistance developed out of a dynamic of conflict and collaboration between natives and Europeans. This dynamic led to the borrowing, adaptation, and appropriation of ideas and tropes of resistance in both directions. As accounts of native resistance, especially from the early days of Spanish conquest of the Americas, filtered back to Europe, European critics of imperialism, such as Bartolomé de las Casas, used them to protest the abuses of natives. Dominican criticisms of Spanish subjugation of Indians were developed into explicit theories of anti-imperial resistance and were subsequently used in European wars of independence, fueling revolutions like the Dutch Revolt, discussed later. Although native resistance most usually has to be recognized in acts rather than in documents, some European writings traveled back to colonial America where they were incorporated into native writing: arguing for his land rights, the Peruvian noble Felipe Guaman Poma de Ayala references de las Casas in his more than 1000-page illustrated chronicle of Andean history in Spanish and in Quechua (Adorno 1986). Native uprisings in the Americas, Asia, and Africa were paralleled by peasant uprisings in Europe, for the consolidation and expansion of European monarchies meant colonization of peripheral lands. Such colonization at home, as well as colonization abroad, fueled explicit theories of anti-imperial resistance while other processes of state centralization, such as the expansion of taxation, sparked anti-monarchical discourses. European peasant uprisings, ideologically inchoate, were themselves responses to the wrenching economic transformations that took place as direct result of overseas imperial expansion.

This essay first considers New World interactions and the variety of Native American resistance to European colonization, covering the gamut of cultural strategies outlined earlier, before turning to how resistance theories focusing on natural law developed in Europe out of that early history of conquest. The final section examines how natural-law arguments were transferred to the East Indies and Africa, where Europeans took advantage of local political rifts to insert themselves in local economic systems, though anti-colonial resistance also took diverse forms, in everyday practice, in diplomatic and legal culture, in religious movements, and in literary works. The circulation of ideas meant that both empire and developing anti-colonial cultures of resistance in Europe and the rest of the world were not wholly separate.

CONQUEST AND COLONY

In the late sixteenth century a small emerging nation-state, seeking to throw off the Spanish yoke, began employing an anti-colonial discourse that drew analogies between themselves and Native Americans. In a manifesto, their leader wrote, "I have bin a witnes of their advise, by which they adjudged all you to death, making no more account of you, than of beastes, if they had had power to have murthered you, as they do in the Indies, where they have miserablie put to death, more than twentie millions of people" (*Apologie* 1581: sig. F4). This leader of an anti-imperial independence movement was no other than William of Orange, the *stadthouder*, steward or lord, of the Netherlands, who further noted that the Spanish "have made desolate & waste, thirtie tymes as much lande in quantitie and greatnes, as the lowe countrie is, with such horrible excesses and ryottes, that all the barbarousnesses, cruelties, and tyrannies, whiche have ever bin co[m]mitted, are but sport, in respect of that, which hath fallen out upon the poore Indians, which thing, even by their owne Bishoppes and Doctours, hath bin left in writing" (*Apologie*, sig. F4). William's *Apologie* was published in 1581, the year of the Act of Abjuration when most of the Dutch provinces declared independence from Hapsburg Spain.

In the decades to follow, warfare on the battleground was accompanied by a war in print. Dutch political pamphlets, histories, poetry, print, and paintings depicted the Low Countries as another America, brutally colonized by the Spanish (Schmidt 2001). The anonymous *Politicq onderwijs* (Political Education, 1582) argued for renouncing Philip II because he would "treat us, our wives, children and their descendants as he has in all cruelty treated the Indians" (van Gelderen 1993b: 209). Georgius Benedicti's 1586 Latin historical poem on the feats of Prince William draws on the comparison in depicting a murderous Duke of Alva:

> Dicta placent: fremit ipse ferox, sitiensque cruoris
> Ducendas in bella acies atque agmina poscit.
> Miles adest, et iam plenis occurrere campis
> Hostem optat, iterum vastari caedibus Indos
> Sperat, et ignotum quaeri nova regna per aequor. (Benedicti 1990: 24–5,
>   ll. 89–93, my English translation)

[The words please [Alva]: he growls ferociously and, thirsting for blood, calls on the keen troop who will be led into wars. The soldier, ready, longs to meet at last the enemy on the full field, hopes once again for the Indians to be laid waste in massacres and new kingdoms found across an unknown sea.]

In this vivid picture of Alva's bloodthirsty slaughter of Indians on the marshy fields of Holland—the modern Dutch edition translates *caedibus* as *in bloedbaden* (in bloodbaths)—Benedicti's poem collapses the distinction between Dutch and Indian. Ironically, Dutch comparison to America had Spanish inspiration. The Duke of Alva told Philip II, "If Your majesty looks closely at what is to be done [in the Netherlands] you will see that it amounts to creating a New World" (quoted in Parker 2014: 196). The Habsburgs took a similar view of their possessions in Italy: an anonymous Spaniard wrote back from Milan, "For these Italians, although they are not Indians, have to be treated as such, so that they will understand that we are in charge of them and not they in charge of us" (quoted in Koenigsberger 1969: 48). Dutch revolutionary discourse inverted Spanish rhetoric of conquest. They even extended this discourse to Asia: writing to the sultan of Aceh in 1600, Prince Maurice, stadtholder of the Dutch Republic, compares Aceh's war with the Portuguese to the war the Dutch waged against the Spanish (at the time Portugal was under Spanish rule with the union of crowns), accusing the Spanish of "seeking to take away your freedom and to put you in subjection as slaves, as he has tried to do in these Provinces for the space of more than thirty continuous years (pretendiendo de quitarles su libertad y ponerles en subiection como a esclavos, como lo han pretendido de hazar en estas Provincias por el espacio de mas de treinta annos continos, Unger 1948: 133).[3] In the Dutch Revolt, anti-imperial discourse found a new geography as it circulated from the New World back to the Old, even as European nomenclature for Asia and the Americas, the East and West Indies, made its recirculation easy.

As I have shown, Dutch and Spanish understanding of their relations to each other as colonial was informed by the dynamics of Spanish New World imperialism. But even as New World relations came to define Old World ones, Old World ideas and institutions were also translated back to the New. Spanish conquistadors turned repeatedly to the example of the ancient Roman empire as a parallel to their own deeds. Bernal Díaz, Hernán Cortés, and others equated the fall of Tenochtitlán to the Roman destruction of Jerusalem in AD 70 (Lupher 2003: 35–6). As J.H. Elliott points out, for both Spain and Britain, which were proto-colonial powers with long histories of internal colonization and renewed early modern expansion—Spain's *Reconquista* of Muslim Granada and Tudor England's reconquest of Catholic Ireland—"the pattern of combined conquest and colonization was equally well established" and was "easily transportable to distant parts of the world in … overseas expansion." (Elliott 2006: 17).[4] Cortés followed *Reconquista* practice, setting aside a fifth of the booty for the royal coffers and referring to Mesoamerican temples as "mosques" (Cortés 1963: 51; quoted in Elliott 2006: 18). Christian Spain's *Reconquista*, which expelled Muslims from the Iberian Peninsula in an attempt to erase its long history of Islamic heritage, was invoked in the New: at his formal entry into Cuzco, Peru in 1570, Viceroy Francisco de Toledo was welcomed with a pageant of Christian knights in mock combat with "Moors" played by Indians in a "metonymical substitution of one Conquista for the other" (Clissold 1954: 64; quoted in Fuchs 2001: 1, 74).

Imperial conquest depended on native help. Considered the most important Spanish conquest, Tenochtitlán's fall traces the familiar pattern of native collaboration with Europeans. Cortés's arrival coincided with the Aztec prophecy of the return of white god Quetzalcoatl; initially welcomed by Montezuma, he then made war on the Aztecs. But the Spanish only defeated the Aztecs with the help of Tlaxcalans, an independent native group whom the Aztecs had tried to subjugate (Thomas 1993; Restall 2003). This alliance was cemented in intimate and sexual relations, including the crucial role of Cortés's interpreter, a Nahua woman given to him as a slave. Named Malinalli, otherwise known as La Malinche or Doña Marina, she was a bilingual who spoke Nahuatl and Mayan and later acquired Castilian. Hugh Thomas writes, "The pair constituted a duet which often combined eloquence with subtlety, piety with menace, sophistication with brutality" (Thomas 1993: 172). Tlaxcalans helped not only in the initial conquest but also in the establishment of a hybrid colonial state, colonizing the frontier by creating "webs of self-replicating colonies that drew nomadic frontier peoples into the emerging colonial society"; in so doing they were both "cultural intermediaries" and "authors of their own local political systems" (McEnroe 2012: 5).[5] Tlaxcalan military resistance was thus first directed against an indigenous empire rather than Europeans. In the process, they created a hybridized political culture.

Aside from armed conflict and violent revolts, resistance also took indirect forms such as escape and suicide, sabotage, work stoppages, thefts, and others. The first American colony, established on the Caribbean island of Hispaniola (Dominican Republic) by Christopher Columbus in 1493, had a difficult start. Native Americans taken to Spain and brought back as interpreters absconded as soon as they could, and the thirty-nine Spaniards left behind were all dead. Two years later, Columbus suppressed a large revolt and sent five hundred of the 1,500 captured Native Americans to Spain as slaves. With gold's discovery in 1499, a system of forced labor was put in place. When disease and desertion depleted the numbers of indigenous slaves, slaves were imported from Africa. These slaves vigorously resisted their captors during transportation in mutinies and shipboard revolts.[6] Hispaniola also saw the first major revolt of African slaves only two decades after its founding. The 1522 Christmas Day revolt started on the sugar plantation of the governor, Diego Columbus, Christopher's son, and involved about twenty slaves, wielding machetes to cut down people and cattle in their path, moving from plantation to plantation, only to be put down harshly by December 28. Led by prisoners of war from Senegal, Wolof men who were predominantly Muslim, the revolt's aim might have been as much escape as anything else (Gomez 2005: 3–4, 16).

Until the 1791 Haitian Revolution, the many slave revolts did not produce a mature ideology of resistance. However, escape was one among the cultural strategies of premodern societies Michael Adas calls "avoidance protest," whereby "dissatisfied groups seek to attenuate their hardships and express their discontent through flight, sectarian withdrawal, or other activities that minimize challenges to or clashes with those whom they view as their oppressors," a mode of protest found from Southeast Asia to Antiguan slave communities (Adas 1981: 217; Gaspar 1993). Although the early documentary evidence is from European sources, we can learn something about the nature of early slave revolts from Spanish fears about them and Spanish cultural taxonomy of their subaltern subjects. As early as 1503 complaints circulated about enslaved *ladinos*, who spoke Spanish or Portuguese and were Muslim, encouraging the indigenous community to resist Christianity. Non-Spanish speaking Africans, *bozales*, believed to be more submissive, were preferred by slave owners. Just as *Reconquista* methods were transferred to the Americas, so too was the greater suspicion of Muslim slaves, especially North and West African, from Iberian Christians' experience of conflicts with Muslim populations and states such as Morocco in the Mediterranean (Gomez 2005: 4–5, 15). In early Hispaniola, rebellion was most often fomented by Muslim Senegambians, resilient and adaptable, who were able to bring their cattle culture to colonial life, becoming cowboys and ranchers (*vaqueros* and *ganaderos*); a contemporary poem describes them as "warlike Gilosos / With the vain arrogance of gentry" (Castellanos 1997: 100, elegy 5, canto 2; quoted in Gomez 2005: 17).[7] Spanish religious discrimination imported from the Old World in the form of a ban on the transportation of Muslims, Jews, and *ladinos* did not stop *bozales* and indigenous peoples from revolting and forming maroon societies (Price 1996; Diouf 2014).

Indigenous peoples also became familiar with European law by resisting through the courts, especially in disputes over land title, and thus developing a legal culture of resistance. Patricia Seed's influential argument that different European groups employed distinct techniques of claiming territorial possession—"Englishmen held that they acquired rights to the New World by physical objects, Frenchmen by gestures, Spaniards by speech, Portuguese by numbers, Dutch by description"—assumes that these ceremonies were incomprehensible across cultures (Seed 1995: 179). Other scholars argue that indigenous peoples also use legal arguments to resist their dispossession, such as the Wabanaki Indians whose opposition to European land titles was unwittingly recorded by the French seeking to pursue their own claims against the English (Belmessous 2012a, 2012b). The Tlaxcalans again provide an important example of indigenous claim-making as anti-colonial resistance. R. Jovita Baber shows they adapted their petitions in response to shifts in Spanish political culture: in the first decade of Spanish conquest, Tlaxcalans used a rhetoric of loyal service to the prince, emphasizing their role in the conquest; when the military government was converted into an imperial bureaucracy, the Tlaxcalans changed their rhetoric to one of supporting good government; later, when the Spanish Crown started using *indios* as a legal category, their rhetoric shifted into pleading for Spanish elites to protect them as vulnerable *indios miserables* (miserable Indians) (Baber 2010, 2012). The Tlaxcalans used their alliance with Cortés to ask for rights and privileges, including protection of their lands by prohibiting Spanish ownership of them: "We appear with this petition and humbly present ourselves and prostrate ourselves at the royal feet of your majesty asking that you ... not award ranches to Spaniards within the limits of our land and province" (Archivo General de Indias [AGI], Mexico, 94, N.2; quoted in Baber 2012: 53). They successfully got the Crown to forbid land grants to Spanish owners near native villages, a royal mandate that was promulgated for all of the American kingdoms and included in *Recopilación de leyes*, a 1680 compilation of colonial laws (Spain 1681: Ley 12, Titulo XII, Libro IV).

In North America the absence of silver and gold meant there were no fabulous fortunes to be made; plantation rather than conquest therefore became the major mode. The English in the early Jamestown colony faced armed resistance from a formidable opponent. Wahunsonacock, the Powhatan chief, whose wars of conquest established his empire over the region's various Algonquian-speaking tribes, took advantage of English military alliance (and muskets) to overawe other tribes and kept the English dependent on him for food supplies (Axtell 1988; Roundtree 1990; Gleach, 1997). William Strachey's account of the Virginia colony testifies to their ferocity by including an Algonquin war-song, which he termed a "scornefull song," celebrating the slaughter of the English: commenting that the natives mocked them for crying, Strachey conceded, "yt is true they never bemoane themselues, nor cry out, giving vp so much as a groane for any death how cruell soever and full of Torment" (Strachey 1953: 85–6).[8] More wily than Montezuma, Wahunsonacock was not so easily overcome. The Powhatans and the English alternated between peace and hostility until the 1622 massacre of 400 of the colonists (Figure 7.1), after which the English slowly gained ascendancy.

In North America, Native Americans' resistance strategies included subterfuge, such as kidnapping and spying, as well as alliance-making, but these were also employed by Europeans. Early Virginia was an example of Richard White's "middle ground," where mutual accommodation created a common cultural arena not dominated by either side (White 1991). Additionally, in the

FIGURE 7.1: Jamestown Massacre. Woodcut by Mattäus Merian, 1628. Credit: MPI/Getty Images.

Algonquians, the English found a people similar to themselves, engaging through what Joyce Chaplin calls a "permeable barrier between self and other," for like the English, the Algonquian martial culture was centered on the bow and arrow (Chaplin 2001: 85).[9] Their chiefdom, which exalted the hereditary leader, was a political structure not dissimilar to Jacobean England's. Andrew Fitzmaurice argues that both Wahunsonacock and James I had to distribute goods to maintain control of powerful subjects, that both contended with scarce resources to do so, and both had to put down rebellions, in James's case the Percy rebellion and in Wahunsonacock's case the unruly tributary *werowances* (leaders); Strachey even defined Wahunsonacock's authority in the language of Jacobean divine right kingship in describing the English being awestruck by "the Impression of divine nature" (Strachey 1953: 60; Fitzmaurice 2012: 93–5) (Figure 7.2). During the Jamestown colony's occupation, both sides sent spies to gather information. Strachey mentions Thomas Savage, a boy of thirteen sent to live with the Powhatans to learn their language, as well as natives who learned English (Strachey 1953: 61–2). Wahunsonacock used Pocahontas as his intermediary and spy, for as a young girl she did not threaten the English colony. Pocahontas's adoption of John Smith as her father was part of a Powhatan strategy of kinship alliance to subsume the English as one of their tributary tribes. The incident of Pocahontas's supposed rescue of John Smith was very likely a ceremony of adoption, and Pocahontas's marriage to John Rolfe was an extension of that tributary alliance-making (Zandt 2008: 65–85).[10]

FIGURE 7.2: Theodore de Bry. Indians testing the immortality of the westerners, 1594. Credit: Rijksmuseum, the Netherlands.

A series of uprisings, conflicts, and wars marked the period of English, French, and Dutch settlement of coastal North America and their competition for resources, from the three Powhatan wars in the early seventeenth century to the devastating King Philip's War in New England in 1676–8 (Oberg 2003; Drake 1999). As cultural boundaries hardened, settlers abandoned Christian evangelism, increasingly viewed Indians as savage, and developed a separate Euro-American identity distinct from their European origins (Lepore 1999). European encroachment became increasingly difficult for Native Americans to resist effectively, though this transformation happened later in places further away from the east coast, whether the Arkansas Valley held by one or another Indian tribe through the eighteenth century, or the Comanche empire that rose up in the American Southwest in the eighteenth and early nineteenth centuries.[11] Michael Witgen even argues that until the middle of the nineteenth century Native Americans controlled most of North America with European colonies largely confined to the eastern seaboard (Witgen 2012). Over time, Native Americans lost the middle ground but the end came at different points in time for different regions.

RESISTANCE THEORIES

Imperial rapacity created the conditions for early European articulations of anti-imperialism. The Dominican critique of New World abuses built on the foundation of natural law (*ius gentium*) to dispute characterization of Native Americans as natural slaves and to assert their right to dominion over their lands. Moreover, justifications advanced for their resisting Spanish empire in the New World supplied key elements for those resisting political authority in Europe. In both cases, tyranny was understood to limit the extent of a ruler's sovereignty. Arguments from natural law were also applied to defend anti-monarchical resistance in European revolutions. But in the East Indies, natural-law arguments supported European colonization. This section considers natural-law arguments as they were developed in Europe while the next will address how they were used for colonizing the East Indies and consequent indigenous responses.

Criticism of Spanish abuses began with the moral quandary posed by Columbus's enslavement of Native Americans. Having depicted them as amenable to conversion, Columbus's shipment of five hundred Native Americans as slaves to Europe called into question the nature of Spain's imperial enterprise. Such enslavement conflicted with the terms of Pope Alexander's bull donating the New World to Spain, whose declared purpose was bringing natives into the Catholic faith. Reports of widespread heresy among the Spanish colonists forced King Ferdinand to send Dominicans, the order most associated with the Inquisition, to investigate; the priests' arrival in the New World in 1510 initiated the Dominican reform movement that focused attention on the Spanish's unjust treatment of Indians. The chronicle of abuses in Bartolomé de las Casas's enormously influential *A Short Account of the Destruction of the Indies* (1552), which was subsequently translated into Dutch, French, English, and German, helped create the Spanish Black Legend that became grist for Protestant literary mills: Edmund Spenser's *Faerie Queene*, for example, depicted Spanish "hunger of gold" (Read 1990; Greer *et al.* 2007). The engravings of Theodore de Bry, a Protestant convert, gave visual life to the Black Legend by depicting scenes of cruelty from las Casas's text as well as scenes of native revolt (de las Casas 1598). Criticisms of Spanish tyranny circulated in Europe as part of Protestant resistance against Catholic Spain. The most spectacular example is one I discussed earlier—the Dutch Revolt that inspired subsequent anti-Hapsburg rebellions, in Naples in 1584, Bohemia in 1619, and Catalonia in the 1640s (Villari 1993; Mastellone 1983; Elliott 1963).

Defenders of empire described natives as Aristotelian natural slaves, without rational autonomy and deserving of enslavement: in his controversy with de las Casas, Juan Ginés de Sepúlveda insisted that all barbarians, including Native Americans, were natural slaves (de Sepúlveda and de las Casas 1975). The Dominicans countered by rehearsing the basic principles of man's natural rights derived from "the central tenet of Thomistic-Humanist philosophy that all humans possessed the common element of reason" (Williams 1990: 93).[12] Christianizing Aristotle's idea that political society exists by nature, Thomas Aquinas argued that God gave everyone reason so that even heathens know right from wrong. In a sermon preached in Hispaniola in 1511, Antonio de Montesinos castigated the colonists and defended the natives' natural rights to their land as rational beings possessed of a soul. Perhaps the most important figure in the debates over the Indians' rational capacity was Francisco de Vitoria, who argued that all men were created in God's image. Pointing to evidence of native social order, and therefore of natural reason, he asserted that they "undoubtedly possessed as true dominion, both public and private, as any Christians." Vitoria considered that the conquistadores "can allege no title other than *the law of war*," which he termed "sheer robbery," for war was waged "not against strangers, but against true vassals of the emperor, as if they were natives of Seville" (Vitoria 1991: 332; see Williams 1990: 93–108).

Natural law (*ius gentium*), the concept central to Vitoria's defense of native dominion, was also key to resisting monarchical tyranny in Europe. Since natural law—Aquinas's amalgamation of Augustine and Aristotle, which insisted that all human beings have God-given capacity for reason—overlaps with divine law—some early modern thinkers like John Milton even equated them, suggesting that "the law of God agrees exactly with the law of nature"—it cannot be contravened by positive law, making it possible to resist temporal authority and even to depose kings (Milton 1991: 149). It was important to

Calvinist resistance theories from Luther to the British Marian exiles of 1550s and the Huguenots writing after the traumatic 1572 St. Bartholomew's Day Massacre; figures like John Knox, John Ponet, and Theodore Beza, all turned to natural law to justify resisting tyrants (Tuck 1979; Shoenberger 1977: 61–76; VanDrunen 2005–6: 143–67; Salmon 1959). These resistance theories, including a particularly influential Huguenot tract, the anonymous *Vindiciae contra tyrannos* (1579) emphasizing the supremacy of natural law or divine law, became the foundation for the Dutch Revolt and the English Revolution (Brutus 1994; van Gelderen 1986; Israel 1982; Parker 1977; Tracy 2008). The ideological conflict in these revolutions was over whether sovereignty was absolute or contractual: in the English Revolution Milton and Parliamentary apologists argued that the king's tyranny invalidates his sovereignty (Sirluck 1959: 12–25; White 1996). European debates paralleling those taking place in the Americas about the right of natives to resist hinged on the legitimacy of Spain's sovereignty. The Tlaxcalans used their alliance with Spain—like the Algonquians—as a resistance strategy. Asserting that they "treated [the Spanish] and loved them as our own brothers," they argued that their voluntary obedience made their relationship to Philip II a contractual one, and thus put limits on Spanish sovereignty (quoted in Baber 2012: 46).

Resistance against Spanish tyranny produced two seminal works of international law (called the law of nations in the early modern period), whose reformulations of the work of Vitoria and other Iberian theologians at the University of Salamanca were translated to European colonies in other parts of the world. While originally natural-law arguments were used to defend the rights of Native Americas, when they were imported to Asia and elsewhere, the force of the arguments were reversed to justify European colonization. The first, Alberico Gentili's *De iure belli* (The right of war, 1589), generalized Vitoria's arguments beyond the American case and secularized them. An Italian Protestant exile at Oxford, Gentili was among the circle of promoters of the Virginia Company, including Samuel Purchas, who also turned to Vitoria to criticize Spanish imperialism. However, Gentili, Purchas, and their circle distinguished between conquest and the right to trade and self-defense, a distinction that opened the door to colonial justifications. Insisting on their right to trade with indigenous peoples, they also justified taking up arms to defend themselves in conflicts with these trading partners. Furthermore, when it came to their own plantations, English colonists shied away from applying Vitoria's argument that Native Americans had reason; instead they recategorized those they encountered from humans with civil society to barbarians similar to wild animals (*ferae bestiae*), and they classified the land as *terra nullius* (empty land); this strand of thought culminated in John Locke's dismissal of Native Americans' natural-law rights in *The Second Treatise of Government* (Fitzmaurice 2007, 2003; Arneil 1996). The English thus inverted the force of the natural-law argument to justify dispossessing indigenous peoples of their lands.

The second foundational work of international law, Hugo Grotius's *De iure belli ac pacis* (The rights of war and peace, 1625), also argues for Europeans' right of self-preservation (Tuck 1999: 68–108; van Gelderen 1993a). But his ideas were motivated by his defense of Dutch mercantilism. In particular, his 1608 *Mare Liberum*, "The Freedom of the Seas, or the Right which belongs to the Dutch to take part in the East Indian trade," turned to natural-rights theories to defend Dutch East India Company (VOC) profit from trade, navigation, and even piracy. His cousin Jacob van Heemskerk had captained the seizure of the Portuguese carrack *Sta. Catarina* in the Straits of Melaka, challenging Portugal's claim to ownership of the oceans. Grotius, a lawyer employed by the VOC, defended the Dutch by arguing that the seas were an open space, unlike land that could be carved out territorially; in the particular case of the *Sta. Catarina*, VOC alliance with the king of Johor, who laid hereditary claim to the throne of Melaka, provided additional legal justification (Borschberg 1999). Grotius established that East Indians have sovereignty over their domain and the freedom to choose their trading partners: "But that the Portugals are not lords of those parts whither the Hollanders go—to wit, of Java, Tabrobana and the greatest part of the Moluccas—. . . These islands we speak of have, and always had, their kings, their commonwealth, their laws and their liberties. Trading is granted to the Portugals as to other nations; therefore, when they both pay tribute and obtain liberty of trade of the princes, they testify sufficiently that they are not lords but arrive there as foreigners" (Grotius 2004: 13). Even if they were infidels, the East Indians had the right to rule themselves and to deprive them of their property "is theft and robbery no less than if the same be done to Christians" (Grotius 2004: 15). Two key elements of his natural law are self-interest and abstaining from injuring others, which "stressed individuality in the area of rights, but communality in the area of obligation" (Tuck 1979: 97; Haakonssen 1996: 26–30). Like the Virginian colonists, Grotius used the natural-law argument of native civil society against the Portuguese but when it came to Dutch trading interests, Grotius defended the justice of exclusive contracts with local rulers, which the VOC enforced with military power and thus encroached on native sovereignty (Ittersum 2006; Borschberg 2011).

Originating in the Americas and generalized for anti-monarchical resistance in Europe, natural-rights arguments that migrated to the East Indies became self-interested. Using natural-law theories against the Iberians, northern Europeans turned them to advantage in their own dealings with indigenous peoples. Furthermore, when the English tried to use free trade arguments, Grotius insisted that VOC contracts with indigenous rulers were binding and exclusive. Proving as rapacious as the Iberians, the Dutch drove a slave trade in the Indian Ocean, adopting indigenous forms of chattel and other slavery, but grafting on them a justifying discourse of Christian humanism (Vink 2003). As a mercantilist commonwealth, the defense of their sovereignty was closely tied to their trading interests. Displacing the Iberians in colonial trade in seventeenth century, the Dutch became the focus of native resistance around the Indian Ocean as the new Spaniards.

COMMERCE AND COMPETITION

European explorers to the East Indies sought direct access to spices, but they were belated arrivals to a thriving Asian-centered world economy.[13] The first Europeans to reach India—Vasco da Gama arrived in Calicut in 1498—the Portuguese conquered a series of port-cities from Goa to Melaka. But *Estado da India* was not gained without native resistance. Despite European attempts at monopoly, Asian trade networks persisted, rerouting to bypass European-controlled ports. Holden Furber has named this the "Age of Partnership," challenging previous Eurocentric views that overestimated European dominance, while other scholars characterize the era as the "Age of Competition" to account for rivalry as well as cooperation (Furber 1969; Chaudhury and Morineau 1999). In the seventeenth century, Northern Europeans pioneering the joint-stock company outpaced Iberians in colonial adventuring. The Dutch and English East India Companies made incursions into the Portuguese colonial empire by cooperating with indigenous allies. Even as they intervened in local conflicts, Europeans brought their own rivalries to Asia. In this multipolar world, non-European responses to European incursions were complex, ranging from armed conflict to more indirect forms of resistance, including counter-claims and even strategic alliances.[14]

Bringing armed trading to the Indian Ocean, the Portuguese met with armed resistance from South Africa to Southeast Asia. At the Cape of Good Hope, the Portuguese came into explosive contact with the Khoikhoi or Khoisan. The Portuguese encroached on Khoikhoi herders' water rights, disregarded their customs about the privacy of women, children, and encampments, and simply offered bad trade. The account of Vasco da Gama's first voyage, attributed to Álvaro Velho, reports that when one of the Portuguese, Bartolomeu Dias, "was taking water from a watering hole, . . . they [the Khoikhoi] sought to prevent this. They pelted him with stones from atop a hill overlooking that spot" (Gama 2009: 40; see also Boonzaier *et al.* 1996: 52–64). Dias then killed one of them with his crossbow. The Portuguese had not gained permission to access water, and the Khoikhoi were defending their water sources. In 1510, the Portuguese had an even greater clash with them: after trading calico and iron for cattle, they visited the Khoikhoi village, where a fight broke out and they were chased back to their ship. While some Portuguese accounts blame the Khoikhoi, Gaspar de Corrêa suggests that "they feared we might wish to build a fortress there also and take their watering place, and thus they would lose their cattle" and even points out that "it is always the character of the Portuguese to endeavor to rob the poor natives of the country of their property" (Theal 1964: 2.46). To exact revenge, the first viceroy of India, Dom Francisco de Almeida and a contingent of 150 men returned to the village to set fire to their huts and kidnap children and cattle, whereupon the enraged Khoikhoi retaliated. Although the Portuguese were armed with swords, lances, and crossbows while the Khoikhoi had only stones and fire-hardened wood, their accuracy at throwing these missiles killed sixty-five Portuguese, including Almeida: João de Barros notes in his *Da Asia* (1553) that they were "killed by sticks and stones, hurled not by giants or armed men but by bestial negroes, the most brutal of all that coast" (Theal 1964: 6.302).[15] After that massacre, the Portuguese avoided Table Bay.

Although more successful elsewhere, the Portuguese nonetheless faced other forms of resistance. While their capture of Melaka was a major coup—Tomé Pires said, "Whoever is lord of Malacca has his hands on the throat of Venice" (Pires 1944: 2.287)—they never had a completely secure hold on the city. Trade dispersed to other regional ports, and between the 1511 Portuguese conquest and their loss of the city in 1641 to an alliance of the Dutch and the native kingdom of Johor, there were numerous attempts at recovering Malacca (Reid 1993: 208–14; Bassett 1960). With Europeans disrupting Islamic trade networks, resistance to them took on a religious aspect; arguably, in such communities the culture of resistance turned into religious practice. This period of commercial expansion went hand-in-hand with intense Islamicization and Christianization in Southeast Asia. Direct contact with missionary Jesuits and with Mecca and the Ottoman caliphate, as Anthony Reid notes, "sharpen[ed] the spirit of confrontation with unbelief as aggressively represented by the Portuguese" (Reid 1993: 133–4). The Ottoman empire aided fellow Muslims in their war against the Portuguese, sending firearms to Ethiopian Muslims in 1527—the Portuguese responded by sending 400 musketeers to the Christian king and the Ottomans countered by sending 900 musketeers the following year—and sending soldiers and gunners to the sultan of Aceh in the 1530s in exchange for four shiploads of pepper. It was as much an Ottoman age of exploration as it was European (Oliver and Atmore 2001: 123–7; Özbaran 1995: 55–70; Casale 2010).

This history was recalled in chronicles and literary romances. The sixteenth-century chronicle *Sejarah Melayu* (Malay Annals) calls the Portuguese "Feringgi," Malay for Franks, a term alluding to medieval Christian crusaders. This association is reinforced by the text's turn to a Persian romance of Prophet Muhammad's uncle, *Hikayat Amir Hamzah*, as a model of anti-European heroism: on the eve of the Portuguese attack on Melaka, the sultan offers this romance as a war story to encourage his men. A. Samad Ahmad suggests that the sultan may be alluding to the episode where Amir Hamzah and his son prince Rastam fight the Portuguese, beating them from Khursand (Saudi Arabia) back to Portugal (Ahmad 1987: ix). While targeting the Portuguese as commercial and religious enemies, the seventeenth-century Acehnese chronicle *Hikayat Aceh* explicitly depicts a geopolitical alignment with the Ottomans, attributing to the Ottoman sultan the praise of Aceh's king as a defender of Islam: "Maka yang daripada pihak maghrib kitalah raja yang besar, dan daripada pihak masyrik itu Seri Sultan Perkasa 'Alam raja yang besar dan raja yang mengeraskan agama Allah dan agama Rasul Allah" (From the western side we are the most great king, and from the eastern side Seri Sultan Perkasa 'Alam is the great king and the one who presses the cause of Allah's religion and the religion of the messenger of Allah) (Iskandar 2001: 96, my translation).

Armed conflicts between natives and Europeans were sometimes the consequence of cross-cultural and cross-religious alliances. One of the earliest examples of armed resistance against Europeans—the 1521 Battle of Mactan in the Philippines fought between Ferdinand Magellan and a chieftain named Lapu-Lapu—was also an example of European-Asian alliance. Lapu-Lapu is now celebrated as the Philippines's first national hero for killing Magellan. This nationalist celebration is anachronistic not only because the Philippines did not yet exist as a nation-state but also because Lapu-Lapu fought not against the Spanish but against a regional centralizing power, the kingdom of Cebu. However, it is telling that Antonio Pigafetta's account of their first meeting with Humabon, facilitated by Magellan's Malay interpreter, depicted the Iberians in the position of power:

> The interpreter told the king that, since his master was the captain of so great a king, he did not pay tribute to any lord in the world, and that if the king wished peace he would have peace, but if war, he would have war. Thereupon, the Moor merchant said to the king 'Cata raia chita,' that is to say, 'Look well, sire, these men are the same who have conquered Calicut, Malacca, and all India Major. If they are treated well, they will give good treatment, but if they are treated badly, they will deliver bad treatment and worse, as they have done to Calicut and Malacca.' (Pigafetta 2007: 43)

What the visiting Muslim merchant said was a simple Malay phrase, "*Kata raja kita*," meaning "So spoke our king."[16] Pigafetta's translation elaborates this short sentence into an extended warning about prior Portuguese conquests, implying that awe of those powers cemented the alliance with Humabon and his people and enabled their conversion to Catholicism. He suggests that even Spain's foes acknowledge her military strength.

But the Battle of Mactan fits uneasily in a simple narrative of anti-colonial resistance against European domination. Rather, Cebu was another centralizing state, expanding economic and political control over neighboring rulers.

Kenneth Hall notes, "Humabon was at the apex of a sequence of datu [chief] relationships, that is, personal alliances among chief who led barangay [village] upstream-downstream networks and were therefore responsible for the flow of local agricultural goods to Humabon's port for the entrepôt trade" and moreover "Humabon solicited Magellan's crew's support against Lapulapu in the attempt to consolidate his political and economic hold over the Cebu and Mactan coasts" (Hall 2010: 322, 338). The two sides' ethnic identities obscure the fact that the battle was first and foremost the effort of a regional king to discipline an unruly vassal. Among Southeast Asian rulers there was a widespread practice of encouraging "Chinese and other foreign traders to move into their states as allies in their struggle for political dominance" (Hall 2010: 338). The pattern of one set of natives welcoming European intervention against local rivals is replicated in many places. The Dutch war with the kingdom of Makassar in the 1660s over the Spice Islands was fought with native allies, most importantly the Bugis and their leader Arung Palakka, while the Makassarese allied with the English (Ng 2012). Like other foreign traders, Europeans found themselves entangled in local politics and participated in local rivalries and conflicts (Figure 7.3).

Trading ports were particular sites of contention between non-Europeans and Europeans. In West Africa, a system of international relations provided immunity for ambassadors to allow European factories limited jurisdiction. In some cases, Africans ceded territory through military coercion, as when in 1482 the local ruler Caramansa permitted the Portuguese fort at São Jorge da Mina (Ghana); other cases may be the opposite, as in 1693 when Queen Tituba of Winneba (Ghana) invited the English Royal African Company to trade (Benton 2012: 31–3; Benton 2001: 55–6). Africans and Asians understood European interest in trading ports as a way to control trade and territory. The Acehnese *Hikayat Aceh* depicts a Portuguese embassy seeking to build a factory at Kota Biram, which is rejected by the sultan: "Kota Biram itu kota yang mengawal Kuala Aceh. Jikalau tempat yang lain dipinta raja pertugal nescaya kami beri" (Kota Biram is the fort that guards Aceh Bay. If the king of Portugal asks for another location surely we would agree) (Iskandar 2001: 73, my translation). But the Portuguese are dismissed empty-handed. The coastal location's strategic importance means that the request is viewed as an encroachment on Acehnese sovereignty. Here Acehnese resistance takes the form of diplomatic maneuvering rather than outright war. Eventually, the Portuguese were pushed out of Southeast Asia; ironically, the exiled court at Johor defeated Melaka with the help of the Dutch (Figure 7.4).

In Asia legal challenges were equally part of the local repertoire of resistance strategies. Although Europeans were unable to make expansive claims to territorial possession, their exercise of sovereign control over port-cities were challenged by locals. In one example, the latter sought a new intra-Asian

FIGURE 7.3: Romeyn de Hooghe, Cornelis Speelman's victories in the Kingdom of Makassar, 1666–9. 1670. Credit: Rijksmuseum, the Netherlands.

alliance. In 1627 Taiwan's Siraya tribe sent a largely-forgotten mission to Nagasaki to oppose VOC territorial claims over their villages in the Bay of Tayouan. The mission was engineered by Zheng Chenggong, a Ming loyalist who, especially after the Qing conquest of the Ming in 1644, wanted to expel the Dutch in order to secure the island as his base (Clulow 2016: 17–38; Andrade 2005, 2008; Blussé 1990).[17] The Dutch tried to organize Chinese pirates preying on shipping between Taiwan and Batavia into a coalition to force China into granting free trade, but were outmaneuvered by Zheng, the heir of a former pirate chief, Zheng Zhilong, who was absorbed into the Chinese imperial bureaucracy. A cultural chameleon, the elder Zheng's career is an object lesson on the strategic use of flexible alliances. Seeking his fortune first in (Portuguese) Macao, he was baptized Nicholas Gaspard there; later he joined a group of pirates while simultaneously working as a translator for the VOC, and perhaps spying on the latter as well; as pirate chief, he transferred

FIGURE 7.4: Jan Luyken, Melaka besieged under the leadership of Cornelis Matelief de Jonge. 1683. Credit: Rijksmuseum, the Netherlands.

allegiance to the new Qing empire. Based in Taiwan, his son Zheng Chenggong warred against the Manchus and defeated the Dutch, thoroughly ejecting them from the island through military and diplomatic means.

Disgruntlement with the VOC also found expression in assertions of Islamic unity. In the 1635–45 war with the VOC over Batavia (Jakarta), the king of nearby Banten in Java sought both firearms—from the English—and religious legitimacy (Figure 7.5). An embassy to Mecca in 1637 returned with two

FIGURE 7.5: Three warriors from Banten, 1596. Soldiers equipped with spear, sword, shields, and musket. Printed from plates made for the original illustrations in the travel account of the First Voyage of Cornelis de Houtman to the East Indies in 1595–7. Credit: Rijksmuseum, the Netherlands.

religious treatises and the title of sultan to be conferred on the king, who adopted an Islamic name (Burhanudin 2006). The Dutch 1669 defeat of Makassar fanned the flames of an anti-*kafir* (unbeliever) movement. In the 1680s, the movement found a leader in Ahmad Shah bin Iskandar, who claimed to be heir of the Minangkabau throne and professed the status of a saint to wage holy war against the Dutch (Kathirithamby-Wells 1970; Andaya 1975: 262–88). He gained widespread support across Sumatra, appearing at one point with an army of 4,000 and a fleet of 300. Writing to Siam, Aceh, Borneo, and Java, Ahmad Shah aimed at an archipelagic alliance. Although his movement petered out, he even conspired with the English in Bengkulen, Sumatra. Dutch strategy of sending dissidents into political exile sometimes backfired when it became another avenue for Islam's transmission. One important figure was Shaykh Yusuf, a member of the royal house of Makassar, who had completed the pilgrimage to Mecca and was educated in mystical Islam. His exile to the Cape at the end of the Dutch-Makassar war was meant to prevent religious uprisings, but instead he propagated Islam in Southern Africa, a cultural transfer that fueled future resistance (Ward 2009: 199–212, 231–7).

At the Cape, Khoisan resistance to the Dutch showed the ambiguous nature of their relations with Europeans. Willing to trade only surplus stock, the Khoisan did not like the bad trade Europeans offered: in 1614 one Khoi who had been taken to Bantam and learned English informed his countrymen that the goods offered were of low value. Native interpreters, such as one Doman sent to Java to learn Dutch, would return to lead the resistance (Marks 1972: 61–2). Khoisan resistance was particularly sustained against the Dutch who were there to settle, with actions ranging from petty pilfering to murder, violence, and raids. In response, the Dutch turned to racial stereotyping, calling them savage *wilden* (wild people) (Romney 2015). In characterizing them as not having a state or civil society, the Dutch reversed natural-law arguments to justify colonization. War finally broke out in 1659, though they submitted to peace in 1660: the complaint that the Dutch were taking "land which had belonged to them from all ages" would be repeated through the next centuries; by the 1730s, there were explicit expressions of political resistance in the calls for expelling the Dutch from their land (Romney 2015: 64, 71). But Dutch success had much to do with Khoi collaboration with them: large numbers of Khoi servants and soldiers also served the Dutch colonial state. In the seventeenth century, the English recycled anti-Spanish stereotypes to transfer the Black Legend onto the Dutch (Nocentelli 2014). The Dutch who had hitherto likened themselves to Native Americans as fellow-victims of the Spanish were now depicted in the same light as their former oppressors.

In the early modern beginnings of European empires, a range of strategies were used to resist their expansion, from armed rebellion to acts of non-cooperation; cultures of resistance expressed themselves in everyday, ordinary life as well as in formal literary works. Anti-colonial resistance was creative, subversive, and culturally hybrid, whether it was Senegambians adapting cattle culture from their homeland to the Americas or Makassarese aristocrats bringing Islam to South Africa. Cultures of resistance developed through engagement with Europeans that included cooperation as well as conflict. If European empires transformed the world system into one whose economic asymmetries benefited Europe, they did in part by taking advantage of rifts in local political dynamics. At the same time, non-Europeans deftly played off different European groups who were each other's traditional enemies or trade competitors. In the cultural middle ground, they shaped each other's strategies and responses.

From the beginning too, resistance to European empires cannot be neatly separated from oppositional discourses in Europe or intra-European politics abroad. Both drew upon each other. In the early modern period, debates over the treatment of Native Americans played particular importance in European political thought, used both to resist monarchical authoritarianism at home and to justify empire elsewhere. As Europe laid the initial foundation for later colonial conquest in the plantations and settlements around the globe, anti-colonial resistance in other parts of the world contributed to resistance against the political elites in Europe. The events and practices of one place entered discourses in another to influence ideas that came to be applied to yet a third space.

By the end of the early modern period, this dynamic interaction led to the development of political theories and discourses—of natural law, social contract, republicanism, and individual liberties—that became the basis of later national and anti-imperial revolutions in the colonies. As Europe diverged further from her colonies, the co-existence of democracy at home and autocratic colonial authority abroad became increasingly untenable, at least in the eyes of some Europeans. The poet William Cowper asked in 1785, "We have no slaves at home—Then why abroad?" (Cowper 2003: 84). Such voices grew louder over the next centuries, just as nationalist movements grew stronger in the colonies on the long road to decolonization. But, profoundly shaped by the earlier circulation of discourses of resistance, later anti-imperial movements were legacies of early modern cultures of resistance.

CHAPTER EIGHT

Race[1]

JONATHAN BURTON

The subject of empire is critical to most histories of race in the early modern period. It is a commonplace—albeit one that this chapter interrogates—that modern ideas about race in the west were honed on the ideological whetstone of empire when "encounters with new peoples in the Americas and the Pacific forced Europeans to create new ways of explaining physical and cultural difference" (Samson 2005: 5). Similarly, it is frequently argued that imperialism cannot "be understood without reference to ideologies of race," since the latter provide categories of difference crucial to arguments for and against the extension of dominion (Loomba 2014: 147). These assertions of mutual contingency urge us to ask questions about how the idea of race is altered or intensified by early modern imperialism, or to what extent empire depends upon the emergence of a particular iteration of race. Was race a crucial factor in the extension of empires in the west? Conversely, was the "Age of Discovery" responsible for a hardening, sharpening, or stabilizing of racial discourses?

"Empire," "race," and "the west" are all disputed terms. Consequently, any consideration of the symbiosis of race and empire has to begin with the fact that each of these terms points to a broad spectrum of discourses and practices, adopted, debated, and recalibrated both within and across cultural traditions. Rather than attempting a comprehensive account of the various intersections of race and empire in the period covered by this volume, this chapter troubles the question before offering some thoughts on our efforts to historicize race.

WHICH EMPIRES?

To begin, we might consider precisely what belongs under the heading of "western empires." Prior to the Portuguese settlement of Madeira (1425) and the Azores (1440), European overseas colonization was limited to Norse settlements in Iceland and Greenland, and the Crusader States that had collapsed by 1300. Madeira and the Azores were uninhabited, so it was with a blend of improvisation and remote precedents that the Portuguese went on to establish settlements in places as varied as Ghana (1482), Kerala (1500), Brazil (1500), Hormuz (1507), Malacca (1511), and Angola (1570), followed by the Spanish in the West Indies (1493), Mexico (1520), and Peru (1542), and the English in Jamestown (1607). These ventures ranged from isolated trading posts and garrisons to formal and expansive colonies whose economic viability relied upon an unprecedented use of chattel slavery. Some were established by force, others in collaboration with indigenous elites. If in some places Europeans discerned no formal system of land tenure, in others they encountered metropolitan cultures with recognizable structures of governance and taxation. Even within a single colonial setting such as New Spain (Mexico) or Peru, practices of inclusion or disenfranchisement were not monolithic but subjective and situational, employing what could be contradictory ideological frameworks in response to varying degrees and sources of resistance. Likewise, consistency was not always found across the disparate territories of a given empire. So, for example, in Spanish America, "the Iberian concept of *limpieza de sangre* would be reformulated and have different implications than in Spain," focusing more on Spanish ancestry than on the absence of Jewish or Moorish blood that preoccupied inquisitors in Sevilla, Jaén, Córdoba, and Ciudad Real (Martinez 2008: 2). And while the Spanish may have linked their New World endeavors to ancient Roman imperialism, they would eschew the same comparisons in their contemporaneous conquest of Naples (Devereux 2015: 113–14).

The sheer number of instances involving European attempts to seize overseas territory in the period covered by this volume signals "a new and distinctive phase in the continent's relationship with the outside world" (Elliott 1998: 140). Yet the diverse authority and scope of the settlements established by the Portuguese, Spanish, English, French, Dutch, and Swedes in this period confound our efforts to pin down a meaning for the term "empire." At what point does privateering or establishing an overseas trading post shade into empire? Do we risk overestimating European power and obscuring the power of South Asian empires when we treat Portugal's *Estado da India* as an empire as opposed to a "loose knit network of Portuguese communities" with designs on "extorting protection money from the seaborne trade" of pepper and other spices (Darwin 2008: 53–4)? Should we place under the same heading Golden Age Spain, whose influence stretched from Manila to the New World where it carved out vast inland empires, and its English counterpart that, at the close of the sixteenth century, controlled no overseas territories beyond the Munster Plantation?

The project of separating out and studying *western* empires also demands some reflection, as proponents of "connected history"—a school of historiography that questions the traditional borders drawn between nations, continents, and other units of geography—point out that, "the early modern period should be considered an Age of Empires in a truly global sense" (Casale 2015: 325). It is salutary to note that to leave outside of our consideration Aztec, Inca, Ming, Mughal, Ottoman, Russian, and Safavid empires of the same period is to ignore the ways in which non-western powers could—with no less force than their European counterparts—act as rivals to and/or foils in the justification and self-fashioning of western empires and their racial ideologies. So, for example, the Ottoman conquest of Constantinople in 1453 cut off western European access to the Black Sea suppliers of light-skinned slaves and created new incentives to develop and justify the nascent Portuguese slave trade in West Africa. Concerns about Ottoman expansion also reorganized ideas about domestic difference, as Christopher Marlowe depicts in his 1592 play, *The Jew of Malta*, where the appearance of an Ottoman fleet off the coast of Malta recalibrates notions of Jewish citizenship and excuses a Spanish colonial presence. When we consider how British imperial self-fashioning depended on a contrast of upright Britons with conquistadors prone to degeneracy, intermarriage, and cruelty, we should remember that this mode of thinking was anticipated by Iberian thinkers anxiously concocting notions of their "commonality of blood" as their countrymen were absorbed into Ottoman fleets or were intermarrying with indigenous women in Asia (Casale 2007: 123). Of course, it was not only the powerful empires of the Near Eastern "old world" that influenced European thinking about race and empire. The force of New World empires is no less evident in Spanish attempts to justify their attacks on the Aztec and Inca empires, whose urban cultures and sophisticated systems of communication and governance gave the lie to European discourses of primitivism previously applied to natives of the Antilles.

Laura Doyle has recently encouraged an exploration of "inter-imperiality," where we "look more directly at the force-field of multiple empires, with their interactive co-formations over the longue durée, including empires that pre-date, prepare, and interact as contemporaries with Anglo-European empires" (Doyle 2014: 160). At the very least, we should recall that the idea of *the west* has always been more cultural than precisely geographic and strive not to erase the classical legacies of Eurasian empires. David Armitage may not have the Russians or the Ottomans in mind when he argues that in "early-modern theories of empire, all roads led to Rome," but a brief detour into empires not typically associated with the European Renaissance helps to identify something distinctive about the racial formations at work in those empires that we more conventionally regard as "western" (Armitage 1998: xv). The scale of the Hapsburg empire at the midpoint of the sixteenth century made it a logical contender for the role of Rome's successor. But the same might be said of the Ottoman empire, especially after it absorbed Greece and the bulk of ancient Rome's African and Near Eastern empire. In terms of their rates of demographic and territorial expansion during the period covered by this volume, it makes good sense to consider the Russian and Ottoman alongside Iberian empires, though the former generally grew across continents instead of oceans, and involved familiar cultures rather than encounters with, as the conquistador Bernal Diaz put it, "things never heard of, seen, or dreamed of before" (Sunderland 2004: 3). In the century following the conquest of Constantinople, the Ottomans doubled their empire in Europe, in addition to expanding across North Africa and east into Asia. For its part, the Russian empire grew by an average of 35,000 square kilometers per year in the two centuries following the late fifteenth-century withdrawal of the Golden Horde.

When Barbara Fuchs explains that "the myth of *translatio imperii* (political power and cultural authority travel from Troy to Rome to the European states that vie for its legacy) undergirds much of European imperialism and national formation in the sixteenth century," she may inadvertently obscure the breadth of such *translatio,* or transmission (Fuchs 2003: 73). Certainly, it is easy to find instances where the Spanish, English, and Portuguese attempted to connect their imperial aspirations to a Roman tradition: Spanish propagandists cast Montezuma II's submission to Hernán Cortés in terms of the donation of Constantine (Pagden 1995: 32), and the Englishman William Strachey defended settlement in the New World by asserting that "[h]ad not this [same] violence and injury been offered to us by the Romans ... [w]e might yet have lived overgrown satyrs, rude, and untutored, wandering in the woods ... prostituting our daughters to strangers, sacrificing our children to idols, nay eating our own children" (Strachey 1849: 18). When the Portuguese grew anxious about interethnic relations in the *Estado da India*, they drew on the "decline literature" of antiquity, where "the enervating power of the Orient was already a trope in the Hellenistic and Roman republican periods" (Nocentelli 2007: 209). Yet western Europeans did not have an exclusive claim on this classical tradition. Upon conquering Constantinople in 1453 (thirty-two years before the birth of Cortés), the Ottoman Sultan Mehmed styled himself *Kayser-i-Rum*, or Roman emperor. Likewise, it is easy to forget that the Russian title "tsar" derives from the Latin cognomen "Caesar." What's more, the concept of *res nullius* that British and French theorists of empire borrowed from Roman common law to justify the seizure of "unoccupied territory" across the Atlantic was also used by Ivan IV (the Terrible) and his successors to enlist Russian peasants and townsmen in Muscovy's eastward expansion, in the third-quarter of the sixteenth century, across the steppe and through Siberian forests occupied by nomadic peoples (Sunderland 2004: 22–3).

Inheriting the Roman tradition of imperium was, of course, more complicated than resurrecting Roman legal traditions and vocabulary. Innovations in navigation meant that the *orbis mundi* known to the Romans was only part of the world known to early moderns. Dutch, English, French, and Iberian theorists were therefore confronted with two difficult questions: First, were the heirs of Rome's empire entitled to extend their authority over newly "discovered" territories? Second, were all peoples—including those unknown to the Romans—capable of traversing the distance between the classical poles of barbarism and civility? These questions put direct pressure on ideas of racial difference, but they exerted different degrees of force for the Ottomans and Russians whose expansion took place across geographically contiguous territories and involved contact only with cultures with whom they were already familiar and often already intermixed. As Willard Sunderland explains for the Russian case, "the steppe and its peoples were simply too well-known to appear exotic" to the Muscovites and too integrated with the Russians to spur new racial vocabularies (Sunderland 2004: 19). Even if orthodox ideology figured the peoples of the steppe as godless pagans, "proximity had created relationships of peaceful exchange along with intermittent conflicts, including intermarriage" of Rus and Tatar peoples for centuries leading up to the sixteenth-century rise of Muscovy (Sunderland 2004: 12–13). It is a mistake to imagine intermarriage as a necessarily benign form of integration, overlooking the ways in which sexual relations can be acts of power. But in this case, the practice of intermarriage dated back even before the occupation of Russian lands by the Golden Horde. Consequently, by the time of Russia's expansion across the steppe, "a variety of ethnic elements ha[d] long flowed in the veins of Russia's blue bloods" (Schimmelpenninck van der Oye 2010: 22). In short, empire did not always or necessarily involve racialization.

By no means do I wish to challenge or displace the important work of figures like Jorge Mariscal, David Nirenberg, Deborah Root and James Sweet demonstrating the centrality of the Portuguese and Spanish empires in the development of early modern racial discourses. Nor do I wish, by placing the Russians and Ottomans alongside the Iberians, to suggest that we treat empire as a transcultural phenomenon. On the contrary, I hope to indicate that even among the various early modern examples that purported to derive from the same archetype, empires were always distinct in terms of regional motives, parameters, and rivalries, and it is those differences that may tell us something interesting about the cultural intersections of race and empire. For if the scope of the Russian and Ottoman empires was comparable with the Spanish, they differed significantly in terms of how they addressed the peoples they encountered. By setting Russian and Ottoman empires alongside the more commonly studied Dutch, English, and Iberian empires, we can see more fully the multiple pathways into and through empire, that race and empire are not invariably (or singularly) bound together, and that empire does not necessarily produce new or more potent racial formations though it can be an engine for the mutability that makes race so potent.

Early modern theorists of empire from London to Lisbon and Istanbul to Moscow shared a tendency to cite classical Roman ideas related to empire and difference. Most important among these was the discourse around universal monarchy (*monarchia universalis*) developed across the writings of Cicero, Virgil, Livy, Polybius, Sallust, and Tacitus. According to this tradition, the empire was obliged to disseminate *civitas* and *virtus* throughout the whole world (*orbis mundi*) (Pagden 1995: 11–62). For the Romans, *civitas* referred to an ethical citizenship that took root in Rome where citizens lived by civil law. But as Anthony Pagden puts it, *civitas* "was crucially a civilization for exportation," and both provincials and slaves could be educated and manumitted into citizenship. Hence, "the frontiers between the world of civil men and that of barbarians was forever dissolving" (Pagden 1995: 22). So, for example, Roman citizenship was extended to Picts in Scotland, Nubians in the Sudan, and Berbers in North Africa. *Virtus* was a concept that shifted in meaning during the Roman era but came to most commonly signify an ethical composite embracing courage, fair-mindedness, and temperance. These were not qualities that the Romans believed they possessed exclusively. Foreigners might just as soon possess or embrace them. Thus, the Roman General Pompeius Strabo awarded citizenship in 89 CE to opposing Spanish cavalrymen in specific recognition of their *virtus* (McDonnell 2006: 160).

In the early modern period, western European citations of Roman authority would differ markedly from the ways in which both the Ottoman and Russian empires drew on Rome's ancient example. Crucial to this division was a detaching of *civitas* and *virtus*, particularly as the latter came to dovetail with piety and the task of preparing for the second coming of Christ those who had no previous access to the gospel. So, where Spaniards justified the *Reconquista* as a recovery of the ancient Roman empire and an extension of piety, or Christian *virtus*, the Ottoman expansion (that coincidentally heightened the perceived urgency of the Iberian reconquest) might be understood as a propagation of *civitas*.

"Self-conscious inheritors of the legacy of the Roman empire," the Ottomans referred to themselves as "*Rumi*," and followed the Roman model of extending the benefits of citizenship to the diverse peoples they conquered from Basra in the east to Algiers in the west, as far south as Mecca and north into Hungary and what is now the Ukraine (Greer, Mignolo and Quilligan 2007: 17). Informed as well by a centuries-old legal tradition of tolerance established in the Pact of Umar, they did not attempt to convert all of their conquered subjects (*dhimmis*), expropriate their land, or control their natural resources as their European neighbors attempted to do in the New World. Instead, they enlisted local elites into the *timar* system of revenue collection, allowed confessional diversity, intermarried at the highest echelon, and most importantly recruited a core of metropolitan elites through the *devşirme*, or child tribute.[2]

By gathering children from the frontiers and raising them to serve the state, the Ottomans created an army of subjects loyal to empire and Sultan above any ethnic, regional, or religious affiliation. Although they were known as "slaves" to the sultan, these *askeri*, in fact, comprised an administrative elite who ascended to the highest echelon of power barring only the role of sultan. As Daniel Goffman explains, this group

> had no basis in ethnicity, race or religion. Its members included individuals of Arab, Greek, Italian, Jewish, Slavic, sub-Saharan African, Turkish and myriad other extractions. The manner in which it carefully distinguished itself from all over whom it ruled—Muslims as well as Christians and Jews—was through the expression of a fastidious and urbane culture (Goffman 2002: 51).

In other words, what made someone *Rumi* was not blood, belief, or skin color but his or her acceptance of and participation in a cosmopolitan meritocracy (Casale 2007: 126). So, for example, Sokollu Mehmed Pasha who served as Grand Vizier under three different sultans from 1565–79 was born an Orthodox Christian in Serbia and taken by the *devşirme* as a ten-year-old boy. Sokollu Mehmed's was not an unusual case: Of the thirty-nine Grand Viziers who served the Ottoman sultanate in the sixteenth century, only three were of Turkish descent, with others hailing from Albania, Bosnia, Greece, Herzegovina, Hungary, Croatia, and Italy.

Just beneath the Grand Vizier in power and influence was the *kizlar ağasi*, chief of the black eunuchs who guarded the Imperial Harem. This post was created by Murad III in 1574 and occupied first by the Ethiopian Mehmed Agha. A 1581 manuscript painting credited to the court's chief miniaturist Nakkaş Osman testifies to the prominence of the *kizlar ağasi*, portraying him on horseback while other court officials remain beneath him, on foot (Figure 8.1). In another painting of the era, he is depicted capturing the full attention of the sultan while smaller, light-skinned members of the court look on from behind a throne that half-obscures them (Kangal 2000: 264).[3] Clearly, skin color was not an inactive force in determining court positions, but it is noteworthy that the dark-skinned men who occupied the post of *kizlar ağasi* for more than two centuries surpassed in power the light-skinned white eunuchs to become "in practice the principal officer of the whole palace" (Bosworth 1995: 243).[4] That the *kizlar ağasi* was not merely an exception is obvious from another miniature found in a *Shāhanshāhnāma* of the early 1590s featuring groups of black eunuchs looking on as Mehmed Agha engages in conversation with the crown prince (Figure 8.2). By comparison, the portrait of James I of England's privy council gathered at Somerset House a decade later to meet with

FIGURE 8.1: Mehmed Agha, *Shāhanshāhnāma of Lokman*, vol. 1. Istanbul, 1581. Credit: Istanbul University Library, F. 1404, fol. 131b.

FIGURE 8.2: Prince Mehmed conversing with Vizier Mehmed Pasha, *Shāhanshāhnāma of Lokman*, vol. 2. Istanbul, 1592–7. Topkapi Palace Library, B. 200, fol. 83a. Credit: Getty Images/Werner Forman/Contributor.

representatives of Spain and the Spanish Netherlands features a strikingly homogeneous group (Figure 8.3). When dark-skinned attendants appeared in European court portraits, it was primarily to mark the prestige or fairness of their white masters (Hall 1995: 211–53) (Figure 8.4). In particular, slaves acquired in Portugal's imperial ventures, "first North African Moors and black

FIGURE 8.3: The Somerset House Conference, 1604, by unknown artist. Credit: National Portrait Gallery.

FIGURE 8.4: Tiziano Vecelli (Titian). Portrait of Laura de'Dianti c. 1523. Public domain: GNU Free Documentation License.

West Africans, and subsequently Amerindians (Tupi) from Brazil—played an important role as an essential labor force and as exotic components at court" but they tended to perform menial tasks or decorate ceremonial occasions, rather than exercising authority like the diverse subjects of the Ottoman empire (Jordan 2005: 155–80).

It was not only at the level of the imperial elite that the Ottomans practiced integration. Nor did integration at all levels require ritual mutilation. In his study of Ottoman ship crews, Giancarlo Casale demonstrates that less than a quarter of the seamen in the Ottoman fleet in 1538 were ethnic Turks (Casale 2007: 129). The remaining *Rumi* included not only Arabs but also sailors from Albania, England, France, Greece, Italy, Portugal, Spain, and Sub-Saharan Africa. It is easy to lose sight of this diversity and inclusiveness since the miniaturists depicting Ottoman military forces typically portrayed soldiers according to archetypes, ignoring entirely the actual, individual features. So, for example, when we look at a 1579 painting of Suleiman's army marching to Belgrade, we might be led to believe that the Ottoman military consisted primarily of quintuplets (Figure 8.5).

FIGURE 8.5: Battle between the Turks, led by Suleiman the Magnificent, and the Hungarians at Mohacs, August 29, 1526, drawing from a manuscript. Credit: De Agostini Picture Library/Getty Images.

It is illuminating to set the multi-ethnic cosmopolitanism and tolerance of the Ottomans against the racial practices that developed in contemporaneous Portuguese, Spanish, English, and Dutch empires. For the Ottoman historian Leslie Pierce, the juxtaposition yields a vision of "inverted racialization," contrasting western practices of hierarchization, marginalization, and segregation with a hybrid and pluralistic Ottoman culture (Peirce 2007: 28). Certainly, race was a consistently active force throughout the early modern history of western empires, but it was also crucially adaptive, mobile, multidirectional, and polymorphous. When we think of an Age of Discovery, or an Age of Empire, we tend to erase the ways in which culture and politics are always contested, polyvocal fields. Empire was itself the subject of intense debate in the early modern world. What's more, internal debates about their legitimacy and reach raise questions about the degree to which any empire represented a consensus on the questions of civility, evangelism, and humanity that transect most discussions of difference. But confronted by skepticism, incredulity, and reason, racism continually reinvents race, rendering it a moving and multilocated target. Thus, while Matthieu Chapman may be right in arguing for "blackness as a stable locus of negation" in western racialism (Chapman 2017: 20), I otherwise join Geralidine Heng in an understanding that race has "no singular or stable referent," but is instead "a structural relationship for the articulation and management of human differences" (Heng 2011a, 262).

WHICH "RACE?"

Race matters in the history of western empires; but it may not matter in the ways we have assumed: what is crucial to recognize about racial discourses deployed in the context and service of western imperialism is that they were almost always inconsistent, have only rarely stabilized and do not necessarily seek or benefit from stability. If empire has an effect on race it is to excite the tendency of racial discourse to shift emphases, take on alternate forms and redefine itself in response to varying cultural circumstances. It does not generate something new so much as it reactivates quiescent ideas and redefines enduring ones. Consequently, western empires never benefited from a hardening of racial discourses but instead from their mutability.

Debates over the contours and history of race are ongoing and vigorous, with arguments for classical, medieval, fifteenth century, and eighteenth century points of origin. Those debates arise primarily from differences of opinion about how precisely to characterize and delimit "race." If we admit all the forms of race discussed in recent scholarship of the early modern period, then race might be inferred from any one or combination of bodily praxes, kinship ties, physiological traits, or social predilections, whether real or fantasized. These include hair type, skin color, and the relative size and strength of body parts, but also dietary, religious, sartorial and sexual practices, family lineage, manners of speech, customs of maintaining a livelihood, public allegiances, and more. Depending on who was citing them, where and why, these factors could be variously activated or dampened as indicators of moral quality or inhumanity, and consequently grant legitimacy to relations of domination or exploitation.

Some would argue, however, that the catalog I have offered here fails to distinguish cultural from 'scientific' ideas of race, and that any treatment of race and empire for the period covered by this volume is anachronistic because "a deep epistemological change took place in Europe ... toward the end of the eighteenth century, producing new scientific representations of race" (Bancel, David and Thomas 2014: 1). At this point, they argue, a "biological doctrine of race invested traditional 'folk' prejudice with a new intellectual authority" (Hudson 1996: 252). For these scholars, race cannot be factored into the early modern history of western empires because "race" meant something else entirely before the rise of Enlightenment science. According to this line of thinking, race becomes a more powerful tool when it is consistently fixed on the body and treated as an inherited trait beyond human behavior, choice, and will.

Others argue that "the concept does not always need biology to 'do its work,'" (Martinez 2008: 3) and that cultural practices could often trump physiological traits. This is apparent in Richard Ligon's account of a seventeenth-century Barbados plantation owner denying his black slave's request to be baptized with the explanation that "being once a Christian, he could no more account him a slave" (Ligon 1657: 47). In addition, an emphasis on scientific thought ignores the fact that "the biological discourse of race was never really biological and that its categories were, in fact, always cultural" (Martinez 2008: 59). In other words, the privileging of science and particularly biological science itself takes place within and as a result of cultural parameters, shaped in part by the history of imperialism. As David Nirenberg points out in his work on the part of race in the consolidation of Spanish imperial identity, "the late fourteenth and fifteenth centuries," a period long preceding the codification of biological science, "witnessed massive attempts to eliminate ... diversity through massacres, segregation, conversion, Inquisition and expulsion" (Nirenberg 2009: 242). From this point of view, it does not matter whether race was scientific or cultural, bound to an unchanging body or to an inconsistent set of habits and mores, only that it possessed the power to divide, hierarchize, and even validate terrible violence. Any reluctance to address these occurrences under the heading of "race" minimizes the ethnic violence of the past and obscures the deep history of cultural forms of race that continue to impact our lives.

Even where authors acknowledge the existence of multiple, overlapping ideas about race in early modern culture, a tendency persists to privilege certain discourses over others. Title pages announce the "birth" or "invention" of race at a particular moment, with the ensuing articles and chapters typically tracing discursive *bildungsromans*, where race matures, hardens, and takes on a fully developed (i.e., modern) form. So, for example, when Diego von Vacano argues that the "birth of race" occurs in the writings of Bartolomé de las Casas on the treatment of native Americans he figures "staunch imperialist" ideology as the vital seed of modern racialization (von Vacano 2012: 401). Nicolas Bancel, Thomas David, and Dominic Thomas argue instead that it was not until "somewhere between 1730 and 1790" that "the concept of race was invented" in conjunction with modern scientific thought (Bancel, David and Thomas 2014: 11). Birth and invention are temporal metaphors; each concerns a point of origin and implies a more developed and potent life or career to follow. They encourage us to think serially about the development or lifespan of their shared tenor, race. And consequently, they give way to a second set of metaphors introduced to explain change across time. These involve terms like "fracture," "rupture," and "break." Thus, we read about the "break with older conceptions" of race (Feerick 2010: 21), the "fracturing of one racial system" precipitating the rise of another (Feerick 2010: 6), and consequently an "epistemic divide" separating racial schemes (Kinoshita 2006, 5). What is noteworthy in this second set of figures is that each of its terms implies a singular and delimited form that is categorically different from its predecessors. After all, what will be broken must first be whole; and what is compared must first be singled out and defined. Consequently, race is described as materializing in singular, static forms that persevere until meeting what is often figured as a violent or even "cataclysmic" end (Feerick 2010: 47).

Even when the terms are less violent—when we hear of a succession or supplanting—race continues to be imagined in terms of teleology. Bloodlines and genealogy, we are told, are supplanted by skin color, culture is succeeded by 'protoracial' science, and a scholarly *battle royale* seeks to determine each particular period's "dominant mode of ethnic distinction" (Floyd-Wilson 2003, 1). In other words, if instability and shifting are common tropes in our histories of race, it is often because they are used to describe what is seen as irreversible change across eras, where race is imagined to take on forms more potent than those allegedly expired categories that have lost their ability to define and organize human differences.

Not only does this sort of thinking conceal the force and resilience of cultural ideas about difference—consider the ongoing associations of certain faith groups with duplicity and violence—it also obscures early appearances of pseudoscientific racial ideologies commonly associated with the eighteenth and nineteenth centuries. So, for example, the prominence of phrenology in nineteenth-century racial pseudoscience, tends to eclipse its appearance as early as 1523 in Johannes ab Indagine's *Briefe introductions ... unto the art of chiromancy or manuel divination, and physiognomy*. Indagine asserts that "thin lips do betoken great talkers, eloquent, witty, prudent and ingenious men" while "[g]reat lips ... do declare dull and foolish people, hard of understanding, unclean, luxurious, inconstant and cruel" (Loomba and Burton 2007: 90). The linkage of Africans and apes that we associate with Victorian imperialism is anticipated in Edward Topsell's 1607 assertion that men "that have low and flat nostrils are libidinous as apes ... and having thick lips ... they are deemed fools, like the lips of asses and apes" (Topsell 1607: 15).[5] And arguments for the seminal transmission of bodily traits long pre-date Mendelian genetics, arguably beginning as far back as Herodotus but certainly as early as Juan Harte's claim in *Examen de ingenios* (1575) that "the Moors communicate the colour of their elders by means of their seed" (Huarte 1594: 199). In other words, many of the concepts that we associate with post-Enlightenment science, or "scientific racism," circulated well before the scientific revolution, and merely grew in standing with the imprimatur of "science." They were not born or invented as a result of either imperialism or Enlightenment science, nor did cultural ideas about difference die out in the face of science or increased cross-cultural contact. It is noteworthy, for example, that the celebrated chemist Robert Boyle—a founding member of the Royal Society and investor in East India, Hudson Bay, and Turkey Companies—would argue against the idea that blackness was derived from the biblical curse of Ham, but continue to give credence to the notion (as old as Heliodorus of Emesa) that skin color might be determined by what a pregnant woman saw around the time of her conception with child (Boyle 1664: 163). In other words, if empires fueled scientific research, science did not necessarily eradicate cultural ideas about difference.

POLYMORPHISM

The (mis)understanding of race as a product of serial elimination is often at work in attempts to correlate the histories of race and empire. Take, for example, Gary Taylor's locating in the Columbian voyages a precise birthdate for modern ideologies of whiteness. Taylor explains that the discovery of light-skinned natives in what would later be Trinidad—at the same latitude where Europeans had previously encountered dark-skinned Africans—"initiated an intellectual chain reaction that eventually produced the modern racial world" (Taylor 2005: 59). In this tidy, causal formulation, Columbus embarks on his voyage to extend the Spanish empire armed with a Ptolomeian worldview that had "dominated European thought for a millennium and a half" (Taylor 2005: 67). But what he finds depletes climatic theories, triggering a search for a replacement that would eventually yield Linnaean taxonomy and scientific racism. In short, empire demands and ultimately generates a racial discourse better equipped to distance and distinguish its subjects.

This is an appealingly trim narrative, but it neglects the fact that race is not only adaptive, but also multifaceted, and this dual versatility is crucial both to its force and its longevity. Columbus may have been informed by Ptolemaic ideas about climate and difference, but they did not saturate his thought to the exclusion of all others. His writings on the Amerindians draw on multiple ideas about difference and to the extent that those ideas were displaced they only went dormant while others did the work of marking and organizing difference for a while. So, if a Ptolemaic model receded it was not to make way for a single, allegedly modern and pseudoscientific understanding of difference but rather for multiple ideas, some resurrected from earlier textual traditions and others exported from domestic scenes. Moreover, as questions arose about the probity of the Spanish project in the New World, it was this multiplicity of active racial discourses that ultimately steered the debate toward resolution.

Columbus left Spain seeking to solve a problem of trade; he brought back a problem of empire. He was expected to return with silk, spices, and gold, unimpeded by Muslim middlemen and without violating the Treaty of Tordesillas. Instead, he appeared in the Spanish court with tobacco, pineapples, some colorful birds, a cotton hammock, so little gold that a court page could carry it around on a tray for all to see (Granzotto 1985: 190), and six Caribbean natives (no pepper, ginger, or cloves). Those six bodies—paraded through Barcelona and Seville, and memorialized in paintings like the one adorning this volume—would initiate a century-long debate over whether and how the Indians might be deprived of their sovereign rights. Informed by Aristotelian logic, Christian theology, *Reconquista* politics, and a long tradition of traveler's narratives, Iberian commentators would variously figure the Amerindians as reasoning subjects or immoral savages, weak and vulnerable innocents, or natural slaves, subhuman monsters, or fellow descendants of Adam. For Columbus, they were offered in support of his promise, in a shipboard letter to the sovereigns Ferdinand and Isabella dated March 4, 1493, that his ventures would "be able to pay Your Highnesses for five thousand cavalry and fifty thousand foot soldiers for the war and conquest of Jerusalem" (Zamora 1993, 195). In other words, Columbus was affixing Spain's Christian imperialism—both in the New World and Old—to a vision of Amerindians as an emblem of Iberian piety and as a valuable commodity. Indeed, a consignment of native slaves would be sent to Spain after Columbus's second voyage (Hanke 1945: 19). Yet where we might expect Columbus to frame Amerindian bodies within a coherent racial narrative crafted in support of the imperial mission, he instead draws on various and even contradictory racial discourses in a letter of just over three thousand words.

Prior to his departure, Columbus studied *The Book of John Mandeville* and the Plinian notions of monstrous races that he encountered there clearly influenced his account. (Bedini 1992: 446). He reports not only on the "whites" that occupy Taylor but also about the presence of Amazons, cannibals, men with tails, and a tribe of people who grow no hair. These are figures derived from a classical tradition of marking outsiders with cultural inversion, taboo, and animality. To figure Amerindians in these terms is to identify in their bodies and bodily praxes cause to treat them as renegades to if not a subspecies of humanity. Moreover, to display native bodies along with unknown species of birds enabled ideas that they too might comprise something categorically different. If native bodies could be more easily imagined uncivil or subhuman, concerns about subjecting them to inhumane labor or about the seizure of their property could be more easily dismissed.

But what appears to be a simple instance of racism forging a path for imperialist domination is complicated by Columbus's assertions—in the same shipboard letter—that the islands "are densely populated with the best people under the sun; they have neither ill will nor treachery" (Zamora 1993: 192). Whereas cultural differences (e.g., eating pork) would be used to identify an alleged impurity of blood on the Iberian Peninsula, Columbus figured cultural difference across the Atlantic as a gulf easily crossed: the Amerindians might "go about naked like their mothers bore them" and "have neither iron nor weapons" but they "know that all powers reside in heaven" and with "very little effort will be converted to our Holy Faith" (Zamora 1993: 192, 195). Representing natives as potential converts rendered Spanish invaders "ministers of grace and liberty" freeing "these new gentiles ... from the bondage of Satan's tyranny" (Eden 1555: aiii^r). At the same time, in order to distinguish Amerindians from the Marranos and Moriscos whose obstinacy and clandestine faith became the bugbear of the Inquisition, Columbus would paradoxically assure his readers that "[n]owhere in these islands have I known the inhabitants to have a religion, or idolatry" (Zamora 1993: 192).

With its apparently diametrical claims for Amerindian humanity and monstrosity, civility and savagery, and piety and godlessness, Columbus's letter might be taken for evidence that racial discourses were not yet stabilized to the point where they could be harnessed to the interests of empire. Yet it is important to keep in mind that empires rarely have a single, shared, and unchanging set of interests. So, for example, ideas about the "wild Irish" circulating in Elizabeth I's court differed widely from those held by their countrymen whose families had occupied Irish lands since the Norman invasion. The Spanish case, in particular, demonstrates the ways in which imperial cultures are not only unstable but also ideologically divided with regard to racial difference. Inconsistency is both a product of and answer to this division. It means that where one racial discourse is questioned, another is always available.

Initially, the Spanish crown insisted on a more respectful approach to the Amerindians, requiring their consent and hence assuming the natives to be capable of reason. Michael Guasco argues in this volume that this course of action came in response to the particular rapaciousness of slave traders in the immediate aftermath of the Spanish arrival. In addition, the crown's preliminary tendency to downplay difference and prohibit slavery might have come from chariness on the part of the crown to cede to conquistadors complete control of such an unprecedentedly large labor force.[6] Yet the extent to which inclusion was encouraged is worth noting. As Kathryn Burns points out, "[o]ne royal decree went so far as to recommend that some Spaniards marry Indian women and some Indian men marry Spanish women" (Burns 2007: 190). Similarly, the Portuguese crown, in support of its earliest settlements in Asia, "not only condoned but actively encouraged interethnic unions by restricting emigration of European women and by providing financial incentives to mixed couples." (Nocentelli 2007: 215). If the English distinguished their fledgling empire by condemning the degeneracy produced by these intermixtures that rendered the Spaniard "the most mingled" of all nations (Spenser 1890: 82), the Iberians assured themselves that in instances of interethnic union the "mightier" seed will prevail (Huarte 1594: 317). As Valerie Traub elaborates elsewhere in this volume (Chapter 6, p. 172), as long as these relationships were temporary, they did not seem to challenge European ideas about the purity of their own race. Thus, Duarte Lopes claimed, "the children of the Portingals, which are born of the women of the Congo, do incline somewhat towards white" (Lopes 1597: 19). What is most noteworthy here is the opportunistic shifting between difference located on the body and difference discovered in chosen ways of life.

Where the crown's initial stance toward Amerindians emphasized compatibility and peaceful incorporation, the conquistadors instead insisted on ontological difference and war. There was not, however, consensus among all who crossed the Atlantic. Missionaries who accompanied the conquistadors, such as Father Antonio Montesinos, asked in 1511, "By what right do you wage such detestable wars on these people who lived idly and peacefully in their own lands, where you have consumed infinite numbers of them with unheard of murders and desolations?" (Gibson 1968: 60). The answers offered by and on behalf of the conquistadors refused even the premise that the natives of the Americas were people. According to the Dominican Bernardino de Minaya, the conquistadors claimed that the natives they encountered were "not true men, but a third species of animal, between man and monkey, created by God for the better service of man" (Pagden 1982: 104). Back in Spain, this argument was represented most forcefully by the scholar, Juan Ginés de Sepúlveda, who resurrected ideas from Aristotle, Pliny, and Albertus Magnus to argue that the Amerindians were subhuman beings perpetrating crimes against nature including human sacrifice, cannibalism, and sodomy. In his 1547 treatise, *Democrates alter,* Sepúlveda made the case for enforced conversion by arguing that "the Spanish have a perfect right to rule these barbarians of the New World and the adjacent islands, who in prudence, skill, virtues, and humanity are as inferior to the Spanish as children to adults, or women to men, for there exists between the two as great a difference as between . . . apes and men" (Columbia College 1954: 495–6).

Sepúlveda's views were contested in a famous mid-century debate at Valladolid by the Bishop of Chiapas, Bartolomé de las Casas, the crown's appointed "Protector of the Indians." Both men took for granted that the Spanish belonged in the New World; their dispute was over the nature of Amerindians and by extension how they should be treated. On one hand, Sepúlveda argued that the Amerindians were "homunculi" and natural slaves. On the other, Las Casas took the position, made dogma in Pope Paul III's *Sublimus Dei* of 1537, that the Amerindians were—like Europeans— descendants of Adam and "truly men." Rejecting the notion of their ontological difference, Las Casas distinguished Amerindians from the Spanish only in as much as they were "most delicate and tender, enjoying such a feeble constitution of body as does not permit them to endure labour" (Casas 1656: 2).

Las Casas was not entirely wrong. In the context of the Columbian exchange, and from an immunological perspective, the Amerindians were, in fact, biologically different from and weaker than Europeans. Long histories of contact with Africans and Asians, combined with agricultural practices involving the keeping of disease-carrying domestic animals, meant that Europeans were immune to pathogens unknown to the geographically isolated peoples of the Americas. So when, in 1519, smallpox arrived in the New World, Amerindians died at rates even greater than those suffered by Europeans during the Black Plague. Ironically, it was their purity of blood that rendered Amerindians vulnerable (Crosby 2003: 21–3). Las Casas knew nothing about epidemiology, but he saw its effects and as a result emphasized throughout his writings the feebleness of the Indians. This emphasis may have inadvertently reified the very notion of Amerindian difference that Las Casas sought to oppose. As Diego von Vacano puts it, Las Casas develops "links to the somatic component of later racial classifications. When moral or mental characteristics are coupled to corporeal or natural traits, we find the origins of racialization" (von Vacano 2012: 425).

Yet, the development of racial discourse across the history of empires does not always involve an attempt to affix internal characteristics to bodily traits. The ideology of race both scavenges and improvises, calibrating to the moment whatever ideas are available. Thus, Sepúlveda would also proffer the claim that Amerindians "are barbaric, uninstructed in letters and the art of government, and completely ignorant, unreasoning and incapable of learning anything but the mechanical arts" (de las Casas 1992b: 11). When claims like these of Amerindian primitivism buckled in the face of Tenochtitlan and Cuzco's complex systems of communication, governance, and record-keeping, Spanish thinkers tapped into the existing ideas about the willful degeneracy of heretics. If, at this point, Iberian writers refer more frequently to the color of Amerindians' skin, it was probably in order to associate them with Moriscos and Marranos. Thus, his opponents would redefine the physical weakness that Las Casas claimed to find in the Amerindians as a moral weakness whereby native people willfully resisted their own salvation. Instead of childlike innocents, they could be seen as rational agents bound to their own vicious depravity. Hence, the chronicler Gonzalo Fernandez de Oviedo y Valdes described the Americas as a land filled with "savage Indians who are so sunk in vice" and "have no knowledge of the all-powerful God and worship the devil" (Parry and Keith 1984: 17). Powerful Amerindian leaders could then be defined through an imported matrix of Near Eastern despotism, emphasizing their allegedly tyrannical rule and practices of polygamy. So, for example, William Strachey describes Powhatan's "seraglio" and his beating his subjects "with cudgels as the Turks do" (Strachey 1612: 52). What is crucial here is that race does not elude demystification by defending its logic and assuaging doubts, but by shifting ground and taking multiple shapes. Oviedo did not restrict himself to the idea of Amerindian savagery; he also continued to proffer evidence that the Amerindians were physiologically different, alleging that native women were impervious to the pain of childbirth and that the natives "have bones of the skulls of their heads four times as thick and much stronger than ours." (Martire d'Anghiera 1555: 209). Las Casas was not so much defeated as he was outflanked.

My point here is not to demonstrate the primacy of one racial discourse over another in the context of empire. Instead, it is to highlight how the racial system that channeled economic power and natural resources into the hands of European settlers depended above all on its mutability. Racism does not abandon racial discourses but accumulates an archive of "remains" that resurface "if not in form, then in intent, keeping more or less the same bodies in place" (Amin 2010: 5). As Ania Loomba and I have argued elsewhere, debates over the nature of difference do not mean that race was not yet formed but that it is always an amalgam of contradictory, unstable, and evolving ideas. It changes in response to time, place, and a host of other factors, distorting facts and mixing up cultural phenomena with physiological traits, recognizing the value of both for enforcing hierarchies (Loomba and Burton 2007: 10). Inconsistency is precisely what made race an effective tool of empires that needed to mollify reservations about coerced labor and the confiscation of property, or to account for and respond to native resistance.

Understanding race to be a dynamic, instrumental strategy allows us to recognize its many manifestations and transformations throughout history. But I am also arguing here for a polymorphism of race that is simultaneous, not successive. *Mutatis mutandis,* race not only assumes various states in response to present conditions (like water becoming ice or steam), it also—and this is crucial—thrives by keeping multiple forms in its active repertoire. In jettisoning our linear models of one schema superseding another and thinking instead about a model of recursive, polyschematic variation, I am attempting to take aboard Stephen Greenblatt's observation that "one of the characteristic powers of a culture is its ability to hide the mobility that is its enabling condition" (Greenblatt 2010, 252). Race does not become effective when it grows more fixed or stable than an older schema for which some substitute must be invented. As Ian Smith and others have indicated, race is always a fiction. But, to say that it is a fiction is not to suggest it can be easily invalidated. Race is a powerful fiction because it is relentlessly adaptive, innovating, and recycling.

FLUIDITY AND RESISTANCE

This chapter does not attempt to offer a conclusive definition or fix a point of origin for race in relation to empire largely because race was not and has never been a stable and transhistorical system of classification. It is better understood as a range of operations, selected for, applied to, and in turn reformulated by diverse ideologies and practices benefiting from the division of populations. Or, as Walter Mignolo puts it more succinctly, race is "an epistemic category to legitimize racism" (Mignolo 2008: 1739). To debate the moment of race's birth or invention then is to obscure the ways in which race is continually reinventing itself.

The situational mutability that I am describing here has raised some concerns among scholars of race in early modern studies. Peter Erickson and Kim Hall warn that an emphasis on race's "fluidity . . . remains a way of isolating the past from the present, reifying a narrative that makes race the regrettable product of modernity" (Erickson and Hall 2016: 10). The concerns here are threefold: First, a contradistinction of fluid (i.e., cultural, early modern) and fixed (i.e., scientific, modern) formulations of race can minimize, where it does not entirely discount, the force in our own world of cultural racism that is not based on strict taxonomies and does not look like genocide, lynching, or segregation. Second, an approach that partitions early modern and modern prejudices obscures the tenacity of race and its long and complex genealogies, allowing the fiction of a single, transhistorical racism instead of acknowledging various types of racism adapted to local conditions and responsive to contestation. Third, if early modern formulations of difference are denied the term "race" on the basis of their fluidity, scholarly scrutiny of early modern racism may be devalued as anachronistic and the violence of early modern racism may be dismissed.

These are serious concerns, yet "removing that concept [of fluidity] from our critical repertoire" (Erickson and Hall 2016: 12) as Erickson and Hall urge us to do is also to give up naming the very quality that has made race so tenacious in the past and arguably continues to sustain it today. For, as Patricia Akhimie argues, "it is the very slipperiness of the concept that makes oppression possible" (Akhimie 2016: 188). And as this chapter has attempted to demonstrate, it is precisely the situational mutability, or fluidity, of race that could make it the handmaid of early modern western empires. Furthermore, to recognize fluidity as a defining *characteristic* of early modern racialism is not the same thing as "identifying fluidity as a defining difference of early modern race" (Erickson and Hall 2016: 10). Racial violence in contemporary settings is no less dependent on fluidity. Consider, for example, the alterable racial valence of a hooded sweatshirt or of non-English speech in Britain and the United States today. To emphasize the fluidity of early modern racialism is not to distinguish between the past and present but rather to acknowledge how "our contemporary ideologies bear traces of older practices and thinking" (Loomba 2016: 235). It helps us to recognize the dynamism of racial ideologies in all times and places, and thus to approach with equal seriousness micro-aggressions and the genocidal imperialism to which they are kin.

What bears further exploration is how and where race's fluidity may have made it an effective weapon for those who sought to contest and negotiate imperial hierarchies. This kind of resistance is depicted in Shakespeare's Othello, who draws attention to "my parts, my title and my perfect soul" (Shakespeare 2008: 1.2.31), pre-empting Iago's proffered racial categories of "clime, complexion and degree" (3.3.234). By seizing on the fluidity and simultaneous multiplicity of race, the Moor of Venice overturns custom and convinces the Italian senators that he is "far more fair than black" (1.3.291). But slippage and performativity were not only the tools of Shakespeare's stage characters. Africans, and particularly Andean Indians in colonial Peru, found ways in legal proceedings to situationally perform, disavow, and move between *casta* categories created by the Spanish in order to improve their own economic and social circumstances (O'Toole 2012: 160–3). Likewise, in colonial Mexico enslaved peoples of African descent "utilized the sacrament of matrimony—imposed as an obligation—in order to appropriate rights for themselves" and insist upon their legal status as Christians (Bennett 2003: 46; and Bennett 2010: 3–4, 166). If the degree of agency imperial subjects exercised in these moments was often feeble or momentary—like Shylock's argument for Jewish similitude in the courtroom scene of *The Merchant of Venice*—they were nevertheless enough to heighten the sense of urgency about racial categories in colonial legislators that Valerie Traub describes in her chapter of this volume (Chapter 6, p. 175). At the very least, moments of racial negotiation should be enough to deter us from abandoning the idea of fluidity, at least until we have illuminated those places where it may have been key not only to racism but also to anti-racism and anti-imperialism.

NOTES

Introduction

1. See Jonathan Burton 2005. The quoted words are from Vitkus 2000: 7.
2. The phrase is Helmut Puff's (2013: 389).

Chapter 1

1. Mallett (1996) provides a concise synthesis of the definition and debate surrounding the military revolution that was originally described as taking place in northern Europe in the period from 1560 to 1660 in a lecture and later article by Michael Roberts in 1955, but later pushed back to the fifteenth and sixteenth centuries and located primarily in Italy and Spain most noticeably by Geoffrey Parker, 1988.
2. For a valuable new contribution to the specifically cultural history of war and empire see the volume of translated poems in *The Battle of Lepanto*, eds, Elizabeth R. Wright, *et al.*, 2014.

Chapter 2

1. Economic historians, historians of global empire, and development theorists have engaged in a long debate about how we might understand "the rise of the West" during the early modern period and yet avoid the pitfalls of Eurocentrism. Some of the most important book-length contributions to this debate include Amin, Anievas and Nisancioglu, Braudel, Davis, Frank, Hoffman, Kamen, Pomeranz, Smith, and Wallerstein.
2. See Jardine, and Jardine and Brotton. On *Worldly Goods*, see the reviews by Rowland and Martines.
3. See Fuller 158ff (where she cites Froude) on Hakluyt's compilation of travel narratives as a kind of "epic" form.

4. On the early history of joint-stock companies and corporations in England, see Barbour, Epstein, Stern, and Turner. On Shakespeare's company as joint-stock corporation, see Gurr 31–6.
5. Two important collections of essays that look at cross-cultural trade and early modern cultural production in ways that balance the light and the dark sides of the "global Renaissance" are Sebek and Deng, and Singh.

Chapter 3

1. The term Anthropocene is a recent term used by scientists to refer to a period of anthropogenically driven climate change when humans have become a geological force transforming the earth's atmosphere.
2. Brian Morris (2006). Studies that do offer global comparisons include W. Beinart and Lotte Hughes, (2007). For the twentieth-century story of conservation see W.M. Adams (2004). See also S. Dovers, R. Edgecomb and B. Guest (2002); W. Beinart and J. Mcgregor, (2003).
3. This carried on into a later period: see Felix Driver (2004) and David Arnold (2000).
4. The Mughal empire was spread over large parts of north and central India and the Deccan plateau with long periods of rule by emperors: Akbar, r. 1556–1605; Jahangir, r. 1605–27; Shahjahan, r. 1628–59; and Aurangzeb, r. 1659–1707.
5. The four articles were William Atwell (1990), Anthony Reid (1990), John Richards (1990) and Neils Steensgaard (1990). See also G. Parker and L.M. Smith (1990).
6. Tanistry refers here to the competition—often military—for power between families, dynasties, siblings, fathers, and sons, rather than inheritance of power.

Chapter 5

1. The manuscript, containing the surviving Arabic fragment, is preserved at the Escorial Library in Spain (Ms. Arabo 598).
2. Carvalho combs the Portuguese Inquisition records and finds in them numerous important details of Orta's life, including the fact that he was married, his sister Catarina's trial, and the names of their relatives.
3. Kathak's transcultural fusions take us back to Andalusia, where we started with Leo Africanus/al-Hasan. And that is because Kathak, or related forms, migrated with the Rajasthani tribes who were later to become known as the Roma or Gypsies; Kathak-like movements form a part of the post-*Reconquista* Andalusian *flamenco*, which also includes elements of Jewish mourning song and Sufi spinning. See Phillips (1991).

Chapter 6

1. I thank Ania Loomba for her crucial responses to drafts of this essay, Antoinette Burton for her help in making judicious cuts, Laurel Billings for compiling a research bibliography, and Joseph Gamble for his timely assistance in preparing the manuscript final publication.

Chapter 7

1. Adorno coined the term "zona de contacto," which Pratt translated into English as "contact zone."
2. Other scholars have contested the idea of centralized states in early modern Southeast Asia on the European model: Chutintaranond 1990; Pelras 2000; Cummings 2007: 9.
3. My translation; Unger provides a modern Dutch translation (134–5).
4. See also Verlinden 1970: 3–32, chapter 1, "The Transfer of Colonial Techniques from the Mediterranean to the Atlantic."
5. On the hybrid colonial system, see Ouweneel 1995; for Nahua views of the conquest, see Wood 2003; and Alsselbergs 1997.
6. For a list of revolts, see Taylor 2006: 179–213.
7. Castellanos (1522–1607) traveled through Puerto Rico, Venezuela, and Colombia.
8. For discussion, see Clements 2011.
9. See also Chaplin 2001: 79–115, chapter 3, "No Magic Bullets: Archery, Ethnography, and Military Intelligence."
10. African slaves in Dutch New Amsterdam also engaged in alliance-making among themselves to resist their Dutch masters (Zandt 2008: 137–65). Harris ("Mobility," this volume) views Pocahontas as the oppressed victim of the English, but contextualizing the episode within Algonquian cultural norms, historians like van Zandt emphasize her status as a Powhatan agent.
11. Extending White 1991, DuVal argues that the Arkansas Valley was the claimed "native ground" of several tribes as well as European groups: "When Indians lost ground, as the Tunicas did in the sixteenth century, Caddoan-speakers did in the eighteenth century, and the Osages did in the early nineteenth century, they lost it to other Indians. Only in the 1820s did Anglo-American settlers outnumber and overwhelm Arkansas Valley Indians" (DuVal 2006: 5); Hämäläinen 2008 argues that the Comanche empire of the American Southwest dominated their European rivals and was only defeated in 1875.
12. Williams ultimately concludes that Vitoria articulated a discourse of conquest; for a contrary view, see Pagden 1982.
13. Revisionist economic historians view Europe as peripheral to a world system centered in Asia, with Europe gaining an edge only in the late eighteenth century or later: Abu-Lughod 1989; Chaudhuri 1990; Wong 1997; Frank 1998; Pomeranz 2000.
14. Scholars are increasingly studying non-European alliances with European: see Harris ("Mobility," this volume) or Meuwese 2012 on Dutch trading alliances with Native Americans and with Africans.
15. For the account of Almeida's defeat, see Johnson 2012: 10–34.
16. My translation; Malay spelling modernized.
17. Clulow also examines Banda, Indonesia, where the elders initially signed treaties with the VOC to counter the Portuguese but then sought protection from the English to counter Dutch expansion.

Chapter 8

1. I am grateful to Ania Loomba for the opportunity to explore the inter-animating lives of race and empire and also to my tenacious and methodical research assistant, Regina Spadoni.
2. On Muscovite efforts at the incorporation of non-Russian elites, see Khodarkovsky 2001, 122–6.
3. See also Fetvacı 2013, pp. 149–90.
4. On western depictions of black eunuchs in the Ottoman court, see Kaplan 2013, 41–66.
5. Connections between apes and Africans also appear in works by Sir Thomas Herbert (1634); John Bulwer (1650); and Edward Tyson (1699), included in Loomba and Burton, *Race in Early Modern England*.
6. That the crown's more respectful approach receded after smallpox devastated native populations suggests that it derived less from worries over native rights than from a concern over the economic power conquistadors would attain given the right to enslave natives.

FURTHER READING

Abulafia, David (2008), *The Discovery of Mankind: Atlantic Encounters in the Age of Columbus*, New Haven: Yale University Press.
Abu-Lughod, Janet (1989), *Before European Hegemony: The World System, A.D. 1250–1350*, New York: Oxford University Press.
Adams, W.M. (2004), *Against extinction: the story of conservation*, London: Earthscan.
Adas, Michael (1981), "From Avoidance to Confrontation: Peasant Protest in Precolonial and Colonial Southeast Asia," *Comparative Studies in Society and History* 23 (2): 217–47.
Adorno, Rolena (1986), *Guaman Poma: Writing and Resistance in Colonial Peru*, Austin: University of Texas Press.
Adorno, Rolena (1987), "Waman Puma: el autor y su obra," in Felipe Guama Poma de Ayala, *Nueva corónica y buen gobierno*, ed. John V. Murra, Rolena Adorno, and Jorge L. Urioste, xvii–xviii, Madrid: Historia 16.1.
Africanus, Leo (1896), *The History and Description of Africa*, trans. John Pory, 3 vols., London: Hakluyt Society.
Agarwal, C.M. (1984), *Natural calamities and the great Mughals*, Delhi: Kanchan Publishers.
Ahmad, A. Samad, ed. (1987), *Hikayat Amir Hamzah*, Kuala Lumpur: Dewan Bahasa dan Pustaka.
Aidoo, Lamonte (2018), *Slavery Unseen: Sex, Power, and Violence in Brazilian History*, Durham and London: Duke University Press.
Akhimie, Patricia (2016), "Bruised with Adversity: reading race in The Comedy of Errors," in Valerie Traub (ed.), *The Oxford Handbook of Shakespeare and Embodiment: Gender, Sexuality and Race*, 186–96, Oxford: Oxford University Press.
Alam, M. (1998), *The Mughal state, 1526–1750*, Delhi: Oxford University Press.
al-Dabagh, Abdulla (2010), *Shakespeare, the Orient, and the Critics*, New York: Peter Lang.
Alfonso, Esperanza (2008), *Islamic Culture through Jewish Eyes: Al-Andalus from the Tenth to the Twelfth Century*, London and New York: Routledge, 2008.

Allen, Richard (2015), *European Slave Trading in the Indian Ocean, 1500–1850*, Ohio University Press.
Alsselbergs, Florine (1997), *Conquered Conquistadors: The Lienzo of Quauhquechollan: A Nahua Vision of the Conquest of Mexico*, Seville: Escuela de Estudios Hispano-Americanos.
Altman, Ida and James Horn (1991), *"To Make America": European Emigration in the Early Modern Period*, Berkeley: University of California Press.
Amer, Sahar (2008), *Crossing Borders: Love Between Women in Medieval French and Arabic Literatures*, Philadelphia, University of Pennsylvania Press.
Amin, Ash (2010), "The Remainders of Race," *Theory, Culture and Society* 27: 1 (March), 1–23.
Amin, Samir (2010), *Eurocentrism: Modernity, Religion, and Democracy: A Critique of Eurocentrism and Culturalism*, 2nd edn trans. Russell Moore and James Membrez, New York: Monthly Review Press.
Amussen, Susan Dwyer (2007), *Caribbean Exchanges: Slavery and the Transformation of English Society, 1640–1700*, Chapel Hill: University of North Carolina Press.
Amussen, Susan Dwyer and Allyson M. Poska (2014), "Shifting the Frame: Transimperial Approaches to Gender in the Atlantic World," *Early Modern Women: An Interdisciplinary Journal* 9 (1): 3–23.
Andaya, Leonard (1975), *The Kingdom of Johor 1641–1723*, Kuala Lumpur: Oxford University Press.
Andrade, Tonio (2005), "The Company's Chinese Pirates: How the Dutch East India Company Tried to Lead a Coalition of Pirates to War against China, 1621–1662," *Journal of World History* 15 (4): 415–44.
Andrade, Tonio (2008), *How Taiwan Became Chinese: Dutch, Spanish, and Han Colonization in the Seventeenth Century*, New York: Columbia University Press.
Andrea, Bernadette (2016), "'Travelling Bodyes': Native Women of the Northeast and Northwest Passage Ventures and English Discourses of Empire," in Ania Loomba and Melissa Sanchez (eds), *Rethinking Feminism in Early Modern Studies: Gender, Race, and Sexuality*, 135–48, New York and London: Routledge.
Anidjar, Gil (2002), *"Our Place in Al-Andalus": Kabbalah, Philosophy, Literature in Arab Jewish Letters*, Stanford, California: Stanford University Press.
Anievas, Alex and Kerem Nisancioglu (2015), *How the West Came to Rule: The Geopolitical Origins of Capitalism*, London: Pluto Press.
Anjum, Faraz (2011), "Strangers' Gaze: Mughal *Harem* and European Travellers of the Seventeenth Century," *Pakistan Vision* 12: 70–113.
Armitage, David, ed. (1998), *Theories of Empire, 1450–1800*, Aldershot, Brookfield USA: Ashgate.
Arneil, Barbara (1996), *John Locke and America: The Defence of English Colonialism*, Oxford: Clarendon Press.
Arnold, David (2000), "Illusory riches: representations of the tropical world, 1840–1950," *Singapore Journal of tropical geography*, 21, 1: 6–18.
Arrighi, Giovanni (1994), *The Long Twentieth Century*, London: Verso.
Arrizabalaga, Jon (2005), "Medical Responses to the 'French Disease' in Europe at the Turn of the Sixteenth Century," in Kevin Siena (ed.), *Sins of the Flesh: Responding to Sexual Disease in Early Modern Europe*, 33–55, Toronto: Centre for Reformation and Renaissance Studies.
Arvas, Abdulhamit (2016), "Travelling Sexualities, Circulating Bodies, and Early Modern Anglo-Ottoman Encounters," Michigan State University dissertation.

Atwell, William (1990), "A Seventeenth Century General Crisis in East Asia," *Modern Asian Studies*, Vol. 21, 4: 621–82.

Axtell, James (1988), "The Rise and Fall of the Powhatan Empire," in *After Columbus: Essays in the Ethnohistory of Colonial North America*, 182–221, New York: Oxford University Press.

Baber, R. Jovita (2010), "Empire, Indians, and the Negotiation for Status in the City of Tlaxcala, 1521–1550," in Ethelia Ruiz Medrano and Susan Kellogg (eds), *Negotiation with Domination: Colonial New Spain's Indian Pueblos Confront the Spanish State*, 34–55, Denver: University Press of Colorado.

Baber, R. Jovita (2012), "Law, Land, and Legal Rhetoric in Colonial New Spain: A Look at the Changing Rhetoric of Indigenous Americans in the Sixteenth Century," in Saliha Belmessous (ed.), *Native Claims: Indigenous Law against Empire, 1500–1920*, 41–62, Oxford: Oxford University Press.

Bakewell, Peter (1984), "Mining in Colonial Spanish America," in Leslie Bethelll (ed.), *The Cambridge History of Latin America*, vol. 2: *Colonial Latin America*, 105–51, Cambridge: Cambridge University Press.

Bancel, Nicolas, Thomas David and Dominic Thomas (2014), *The Invention of Race: Scientific and Popular Representations*, New York: Routledge.

Banerjee, Pompa (2003), *Burning Women: Widows, Witches, and Early Modern European Travelers in India*, New York: Palgrave Macmillan.

Banks, Kenneth (2002), *Chasing Empire Across the Sea: Communications and the State in the French Atlantic, 1713–63*, Montreal: McGill-Queen's University Press.

Barbour, Richmond (2009), *The Third Voyage Journals: Writing and Performance in the London East India Company, 1607–10*, New York: Palgrave Macmillan.

Bartlett, Robert (1993), *The Making of Europe, Conquest, Colonization and Cultural Change 950–1350*, Princeton, NJ: Princeton University Press.

Bassett, D.K. (1960), "European Influence in the Malay Peninsular 1511–1786," *Journal of the Malayan Branch, Royal Asiatic Society* 33 (3): 9–31.

Bayly, Chris (1993), *Rulers, townsmen and bazars, North Indian Society in the age of expansion*, Cambridge: Cambridge University Press.

Beckles, Hilary McD. (1989), *White Servitude and Black Slavery in Barbados, 1627–1715*, Knoxville: University of Tennessee Press.

Bedini, Silvio A., ed. (1992), *The Christopher Columbus Encyclopedia*, New York: Macmillan.

Beeching, Jack (1982), *The Galleys at Lepanto*, London: Hutchinson.

Beinart, W. and J. Mcgregor (2003), *Social History and African environments*, Oxford: James Curry.

Beinart, William and Lotte Hughes (2007), *Environment and empire*, Oxford: Oxford University Press.

Belmessous, Saliha (2012a), "Introduction: The Problem of Indigenous Claim Making in Colonial History," in Belmessous (ed.), *Native Claims: Indigenous Law against Empire, 1500–1920*, 3–18, Oxford: Oxford University Press.

Belmessous, Saliha (2012b), "Wabanaki versus French and English Claims in Northeastern North America, c. 1715," in Belmessous (ed.), *Native Claims: Indigenous Law against Empire, 1500–1920*, 107–28, Oxford: Oxford University Press.

Benedicti, Georgius (1990), *De rebus gestis Principis, Guilielmi comitis Nassovii, . . .* (1586), *De Krijgsdaden van Willem van Oranje*, ed. and trans. EDEPOL, Leiden: EDEPOL.

Benjamin, Walter (1969), "Theses on the Philosophy of History," *Illuminations: Essays and Reflections*, New York: Schocken.
Bennett, Herman L. (2003), *Africans in Colonial Mexico: Absolutism, Christianity, and Afro-Creole Consciousness, 1570–1640*, Bloomington, IN: Indiana University Press.
Bennett, Herman L. (2003), *Africans in Colonial Mexico: Absolutism, Christianity, and Afro-Creole Consciousness, 1570–1640*, Bloomington: Indiana University Press.
Bennett, Herman L. (2010), *Colonial Blackness: A History of Afro-Mexico*, Bloomington: Indiana University Press.
Bennett, Judith M. (1997), "Confronting Continuity," *Journal of Women's History* 9 (3): 73–94.
Bennett, Judith M., and Amy Froide, eds (1999), *Singlewomen in the European Past, 1250–1880*, Philadelphia: University of Pennsylvania Press.
Benton, Lauren (2001), *Law and Colonial Cultures: Legal Regimes in World History, 1400–1900*, Cambridge: Cambridge University Press.
Benton, Lauren (2012), "Possessing Empire: Iberian Claims and Interpolity Law," in Saliha Belmessous (ed.), *Native Claims: Indigenous Law against Empire, 1500–1920*, 19–40, Oxford: Oxford University Press.
Beveridge, Henry, ed. (1989), *Tuzuk-i-Jahangri or Memoirs of Jahangir*, trans. Alexander Rogers, Delhi: Low Price Publications.
Biddulph, William and Peter Biddulph (1608), "The Travels of foure English men and a preacher" in Thomas Osborne, *A Collection of Voyages and Travels*," Vol 1: XII, 761–830, London, 1745.
Black, Jeremy (1997), *Maps and History; constructing images of the past*, Yale: Yale University Press.
Blackburn, Robin (1997), "The Old World Background to European Colonial Slavery," *The William and Mary Quarterly*, 54 (1), 65–102.
Blackburn, Robin (1997), *The Making of New World Slavery: From the Baroque to the Modern, 1492–1800*, New York: Verso Press.
Blackmore, Josiah (2002), *Manifest Perdition: Shipwreck Narrative and the Disruption of Empire*, University of Minnesota Press.
Blaxton, John (1634), *The English Usurer*, London.
Bleys, Rudi C. (1996), *The Geography of Perversion: Male-to-male Sexual Behaviour outside the West and the Ethnographic Imagination, 1750–1918*, New York and London: Cassell.
Blount, Sir Henry (1636), *A Voyage into the Levant*, London.
Blussé, Leonard (1990), "Minnan-jen or Cosmopolitan? The Rise of Cheng Chih-lung Alias Nicolas Zhilong," in E.B. Vermeer (ed.), *Development and Decline of Fukien Province in the 17th and 18th Centuries*, 245–64, Leiden: Brill.
Bodin, Jean (1606), *The Six Bookes of a Commonweale*, trans. Richard Knolles, London: G. Bishop.
Boone, Joseph Allen (2014), *The Homoerotics of Orientalism*, New York: Columbia University Press.
Boonzaier, Emile, Candy Malherbe, Andy Smith, and Penny Berens (1996), *The Cape Herders: A History of the Khoikhoi of Southern Africa*, Cape Town & Johannesburg: David Philip; Athens: Ohio University Press.
Borschberg, Peter (1999), "Hugo Grotius, East India Trade and the King of Johor," *Journal of Southeast Asian Studies* 30 (2): 225–48.
Borschberg, Peter (2011), *Grotius, the Portuguese and Free Trade in the East Indies*, Singapore: NUS Press.

Borucki, Alex, David Eltis and David Wheat (2015), "Atlantic History and the Slave Trade to Spanish America," *American Historical Review*, 120 (2): 433–61.
Bosworth, C.E. (1995), "Ḳîz," in *The Encyclopedia of Islam*, 243. New Edition, Volume V: Khe–Mahi, Leiden and New York: Brill.
Boucher, Philip P. (2007), "Revisioning the 'French Atlantic': Or, How to think about the French Presence in the Atlantic, 1550–1625," in Peter C. Mancall (ed.), *The Atlantic World and Virginia, 1550–1624*, 274–306, Chapel Hill: University of North Carolina Press.
Boxer, C.R. (1963), *Two Pioneers of Tropical Medicine: Garcia d'Orta and Nicolás Monarde*, London: Wellcome Institute.
Boyle, Robert (1664), *Experiments and considerations touching colours*, London: Henry Herringman.
Braude, Benjamin (1997), "The Sons of Noah and the Construction of Ethnic and Geographical Identities in the Medieval and Early Modern Periods," *The William and Mary Quarterly*, 54 (1): 103–42.
Braudel, Fernand (1999), *The Perspective of the World, Vol. 3: Civilization and Capitalism, 15th–18th Century*, trans. Sian Reynolds, New York: Harper & Row.
Bray, Alan (1982), *Homosexuality in Renaissance England*, London: Gay Men's Press.
Bray, Alan (2003), *The Friend*, Chicago: University of Chicago Press.
Britton, Dennis (2014), *Becoming Christian: Race, Reformation, and Early Modern English Romance*, New York: Fordham University Press.
Brotton, Jerry (2006), *The Renaissance, A Very Short Introduction*, Oxford University Press.
Brown, Kathleen M. (1996), *Good Wives, Nasty Wenches, and Anxious Patriarchs: Gender, Race, and Power in Colonial Virginia*, Chapel Hill and London: University of North Carolina Press.
Brutus, Stephanus Junius, the Celt (1994), *Vindiciae, contra tyrannos*, ed. and trans. George Garnett, Cambridge: Cambridge University Press.
Bryant, Sherwin K. (2014), *Rivers of Gold, Lives of Bondage: Governing Through Slavery in Colonial Quito*, Chapel Hill: University of North Carolina Press.
Bryant, Sherwin K., Ben Vinson III and Rachel Sarah O'Toole, eds (2012), *Africans to Spanish America: Expanding the Diaspora*, Urbana, IL: University of Illinois Press.
Burbank, Jane, and Frederick Cooper (2010), *Empires in World History: Power and the Politics of Difference*, Princeton and Oxford: Princeton University Press.
Burhanudin, Jajat (2006), "*Kerajaan*-Oriented Islam: The Experience of Pre-Colonial Indonesia," *Studia Islamika* 13 (1): 31–60.
Burns, Kathryn (2007), "Unfixing Race," in Margaret R. Greer, Walter D. Mignolo, and Maureen Quilligan (eds), *Rereading the Black Legend*, 188–202, Chicago and London: University of Chicago Press.
Burton, Jonathan (2005), *Traffic and Turning: Islam and English Drama, 1579–1624*, Newark: University of Delaware Press.
Burton, Jonathan (2013), "Western Encounters with Sex and Bodies in Non-European Cultures, 1500–1750," in Sarah Toulalan and Kate Fisher (eds), *The Routledge History of Sex and the Body: 1500 to the Present*, 496–510, London and New York: Routledge.
Bush, Michael (1996), "Serfdom in Medieval and Early Modern Europe: A Comparison," in M.L. Bush (ed.), *Serfdom & Slavery: Studies in Legal Bondage*, 199–224, London: Longman.
Caesar, Caius Julius (1488), *Les Commentaires de Julius Cesar*, trans. Robert Gaguin, Paris: Anthoine Verad.

Caldwell, Ian (1995), "Power, state and society among the pre-Islamic Bugis," *Bijdragen tot de Taal-, Land- en Volkenkunde* 151: 394–421.
Camões, Luís Vaz de [Camoens] (2008), *The Lusiads*, trans. Landeg White, Oxford: Oxford University Press.
Carrasco, Pedro (1997), "Indian-Spanish Marriages in the First Century of the Colony," in Susan Schroeder, *et al.* (eds), *Indian Women of Early Mexico*, 87–103, Norman and London: University of Oklahoma Press.
Carvalho, Augusto da Silva (1934), "Garcia d'Orta," *Revista da Universidade de Coimbra* 12: 61–246.
Casale, Giancarlo (2007), "The Ethnic Composition of Ottoman Ship Crews and the 'Rumi Challenge' to Portuguese Identity," *Medieval Encounters* 13, 122–44.
Casale, Giancarlo (2010), *The Ottoman Age of Exploration*, Oxford: Oxford University Press.
Casale, Giancarlo (2015), "The Islamic empires of the early modern world," in Jerry H. Bentley, Sanjay Subrahmanyam and Merry E. Weisner-Hanks (eds), *The Cambridge World History: Volume VI: The Construction of a Global World, 1400–1800 CE: Part 1: Foundations*, 323–44. Cambridge: Cambridge University Press.
Castellanos, Juan (1997), *Elegíade varones ilustres de Indias*, Bogota: Gerardo Rivas Moreno.
Chakrabarty, Dipesh (2000), *Provincializing Europe: Postcolonial Thought and Historical Difference*, Princeton: Princeton University Press.
Chang, Kuei-Sheng (1974), "The Maritime Scene in China at the Dawn of Great European Discoveries," *Journal of the American Oriental Society*, Vol. 94, No. 3 (July–Sept), pp. 347–59.
Chaplin, Joyce E. (2001), *Subject Matter: Technology, the Body, and Science on the Anglo-American Frontier, 1500–1676*, Cambridge, MA: Harvard University Press.
Chapman, Matthieu (2017), *Anti-Black Racism in Early Modern English Drama: The Other "Other."* New York and London: Routledge.
Chaudhuri, K.N. (1985), *Trade and civilization in the Indian Ocean: an economic history from the rise of Islam*, Cambridge: Cambridge University Press.
Chaudhuri, K.N. (1990), *Asia before Europe: Economy and Civilisation of the Indian Ocean from the Rise of Islam to 1750*, Cambridge: Cambridge University Press.
Chaudhury, Sushil and Michel Morineau, eds (1999), *Merchants, Companies, and Trade: Europe and Asia in the Early Modern Era*, Cambridge: Cambridge University Press.
Chutintaranond, Sunait (1990), "'Mandala,' 'Segmentary States,' and Politics of Centralization in Medieval Ayudhya," *Journal of the Siam Society* 78 (1): 89–100.
Clark, Anna (2008), *Desire: A History of European Sexuality*, New York and London: Routledge.
Clements, William M. (2011), "Translating Context and Situation: William Strachey and Powhatan's 'Scorneful Song,'" in Brian Swann (ed.), *Born in the Blood: On Native American Translation*, 398–418, Lincoln: University of Nebraska Press.
Clingingsmith, David and Jeffery G. Williamson (2009), "Deindustrialization in 18th and 19th century India: Mughal decline, climate shocks and British industrial ascent," *Explorations in Economic History*, Vol. 45, issue 3: 209–34.
Clissold, Stephen (1954), *Conquistador*, London: Derek Verschoyle.
Clulow, Adam (2016), "The Art of Claiming: Possession and Resistance in Early Modern Asia," *American Historical Review* 121 (1): 17–38.

Columbia College (1954), *An Introduction to Contemporary Civilization in the West: A Source Book*. Vol. 1, Second Edition, New York: Columbia University Press.

Constanza, Robert, Lisa J. Graumlich and Will Steffan, eds (2006), *Sustainability or collapse; Integrated history and future of people on earth*, Cambridge: MIT Press.

Coombs, John C. (2011), "The Phases of Conversion: A New Chronology for the Rise of Slavery in Early Virginia," *The William and Mary Quarterly*, 68 (3): 332–60.

Coppi, A. (1855), *Memoriae Colonessi*, Rome: Salviucci.

Corn, Charles (1998), *The Scents of Eden, A History of the Spice Trade*, New York: Kodanasha America.

Corona, Gabriella, ed. (2008), "What is global history?" Global Forum, *Global Environment*, no. 2, accessible at http://www.environmentandsociety.org/mml/corona-gabriella-ed-what-global-environmental-history.

Cortés, Hernán (1963), *Cartas y documentos*, ed. Mario Sánchez-Barba, Mexico City.

Coryate, Thomas (1616), *Thomas Coriate traveller for the English wits: greeting From the court of the Great Mogul, resident at the towne of Asmere, in easterne India*, London.

Cott, Nancy F., *et al.*, eds (1996), *Roots of Bitterness: Documents of the Social History of American Women*, 2nd edn, Boston: Northeastern University Press.

Cowper, William (2003), *William Cowper: Selected Poems*, ed. Nick Rhodes, New York: Routledge.

Crosby, Alfred (2003), *The Columbian Exchange: Biological and Cultural Consequences of 1492. 30th Anniversary Edition*, Westport, CT: Praeger.

Crosby, Alfred (2004), *Ecological imperialism, the biological expansion of Europe, 900–1900*, Cambridge: Cambridge University Press.

Cummings, William P., ed. and trans. (2007), *A Chain of Kings: The Makassarese Chronicles of Gowa and Talloq*, Leiden: KITLV.

Curione, Celio Augustino (1575), *A Notable History of Saracens*, London, Thomas Newton.

Curtin, Philip D. (1990), *The Rise and Fall of the Plantation Complex: Essays in Atlantic History*, Cambridge: Cambridge University Press.

Dainotto, Roberto M (2006), "On the Arab Origins of Modern Europe: Giammaria Barbieri, Juan Andres, and the Origin of Rhyme," *Comparative Literature*, 58: 4 271–92, 275.

Damodaran, Vinita, Rob Allan and James Hamilton (forthcoming), "Climate signals, environment and livelihoods in seventeenth century India in a comparative context," in Ayesha Mukherjee ed. *A Cultural History of Famine*, Routledge.

Dandelet, Thomas (2014), *The Renaissance of Empire in Early Modern Europe*, Cambridge and New York: Cambridge University Press.

Darwin, John (2008), *After Tamerlane: The Global History of Empire since 1405*, New York: Bloomsbury Press.

Davis, Natalie Zemon (2007), *Trickster Travels: A Sixteenth-Century Muslim between Worlds*, New York: Hill and Wang.

Davis, Ralph (1973), *The Rise of the Atlantic Economies*, Ithaca, NY: Cornell University Press.

de Barros, João (1553), *Da Asia, Of the Deeds which the Portuguese Performed in the Conquest and Exploration of the Lands and Seas of the East*, in Theal, G.M. trans. and ed. (1964), *Records of South-Eastern Africa*, 9 vols., Cape Town: Struik, first published 1898.

Deeds, Susan M. (1997), "Double Jeopardy: Indian Women in Jesuit Missions of Nueva Vizcaya," in Susan Schroeder, *et al.* (eds), *Indian Women of Early Mexico*, 255–72, Norman and London: University of Oklahoma Press.

de las Casas, Bartholomé (1598), *Narratio regionum indicarum per Hispanos . . .*, Frankfurt: Theodor de Bry.
de las Casas, Bartolemé (1992a), *A Short Account of the Destruction of The Indies, 1542*, ed. and trans. Nigel Griffin, London: Penguin.
de las Casas, Bartolomé (1552), *Brevísima relación de la destrucción de las Indias*, Seville.
de las Casas, Bartolomé (1656), *The tears of the Indians being an historical and true account of the cruel massacres and slaughters of above twenty millions of innocent people, committed by the Spaniards . . . .* London: Printed by J.C. for Nath. Brook.
de las Casas, Bartolomé (1992b), *In Defence of the Indians*, ed. and trans. Stafford Poole, De Kalb: Northern Illinois University Press.
Degenhardt, Jane Hwang (2010), *Islamic Conversion and Christian Resistance on the Early Modern Stage*, Edinburgh: University of Edinburgh.
della Valle, Pietro (1650–1658). *Viaggi di Pietro Della Valle il pellegrino, con minuto ragguaglio di tutte le cose notabili osservate in essi: descritti da lui medesimo in 54 lettere familiari all'erudito suo amico Mario Schipano, divisi in tre parti cioè: la Turchia, la Persia e l'India*, Rome, 1650–1658; Torino, 1843.
de Sepúlveda, Juan Ginés and Bartolomé de las Casas (1975), *Apología de Juan Ginés de Sepúlveda contra Fray Bartolomé de las Casas y de Fray Bartolomé de las Casas contra Juan Ginés de Sepúlveda* (1550, 1552–3), ed. and trans. Ángel Losada, Madrid: Editora Nacional.
DeSouza, Teotonio R. (1989), *Goa through the Ages: An Economic History*, 2 vols, New Delhi: Concept Publishing.
Devereux, Andrew (2015), "The ruin and slaughter of . . . fellow Christians: The French as Threat to Christendom in Spanish Assertions of Sovereignty in Italy, 1479–1516," in Barabara Fuchs and Emily Weissbourd (eds), *Representing Imperial Rivalry in the Early Modern Mediterranean*, 101–25, Toronto: University of Toronto Press.
Dijk, Wil O (2008), "An end to the history of silence? The Dutch Trade in Asian slaves: Arakan and the Bay of Bengal, 1621–1665," *IIAS Newsletter* 46, Winter, 16.
Diouf, Sylviane A. (2014), *Slavery's Exiles: The Story of the American Maroons*, New York: New York University Press.
Divyabhanusinh (2012), "At the court of the great Mughals," in Rangarajan, M. and K. Sivaramakrishnan, *India's environmental history from ancient times to the colonial period*, Ranikhet: Permanent Black.
Donoghue, John (2013), "Indentured Servitude in the 17th Century English Atlantic: A Brief Survey of the Literature," *History Compass* 11/10: 893–910.
Dovers, S., R. Edgecomb and B. Guest (2002), *South Africa's environmental history, cases and comparisons*, Ohio: Ohio University Press.
Doyle, Laura (2014), "Inter-Imperiality: Dialectics in a Postcolonial World History," *Interventions: International Journal of Postcolonial Studies* 16.2, 159–96.
Drake, James David (1999), *King Philip's War: Civil War in New England, 1676–76*, Amherst: University of Massachusetts Press.
Driver, Felix (2004), "Imagining the tropics: views and visions of the tropical world," *Singapore Journal of tropical geography*, 25, 11: 1–17.
DuVal, Kathleen (2006), *The Native Ground: Indians and Colonists in the Heart of the Continent*, Philadelphia: University of Pennsylvania Press.
Eden, Richard (1555), "To the Reader," *The decades of the newe worlde or West India . . .*, translated by Richard Eden, London: Guilhelmi Powell.

Edwards, S.M. and H.M.O. Garrett, (1974), *Mughal rule in India*, London: Luzac.
Eisenberg, José (2003), "Antonio Vieira and the Justification of Indian Slavery," *Luso-Brazilian Review*, 40 (1): 89–95.
Eliot, Charles W (2005), *Voyages and Travels, Ancient and Modern*, volume 33, New York: Cosimo.
Ellingson, Ter (2001), *The myth of the Noble savage*, Berkley and California: University of California Press.
Elliott, J.H. (1963), *The Revolt of the Catalans*. Cambridge: Cambridge University Press.
Elliott, J.H. (1992), "A Europe of Composite Monarchies," *Past and Present* 137: 48–71.
Elliott, J.H. (1998), "The Seizure of Overseas Territories by the European Powers," in David Armitage (ed.), *Theories of Empire, 1450–1800*, 139–58, Aldershot, Brookfield USA: Ashgate.
Elliott, J.H. (2006), *Empires of the Atlantic World: Britain and Spain in America, 1492–1830*, New Haven: Yale University Press.
Eltis, David (2001), "The Volume and Structure of the Transatlantic Slave Trade: A Reassessment," *The William and Mary Quarterly*, 58 (1): 17–46.
Epstein, Mortimer (1908), *The Early History of the Levant Company*, London: George Routledge and Sons.
Ercilla y Zuniga, Alonso de. (1945), *La Araucana*, 1589, trans. Charles M. Lancaster and Paul T. Manchester, Nashville: Vanderbilt University Press.
Erickson, Peter and Kim F. Hall (2016), "'A New Scholarly Song': Rereading Early Modern Race," *Shakespeare Quarterly* 67, no.1: 10.
Evelyn, John (1674), *Navigation and Commerce, Their Original and Progress, Containing a Succinct Account of Traffick in General*, London.
Faria y Sousa, Manuel de. (1695), *The Portuguese Asia*, trans. John Stevens, London.
Faroqhi, Suraiya (2006), *The Ottoman Empire and the World Around It*, London and New York: I.B. Tauris.
Fazl, Abu'l (1927), *The A'in-i-Akbari of Abu'l Fazl*, 2 vols, Calcutta: Asiatic Society.
Feerick, Jean (2010), *Strangers in Blood: Relocating Race in the Renaissance*, Toronto: University of Toronto Press.
Fernandez-Armesto, Felipe (1987), *Before Columbus: Exploration and Colonisation from the Mediterranean to the Atlantic, 1229–1492*, (Macmillan).
Fernández-Armesto, Felipe (1988), *The Spanish Armada*, Oxford: Oxford University Press.
Fetvacı, Emine (2013), *Picturing History at the Ottoman Court*, Bloomington: Indiana University Press.
Fisher, Michael H. (2004), *Counterflows to Colonialism: Indian Travellers and Settlers in Britain, 1600–1857*, Delhi: Permanent Black.
Fitzmaurice, Andrew (2003), *Humanism and America: An Intellectual History of English Colonisation, 1500–1625*, Cambridge: Cambridge University Press.
Fitzmaurice, Andrew (2007), "Moral Uncertainty in the Dispossession of Native Americans," in Peter C. Mancall (ed.), *The Atlantic World and Virginia, 1550–1624*, 383–409, Chapel Hill: University of North Carolina Press.
Fitzmaurice, Andrew (2012), "Powhatan Legal Claims," in Saliha Belmessous (ed.), *Native Claims: Indigenous Law against Empire, 1500–1920*, 85–106, Oxford: Oxford University Press.
Floyd-Wilson, Mary (2003), *English Ethnicity and Race in Early Modern Drama*, Cambridge, UK; New York, NY: Cambridge University Press.

Flynn, Dennis O. and Arturo Giraldez (2001), "Latin American Silver and the Early Globalization of World Trade," in Mercedes F. Duran-Cogan and Antonio Gomez-Moriana (eds), *National Identities and Socio-Political Changes in Latin America*. New York and London: Routledge, 140–59.

Ford, Caroline, (2007), "Natures fortunes: new directions in the writing of European environmental history," *The journal of modern history*, 79, March 2: 112–33.

Frank, Andre Gunder (1998), *ReORIENT: Global Economy in the Asian Age*, Berkeley: University of California Press.

Friedman, Jerome (1987), "Jewish Conversion, the Spanish Pure Blood Laws and Reformation: A Revisionist View of Racial and Religious Antisemitism," *The Sixteenth Century Journal* 18 (1): 3–30.

Friedman, John Block (1981), *The Monstrous Races in Medieval Thought and Art*, Cambridge: Harvard University Press.

Fuchs, Barbara (2001), *Mimesis and Empire: The New World, Islam, and European Identities*, Cambridge: Cambridge University Press.

Fuchs, Barbara (2003), "Imperium Studies: Theorizing Early Modern Expansion," in Patricia Clare Ingham and Michelle R. Warren (eds), *Postcolonial Moves: Medieval through Modern*, 71–90, New York: Palgrave MacMillan.

Fuchs, Barbara and Emily Weissbourd (2015), *Representing Imperial Rivalry in the Early Modern Mediterranean*, Toronto: University of Toronto Press.

Fuller, Mary (1995), *Voyages in Print: English Narratives of Travel to America 1576–1624*, Cambridge: Cambridge University Press.

Furber, Holden (1969), "Asia and the West as Partners before 'Empire' and After," *Journal of Asian Studies* 28 (4): 711–21.

Gallay, Alan (2002), *The Indian Slave Trade: The Rise of the English Empire in the American South, 1670–1717*, New Haven: Yale University Press.

Gama, Vasco (2009), *Em nome de Deus: The Journal of the First Voyage of Vasco da Gama to India, 1497–1499*, trans. and ed. Glenn J. Ames, Leiden: Brill.

Games, A. (1999), *Migration and the Origins of the English Atlantic World*, Cambridge, MA: Harvard University Press.

Games, Alison (2008), *The Web of Empire: English Cosmopolitanism in an Age of Expansion, 1560–1660*, Oxford: Oxford University Press.

Garofalo, Leo J. (2012), "The Shape of a Diaspora: The Movement of Afro-Iberians to Colonial Spanish America," in Sherwin K. Bryant, Ben Vinson III, and Rachel Sarah O'Toole (eds), *Africans to Spanish America: Expanding the Diaspora*, Urbana, IL: University of Illinois Press.

Garza Carvajal, Federico (2003), *Butterflies Will Burn: Prosecuting Sodomites in Early Modern Spain and Mexico*, Austin: University of Texas Press.

Gaspar, David Barry (1993), *Bondmen and Rebels: A Study of Master-Slave Relations in Antigua*, Durham: Duke University Press.

Gibson, Charles (1968), *Spain in America*, New York: Harper & Row.

Gleach, Frederic W. (1997), *Powhatan's World and Colonial Virginia: A Conflict of Cultures*, Lincoln: University of Nebraska Press.

Godbeer, Richard (2002), *Sexual Revolution in Early America*, Baltimore, MD: Johns Hopkins University Press.

Goffman, D. and C. Stroop (2004), "Empire as Composite: The Ottoman Polity and the Typology of Dominion," in Balachandra Rajan and Elizabeth Sauer (eds), *Imperialisms: Historical and Literary Investigations, 1500–1900*, 129–45, New York: Palgrave Macmillan.

Goffman, Daniel (2002), *The Ottoman Empire and Early Modern Europe*, Cambridge: Cambridge University Press.
Goldberg, Jonathan (1992), *Sodometries: Renaissance Texts, Modern Sexualities*, Stanford: Stanford University Press.
Gomez, Michael A. (2005), *Black Crescent: The Experience and Legacy of African Muslims in the Americas*, Cambridge: Cambridge University Press.
Gommans, Jos (2002), *Mughal Warfare*, London: Routledge.
Goodman, Anthony (1988), *The New Monarchy: England 1471–1532*, Oxford: Blackwell.
Goodman, Lenn E. (2005), *Avicenna*, Ithaca, New York: Cornell University Press.
Goody, Jack (1996), *The East in the West*, Cambridge: Cambridge University Press.
Gould, Virginia Meacham (1997), "'A Chaos of Iniquity and Discord': Slave and Free Women of Color in the Spanish Ports of New Orleans, Mobile, and Pensacola," in Catherine Clinton and Michele Gillespie (eds), *Devil's Lane: Sex and Race in the Early South*, Oxford: Oxford University Press.
Grady, Kyle (2017), "Moors, Mulattos, and Post-Racial Problems: Reconstructing Racialization in Early Modern England," University of Michigan dissertation.
Graeber, David (2014), *Debt: The First 5000 Years*, New York: Melville House.
Grafton, Anthony (1992), *New World, Ancient Texts, The power of tradition and the shock of discovery*, Harvard University Press.
Granzotto, Gianni (1985), *Christopher Columbus*, New York: Doubleday & Co.
Greenblatt, Stephen (2010), *Cultural Mobility: A Manifesto*, New York: Cambridge University Press.
Greenblatt, Stephen J (1980), *Renaissance Self-fashioning*, Chicago: University of Chicago Press.
Greer, Margaret R., Walter d. Mignolo, and Maureen Quilligan, eds (2007), *Rereading the Black Legend: The Discourses of Religious and Racial Difference in the Renaissance Empire*. Chicago and London: The University of Chicago Press.
Grotius, Hugo (2004), *The Free Sea*, trans. Richard Hakluyt, ed. David Armitage, Indianapolis: Liberty Fund.
Grove, Richard (1995), *Green imperialism, colonial expansion, tropical island Edens and the origins of environmentalism, 1600–1860*, Cambridge: Cambridge University Press.
Grove, Richard and V. Damodaran (2006), "Imperialism, intellectual networks and environmental change, origins and evolution of global environmental history, 1676–2000," *Economic and Political Weekly*. Part 1, October 14, Vol. 41: 4345–54, and Part 2, October 21, Vol. 42: 4497–4505.
Gruzinski, Serge (2003), "The Ashes of Desire: Homosexuality in Mid-Seventeenth-Century New Spain," in Pete Sigal (ed.), *Infamous Desire: Male Homosexuality in Colonial Latin America*, 197–214, Chicago and London: University of Chicago Press.
Guasco, Michael (2014), *Slaves and Englishmen: Human Bondage in the Early Modern Atlantic World*, Philadelphia: University of Pennsylvania Press.
Guicciardini, Frencesco (1969), *The History of Italy*, trans. Sidney Alexander, New York: Macmillan.
Gunder Frank, Andre (1998), *Re-Orient, Global Economy in the Asian Age*, Berkeley: University of California Press.
Gurr, Andrew (2004), *The Shakespeare Company, 1594–1642*, Cambridge: Cambridge University Press.
Haakonssen, Knud (1996), *Natural Law and Moral Philosophy: From Grotius to the Scottish Enlightenment*, Cambridge: Cambridge University Press.

Habib, I. (1963), *The Agrarian System of Mughal India*, Aligarh: Asia Publishing House.
Habib, Irfan (1990. "Merchant communities in pre-colonial India,' in James D. Tracy (ed.) *The Rise of Merchant Empires*. Cambridge, Cambridge University Press, 371–99.
Habib, Imtiaz (2008), *Black Lives in the English Archives, 1500–1677: Imprints of the Invisible*, Aldershot: Ashgate.
Hakluyt, Richard (1904), *Principal Navigations, Voyages and Discoveries of the English Nation*, 1598–1600, 12 vols., Glasgow: James Maclehose and Sons.
Hale, J.R. (1961), *The Art of War in Renaissance England*, Washington: Folger Shakespeare Library.
Hale, J.R. (1985), *War and Society in Renaissance Europe 1450–1620*, Leicester: Leicester University Press.
Hale, J.R. (1990), *Artists and Warfare in the Renaissance*, New Haven and London: Yale University Press.
Hale, Sir Matthew (1677), *The Primitive Origination of Mankind*, London: William Bodbid.
Hall, Joseph (1617), *Quo Vadis? A Just Censure of Travel as It Is Commonly Undertaken by the Gentlemen of Our Nation*, London.
Hall, Kenneth R. (2010), *A History of Early Southeast Asia: Maritime Trade and Societal Development*, Lanham: Rowman & Littlefield.
Hall, Kim (1995), *Things of Darkness, Economies of Race and Gender in Early Modern England*, Ithaca: Cornell University Press.
Halley, Edmond (1694), "An account of the circulation of watry vapours of the sea and of the cause of springs," *Philosophical Transactions of the Royal Society*, 192: 17: 468–73.
Hämäläinen, Pekka (2008), *The Comanche Empire*, New Haven: Yale University Press.
Handler, Jerome S. and Matthew C. Reilly (2017), "Contesting 'White Slavery' in the Caribbean: Enslaved Africans and European Indentured Servants in Seventeenth-Century Barbados," *NWIG: New West Indian Guide/Nieuwe West-Indische Gids*, 91 (1–2): 3–55.
Hanke, Lewis (1945), *The Spanish Struggle for Justice in the Conquest of America*, Philadelphia: University of Pennsylvania Press.
Hardiman, David (1998), "Well irrigation in Gujerat; systems of use, hierarchies of control," *Economic and Political weekly*, Vol. 33, no. 25: 1533–44.
Harris, Jonathan Gil (2014), *The First Firangis: Remarkable Stories of Heroes, Healers, Charlatans, Courtesans, and Others Who Became Indian*, New Delhi: Aleph Books.
Harris, Jonathan Gil (2015), "When Christian Power Was Arrayed against a Judeo-Muslim Ideology," *YaleGlobal*, July 30, 2015, http://yaleglobal.yale.edu/content/when-christian-power-was-arrayed-against-judeo-muslim-ideology.
Hatfield, April Lee (2004), *Atlantic Virginia: Intercolonial Relations in the Seventeenth Century*, Philadelphia: University of Pennsylvania Press.
Hawkes, David (2010), *The Culture of Usury in Renaissance England*, New York: Palgrave Macmillan.
Hemming, John (1978), *Red Gold: The Conquest of the Brazilian Indians, 1500–1760*, Cambridge, MA: Harvard University Press.
Heng, Geraldine (2003), *Empire of Magic: Medieval Romance and the Politics of Cultural Fantasy*, New York: Columbia University Press.
Heng, Geraldine (2011a), "The Invention of Race in the European Middle Ages I: Race Studies, Modernity, and the Middle Ages," *Literature Compass* 8:5, 258–74.

Heng, Geraldine (2011b), "The Invention of Race in the European Middle Ages II: Locations of Medieval Race," *Literature Compass* 8:5, 275–93.
Hewlett, Mary (2005), "The French Connection: Syphilis and Sodomy in Late-Renaissance Lucca," in Kevin Siena (ed.), *Sins of the Flesh: Responding to Sexual Disease in Early Modern Europe*, 33–55, Toronto: Centre for Reformation and Renaissance Studies.
Heywood, Thomas (1964), *If You Know Not Me, Part II. 1605. The Dramatic Works of Thomas Heywood*, Vol. 1., New York: Russell & Russell.
Hing, Hui Chun (2010), "Hunagming zuxun and Zheng He's Voyages to the Western Oceans," *Journal of Chinese Studies* (Institute of Chinese Studies), 67–85.
Hite, Katherine (2012), *Politics and the Art of Commemoration, Memorials to Struggle in Latin America and Spain*, Milton Park: Routledge.
Hobsbawm, E.J. (1954), "The general crisis of the seventeenth century," *Past and Present*, no. 5: 33–53.
Hodes, Martha (1997), *White Women, Black Men: Illicit Sex in the Nineteenth-Century South*, New Haven: Yale University Press.
Hodes, Martha, ed. (1999), *Sex, Love, Race: Crossing Boundaries in North American History*, New York: New York University Press.
Hoffman, Philip T. (2015), *Why Did Europe Conquer the World?* Princeton: Princeton University Press.
Hopkins, Lisa (2008), *Cultural Uses of the Caesars on the English Renaissance Stage*, Abingdon: Ashgate.
Horswell, Michael J., "Toward an Andean Theory of Ritual Same-Sex Sexuality and Third-Gender Subjectivity," in Pete Sigal (ed.), *Infamous Desire: Male Homosexuality in Colonial Latin America*, 25–69, Chicago and London: University of Chicago Press.
Howard, Jean E. (2007), *Theater of a City: The Places of London Comedy 1598–1642*, Philadelphia: University of Pennsylvania Press.
Huarte, Juan (1594), *Examen de ingenious*, trans. by M. Camillo Camilli and R.C. Esquire, London: Adam Islip.
Hudson, Nicholas (1996), "From 'Nation' to 'Race': The Origin of Racial Classification in Eighteenth-Century Thought." *Eighteenth Century Studies* 29, no. 3 (Spring): 252.
Hulme, Peter (1985), "Polytropic Man: Tropes of Sexuality and Mobility in Early Colonial Discourse," *Europe and Its Others* edited Francis Barker *et al.* Colchester: University of Essex Press. 17–32.
Hulme, Peter (1986), *Colonial Encounters: Europe and the Native Caribbean, 1492–1797*, London: Methuen.
Hulme, Peter (1999), "Voice from the margins?: Walter Mignolo's *The Darker Side of the Renaissance*," *Journal of Latin American Cultural Studies*, 8:2, 219–33.
Inden, R. (2000), *Imagining India*, Bloomington: Indiana University Press.
Iskandar, Teuku, ed. (2001), *Hikayat Aceh*, Kuala Lumpur: Yayasan Karyawan.
Israel, J. (1974), *Mexico and the General Crisis of the Seventeenth Century, Past and Present*, 63: 33–57.
Israel, Jonathan (1982), *The Dutch Republic and the Hispanic World, 1606–1661*, Oxford: Clarendon Press.
Ittersum, Martine Julia (2006), *Profit and Principle: Hugo Grotius, Natural Rights Theories and the Rise of Dutch Power in the East Indies (1595–1615)*, Leiden: Brill.
Jacquart, Danielle, and Claude Thomasset (1988), *Sexuality and Medicine in the Middle Ages*, Princeton: Princeton University Press.

Jardine, Lisa (1998), *Worldly Goods: A New History of the Renaissance*, New York: Norton.

Jardine, Lisa and Jerry Brotton (2000), *Global Interests: Renaissance Art between East and West*, London: Reaktion Books.

Jefferson, Ann and Paul Lokken (2011), *Daily Life in Colonial Latin America*, Santa Barbara, CA: Greenwood Press.

Jehlen, Myra (1993), "History before the Fact; Or, Captain John Smith's Unfinished Symphony," *Critical Inquiry* 19, no. 4 (Summer): 677–92.

Johnson, David (2012), *Imagining the Cape Colony: History, Literature, and the South African Nation*, Edinburgh: Edinburgh University Press.

Jordan, Annemarie (2005), "Images of empire: slaves in the Lisbon household and court of Catherine of Austria," in T.F. Earle and K.J.P. Lowe (eds), *Black Africans in Renaissance Europe*, 155–80, Cambridge: Cambridge University Press.

Kamen, Henry (2003), *Empire: How Spain Became a World Power, 1492–1763*, New York: HarperCollins.

Kangal, Selim, ed. (2000), *The Sultan's Portrait: Picturing the House of Osman*. Istanbul: Isbank.

Kaplan, M. Lindsay (2016), "Constructing the Inferior Body: Medieval Theology in *The Merchant of Venice*," in Valerie Traub (ed.), *Oxford Handbook of Shakespeare and Embodiment*, 155–69, Oxford: Oxford University Press.

Kaplan, M. Lindsay (2018), *Theological Inferiority and the History of Racism*, Oxford: Oxford University Press.

Kaplan, Paul H.D. (2013), "Black Turks: Venetian artists and perceptions of Ottoman ethnicity," in James G. Harper (ed.) *The Turk and Islam in the Western Eye, 1450–1750: Visual Imagery before Orientalism*, 41–66, Farnham Burlington, VT: Ashgate.

Karras, Ruth Mazo (1996), *Common Women: Prostitution and Sexuality in Medieval England*, New York and Oxford: Oxford University Press.

Karttunen, Frances (1997), "Rethinking Malinche," in Susan Schroeder, *et al.* (eds), *Indian Women of Early Mexico*, 291–312, Norman and London: University of Oklahoma Press.

Kathirithamby-Wells, J. (1970), "Ahmad Shah Ibn Iskandar and the Late 17th Century 'Holy War' in Indonesia," *Journal of the Malaysian Branch of the Royal Asiatic Society* 43 (1): 48–63.

Kelly, Joan (1986), "Did Women Have a Renaissance?," in *Women, History and Theory*, 19–50. University of Chicago Press.

Kendi, Ibram X. (2016), *Stamped from the Beginning: The Definitive History of Racist Ideas in America*, New York: Nation Books.

Khodarkovsky, Michael (2001), "The Conversion of Non-Christians in Early Modern Russia," in Robert P. Geraci and Michael Khodarkovsky (eds), *Of Religion and Empire: Missions, Conversion and Tolerance in Tsarist Russia*, 122–6, Ithaca and London: Cornell University Press.

Kinoshita, Sharon (2006), *Medieval Boundaries: Rethinking Difference in Old French Literature*, Philadelphia: University of Pennsylvania Press.

Klein, Herbert S. and Ben Vinson III (2007), *African Slavery in Latin America and the Caribbean*, 2nd edn, New York: Oxford University Press.

Koenigsberger, H.G. (1969), *The Practice of Empire*, Ithaca: Cornell University Press.

Kruger, Steven F. (1997), "Conversion and Medieval Sexual, Religious, and Racial Categories," in Karma Lochrie, Peggy McCracken, and James A. Schultz (eds),

Constructing Medieval Sexuality, 158–79, Minneapolis and London: University of Minnesota Press.
Kulku, Hermann (1986), "The Early and the Imperial Kingdom in Southeast Asian History," in David G. Marr and A. C. Milner (eds), *Southeast Asia in the 9th to 14th Centuries*, 1–22, Singapore: Institute of Southeast Asian Studies.
Kumar, Deepak (2015), "Botanical explorations and the East India Company: revisiting 'Plant colonialism,'" in Vinita Damodaran, Anna Winterbottom and Alan Lester eds, *The East India Company and the Natural World*, London: Palgrave.
Kupperman, Karen Ordahl (2000), *Indians and English: Facing Off in Early America*, Ithaca and London: Cornell University Press.
Lach, Donald Frederick and Edwin J. Van Kley (1998), *Asia in the Making of Europe, Vol III: A Century of Advance*, Chicago: Chicago University Press.
Lal, Ruby (2005), *Domesticity and Power in the Early Mughal World*, Cambridge: Cambridge University Press.
Lampert, Lisa (2010), *Medieval Literature and Postcolonial Studies*, Edinburgh: University of Edinburgh Press.
Lanser, Susan S. (2014), *The Sexuality of History: Modernity and the Sapphic, 1565–1830*, Chicago: University of Chicago Press.
Lawrence, Jeremy (2005), "Black Africans in Renaissance Spanish Literature," in T.F. Earle and K.J.P. Lowe (ed.) *Black Africans in Renaissance Europe*, 70–93, Cambridge: Cambridge University Press.
Leapman, Michael (2003), *Inigo*, London: Review.
Lefroy, J.H. (1879), *Memorials of the discovery and early settlement of the Bermudas or Somers Islands, 1515–1685. Comp. from the colonial records and other original sources*, London: Longmans, Green, and co.
Lepore, Jill (1999), *The Name of War: King Philip's War and the Origins of American Identity*, New York: Vintage.
Lewis, Martin W. and Kären Wigen (1997), *The myth of continents: a critique of metageography*, University of California Press.
Ligon, Richard (1657), *A true and exact history of the island of Barbados*, London: Peter Parker.
Ligon, Richard (1673), *A True & Exact History of the Island of Barbados*, London.
Linton, Joan Pong (2006), *The Romance of the New World: Gender and the Literary Formations of English Colonialism*, Cambridge: Cambridge University Press.
Lochrie, Karma (2005), *Heterosynchrasies: Female Sexuality When Normal Wasn't*, Minneapolis: University of Minnesota Press.
Lokken, Paul (2013), "From the 'Kingdom of Angola' to Santiago de Guatemala: The Portuguese Asientos and Spanish Central America, 1595–1640," *Hispanic American Historical Review* 93 (2): 171–203.
Loomba, Ania (2002), "'Break her will, and bruise no bone, sir': Colonial and Sexual Mastery in *The Island Princess*," *Journal of Early Modern Cultural Studies* 2 (1): 68–108.
Loomba, Ania (2007), "Periodization, Race, and Global Contact," *Journal of Medieval and Early Modern Cultural Studies* 37 (3): 595–620.
Loomba, Ania (2009), "Race and the Possibilities of Comparative Critique," *New Literary History* 40 (3): 501–22.
Loomba, Ania (2014), "Early Modern or Early Colonial?" *JEMCS* 14, no. 1 (Winter): 143–8.

Loomba, Ania (2016), "Identities and Bodies in Early Modern Studies," in Valerie Traub (ed.), *The Oxford Handbook of Shakespeare and Embodiment: Gender, Sexuality and Race*, 228–45, Oxford: Oxford University Press.
Loomba, Ania, and Jonathan Burton, eds (2007), *Race in Early Modern England: A Documentary Companion*, New York: Palgrave Macmillan.
Lopes, Duarte (1597), *A report of the kingdome of the Congo*. London: John Wolfe.
Louis XIV (1651), *La Guerre des Suisses traduite du I. Livre des Commentaires de Jule Cesar par Louis XIV*, Paris: Imprimerie Royale.
Lovejoy, Arthur (1936), *The great chain of being, a study of the history of an idea*, Cambridge: Cambridge University Press.
Lovejoy, Paul (2004), "Ethnic Designations of the Slave Trade and the Reconstruction of the History of Trans-Atlantic Slavery," in Paul Lovejoy and David Trotman (eds), *Trans-Atlantic Dimensions of Ethnicity in the African Diaspora*, London: Bloomsbury Academic.
Lowney, Chris (2005), *A Vanished World: Muslims, Christians and Jews in Medieval Spain*, Oxford: Oxford University Press.
Lupher, David A. (2003), *Romans in a New World: Classical Models in Sixteenth-century Spanish America*, Ann Arbor: University of Michigan Press.
Machiavelli, Niccolò (2003), *The Art of War*, ed. Christopher Lynch, Chicago: University of Chicago Press.
Macinnes, Allan I. (2007), *Union and Empire*, Cambridge: Cambridge University Press.
Mackay, D. (1985), *In the wake of cook; exploration, science and Empire, 1780–1801*, Wellington: Victoria University Press.
MacLean, Gerald, ed. (2005), *Reorienting The Renaissance: Cultural Exchanges With the East*, Basingstoke and New York: Palgrave Macmillan.
Macpike, E.F., ed. (1932), *Correspondence and papers of Edmond Halley, preceded by an unpublished memoir of his life by one of his contemporaries and the 'Éloge' by D'Ortous de Mairan*, Oxford, The Clarendon Press.
Malieckal, Bindu (2011), "Mariam Khan and the Legacy of Mughal Women in Early Modern India," in Linda McJannet and Bernadette Andrea (eds), *Early Modern England and Islamic Worlds*, New York: Palgrave Macmillan, 97–121.
Mallett, Michael E. (1996), "The Art of War," in Thomas A. Brady, Heiko A. Oberman, James D. Tracy (eds) *Handbook of European History, 1400–1600*, vol. 1, Grand Rapids, William B. Eerdmans, 535–62.
Mallett, Michael E. and Christine Shaw (2012), *The Italian Wars, 1494–1559*, New York, Pearson.
Mancall, Peter C. (2007), *Hakluyt's Promise: An Elizabethan's Obsession for an English America*, New Haven: Yale University Press.
Mangan, Jane E. (2005), *Trading Roles: Gender, Ethnicity, and the Urban Economy in Colonial Potosí*, Durham: Duke University Press.
Marcus, Leah S (1992), "Renaissance/Early Modern Studies," in *Redrawing the Boundaries*, edited Stephen J. Greenblatt and Giles Gunn. New York: MLA, 41–63.
Mariscal, Jorge (1998), "The Role of Spain in Contemporary Race Theory," *Arizona Journal of Hispanic Cultural Studies*, 2: 7–23.
Marks, Shula (1972), "Khoisan Resistance to the Dutch in the Seventeenth and Eighteenth Centuries," *Journal of African History* 13 (1): 55–80.
Marlowe, Christopher (2009), *The Jew of Malta*. 1592, ed. James R. Siemon, London: A & C Black.
Marshall, Peter and Glyndwyr Williams (1972), *The great map of mankind; British perceptions of the world in the age of enlightenment*, Dent.

Martin, Jerry L (1996), *The Shakespeare File, What American Majors are Really Studying*, available at https://www.goacta.org/images/download/shakespeare_file.pdf.
Martines, Lauro (1998), "Review of Lisa Jardine, *Worldly Goods*," *Renaissance Quarterly* 51:1 (Spring) 193–204.
Martinez, Maria Elena (2008), *Genealogical Fictions: Limpieza de Sangre, Religion and Gender in Colonial Mexico*, Stanford, CA: Stanford University Press.
Martínez, Miguel (2016), *Front Lines*, Philadephia: University of Pennsylvania Press.
Martire d'Anghiera, Pietro (1555), *The decades of the newe world or West India . . .*, trans. by Richard Eden, London: Guilhelmi Powell.
Marx, Karl (1977), *Capital*, Vol. I. New York: Vintage Books.
Masonen, Pekka (2001), "Leo Africanus: The Man with Many Names," *Al-Andalus Magreb* 8: 115–43.
Massey, Reginald (1999), *India's Kathak Dance, Past, Present and Future*, New Delhi: Abhinav Publications.
Mastellone, S. (1983), "Holland as a political model in Italy in the seventeenth century," *BMGN* 98 (4): 568–82.
McDonnell, Myles (2006), *Roman Manliness: Virtus and the Roman Republic*, Cambridge: Cambridge University Press.
McEnroe, Sean F. (2012), *From Colony to Nationhood in Mexico: Laying the Foundations, 1560–1840*, Cambridge: Cambridge University Press.
Menocal, Rosa (1985), "Pride and Prejudice in Medieval Studies: European and Oriental," *Hispanic* Review, 53: 1. 61–78.
Metlitzki, Dorothee (1977), *The Matter of Araby in Medieval England*, New Haven and London: Yale University Press.
Meuwese, Mark (2012), *Brothers in Arms, Partners in Trade: Dutch-Indigenous Alliances in the Atlantic World, 1595–1674*, Leiden: Brill.
Mignolo, Walter (1995), *The Darker Side of the Renaissance, Literacy, Territoriality and Colonization*, Ann Arbor: University of Michigan Press.
Mignolo, Walter D. (2008), "Racism As We Sense It Today," *PMLA* 123, no. 5, Special Topic: Comparative Racialization (Oct.): 1737–42, 1739.
Milton, John (1991), *Political Writings*, ed. Martin Dzelzainis, trans. Claire Gruzelier, Cambridge: Cambridge University Press.
Miquelon, Dale (Fall 2001), "Envisioning the French Empire: Utrecht 1711–13," in *French Historical Studies*, Vol. 24, No. 4, 653–77.
Miranda, Deborah H. (2013), "Extermination of the *Joyas*: Gendercide in Spanish California," in Stryker, Susan, and Aren Z. Aizura, eds, *The Transgender Studies Reader 2*, 350–63, New York and Abingdon: Routledge.
Mitter, Partha (1992), *Much Maligned Monsters; history of Western reactions to Indian Art*, Chicago; Chicago University Press.
Montaigne, Michael de (2002), *The Complete Essays of Michael de Montaigne*, trans. by Donald Frame, Stanford: Stanford University Press.
Montaigne, Michel de (1957 [1603]), *The Complete Essays of Montaigne*, translated Donald M. Frame. Stanford, Stanford University Press.
Monter, William (1990), *Frontiers of Heresy: The Spanish Inquisition from the Basque Lands to Sicily*, Cambridge: Cambridge University Press.
Morgan, Jennifer L. (2004), *Laboring Women: Reproduction and Gender in New World Slavery*, Philadelphia: University of Pennsylvania Press.
Morgan, Kenneth (2001), *Slavery and Servitude in Colonial North America: A Short History*, New York: New York University Press.

Morley, Henry, ed. (1890), *Ireland under Elizabeth and James the First*. London: Routledge.
Morris Brian (2006), "The ivory trade and chiefdoms in pre-colonial Malawi," in *The Society of Malawi Journal*, Vol. 55, no. 2: 6–23.
Mott, Luiz (2003), "Crypto-Sodomites in Colonial Brazil," in Pete Sigal (ed.), *Infamous Desire: Male Homosexuality in Colonial Latin America*, 168–96, Chicago and London: University of Chicago Press.
Mukherjee, Soma (2001), *Royal Mughal Ladies and Their Contributions*, New Delhi: Gyan Publishing.
Mustakeem, Sowande M. (2016), *Slavery at Sea: Terror, Sex, and Sickness in the Middle Passage*, Urbana, IL: University of Illinois Press.
Muthu, Shankar (2009), *Enlightenment against Empire*, Princeton: Princeton University Press.
Nash, Elizabeth (2005), *Seville, Cordoba, and Granada: A Cultural History*, Oxford: Oxford University Press.
Nerlich, Michael (1988), *Ideology of Adventure: Studies in Modern Consciousness, 1100–1750*, 2 vols., Minneapolis: University of Minnesota Press.
Newman, Simon P. (2013), *A New World of Labor: The Development of Plantation Slavery in the British Atlantic*, Philadelphia: University of Pennsylvania Press.
Ng, Su Fang (2006), "Global Renaissance: Alexander the Great and Early Modern Classicism from the British Isles to the Malay Archipelago," *Comparative Literature* 58 (4): 293–312.
Ng, Su Fang (2012), "Dutch Wars, Global Trade, and the Heroic Poem: Dryden's *Annus mirabilis* (1666) and Amin's *Sya'ir Perang Mengkasar* (1670)," *Modern Philology* 109 (3): 352–84.
Nirenberg, David (1996), *Communities of Violence: Persecution of Minorities in the Middle Ages*, Princeton: Princeton University Press.
Nirenberg, David (2007), "Race and the Middle Ages: The Case of Spain and Its Jews," in Margaret R. Greer, Walter D. Mignolo, and Maureen Quilligan, *Rereading the Black Legend: The Discourses of Religious and Racial Difference in Renaissance Empires*, 71–87, Chicago and London: University of Chicago Press.
Nirenberg, David (2009), "Was there race before modernity?" in Miriam Eliav-Feldon, Benjamin Isaac and Joseph Ziegler (eds), *The Origins of Racism in the West*, 232–64, Cambridge: Cambridge University Press.
Nocentelli, Carmen (2013), *Empires of Love: Europe, Asia, and the Making of Early Modern Identity*, Philadelphia: University of Pennsylvania Press.
Nocentelli, Carmen (2014), "The Dutch Black Legend," *Modern Language Quarterly* 75 (3): 355–83.
Nocentelli-Truett, Carmen (2007), "Discipline and Love: Linschoten and the *Estado da India*," in Margaret R. Greer, Walter D. Mignolo, and Maureen Quilligan (eds), *Rereading the Black Legend*, 205–24, Chicago and London: University of Chicago Press.
Northrup, David (2002), *Africa's Discovery of Europe, 1450–1850*, New York: Oxford University Press.
O'Toole, Rachel Sarah (2007), "From the Rivers of Guinea to the Valleys of Peru: Becoming a *Bran*Diaspora within Spanish Slavery," *Social Text* 92 (25): 19–36.
O'Toole, Rachel Sarah (2012), *Bound Lives: Africans, Indians and the Making of Race in Colonial Peru*, Pittsburgh: University of Pittsburgh Press.
Oberg, Michael Leroy (2003), *Dominion and Civility: English Imperialism and Native America, 1585–1685*, Ithaca: Cornell University Press.

Oliver, Roland and Anthony Atmore (2001), *Medieval Africa 1250–1800*, Cambridge: Cambridge University Press.
Orta, Garcia da (1913), *Colloquies on the Simples and Drugs of India by Garcia da Orta*, ed. Clement Markham, London: Henry Sotheran and Co.
Ouweneel, Arij (1995), "From *Tlahtocayotl* to *Gobernadoryotl*: A Critical Examination of Indigenous Rule in 18th-Century Central Mexico," *American Ethnologist* 22 (4): 765–85.
Owens, Sarah E. and Jane E. Mangan, eds (2012), *Women of the Iberian Atlantic*, Baton Rouge: Louisiana State University Press.
Özbaran, Salih (1995), "Ottoman naval policy in the south," in Metin Kunt and Christine Woodhead (eds), *Suleyman the Magnificent and His Age: The Ottoman Empire in the Early Modern World*, 55–70, London: Longman.
Pagden, Anthony (1982), *The Fall of Natural Man: The American Indian and the origins of comparative ethnology*, Cambridge: Cambridge University Press.
Pagden, Anthony (1995), *Lords of all the World: Ideologies of Empire in Spain, Britain and France c. 1500-c.1800*, New Haven and London: Yale University Press.
Park, Katherine (1997), "The Rediscovery of the Clitoris: French Medicine and the Tribade, 1570–1620," in David Hillman and Carla Mazzio (eds), *The Body in Parts: Fantasies of Corporeality in Early Modern Europe*, 171–93, New York and London: Routledge.
Parker, Geoffrey (1977), *The Dutch Revolt*, Ithaca: Cornell University Press.
Parker, Geoffrey (1988), *Military Revolution: Military Renovation and the Rise of the West, 1500–1800*, Cambridge: Cambridge University Press.
Parker, Geoffrey (2004), *The Army of Flanders and the Spanish Road, 1567–1659*, Cambridge: Cambridge University Press.
Parker, Geoffrey (2013), in *Global Crisis, War, Climate change and catastrophe in the seventeenth century*, Yale University Press: Yale.
Parker, Geoffrey (2014), *The Imprudent King: A New Life of Philip II*, New Haven: Yale University Press.
Parker, Geoffrey and L.M. Smith, eds (1997), *The General Crisis of The Seventeenth Century*, London: Routledge.
Parrott, David (2001), *Richelieu's Army: War Government and Society in France, 1624–1642*, Port Chester: Cambridge University Press.
Parry, J.H. (1982), *The Age of Reconnaissance: Discovery, Exploration and Settlement, 1450–1650*, Berkeley: University of California Press.
Parry, John H. and Robert G. Keith, eds (1984), *New Iberian World: A Documentary History of the Discovery and Settlement of Latin America to the Early 17th Century, Vol. 1*, New York: Times Books.
Paul III, *"Sublimus Dei." Papal Encyclicals Online*, http://www.papalencyclicals.net/Paul03/p3subli.htm (accessed March 1, 2017).
Pearson, Michael (1979), "Corruption and Corsairs in Sixteenth-Century Western India: A Functional Analysis," in Blair B. Kling and Pearson (eds) *The Age of Partnership: Europeans in Asia before Domination*, 15–41, Honolulu: University of Hawaii Press.
Pearson, Michael (1988), *The Portuguese in India: New Cambridge History of India*, Cambridge: Cambridge University Press.
Peirce, Leslie P. (1993), *The Imperial Harem: Women and Sovereignty in the Ottoman Empire*, New York and Oxford: Oxford University Press.
Peirce, Leslie (2007), "An Imperial Caste: Inverted Racialization in the Architecture of Ottoman Sovereignty," in Margaret R. Greer, Walter d. Mignolo, and Maureen

Quilligan (eds), *Rereading the Black Legend: The Discourses of Religious and Racial Difference in the Renaissance Empire*, 27–47, Chicago and London: The University of Chicago Press.

Pelras, Christian (2000), "Patron-Client Ties among the Bugis and Makassarese of South Sulawesi," in Roger Tol, Kees van Dijk, and Greg Acciaioli (eds), *Authority and Enterprise among the Peoples of South Sulawesi*, 15–54, Leiden: KITLV Press.

Perry, Mary Elizabeth (1999), "From Convent to Battlefield: Cross-Dressing and Gendering the Self in the New World of Imperial Spain," in Josiah Blackmore and Gregory S. Hutchenson (eds), *Queer Iberia: Sexualities, Cultures, and Crossings from the Middle Ages to the Renaissance*, 394–419, Durham and London: Duke University Press.

Petrarch, Francesco (2005), *Letters on Familiar Matters*, Vol. 3: Books XVII–XXIV, trans. by Aldo S. Bernardo, New York: Italica Press.

Petrarch, Francesco (2007), *Gli Uomini Illustri Vita Di Giulio Cesare*, ed. Ugo Dotti, Torino: Einaudi.

Phillips, Jr., William D. (1985), *Slavery from Roman Times to the Early Transatlantic Slave Trade*, Minneapolis: University of Minnesota Press.

Phillips, Miriam S. (1991), "A Shared Technique/Shared Roots? A Comparison of Kathak and Flamenco Dance History," *Proceedings of the Society of Dance History Scholars: Dance in Hispanic Cultures*, Riverside, California: Society of Dance History Scholars, 147–53.

Pigafetta, Antonio (2007), *The First Voyage Around the World, 1519–1622: An Account of Magellan's Expedition* (ed.) Theodore J. Cachey, Jr., Toronto: University of Toronto Press.

Pires, Tomé (1944), *The Suma Oriental of Tomé Pires*, trans. and ed. Armando Cortesão, 2 vols., London: Hakluyt Society.

Pomeranz, Kenneth (2000), *The Great Divergence: China, Europe, and the Making of the Modern World Economy*, Princeton: Princeton University Press.

Poska, Allyson (2016), *Gendered Crossings: Women and Migration in the Spanish Empire*, Albuquerque: University of New Mexico Press.

Powers, Karen Vieira (2005), *Women in the Crucible of Conquest: The Gendered Genesis of Spanish American Society, 1500–1600*, Albuquerque: University of New Mexico Press.

Prasannan, Parthasarthi (2011), *Why Europe grew rich and Asia did not; global economic divergence, 1600–1850*, New York: Cambridge University Press.

Pratt, Mary Louis (1991), *Imperial Eyes: Travel Writing and Transculturation*, New York: Routledge.

Price, Richard, ed. (1996), *Maroon Societies: Rebel Slave Communities in the Americas*, 3rd edn, Baltimore: Johns Hopkins University Press.

Priolkar, Anant (1961), *The Goa Inquisition, Being a Quartercentenary Commemoration Study of the Inquisition in India*, Bombay: University of Bombay Press.

Puff, Helmut (2003), *Sodomy in Reformation Germany and Switzerland, 1400–1600*, Chicago: University of Chicago Press.

Puff, Helmut (2013), "Same–Sex possibilities," in *Women and Gender in Medieval Europe*, (eds) Judith M. Bennett and Ruth Mazo Karras. Oxford: Oxford University Press, 379–95.

Purchas, Samuel (1905), *Hakluytus Posthumus or Purchas His Pilgrimes*, Vol. 1, Glasgow: James MacLehose and Sons.

Quatrefages, René (1983a), *La revolucíon military moderna: el crisol español*, Madrid: Ministerio de Defensa.

Quatrefages, René (1983b), *Los tercios*, Madrid: Estado Mayor de Ejército.
Rabb, Theodore K. (2006), *The Last Days of the Renaissance & the March to Modernity*, Cambridge, MA: Basic Books.
Rabreau, Daniel (1984), "Monumental Art, or the Politics of Enchantment," in *The Sun King: Louis XIV and the New World*, ed. Robert R. McDonald, New Orleans: Louisiana Museum Foundation.
Raiskin, Judith (1993), "The Art of History: An Interview with Michelle Cliff," *Kenyon Review* 15: 1, 57–71.
Read, David T. (1990), "Hunger of Gold: Guyon, Mammon's Cave, and the New World Treasure," *English Literary Renaissance* 20 (2): 209–32.
Rediker, Marcus (2007), *The Slave Ship: A Human History*, New York: Viking Press.
Reid, Anthony (1990), "The Crisis of the Seventeenth Century in Southeast Asia," *Modern Asian Studies*, Vol. 24, 4: 639–59.
Reid, Anthony (1993), *Southeast Asia in the Age of Commerce 1450–1680: Volume Two: Expansion and Crisis*, New Haven: Yale University Press.
Reséndez, Andrés (2016), *The Other Slavery: The Uncovered Story of Indian Enslavement in America*, Boston: Houghton Mifflin Harcourt.
Restall, Matthew (2003), *Seven Myths of the Spanish Conquest*, New York: Oxford University Press.
Richards, John (1990), "The Seventeenth Century Crisis in South Asia," *Modern Asian Studies*, Vol. 24, 4: 625–38.
Richards, John F. (2003), *The unending frontier; an environmental history of the early modern world*, University of California Press: Berkeley.
Robertson, Karen (1996), "Pocahontas at the Masque," *Signs* 21 (3): 551–83.
Robinson, Cedric (1993), *Black Marxism, The Making of The Black Radical Tradition*, Chapel Hill and London: University of North Carolina Press.
Rocke, Michael (1996), *Forbidden Friendships: Homosexuality and Male Culture in Renaissance Florence*, Oxford: Oxford University Press.
Romney, Susanah Shaw (2015), "Savage Comparisons: Dutch Cultural Distinctions in Seventeenth-Century Southern Africa and North America," *Genre* 48 (2): 315–40.
Root, Deborah (1988), "Speaking Christian: Orthodoxy and Difference in Sixteenth-Century Spain," *Representations* 23 (Summer): 118–34.
Roundtree, Helen C. (1990), *Pocahontas's People: The Powhatan Indians of Virginia Through Four Centuries*, Norman: University of Oklahoma Press.
Rowland, Ingrid D. (6 Nov. 1997), "The Renaissance Revealed," *New York Review of Books* 44.17.
Rubin, Gayle (1975), "The Traffic in Women: Notes on the 'Political Economy' of Sex," in Rayna Reiter, ed., *Toward an Anthropology of Women*, New York, Monthly Review Press.
Rushforth, Brett (2012), *Bonds of Alliance: Indigenous and Atlantic Slaveries in New France*, Chapel Hill: University of North Carolina Press.
Said, Edward (1978), *Orientalism*, London: Routledge.
Salmon, J.H.M. (1959), *The French Religious Wars in English Political Thought*, Oxford: Clarendon Press.
Samson, Jane (2005), *Race and Empire*, New York: Pearson Education Limited.
Sauer, Carl Ortwin (1992), *The Early Spanish Main*, Berkeley: University of California Press.
Schimmelpenninck van der Oye, David (2010), *Russian Orientalism: Asia in the Russian Mind from Peter the Great to the Emigration*, New Haven and London: Yale University Press.

Schmidt, Benjamin (2001), *Innocence Abroad: The Dutch Imagination and the New World, 1570–1670*, Cambridge: Cambridge University Press.
Schwartz, Stuart B. (1985), *Sugar Plantations in the Formation of Brazilian Society: Bahia, 1550–1835*, Cambridge: Cambridge University Press.
Schwartz, Stuart B. (2004), "A Commonwealth within Itself: The Early Brazilian Sugar Industry, 1550–1670," in Stuart B. Schwartz (ed.), *Tropical Babylons: Sugar and the Making of the Atlantic World, 1450–1680*, 158–200, Chapel Hill: University of North Carolina Press.
Schwarz, Kathryn (2000), *Tough Love: Amazon Encounters in the English Renaissance*, Durham, NC: Duke University Press.
Scott, James (1985), *Weapons of the Weak: Everyday Forms of Peasant Resistance*, New Haven: Yale University Press.
Sebek, Barbara and Stephen Deng, eds (2016), *Global Traffic: Discourses and Practices of Trade in English Literature and Culture from 1550 to 1700*, Springer.
Seed, Patricia (1995), *Ceremonies of Possession in Europe's Conquest of the New World, 1492–1640*, Cambridge: Cambridge University Press.
Seth, Mesrovb Jacob (2005), *Armenians in India: From the Earliest Times to the Present*, New Delhi: Asian Educational Services.
Shakespeare, William (2006), *Othello*, ed. Michael Neill, Oxford: Oxford University Press.
Shakespeare, William (2008), *Othello*, ed. E.A.J. Honigmann, London: Arden Shakespeare.
Shakespeare, William (2010), *The Merchant of Venice*. 1597, ed. John Drakakis, London: Bloomsbury.
Shoenberger, Cynthia Grant (1977), "The Development of the Lutheran Theory of Resistance: 1523–1530," *Sixteenth Century Journal* 8 (1): 61–76.
Siena, Kevin, ed. (2005), *Sins of the Flesh: Responding to Sexual Disease in Early Modern Europe*, Toronto: Centre for Reformation and Renaissance Studies.
Sigal, Pete, ed. (2003), *Infamous Desire: Male Homosexuality in Colonial Latin America*, Chicago and London: University of Chicago Press.
Singh, Jyotsna G., ed. (2009), *A Companion to the Global Renaissance: English Literature and Culture in the Era of Expansion*, Malden, MA. and Oxford: Wiley-Blackwell.
Sirluck, Ernest (1959), "Introduction," *Complete Prose Works of John Milton*, Vol. 2, 1–216, New Haven: Yale University Press.
Slavin, Arthur J., ed. (1964), *The New Monarchies and Representative Assemblies: Medieval Constitutionalism or Modern Absolutism?*, Boston: Heath.
Smallwood, Stephanie (2007), *Saltwater Slavery: A Middle Passage from Africa to American Diaspora*, Cambridge, MA: Harvard University Press.
Smith, Adam (1776), *An Inquiry into the Nature and Causes of the Wealth of Nations*. London.
Smith, Alan K. (1981), *Creating a World Economy: Merchant Capital, Colonialism, and World Trade, 1400–1825*, Boulder, CO: Westview Press.
Smith, Ian (2009), "The Queer Moor: Bodies, Borders, and Barbary Inns," in Jyotsna Singh (ed.), *A Companion to the Global Renaissance: English Literature and Culture in the Era of Expansion*, 190–204, Malden, MA: Blackwell.
Snow, Dean R. (n.d.), "Disease and Population Decline in the Northeast," in *Disease and Demography in the Americas*.
Snyder, Christina (2010), *Slavery in Indian Country: The Changing Face of Captivity in Early America*, Cambridge, MA: Harvard University Press.

Solomon, Michael (1999), "Fictions of Infection: Diseasing the Sexual Other in Francesc Eiximenis's *Lo llibre de les dones*," in Josiah Blackmore and Gregory S. Hutchenson (eds), *Queer Iberia: Sexualities, Cultures, and Crossings from the Middle Ages to the Renaissance*, 277–90, Durham and London: Duke University Press.
Spain (1681), *Recopilación de leyes de los reynos de las Indias, mandada imprimir y publicar por la Magestad Católica del Rey Don Carlos II, nuestro Señor*, 4 vols., Madrid: Julián de Paredes.
Spenser, Edmund (1890), "A View of the State of Ireland (Part 1)," in Henry Morley (ed.), *Ireland under Elizabeth and James the First*, 33–212, London: Routledge.
Spenser, Edmund (2006), *The Faerie Queene*, 2nd edn., ed. A. C. Hamilton *et al.*, New York: Longman.
Spiess, Stephen (2013), "Shakespeare's Whore: Language, Prostitution, and Knowledge in Early Modern England," University of Michigan Dissertation.
Stavig, Ward (2003), "Political 'Abomination' and Private Reservation: The Nefarious Sin, Homosexuality, and Cultural Values in Colonial Peru," in Pete Sigal, *Infamous Desire: Male Homosexuality in Colonial Latin America*, 135–51, Chicago and London: University of Chicago Press.
Steensgaard, Neils (1990), "The Seventeenth Century Crisis and Unity in Eurasian History," *Modern Asian Studies*, Vol. 24, 4: 683–97.
Steinfeld, Robert J. (1991), *The Invention of Free Labor: The Employment Relation in English & American Law and Culture, 1350–1870*, Chapel Hill: University of North Carolina Press.
Stepto, Michele, and Gabriel Stepto (1996), *Lieutenant Nun: Memoir of a Basque Transvestite in the New World, Catalina de Erauso*, Boston: Beacon Press.
Stern, Philip (2012), *The Company-State: Corporate Sovereignty and the Early Modern Foundations of the British Empire in India*. Oxford: Oxford University Press.
Stern, Philip J. (2009), "Neither East nor West, Border, nor Breed, nor Birth: Early Modern Empire and Global History," *Huntington Library Quarterly*, 72, no. 1, 113–26.
Stoler, Ann Laura (2002), *Carnal Knowledge and Imperial Power: Race and the Intimate in Colonial Rule*, Berkeley: University of California Press.
Strachey, William (1612), *For the Colony in Virginea Britannia. Lawes diveine, morall and martiall . . .*, London: W. Stansby.
Strachey, William (1849), *The historie of travaile into Virginia Britannia . . .*, ed. R.H. Major, London: Hakluyt Society.
Strachey, William (1953), *The Historie of Travell into Virginia Britania* (1612), ed. Louis B. Wright and Virginia Freund, London: The Hakluyt Society.
Stryker, Susan, and Aren Z. Aizura, eds (2013), "Introduction: Transgender Studies 2.0," *The Transgender Studies Reader* 2, New York and Abingdon: Routledge.
Subrahmanyam, Sanjay (1997), "Connected Histories: Notes toward a Reconfiguration of Early Modern Eurasia," *Modern Asian Studies* 31: 735–62.
Subrahmanyam, Sanjay (2005), "On World Historians in the Sixteenth Century," *Representations*, 91 (Summer): 26–57, 28.
Subrahmanyam, Sanjay (2005a), *Explorations in Connected History: From the Tagus to the Ganges*, New Delhi: Oxford University Press.
Subrahmanyam, Sanjay (2005b), *Explorations in Connected History: Mughals and Franks*, New Delhi: Oxford University Press.
Subrahmanyam, Sanjay (2007), "Holding the World in Balance: The Connected Histories of the Iberian Overseas Empires, 1500–1640," *American Historical Review* 112: 339–59.

Sullivan, Ceri (2002), *The Rhetoric of Credit: Merchants in Early Modern Writing*, Madison, NJ: Fairleigh Dickinson University Press; London: Associated University Presses.

Sunderland, Willard (2004), *Taming the Wild Field: Colonization and Empire on the Russian Steppe*, Ithaca and London: Cornell University Press.

Sweet, James H. (1997), "The Iberian Roots of American Racist Thought," *The William and Mary Quarterly*, 54 (1): 143–66.

Swingen, Abigail L. (2015), *Competing Visions of Empire: Labor, Slavery, and the Origins of the British Atlantic Empire*, New Haven: Yale University Press.

Taylor, Eric Robert (2006), *If We Must Die: Shipboard Insurrections in the Era of the Atlantic Slave Trade*, 179–213, Baton Rouge: Louisiana State University Press.

Taylor, Gary (2005), *Buying Whiteness: Race, Culture and Identity from Columbus to Hip-Hop*, New York: Palgrave.

The Apologie or Defence, of the Most Noble Prince William, by the grace of God, Prince of Orange, . . . (1581), Delft.

Theal, G.M. (1964), trans. and ed., *Records of South-Eastern Africa*, 9 vols., Cape Town: Struik, first published 1898.

Thomas, Hugh (1993), *Conquest: Montezuma, Cortés, and the Fall of Mexico*, New York: Simon & Schuster.

Thompson, I.A.A. (1976), *War and Government in Habsburg Spain, 1560–1620*, London: Athlone Press.

Thrower, Norman J.W. and Clarence Glacken (1968), *The terraqueous globe: the history of geography and cartography*, papers read at a Clark Library seminar, April 27.

Tilley, Morris Palmer (1950), A *Dictionary of the Proverbs in England in the Sixteenth and Seventeenth Centuries*, Ann Arbor: University of Michigan Press.

Tinsley, Omise'eke Natasha (2010), *Thiefing Sugar: Eroticism Between Women in Caribbean Literature*, Durham and London: Duke University Press.

Todorov, Tzvetan (1984), *The Conquest of America: The Question of the Other*, translated by Richard Howard. New York: Harper & Row.

Tomlins, Christopher (2010), *Freedom Bound: Law, Labor, and Civic Identity in Colonizing English America, 1580–1865*, Cambridge: Cambridge University Press.

Topsell, Edward (1607), *The historie of foure-footed beastes*, London: William Jaggard.

Townsend, Camilla (2004), *Pocahontas and the Powhatan Dilemma*, New York: Hill and Wang.

Townsend, Camilla (2006), *Malintzin's Choices: An Indian Woman in the Conquest of Mexico*, Albuquerque: University of New Mexico Press.

Tracy, James (2002), *Charles V, Impresario of War*, Cambridge: Cambridge University Press.

Tracy, James D. (2008), *The Founding of the Dutch Republic: War, Finance, and Politics in Holland, 1572–1588*, Oxford: Oxford University Press.

Traub, Valerie (1992), *Desire & Anxiety: Circulations of Sexuality in Shakespearean Drama*, London and New York: Routledge.

Traub, Valerie (1995), "The Psychomorphology of the Clitoris," *GLQ* 2, no. 1/2, 81–113.

Traub, Valerie (2002), *The Renaissance of Lesbianism in Early Modern England*, Cambridge: Cambridge University Press.

Traub, Valerie (2015), *Thinking Sex with the Early Moderns*, Philadelphia: University of Pennsylvania Press.

Trevor-Roper, H.R. (1959), "The general crisis of the seventeenth century," *Past and Present*, no. 16: 31–64.

Trexler, Richard (1995), *Sex and Conquest: Gendered Violence, Political Order and the European Conquest of the Americas*, Ithaca: Cornell University Press.

Tryon, Thomas (1684), *Friendly advice to the gentlemen-planters of the East and West Indies: in three parts* by Philotheos Physiologus [alias]. Printed by Andrew Sowle, London.

Tuck, Richard (1979), *Natural Rights Theories: Their Origin and Development*, Cambridge: Cambridge University Press.

Tuck, Richard (1999), *The Rights of War and Peace: Political Thought and the International Order from Grotius to Kant*, Oxford: Oxford University Press.

Tucker, Richard (1989), "The depletion of India's forests under British imperialism: plantation forestry and peasants in Assam and Kerala," in Donald Worster, *The ends of the earth*, 118–40.

Turner, Henry S. (2016), *The Corporate Commonwealth: Pluralism and Political Fictions in England, 1516–1651*. Chicago: University of Chicago Press.

Unger, W.S. (1948), *De Oudste Reizen van de Zeeuwen Naar Oost-Indië, 1598–1604*, The Hague: Martinus Nijhoff.

van Deusen, Nancy E. (2015), "Coming to Castile with Cortés: Indigenous 'Servitude' in the Sixteenth Century," *Ethnohistorian*, 62 (2): 285–308.

van Gelderen, Martin (1986), "A Political Theory of the Dutch Revolt and the *Vindiciae Contra Tyrannos*," *Il Pensiero Politico* 19 (2): 163–82.

van Gelderen, Martin (1993a), "Vitoria, Grotius and human rights: The Early Experience of Colonialism in Spanish and Dutch Political Thought," in Wolfang Schmale (ed.), *Human Rights and Cultural Diversity: Europe, Arabic-Islamic World, Africa, China*, 215–38, Goldbach: Keip.

van Gelderen, Martin, ed. and trans. (1993b), *The Dutch Revolt*, Cambridge: Cambridge University Press.

VanDrunen, David (2005–6), "The Use of Natural Law in Early Calvinist Resistance Theory," *Journal of Law and Religion* 21 (1): 143–67.

Velasco, Sherry (2000), *The Lieutenant Nun: Transgenderism, Lesbian Desire & Catalina de Erauso*, Austin: University of Texas Press.

Velasco, Sherry (2011), *Lesbians in Early Modern Spain*, Nashville: Vanderbilt University Press.

Verlinden, Charles (1970), *The Beginnings of Modern Colonization*, trans. Yvonne Freccero, Ithaca: Cornell University Press.

Vieira, Alberto (2004), "Sugar Islands: The Sugar Economy of Madeira and the Canaries, 1450–1650," in Stuart B. Schwartz (ed.), *Tropical Babylons: Sugar and the Making of the Atlantic World, 1450–1680*, 42–84, Chapel Hill: University of North Carolina Press.

Villagra, Gaspar Perez de. (2004), *Historia de la Nueva Mexico. 1610. Historia de la Nueva Mexico, 1610: A Critical and Annotated Spanish/English Edition*. Albuquerque: University of New Mexico Press.

Villari, Rosario (1993), *The Revolt of Naples*, Cambridge: Polity Press.

Vink, Markus (2003), "'The World's Oldest Trade': Dutch Slavery and Slave Trade in the Indian Ocean in the Seventeenth Century," *Journal of World History* 14 (2): 131–77.

Virilio, Paul (2006), *Speed and Politics*, trans. Mark Polizzotti, Los Angeles: Semiotext(e).

Vitkus, Daniel J. (2000), "Introduction," *Three Turk Plays from Early Modern England*, New York, Columbia University Press

Vitkus, Daniel (2003), *Turning Turk: English Theater and the Multicultural Mediterranean, 1570–1630*, New York: Palgrave Macmillan.

Vitoria (1991), *Vitoria: Political Writings*, ed. Anthony Pagden, Cambridge: Cambridge University Press.
von Vacano, Diego (2012), "Las Casas and the birth of race," *History of Political Thought* 33.3: 401–26.
Voyages: The Trans-Atlantic Slave Trade Database. www.slavevoyages.org.
Wade, Bonnie C. (1998), *Imaging Sound: An Ethnomusicological Study of Music, Art and Culture in Mughal India*, Chicago: University of Chicago Press, 1998.
Wakeman, F. (1986), "China and the Seventeenth Century Crisis," *Late Imperial China* Vol. 7.1: 1–26.
Wallace, David (2004), *Premodern Places: Calais to Surinam, Chaucer to Aphra Behn*, Malden, MA. and Oxford: Blackwell.
Wallerstein, Immanuel (2011a), *The Modern World System, 1: Capitalist agriculture and the origins of the European world economy*, Berkley: University of California Press.
Wallerstein, Immanuel (2011b), *The Modern World-System II: Mercantilism and the Consolidation of the European World-Economy, 1600–1750*, Berkeley: University of California Press.
Ward, Kerry (2009), *Networks of Empire: Forced Migration in the Dutch East India Company*, Cambridge: Cambridge University Press.
Wareing, John (2017), *Indentured Migration and the Servant Trade from London to America, 1618–1718: "There is Great Want of Servants,"* Oxford: Oxford University Press.
Watts, Pauline Moffitt (1985), "Prophecy and Discovery: On the Spiritual Origins of Christopher Columbus's 'Enterprise of the Indies,'" *The American Historical Review*, Vol. 90, No. 1 (Feb. 1985), pp. 73–102.
Wheat, David (2011), "The First Great Waves: African Provenance Zones for the Transatlantic Slave Trade to Cartagena de Indias, 1570–1640," *Journal of African History*, 52 (1): 1–22.
White, R.S. (1996), *Natural Law in English Renaissance Literature*, Cambridge: Cambridge University Press.
White, Richard (1991), *The Middle Ground: Indians, Empires, and Republics in the Great Lakes Region, 1650–1815*, Cambridge: Cambridge University Press.
White, Sam (2011), *Climate of Rebellion in the Early Modern Ottoman Empire*, New York: Cambridge University Press.
Wiesner-Hanks, Merry (2008), *Women and Gender in Early Modern Europe*, Cambridge: Cambridge University Press.
Will, George (1981), "Literary Politics," *Newsweek*, April 2, accessed at http://www.newsweek.com/literary-politics-202084 on August 20, 2017.
Williams, Robert A., Jr. (1990), *The American Indian in Western Legal Thought: The Discourses of Conquest*, New York: Oxford University Press.
Williams, William Appleman (1980), "Empire as a way of life," *The Nation*, 2–9 August.
Wilson, Robert (2009), *The Three Ladies of London. 1582*, in Lloyd Edward Kermode, ed. *Three Renaissance Usury Plays*, Manchester: Manchester University Press.
Winterbottom, Anna (2016), *Hybrid knowledge in the early East India Company World*, London: Palgrave.
Witgen, Michael (2012), *An Infinity of Nations: How the Native New World Shaped Early North America*, Philadelphia: University of Pennsylvania Press.
Wong, R. Bin (1997), *China Transformed: Historical Change and the Limits of European Experience*, Ithaca: Cornell University Press.

Wood, Stephanie (2003), *Transcending Conquest: Nahua Views of Spanish Colonial Mexico*, Norman: University of Oklahoma Press.

Worster, Donald (1994), *Nature's economy, a history of ecological ideas*, Cambridge: Cambridge University Press.

Wright, Elizabeth R., Sarah Spence, and Andrew Lemons, eds (2014), *The Battle of Lepanto*, Cambridge, MA: Cambridge University Press.

Zamora, Margarita (1993), *Reading Columbus*, Berkeley: University of California Press.

Zandt, Cynthia J. (2008), *Brothers Among Nations: The Pursuit of Intercultural Alliances in Early America, 1580–1660*, Oxford: Oxford University Press.

Zurita, Jeronimo (1610), *Los Cinco Libros Postreros de la Historia del Rey Don Hernando El Catholico de las empresas y ligas de Italia*, Zaragoza: Domingo de Portonariis y Ursino.

NOTES ON CONTRIBUTORS

Jonathan Burton is Professor of English at Whittier College. He is the author of *Traffic and Turning: Islam and English Drama, 1579–1624* (2005) and co-editor with Ania Loomba of *Race in Early Modern England: A Documentary Companion* (2007). His recent publications include "Christopher Sly's Arabian Night: Shakespeare's *The Taming of the Shrew* as World Literature" and "Bodies, sex and race: western encounters with sex and bodies in non-European cultures" in *The Routledge History of Sex and the Body in the West, 1500 to the Present*.

Thomas James Dandelet is Professor of History at the University of California, Berkeley. He is the author of *The Renaissance of Empire in Early Modern Europe* (2014); *Spanish Rome, 1500–1700* (2001); co-editor with John Marino of *Spain in Italy, 1500–1700* (2006), and author of twenty articles and book chapters on the broad themes of the political, intellectual, and cultural history of Renaissance Europe, the early modern Mediterranean world, the Spanish Empire, and early modern Italy. He is a fellow of the American Academy in Rome and a recipient of a Guggenheim fellowship.

Vinita Damodaran is a historian of modern India whose work ranges from the social and political history of Bihar to the environmental history of South Asia, including using historical records to understand climate change in the Indian Ocean World. Her books include *Broken Promises, Indian Nationalism and the Congress Party in Bihar* (1992); *Nature and the Orient; environmental histories of South and South East Asia* (1998); *Post Colonial India, History Politics and Culture* (2000); *British empire and the natural world: environmental encounters in South Asia* (2010); *East India Company and the Natural World* (2014); and

Climate change and the Humanities (2017). She is also the author of several articles in established journals. She is particularly interested in questions of environmental change, identity, and resistance in Eastern India. Currently, she is the director of the Centre for World Environmental History at Sussex an internationally recognized center with a specialist focus on the Global South.

Jonathan Gil Harris is Professor of English at Ashoka University in India. He has published widely on early modern cultural production and globalization. His recent books include *Indography: Writing the "Indian" in Early Modern England* (Palgrave Macmillan, 2012); *Marvellous Repossessions: The Tempest and the Waking Dream of Paradise* (Ronsdale, 2012); and *The First Firangis: Remarkable Stories of Heroes, Healers, Charlatans, Courtesans and Other Foreigners Who Became Indian* (Aleph Book Company, 2015). His next book, *Masala Shakespeare: Bollywood, the Bard, and the Promise of the More-Than-One*, is forthcoming from Aleph later this year.

Richard Grove is a pioneer in the field of tropical environmental history. He has an extensive publications and teaching record on many areas of the British Empire and Commonwealth, and a specialist knowledge of the political, environmental, and economic history of India, Pakistan, Sri Lanka, Mauritius and other Indian Ocean islands, Malawi, Ghana, Nigeria, the Southern Caribbean (especially St. Vincent, Montserrat, Dominica, and Tobago), Australia, and New Zealand. His many books and articles include his now classic monograph, *Green Imperialism; colonial expansion, tropical island Edens and the origins of environmentalism 1600–1860* (Cambridge University Press, Cambridge) and *New York, Studies in Environment and History* series, 550pp (1995).

Michael Guasco is Professor and Chair of the Department of History at Davidson College. He is the author of *Slaves and Englishmen: Human Bondage in the Early Modern Atlantic World* (2014). He has published several articles and book chapters related to the history of race and slavery in the early modern Atlantic world, including most recently "Agents of Empire: Africans and the Origins of English Colonialism in the Americas," in Jorge Cañizares-Esguerra, ed., *Entangled Empires: The Anglo-Iberian Atlantic, 1500–1830* (2018).

Ania Loomba is Catherine Bryson Professor of English at the University of Pennsylvania. She is the author of *Revolutionary Desires: Women, Communism and Feminism in India* (2018); *Shakespeare, Race, and Colonialism* (2002); *Colonialism–Postcolonialism* (1998, 2005, 2015); *Gender, Race, Renaissance Drama* (1989, 1992), and numerous articles on early modern studies, race, colonial histories, and feminism. She has co-edited *Rethinking Feminism in Early Modern Studies* (2016); *South Asian Feminisms* (Duke, 2012); *Race in Early*

Modern England: A Documentary Companion (Palgrave, 2007); *Postcolonial Studies and Beyond* (Duke 2005); and *Post-Colonial Shakespeares* (Routledge, 1998).

Su Fang Ng is Clifford A. Cutchins III Professor and Associate Professor of English at Virginia Polytechnic and State University. She is the author of *Literature and the Politics of Family in Seventeenth-Century England* (2007) and articles on early modern, medieval, and post-colonial topics; she guest-edited a special journal issue on Transcultural Networks in the Indian Ocean. The recipient of fellowships at the Radcliffe at Harvard, the National Humanities Center, Texas at Austin, Heidelberg, Oxford, Wisconsin at Madison, and elsewhere, her book on *Alexander the Great from Britain to Southeast Asia: Peripheral Empires in the Global Renaissance* is forthcoming from Oxford University Press.

Valerie Traub is the Adrienne Rich Distinguished University Professor and Frederick G. L. Huetwell Professor of English and Women's Studies at the University of Michigan. She is the author of *Thinking Sex with the Early Moderns* (2015); *The Renaissance of Lesbianism in Early Modern England* (2002); and *Desire & Anxiety: Circulations of Sexuality in Shakespearean Drama* (1992, reissued 2014). Her most recent edited collection is *The Oxford Handbook of Shakespeare and Embodiment* (2016). Forthcoming from Edinburgh University Press is the co-edited *Ovidian Transversions: Iphis and Ianthe, 1350–1650*.

Daniel Vitkus holds the Rebeca Hickel Endowed Chair in Early Modern Literature at the University of California, San Diego. He is the author of *Turning Turk: English Theater and the Multicultural Mediterranean, 1570–1630* (Palgrave) and of numerous articles and book chapters on the cross-cultural history of the sixteenth and seventeenth centuries. Vitkus has also edited *Three Turk Plays from Early Modern England* (Columbia University Press) and *Piracy, Slavery and Redemption: Barbary Captivity Narratives from Early Modern England* (Columbia University Press). He serves as the Editor of *The Journal for Early Modern Cultural Studies*. His current research is focused on "The Global Renaissance."

INDEX

Abdul Hai Firangi 142–3
Abu-Lughod, Janet 17
Abul Fazl ibn Mubarak 96
Act of Abjuration (1581) 183
Adas, Michael 186
Adrian VI, Pope 132
adventuring 8, 51
Africa, and trade 82
African slavery/transatlantic slave trade
    111–19, 205
Africans, occupying positions of power and
    learning 25
Africanus, Leo 129–35, 165–6, 205
agency
    of imperial subjects 223
    and mobility 145
    subaltern 128
    of women 145
aggression, European 22 (*see also* violence)
Agnadello (1509) 35
Agrarian System of Mughal India, The 97
agriculture, plantation 43, 90, 109, 110,
    111, 117–18, 124
Ahmad, A. Samad 195
Ahmad Shah bin Iskandar 200
Akbar, Emperor 96, 142, 144
Akhimie, Patricia 222–3
Alarcón, Hernando de 162
Albuquerque, Afonso de 135
Alcazar Al-Kabir (1578) 66
Alexander VI, Pope 190

Alexander, William 170
Alfonso of Naples 32
Algonquians 44, 187–9, 192
Allen, Richard 23
alliances, cross-cultural and cross-religious
    196 (*see also* networks)
Almeida, Dom Francisco de 195
Amazons 153–4
Amer, Sahar 19
America, rediscovery of 6, *8*, 12, 54
Amerindians 44, 88–9, 102–3, 106–7, 114,
    115, 119, 217, 218–21
Andalusia 132–3, 139
anti-imperialism 190
anti-Semitism 62 (*see also* Jewish people)
Apologie 183
apprenticeship system 120
armies
    French 45, 46–7
    Spanish 38–9, 40
Armitage, David 205
Arrighi, Giovanni 20
Art of War, The 35, 36, 45
artistic production 53
Asia, decline of 84, 86
Asian empires, and trade 17, 53–4, 55
astronomy, nautical 3
asymmetry, between world economies 19
Atlantic trade 47
Auncibay, Francisco 117
Aurangzeb, Shah 94, 96

Averroës 139
Avicenna (Ibn Sina) 138, 139
Azores 204
Aztec empire 33, 40, 55, 185

Baber, R. Jovita 187
Bacon, Francis 2
Badauni, Abdul Qadit 96
Balboa, Vasco Núñez de 163
Bancel et al. 215
Barbados 122, 123, 124
Barros, João de 195
Bartlett, Robert 24
Bellini, Gentile 5
Benedicti, Georgius 184
Benjamin, Walter 75
berdaches 161–3, 172
Berlinghieri, Francesco 5
Bermuda 90, 91
Bersuire, Pierre 30
Best, George 173
Biddulph, William 168
bigamy 179
Black Death 119
Black Legend, Spanish 176, 191, 201
Blackburn, Robin 25
blackness 25, 114, 172–3 (*see also* race)
Blaxton, John 61
Blount, Henry 58
Boccaccio, Giovanni 13
Bodin, Jean 44, 154
Book of John Mandeville, The 217
borders, and race 25
botanical gardens, and plant exchange 79–80, 84–7
Boyle, Robert 216
Braudel, Fernand 17, 19
Brazil 109, 110, 113, 117, 118
Breda, surrender of 39
Briefe introductions . . . unto the art of chiromancy or manuel divination, and physiognomy 215–16
Britain and the British empire 42–4, 86 (*see also* England)
    colonialism of 43, 84, 119, 122–3
Brotton, Jerry 17
Browne, Samuel 86
Browne, Thomas 25
brutality, towards native populations 20 (*see also* violence)

Buckley, Edward 86
Bullock, William 123
Bulwer, John 158
Burkhardt, Jakob 4, 11
Burns, Kathryn 219
Burton, Jonathan 179

Camões, Luís Vaz de 63–5, 138
Canary Islands 12–13, 113
Canterbury Tales, The 59
Capital 19
capitalism
    changes and tensions of 74
    and colonialism 19
    and debt 70, 72
    and globalization 49
    harmfulness of 62
    ideology of emergent 69
    indigenous capital accumulation 83–4
    and individualism 69, 75
    and morality 71
    and the natural world 77
    origins of 17–18
    and power 21
    primitive accumulation of wealth 19, 51
    proto-capitalism 67
    representations of 63
    and trade 49, 50, 55, 59
    Western 21
Caribbean islands (*see also* islands; names of individual islands) 33, 45, 90, 102–3, 106
cartography 89
Casale, Giancarlo 212
Cerignola (1503) 35
Cervantes, Miguel 41
Chaplin, Joyce 189
Chapman, Matthieu 213
Charles I of England (r. 1625–49) 43, 44
Charles II of England (r. 1660–85) 43
Charles IV, Holy Roman Emperor (r.1355–78) 31
Charles V of Spain (r. 1517–57) 7, 18, 33, 34, 35, 36, 43, 56
Charles VIII of France (r.1483–98) 32, 44
Chaucer, Geoffrey 59
Chaudhuri, K.N. 22
Chesapeake 123
children
    child tribute 209

forced labor of 107
mixed race 175, 180
and slavery 115
China 20–2, 53–4
Choice of Emblemes, A 60
Christianity
  forced conversion to 140, 149, 219 (see also *Reconquista*)
  and Islam 14
  and Muslims/Jews 25
  and native peoples 8–9, 13
  and sexuality 155–6, 158, 178
  and wealth 59
Cieza de Leon, Pedro 155, 161
circumcision 158, 159
citizenship, Roman 208
civitas 208
Clark, Anna 148
class
  capitalist class 51–2, 59, 75
  and the Renaissance 4
Clement VI, Pope 13
Cliff, Michelle 1
climate (see also environment)
  climate change 78, 91–9
  and culture 89
  Little Ice Age (LIA) 93, 98
  and resources 88–9
Clingingsmith, David 98
Coen, Jan Pietersz 23
coercion
  sexual 174
  and trade 22–3, 58
Colbert, Jean-Baptiste 46
Colloquies on the Simples and Drugs of India 136–7, 138, 139
colonialism and colonization (see also imperialism)
  anti-colonial resistance 183, 201–2
  British 43, 84, 119, 122–3
  and capitalism 19
  colonial economies 113
  and the environment 77–8, 90, 99
  European 203–4
  French 45, 47
  and humanism and modernity 5–15
  and ideologies 20–1
  and indigenous peoples 90
  and individuality 10–11
  justification of 201, 205, 206–7

in the New World 12, 19
Portuguese 203–4
and power 6–7
and pre-modern ideologies/practices 24
and race 24
revisionist scholarship on 12
Spanish 103
and trade 50
and wealth 181
Colonna, Fabrizio 35, 36
Colonna, Stephano 31
Columbus, Christopher 6, 12, 14, 54, 87, 90, 101–2, 103, 111, 186, 190, 216–18
Commentaries on the Gallic and Civil Wars 29, 32, 36, 44
commerce
  and competition and resistance 194–202
  and theatre 67
commercialization, of society 51–2
commodification 62, 69, 70
compasses 2–3
concubinage 176–7
conquistadors 40–1
conservationism, early 91
consumerism 51, 53
Cordoba, Gonzalo Fernández de 38
Corrêa, Gaspar de 194–5
Cortés, Hernan 33, 40, 41, 55, 56, 106, 161, 169, 170, 180, 185, 206
Cortés, Martín 180
Coryate, Thomas 58
Cowper, William 202
crisis, seventeenth century 91–9
Crosby, Alfred 81, 82
culture(s)
  and climate 89
  cultural downgrading of other societies 87
  cultural racism 222
  cultural responses to new economic practices 59–63
  cultures of savagery 87–9
  and economics 19–25
  global cultural relations 18
  imperial and global relations 15–19
  mestizo 108
  military literary 41
  and nature 78

Renaissance 4, 10, 11
  of resistance 181–2, 195, 201–2
  Roman military 30
  and slavery 114
  and the Spanish empire 41
  and trade 58, 75
  transculturation and trade 50
  of war 33

Da Asia 195
Da Gama, Vasco 17, 22, 54, 63–5, 85, 136, 194
Da Orta, Gracia 85
Damodaran, Vinita 90
dance, Kathak dance tradition 144–5
Dark Ages 4
Davenant, Charles 17
Davis, Ralph 50
De Bry, Theodor 52
de' Conti, Niccolò 157–8, 166
De iure belli ac pacis (rights of war and peace) 193
De iure belli (The right of war) 192
de Marees, Pieter 155, 157
debt
  and capitalism 70, 72
  empires founded on 56
Defoe, Daniel 89
deforestation 90, 91, 94
Dekker, Thomas 127
Democrates alter 219–20
Description of Africa 130–2
D'Este family 31–2
Dias, Bartolomeu 54, 85, 194
Díaz del Castillo, Bernal 41, 155, 206
difference 108, 205, 207, 216–18
Dijk, Wil O. 22–3
diplomacy, and trade 50
"Discourse on Western Planting, A" 122
Discoverie of the large, rich and bewtiful empire of Guiana, The 7
disease
  Black Death 119
  and empires 77
  and native peoples 110, 111, 160, 220
  and sexuality 159–60
  smallpox 220
diversity, elimination of 214
domination
  European 26
  and rape of slaves 174
  Western imperial 4
Dominicans 115, 190–1
Don Juan of Austria 39
Donne, John 49
Doyle, Laura 205
Drake, Francis 42, 55, 130
drama, staging of trade 67–74
Dutch East India Company (VOC) 22–3, 84, 149, 171, 172, 193, 194, 198–9
Dutch republic (*see also* Netherlands)
  coercive trade of 22
  Indian Ocean trade 86
  shipping 83–4

early modern period 11, 17
East in the West, The 17–18
East India Company, Dutch. *See* Dutch East India Company (VOC)
East India Company, English 86, 97, 98, 142, 145, 171, 194
Ecological Imperialism 81
ecological pressures 90 (*see also* climate; environment)
economics, and culture 19–25
economy(ies)
  colonial 113
  cultural responses to economic practices 59–63
  development of a world economy 51
  economic exchange 53
  economic power 61
  economic techniques and trade 50–1
  global 80
  political economy 75
El Niño Southern Oscillation current (ENSO) 93
Eliot, Charles 7–8
elites
  economic 56
  gifts of captives to 171
  indigenous 204
  merchants 70
  power of male European 6–7
  and the Renaissance 4
  resistance against 202
  and sexuality 162
  and slavery 108
  and trade 51, 53, 55, 75

Elizabeth I of England (1533–1603) 15, 42–4, 122, 154, *155*, 171
emigration, to the New World 44
empire(s) (*see also* colonialism and colonization; imperialism)
  empire-thinking 21
  and environmental history 78–80
  epic representations of 63–6
  founded on debt 56
  and the natural world 77–8
  oppression by 51, 181, 184
  and race 203, 207–13, 223
  Renaissance Empire 43, 48
  resistance to 201–2
  and sexuality 149–50, 177, 180
  term 204
  and warfare 28–9
  which empires are Western empires? 203–13
encomienda system 106, 107
England (*see also* Britain and the British empire; East India Company, English)
  coercive trade of 22
  English Revolution 192
  expulsion of Jewish people 173
  labor crisis and colonialism 119, 122
  labor system of 120–1
  London as a world-city 73
  patriarchy 145
  slave trade of 23
English Royal African Company 197
English Usurer, The 61
environment (*see also* climate)
  anthropogenic-induced changes to 82
  and colonialism 77–8, 90, 99
  early environmental enquiry/cultures of savagery 87–9
  environmental change 90
  environmentalism 82–3, 91
environmental history
  and empire 78–80
  and European expansion/globalization 89–90
  tropical 82
Erauso, Catalina de 164, *165*
Ercilla, Alonso de 66
Erickson, Peter 222
Eschenbach, Wolfram von 4

Europe
  aggression of 22
  European colonialism 203–4
  hegemony of 19–20, 26
  and its Others 16–17, 18
  rise of 84
European empires, and the slave trade/New World trade 47–8
Europeans, encounters with non-Europeans 13–14
Evelyn, John 49
Examen de ingenios 216
exploitation
  of Amerindians and Africans 106–7, 119
  of natural resources 81
  of slave women by white men 174
  and trade 58, 74–5
  by Western empires 51
  of white indentured servants 122–4

factories, establishment of commercial 50
Faerie Queene 66, 191
Faroqhi, Suraiya 17
fear, of foreigners 153 (*see also* others)
Ferdinand II of Aragon (r.1475–1504) 14, 32, 33, 36, 54, 103, 133, 190, 218–19
Fernandez-Armesto, Felipe 8
Fernández Navarrete, Domingo 167
feudal order, weakening of 52
Fez 133, 134, 165–6, 179
financial techniques, and trade 50–1
Fitzmaurice, Andrew 189
Florence 35
Ford, Caroline 79
foreigners, fear of 153 (*see also* others)
forest clearance 90, 94
Foster, William 96
Foucault, Michel 10
Fracastoro, Girolamo 159
France
  empire-building in the 17c. 44–8
  Roman influence on 44
  servants and servitude 124–5
  slavery 45, 47, 48
  and Spain 45, 47
  and warfare 37–8
Francis I of France (1494–1547) 15, 33
Francis Xavier, Saint 138, 166
Frank, Andre Gunder 17

Frobisher, Martin 171
Fuchs, Barbara 206
Furber, Holden 194

Gage, Thomas 115, 117
Gaguin, Robert 32
Galle, Theodore 2, 3, 6
gardens, botanical 79–80, 84–7
Garigliano (1504) 35
gender (*see also* men; women)
   and labor 106–7, 125
   and sexuality 151
General Crisis theory 92, 98
Gentili, Alberico 192
Geographia 5
geohumoralism 154
globalization
   and capitalism 49
   of imperial history 23
   and indigenous peoples 82
   and the natural world 89–90
   and resource extraction 87
Globe Theater 67
Goa 135–9
Goffman, Daniel 209
gold
   funding war 34
      gold medal of Charles II 43
   and slavery 115–17
   and the Spanish empire 103, *105*, 106
Goldberg, Jonathan 151
Golden Age, mythical 13
Gómara, Lopez de 161
Gonzaga family 31–2
Goody, Jack 17–18
Graeber, David 56
Grafton, Anthony 2
Granada 132–3
Greece, influence of ancient 2, 3
Greenblatt, Stephen 10, 222
Gresham, Thomas 72
Grotius, Hugo 193
Grove, Richard 78, 79, 80, 81, 85, 87–8, 89–90, 91
Guarini, Guarino 32
Guasco, Michael 218–19
Guiana 7, 154
Gulliver's Travels 89
gunpowder 2–3

Habib, Irfan 22, 97
Habsburg empire 205–6
Habsburgs, Austrian 47–8
Haitian Revolution (1791) 186
Hakluyt, Richard 66, 121–2
Hale, John R. 4, 27, 28
Hale, Matthew 9
Hall, Joseph 58
Hall, Kenneth 197
Hall, Kim 222
Halley, Edmond 91
Ham 9, 23–4, 25, 173
harems 140, 164
Harte, Juan 216
al-Hasan ibn Muhammad al-Wazzan 129–35, 165–6, 205
Hawkes, David 61, 62
Hawkins, William 141–2, 145
Heemskerk, Jacob van 193
Heng, Geraldine 213
Henry the Navigator, Prince 64
hermaphrodites 161–3
Herrera, Antonio 41
Heywood, Thomas 71
Hikayat Aceh 196, 197
Hikayat Amir Hamzah 195
Hispaniola 103, 106, 186
Historia de la Nueva Mexico 66
historical consciousness 18
history, connected histories 23
History of Travel into Virginia Britania, The 25
history-writing 18
Hobsbawm, E.J. 92
Holy Land, reconquest of 14
Horn, Andrew 25
Hortus Malabaricus 85
Howard, Jean 71
Hulme, Peter 6, 10, 12
human trafficking 170–1 (*see also* slavery)
humanism 5–15, 41, 51, 53, 75
Huys, Frans 57

Iberia 54, 111, 114
Ibn Battuta 133
Ibn Juzayy 133
Ibn Khaldoun 13
Ibn Majid, Shihab Al-Din Ahmad 17
identity(ies)
   African American and slavery 114

INDEX

Euro-American 190
European 4–5
French 44
Hindustani musical identity 144
racial 173
religious 24, 173
sexual 147, 150, 179
Spanish imperial 214
ideologies, and colonialism 20–1
If You Know Not Me, Part II 71–3
immigration
    of Europeans 179
    female 168–9
imperialism (*see also* colonialism and colonization; empire(s))
    anti-imperialism 190
    the beginning of imperial contest 32–5
    glorification of 66
    imperial culture and global relations 15–19
    inter-imperiality 205
    justification of 219–21
    native collaboration with 185–8, 197, 201, 204
    natives contesting European 182
    and the natural world 81–2
    and piracy 130
    of Portugal 65–6
    and race 24, 203, 214, 215, 217–18
    and silver 19
    Spanish New World 185
    and warfare 28–9, 40–2
imperium 206–7
Inca empire 33, 40, 55, 161
Indagine, Johannes ab 215–16
India
    colonization of 84
    Mughal empire 83, 86, 93–8, 140, 143, 226n.4:4
    and Portugal 54, 63–5
    slave trade in 23
Indian Ocean
    Sea Surface Temperatures (SSTs) 93
    slave trade in 22–3
    trade 22, 65, 86
Indian peoples. *See* Amerindians
indigenous/native peoples (*see also* names of individual peoples e.g. Amerindians)
    Canary Islanders 13
    and Christianity 8–9, 13
    collaboration with imperial forces 185–8, 197, 201, 204
    and colonialism 90
    and disease 110, 111, 160, 220
    dispossession of 193
    and the French 47
    and globalization 82
    infantilization of 89
    and missionaries 219
    and natural law 190, 191–3
    natural rights of 191
    as natural slaves 191
    North America 44, 88–9 (*see also* Amerindians)
    oppression by Western empires 181, 184
    as potential converts 218
    protections for 107–8
    resistance of 182–3, 188–9, 194–5
    and the Spanish empire 40, 66, 103, 107–8
    subjugation of 9–10
    technical knowledge of 85–6
    and trade 80, 81
    violence towards 20, 23, 40, 66
individualism, and capitalism 69, 75
individuality, and colonialism 10–11
inequalities, economic/financial 55, 70
information, imperial networks of 91
Inquisition
    Portuguese 136, 138, 139, 172
    Spanish 148, 151, 218
Integrated History and People of the World project (IHOPE) 78
inter-imperiality 205
Iroquois peoples 47
Isabella I of Castile (r.1474–1504) 14, 33, 54, 103, 133, 218–19
Isla, Diaz de 159
Islam, and Christianity 14
islands (*see also* Caribbean islands; names of individual islands)
    European impact on 89
    newly discovered 87
Israel, Jonathan 92
Italian Wars (1492–1559) 32–5
Italy, Spanish armies/navy in 38–9
Ivan IV (the Terrible) (r.1547–1584) 206

Jagirdari system 97
Jahan, Shah 94
Jahangir, Emperor 95, 142–3
James I of England (r. 1603–25) 43, 44, 189
James of Compostela, Saint 14
Jamestown Massacre 188
Jardine, Lisa 17, 53
Jehlen, Myra 25
Jenkinson, Anthony 171
Jesuits 109, 115
Jew of Malta, The 62, 205
Jewish people
   anti-Semitism 62
   and Christians 25
   expulsion from England 173
   expulsion from Spain 14
   Goa 135–9
   mass conversion of 149 (*see also* Reconquista)
Jobson, Richard 157
Julius Caesar 29, 30, *31*, 31–2, 35, 44
Julius II, Pope 33

Kathak dance tradition 144–5
Khan, Mariam 140–5
Khan, Mubarak 142
Khoikhoi (Khoisan) 194, 201
King Philip's War in New England (1676–8) 190
kingship 189
kinship alliance 189
Kitab al-Kulliyat fi al-Tibb (Book of Generalities) 139
knowledge
   filtering in to Europe 3–4
   indigenous technical knowledge 85–6
   new and traditional 87
Kumar, Deepak 86

La Araucana 66
labor
   African slavery/transatlantic slave trade 111–19
   apprenticeship system 120
   and children 107
   free blacks 117
   and gender 125
   indigenous female 106–7
   maritime 57

   new 101–11
   and race 125
   serfdom 119–20
   servants and servitude 119–25
   of slaves 19, 115 (*see also* slavery)
   wage laborers 120
Lahori, Abdul Hamid 96
Lal, Ruby 144
language, multilingualism 134
Lanser, Susan 179, 180
Lapu-Lapu 196–7
Las Casas, Bartolomé de 9, 14, 20, 66, 107, 114, 161, 182, 191, 220, 221
Le Moyne de Morgues, Jacques 161
learning, filtering in to Europe 3–4
Legazpi, Miguel 41
legislation
   blood purity laws 173
   early environmental 89–91
   Laws of Burgos (1512) 103
   New Laws (1542) 103, 108
   Recopilación de leyes (1680) 187
Leo X, Pope 130
Lepanto (1571) 15, *16*, 39–40
Ligon, Richard 124, 214
Linschoten, Jan Huygen van 158
literature
   of anti-European heroism 195–6
   imperialist epic poems 63–6
   love poetry 133
   Renaissance 11–12
   and resistance 182, 184
   Roman texts 29
   and the Spanish Black Legend 191
   travel writing 58, 66–74
   utopian 89
   writings of soldiers 41
Lithgow, William 164
Little Ice Age (LIA) 93, 98
Lives of Illustrious Men 30
Livy 29
Lizárraga, Reginaldo de 160
Locke, John 89, 192
Lomba, Baltazar da 172
London, as a world-city 73
Lopes, Duarte 219
Louis XIII of France (r.1610–1643) 45
Louis XIV of France (r.1643–1715) 44–8

Lusiads, The 63–4
Luther, Martin 168

Machiavelli, Niccolò di Bernardo 35–7, 45
Mackay, David 84
Mactan (1521) 196
Madeira Islands 111, 113, 203–4
Magellan, Ferdinand 196–7
Making of Europe: Conquest, Colonialism and Cultural Change, 950–1350, The 24
Malabar Coast 86–7
Malacca 195
Malintzin (Malinalli; La Malinche or Doña Marina) 170–1, 180, 185
Mantegna, Andrea 32
Mantino, Jacob 134
Manuel I of Portugal (r.1495–1521) 135–6
maps 89
Marcus, Leah 11
Mare Liberum 193
Marees, Pieter de 155
Mariana, Juan de 41
maritime capabilities, of China 53–4
maritime technologies 57, 80
maritime trade 51, 55, 80–1, 83–4
Marlowe, Christopher 62, 205
marriage
  interfaith 166–7
  intermarriage 169–70, 172, 207, 209, 219
  and mobility 169
  monogamous 177
  and political alliances 169, 171
  and the theater 68
Martyr d'Anghiera, Peter 163
Marx, Karl 19
Maunder Minimum (1645–1715) 93
Maurice, Prince of Orange 184
Mazarin, Cardinal 45
Mcneill, John 78–9
medicine
  Jewish practitioners 136–8
  and the pharmacological trade 84–6
medieval period 2
Mediterranean, and the Spanish and Ottoman empires 39
Mehmed Agha 209–10
Mehmet II (the Conqueror), Sultan 5, 206
Melanchon, Philip 168

men
  male-male sex 150, 151, 160–1, 162, 166, 176
  and power 6–7
Menocal, Maria Rosa 4
mercenaries 57
Merchant of Venice, The 70–1, 223
merchants 50, 52, 57, 59–63, 67, 70
mestizaje 175
mestizos 108, 180
Mexico 19, 33, 37, 115
Middle Ages 4
Mignolo, Walter 10, 222
Milan 33
military revolution 29, 35, 38
Milton, John 191
Minaya, Bernardino de 219
Ming Dynasty 20
Mirrour of Justices, The 25
missionaries, and native peoples 219
mobility
  and agency 145
  fugitive mobility 127–8, 135, 142, 145–6
  of laborers 120
  and marriage 169
  and the natural world 80
  social mobility 127, 128
  and trade 50
  transculturalism 128–9
  transculturalism of the expelled Andalusian 129–35
  transculturalism of the expelled Arabophone religious refugee 135–9
  transculturalism of the Mughal harem lady 140–5
  of women 140–5
Modern Asian Studies 92
modernity 5–15, 18
monarchy, universal 208
monetization 51–2, 62, 81
Monson, William 121
monstrous races 153, 217–18
Montaigne, Michel de 10, 11, 88
Montesinos, Antonio de 191, 219
Montezuma II (c.1466–1520) 185, 206
Moors, ordered to leave Spain 14
morality, and capitalism 71
More, Thomas 121

Mughal empire 83, 86, 93–8, 140, 143, 226n.4:4
multiculturalism
   Goa 136, 138
   Granada 132–3
   Mughal empire 140
multilingualism 134
Murad III (r.1574–1595), Sultan 209
music, Hindustani musical identity 144
Muslims, and Christians 25
Muthu, Shankar 89

Naples 35
Nashe, Thomas 59
nation, idea of 125
native peoples. *See* indigenous/native peoples
natural law 190, 191–3
natural rights 191, 193
natural worlds
   botanical gardens and plant exchange 79–80, 84–7
   and capitalism 77
   early environmental enquiry/cultures of savagery 87–9
   early environmental legislation 89–91
   and empires 77–8
   and globalization 89–90
   introduction of foreign plants/animals 82
   resource frontier of the early modern world 80–3
nautical astronomy 3
Navarre 33
navies
   French 45, 47
   of Spanish empire 38–9, 40, 42
Nerlich, Michael 51
Netherlands (*see also* Dutch republic)
   Dutch revolts 38, 184–5, 191, 192
   and silver 20
   slave trade in the Indian Ocean 193–4
   and the Spanish empire 183–4
networks
   Andalusian Judeo-Muslim 136, 139
   commercial 67
   of cosmopolitan exchange 132
   imperial 91
   long-distance oceanic trade 84
   trading 142, 194

New Granada (Colombia) 117
New World
   conquest of shaping European culture 11
   encounters between Europeans and Amerindians 88–9
   Europeans reaching the New World 12
   French colonization of 45, 47
   gold and silver from funding war 34
   plundering of the civilizations 54–5
   silver 19–20
   slavery 102, 108
   and sodomy 161
   wars of conquest in 40–2
Nirenberg, David 214
North America
   British plantation colonies 43 (*see also* plantation agriculture)
   French colonization of 47
Notable History of Saracens, The 14
Nova Reperta (New Inventions of Modern Times) 2, 3, 6, 8
Núñez Vela, Blasco 108

oceanic islands, European impact on 89
"Of Cannibals" 88
Olmos, Juan de 163
oppression, by Western empires 51, 181, 184
Orientalism 10, 16
Orta, Garcia da 136–9
Ortelius, Abraham 6
Othello 129, 130, 223
Others
   Europe and it's Others 16–17, 18
   exchanges with foreigners 59
   Othering and sexuality 147, 148
   threat of 10
Ottoman empire
   and citizenship/integration 208–13
   conquest of Constantinople 205
   cultural sophistication of 5
   domination of 14–15
   and the Mediterranean 39
   and Portugal 195
   as Rome's successor 206
Ovando, Nicolás de 106
Oviedo, Gonzalo Fernández de 156, 160
Oviedo y Valdes, Gonzalo Fernandez de 220

Pacheco, Francisco 163
Pacific Ocean, Sea Surface Temperatures (SSTs) 93
Pacific territories, of Spain 41–2
Pact of Umar 208
Pagden, Anthony 208
Parker, Geoffrey 92, 93–4, 96–7, 98
Parry, J.H. 22
Parzival 4
patriarchy
   English 145
   patriarchal power 7
   and sexuality 168, 176
Paul III, Pope 220
Pavia (1525) 35
Peace of Cateau-Cambresis 38
peasantry
   alienation of from the land 19
   peasant uprisings 183
   syphilis 159
persecution, religious 108
Persia, Armenian Christian communities of 142 (*see also* Ottoman empire)
Peru 19, 114, 115, 117
Petrarch, Francesco 13, 29–32, 35–6
pharmacological trade 84–6
Philip II of Spain (1527–1598) 33, 40, 41, 42–3, 113, 184
Philip IV of Spain (1605–1665) 45
Philip V of Spain (1683–1746) 48
Philippine islands 41
philosophical "adjustments" 8–9
Pierce, Leslie 213
Pietro della Valle 58
Pigafetta, Antonio 157, 196
piracy 42, 130, 181
Pires, Tomé 164, 195
Pizarro, Francisco 33, 40
plant exchange, and botanical gardens 84–7
plantation agriculture 43, 90, 109, 110, 111, 117–18, 124
Pocahontas 140–1, 169–70, 180, 189, 227n.7:10
political disorders, and climate change 91–9
political economy 75
political power, and warfare 36
Politicq onderwijs (political Education) 184
polygyny 168, 177, 178

polymorphism 216–22
Pomeranz, Kenneth 17, 84
Portugal
   coercive trade of 22
   colonization by 203–4
   conquest of (1580) 38, 41
   conquest of Goa 135–6
   ideology of 21
   imperialism of 65–6
   and India 54, 63–5
   innovation of and Spanish conquest 54–6
   Inquisition 136, 138, 139, 172
   native resistance to 194–5
   and the Ottoman empire 195
   regaining its independence (1640) 45
   and silver 20
   slavery 55, 109–11, 113, 118, 205
   and trade 63–5
power
   and capitalism 21
   and colonialism 6–7
   economic 61
   imperial of male Europeans 7
   and interracial sex 174
   patriarchal 7
   political and war 36
Powhatans 187–8
Prasannan, Parthasarthi 84
primitive accumulation 51
Prince, The 36
Principal Navigations, Voyages and Discoveries of the English Nation 66
printing 2–3
prostitution 166–7, 177
Prouville, Alexander de 47
Pseudodoxia Epidemica 25
Punic Wars 29
Purchas, Samuel 192
Pyrard, François 164–5

Quo Vadis? A Just Censure of Travel as It Is Commonly Undertaken by the Gentlemen of Our Nation 58

race
   blood purity 149, 170, 173
   climatic theories 216–17
   and colonialism 24

cultural racism 222
emergence of racial language 114
and empire 203, 207–13, 223
fluidity of and resistance to 222–3
forms of 213–16
and imperialism 24, 203, 214, 215, 217–18
invention of the concept 215
and labor 125
monstrous races 153, 217–18
mutability of racism 221–2
polymorphism of 216–22
race-thinking 24, 173
racial classification 175
racial discourses 213, 218, 220
racial identity 173
racial ideologies and imperialism 24
racial pseudoscience 215–16
racial stereotyping 114, 201
racial violence 223
racialized beliefs crossing borders 25
and religion 24, 152
scientific/cultural representations of 214–16
and sexuality 151–2, 158–9, 177, 178
skin color 24, 114, 172–3, 209–12
slavery and the sexual (re)production of race 172–5
Raleigh, Walter 7, 154
rape, and slaves 174
Ravenna (1512) 35
Reconquista 14, 40–1, 108, 134, 135, 149, 160, 185, 208
Recopilación de leyes (1680) 187
refugees 127–8, 133
regulation, of sexuality 150, 175, 178
Reid, Anthony 195
religion
    forced conversions 109, 149, 177 (*see also Reconquista*)
    and race 24, 152
    religious identity 24, 173
    religious orders as slave owners 115
    religious persecution 108
    and resistance 195
    and sexuality 150, 152, 155–6, 158, 161–2, 166–7
    and slavery 25
Renaissance
    darker side of 10, 75
    imperial 28–9
    Renaissance Empire 43, 48
    Renaissance Man 10–11
    and trade 51
    whose Renaissance? 2–6
Reséndez, Andrés 102
resistance
    against elites 202
    anti-colonial 183, 201–2
    avoidance protest 186
    Calvanist 192
    and commerce and competition 194–202
    and conquest and colony 183–90
    and cross-cultural and cross-religious alliances 196
    cultures of 181–2, 195, 201–2
    to empires 201–2
    indirect/ordinary expressions of 181–2, 186
    legal challenges as 197–8
    legal culture of 187
    and literature 182, 184
    native 182–3, 188–9, 194–5
    Protestant against Catholic Spain 191
    to racism 223
    and religion 195
    resistance theories 190–4
    against the Spanish empire 192
resources
    and climate 88–9
    natural 80–3
    resource extraction 84
Ricci, Matteo 166
Richards, John 80, 81, 83, 92, 97
Richelieu, Cardinal 45
risk, sharing of 67
Robinson Crusoe 89
Rocroi (1643) 45
Rolfe, John 124, 140–1, 169–70, 189
Rome
    citizenship 208
    influence of ancient Rome 2, 30, 44, 206–7, 208
Rubens, Peter Paul 31, *34*
Rubin, Gayle 68
Russian empire 206, 207

Said, Edward 10, 16
sailors 57

Sandys, Edwin 168
savagery 88
Schouten, Joost 179
Schwartz, Stuart 109
science
  botanical science 85
  and indigenous technical knowledge 85–6
  Islamic and Jewish 3
  and racism 216
  Western 84
Scott, James 181–2
Sea Surface Temperatures (SSTs) 93
seas, domination of 3
Sebastiao I of Portugal (r.1557–1578) 65–6
Second Treatise of Government, The 192
Seed, Patricia 3, 187
Sejarah Melayu (Malay Annals) 195
self-consciousness
  of being European 4–5
  and imperial ambitions 18
self-definition, European 17
self-fashioning 10
self-preservation, Europeans' right of 193
Sepúlveda, Juan Ginés de 191, 219–20
serfdom 119–20
servants and servitude 119–25
seventeenth century crisis 91–9
sexuality
  bodily morphologies 154–9
  and Christianity 155–6, 158, 178
  complexity of 147–8
  contamination and disease 159–60
  and elites 162
  and empire 149–50, 177, 180
  female-female sex 150, 163–5
  and gender 151
  geospatial figurations 152–4
  history of 18–19
  indigenous and travelling women 168–72
  interracial sex 172, 174–5, 176, 179–80
  male-male sex 150, 151, 160–1, 162, 166, 176
  and Othering 147, 148
  and patriarchy 168, 176
  polygyny 168, 177, 178
  prostitution, concubinage, marriage, polygyny and conversion 166–8
  and race 151–2, 158–9, 177, 178

  regulation of 150, 175, 178
  and religion 150, 152, 155–6, 158, 161–2, 166–7
  same-sex desire 150
  sexual identity 147, 150, 179
  sexual relationships with native women 149
  slavery and the sexual (re)production of race 172–5
  sodomy 150–1, 160–6, 177, 179
Shakespeare, William 10, 11–12, 67, 70–1, 87, 129, 130, 223
ships, tall ships 56–7 (*see also* navies)
Shoemaker's Holiday, The 127
Short Account of the Destruction of the Indies 66, 191
Sicily 35
Silk Road 3, 49
silk weaving 2–3
silver
  funding war 34
  and imperialism 19–20
  and the Spanish empire 103, *104*, 106, 107
sin, and sexuality 150
slavery
  African slavery 111–19, 205
  Amerindians 114, 115, 190, 217, 218–19
  Atlantic 23
  Canary Islanders 13
  chattel slavery 55, 204
  and children 115
  Dutch in the Indian Ocean 193–4
  and economic growth of Europe 19
  and elites 108
  English 23
  French 45, 47, 48
  global dimension of 23
  and gold 115–17
  Amerindian v. African slaves 114, 115
  justification of 23–4, 25, 103, 106, 108, 173, 191
  New World 102, 108
  and philosophical "adjustments" 9
  by pirates 130
  Portuguese 55, 109–11, 113, 118, 205
  and pre-modern ideologies/practices 24
  and religion 25
  in the Renaissance 1

revolts by slaves 186–7
and the sexual (re)production of race 172–5
slave labor in silver mines 19
slave trade in the Indian Ocean 22–3
Spanish 55, 107, 112, 113, 115
and trade 55, 109
transatlantic slave trade 19–20, 102–3
and violence 174
and Western empires 204
Smith, Adam 181
Smith, John 124, 189
social crisis, and sexual scapegoating 153
social exclusion 152
social mobility 127, 128
sodomy 150–1, 160–6, 177, 179
Sokollu Mehmed Pasha 209
sovereignty
    absolute or contractual 192
    deprivation of 13
    and trading interests 194
Spanish empire (*see also* Granada; Iberia)
    abuses by 190–1
    armies and navies of 38–9, 40, 42
    blood purity laws 173
    colonialism of 103
        expansion of 33–5
    expulsion of Jewish people 14
    and France 45, 47
    free blacks in 117
    and gold/silver 20, 103, *104*, *105*, 106, 107
    and indigenous peoples 40, 66, 103, 107–8
    and the Mediterranean 39
    and the Netherlands 183–4
    Pacific territories of 41–2
    planned invasion of England 42
    and Renaissance war 37–40
    resistance against 192
    Roman influence on 41
    and slavery 55, 107, 112, 113, 115
        Spanish Armada 42
    Spanish New World imperialism 185
    Spanish imperial identity 214
        Spanish Inquisition 148, 151, 218
    treaties with Britain 44
Spenser, Edmund 66, 191
spice trade 65, 194
Spörer Minimum (1450–1540) 93

St. Helena 91
Statute of Artificers (1562) 120
Statute of Laborers (1351) 120
Steensgaard, Neils 92
Steinfeld, Robert 120
stereotyping
    anti-Spanish 201
    racial 114, 201
    and relations of exchange/reciprocity 24–5
Stern, Philip 23
Stoler, Ann Laura 18
Strachey, William 25, 188, 206, 220
Straet, Jan van der (Stradanus) 2
Stuart monarchy 43–4
Su Fang Ng 16–17
subjugation, of native peoples 9–10
Subrahmanyam, Sanjay 18, 129
sugar plantations 110, 111, 117–18 (*see also* plantation agriculture)
Suleiman I (the Magnificent) (r.1520–1566) 15, 18
Sullivan, Ceri 72
Sunderland, Willard 207
superiority
    European 2, 6
    Western 4
Swift, Jonathan 89
Symonds, William 169
syphilis 159–60

taxation 45, 97
Taylor, Gary 216
technologies, and trade and warfare 54, 57
Tempest, The 10, 11, 87–8
tercios 38
theater
    city/citizen comedy 69–74
    dramatic character presentation 69
    morality plays 68
    staging of trade 67–74
    theater companies 67
Theatrum Orbis Terrarum 6, 7
Theses on the Philosophy of History 75
Thirty Years War (1618–48) 45
Thomas Aquinas 191
Thomas, Hugh 185
Three Ladies of London, The 68–9
Tlaxcalans 185–6, 187, 192
Toledo, Francisco de 185

Topsell, Edward 216
Towerson, Gabriel 142, 145
trade
   armed 194
   and Asian empires 17, 53–4, 55
   Atlantic 47
   and capitalism 49, 50, 55, 59
   and coercion 22–3, 58
   and colonialism 50
   cultural responses to new economic practices 59–63
   and culture 58, 75
   and elites 51, 53, 55, 75
   and epic representations of empire 63–6
   and exploitation 58, 74–5
   and extortion 54
   financial techniques 50–1
   Indian Ocean 22, 65, 86
   and indigenous peoples 80, 81
   long-distance 57–8, 67, 84
   in luxury goods 49, 53
   maritime trade 51, 55, 80–1, 83–4
   and mobility 50
   networks 142, 194
   pharmacological trade 84–5
   and slavery 55, 109
   spice trade 65, 194
   trade agreements 50
   trading ports 197
   travel narratives and the staging of trade 66–74
   and violence 55, 56–8, 65
   and war 22
transculturalism
   of the expelled Andalusian 129–35
   of the expelled Arabophone religious refugee 135–9
   and fugitive mobility 128–9
   in Mughal harems 140–5
translatio imperii 206
Traub, Valerie 19, 219
travel writing 58, 66–74
Travels of Sir John Mandeville 177–8
Treaty of Tordesillas (1494) 15, 113
tropics, risk of 87
Two-Spirit people 161–3
tyranny 190

universal monarchy 208
usury 59, 61–2

Van Reede, Henrick 85
Vasari, Giorgio 2
Vega, Garcilaso de la 161
Velazquez, Diego Rodriguez 39
Venice 130
Veronese, Paolo 16
Vespucci, Amerigo 6, 8
Villagra, Gaspar Perez de 66
Vindiciae contra tyrannos 192
Vink, Markus 23–4
violence
   to eliminate diversity 214
   racial 223
   and resistance 181
   and slavery 174
   towards native populations 20, 23, 40, 66
   and trade 55, 56–8, 65
   Of Western empires 55–6
Virginia Company 192
Virilio, Paul 56–7
virtus 208
Vitoria, Francisco de 9, 191
von Vacano, Diego 215, 220
Voyage into the Levant 58
voyages of "discovery", motivations for 15
Voyages: The Trans-Atlantic Slave Trade Database 112

Wahunsonacock 187–8, 189
Wakeman, Frederick 92
Wallace, David 13
Wallerstein, Immanuel 21, 80, 84
War and Society in Renaissance Europe, 1450–1620 28
War of the Spanish Succession (1700–1713) 47–8
warfare (*see also* names of individual wars and battles)
   in the early modern period 27, 28
   and empire 28–9
   and France 37–8, 44–8
   funding of 34–5, 45, 47, 48
   Great Britain under Elizabeth and the Stuarts 42–4
   and imperialism 28–9, 40–2
   intra-European 57
   Italian Wars and beginning of imperial contest 32–5
   Machiavelli and the art of war 35–7

maritime 57
military revolution 29, 35, 38
  Petrarch and the rebirth of the Roman military ideal 29–32
  and the Renaissance 27–8
  Spanish empire and Renaissance war 37–40
  and trade 22
Warin, Jean III 46
wars of succession (1658–62), Mughal empire 94
wealth
  accumulation of 52, 59–60
  and colonialism 181
  primitive accumulation of 19, 51
Wealth of Nations, The 181
weaponry 40, 56–7
West Africa 197
West India Company, French 47
Western empires (*see also* empire(s))
  beginnings of 15
  interaction between 49–50
  oppression by 51, 181, 184
  racialization of 213
    and slavery 204 (*see also* slavery)
  violence of 55–6
  which empires are Western empires? 203–13
Western Europe, and the Renaissance 2
White, Richard 188
White, Sam 92
whiteness 172–3 (*see also* race)

Whitney, Geoffrey 60
Will, George 11
William I, Prince of Orange (1533–1584) 183
Williams, William Appleman 21–2
Williamson, Jeffery G. 98
Wilson, Robert 68–9
Witgen, Michael 190
women
  agency of 145
  decline in status of 177
  female-female sex 150, 163–5
  indigenous and travelling women 106–7, 168–72
  labor opportunities of 107
  marriage. *See* marriage
  migrants 168–9
  mobility of 140–5
  in Mughal harems 144
  prostitution 166–7, 177
  and the Renaissance 4
  slaves 174
Worldly Goods 53
Worster, Donald 77, 78, 80

xenophobia 152

Zacuto, Abraão 136
Zheng Chenggong 198, 199
Zheng He (Cheng Ho) 20–1, 54
Zheng Zhilong 198
Zorita, A. de 160